1992

TWENTIETH CENTURY MUSIC

By Marion Bauer

TWENTIETH CENTURY MUSIC

MUSICAL QUESTIONS AND QUIZZES

In collaboration with Ethel Peyser

HOW MUSIC GREW

MUSIC THROUGH THE AGES

TWENTIETH CENTURY
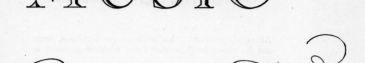
MUSIC

HOW IT DEVELOPED
HOW TO LISTEN TO IT

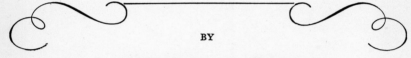

BY

MARION BAUER

ASSOCIATE PROFESSOR, DEPARTMENT OF MUSIC,
NEW YORK UNIVERSITY

A NEW EDITION, COMPLETELY REVISED

G. P. PUTNAM'S SONS

NEW YORK · LONDON

To *the memory of*

EUGENE HEFFLEY
(1862–1925)

valiant pioneer
in the cause of
Twentieth Century Music
whose wise guidance and teachings
have made this book possible

"To musical novelty no man can see an end, because the language of music is not a fixed but a fluid one."

ERNEST NEWMAN
(*The Elastic Language—A Musical Motley*)

"Only a vigorous tree has the vitality to put forth new branches."

AMY LOWELL
(*Sword Blades and Poppy Seeds*)

ACKNOWLEDGMENTS

I am indebted to the following music publishers for the use of music illustrations quoted from copyrighted works: G. Schirmer, Inc., New York; Arthur P. Schmidt Co., Boston; A. Durand & Fils, Paris; Max Eschig, Paris; J. Curwen & Sons, Ltd., London; Universal-Edition, Vienna; C. F. Peters, Leipzig; J. & W. Chester, Ltd., London; Edition Russe de Musique, Paris; F. E. C. Leuckart, Leipzig; Adolph Fürstner, Berlin; Cos Cob Press, New York; New Music Quarterly, San Francisco. I wish also to express my thanks to the Associated Music Publishers, Inc., to Boosey & Hawkes, and to the Galaxy Music Corporation, New York, for permission to quote from copyrighted publications in their domain.

The following publishers have generously granted me permission to quote a few phrases from books in their catalogues: A. A. Knopf, New York; E. P. Dutton & Co., New York; Lincoln MacVeagh, The Dial Press, New York; Henry Holt & Co., New York; Oxford University Press, London; W. W. Norton, New York; Macmillan Co., New York; Houghton Mifflin Co., New York; Whittlesey House, New York; E. C. Schirmer, Boston; Thomas Y. Crowell, New York; Dodd, Mead & Co., New York. (See Bibliography.)

My thanks also to Joseph Yasser for permission to quote from *A Theory of Evolving Tonality* (American Library of Musicology); to Henry Cowell, André Coeuroy, of Paris, Robert Haven Schauffler, Aaron Copland, and the late Katherine Heyman for quotations from their writings; to the late Henry Prunières, editor of *La Revue musicale;* to Minna Lederman, editor of *Modern Music;* to the editors of *The Musical Quarterly;* to Nina Naguid and Flora Bauer, who copied my manuscript and read proof; and to Harrison Potter, also an eagle-eyed proofreader.

Another debt of gratitude must be discharged to Mrs. Edward

MacDowell for a fortnight spent at the MacDowell Colony in June, and to Mrs. Elizabeth Ames for three invaluable weeks at Yaddo, Saratoga Springs, in August (1933), without which TWENTIETH CENTURY MUSIC would not have been completed.

MARION BAUER

AUTHOR'S FOREWORD

Recently, a young woman who, although not a musician, has attended concerts regularly, said to me almost despairingly: "What can I do to grow to like modern music? I don't understand it. I have tried to listen to it, but it means nothing to me; in fact, it takes away much of my pleasure in going to concerts." She is one of many who love music, who know how to listen but do not know how to adjust themselves to the new conditions. They do not know how to *exchange old ears for new*.

Therefore, I offer this book, not as a scientific treatise on ultramodern methods of composition, but as an attempt to guide the rapidly growing army of listeners in concert halls and over the air, through some of the paths along which the music of the twentieth century is traveling. Nor is it intended to be biographical or critical, but principally explanatory.

To many, the present day music seems to break completely with the past, to have no logical connection with former accepted methods. While it must be acknowledged that we are in a stage of transitional upheaval, the change when reviewed step by step is not mere chaos, but presents a front of progressive and reasonable evolution. ·

The tracing of this sequence supplies material for the chapters which follow. They deal with innovations of the past; with the impressionistic methods of Debussy, Ravel, Griffes, and others; with the appearance of new scales, melodic lines, and chordal combinations; with the extended boundaries of tonality and key relationships; with the new rhythmic freedom, the breaking down of accepted conventions, and the gradual framing of a new aesthetic which is the reflection of obvious changes in world thought, sociological conditions, and economic readjustments.

To avoid the use of technical terms entirely is impossible, because another reason for writing Twentieth Century Music: How It Developed, How to Listen to It is to try to explain directly and simply the new musical vocabulary, such as polytonality, atonality, linear counterpoint, whole tone scales, etc. To make these explanations more clear, the text is freely illustrated with examples from frequently programmed works of twentieth century composers—Debussy, Ravel, Scriabin, Stravinsky, Strauss, Kodaly, Schoenberg, Milhaud, Gruenberg, Hindemith, Copland, Harris, etc.

I have quoted frequently from How Music Grew and Music through the Ages, which I wrote in collaboration with Ethel Peyser; also, in Chapter 1, from an article which Rose Heylbut Wollstein and I contributed to The Gamut; I have drawn on material from articles of mine which appeared in Modern Music, Musical Quarterly, La Revue musicale, Musical Leader, Æolian Review, Theatre Magazine, etc.

If these pages enable my readers to listen to our contemporary music with more understanding of its intention, and, therefore, with greater enjoyment, Twentieth Century Music: How It Developed, How to Listen to It will have served its purpose.

Marion Bauer

FOREWORD TO REVISED EDITION

So much has happened in the music world since 1933, when this book first came off the press, that a complete revision has been necessary.

Many of the composers who were discussed in the original edition have added greatly to their contributions. Among these are Stravinsky; Schoenberg and his development of the twelve tone technic; Hindemith, who has written important scores and books such as *The Craft of Musical Composition,* the late Béla Bartók, Bohuslav Martinu, Sergei Prokofieff, Dmitri Shostakovich, Darius Milhaud, Louis Gruenberg, Roy Harris, Aaron Copland, and many others.

In the natural course of human events many composers have died. The most recent of these were Béla Bartók, Manuel de Falla, and Charles Wakefield Cadman.

The period of terrorism inflicted by Nazism and Fascism and the consequent World War II occasioned changes in our civilization which were registered in important ways in music history. Most of the leading composers of Europe and many performers, conductors, teachers, musical scholars, and writers migrated to the Americas, where they found haven and the opportunity to pursue their careers.

As though challenged by the influx of foreigners, many of whom have become American citizens, and by their vast production of works, American composers have shown unprecedented activity. The composers who were young a decade ago have written new works, and new names among the still younger generation have appeared on the programs of important orchestras and other musical organizations.

Radio, motion pictures, and the ballet have offered opportunities to Americans. While many have traveled along established roads, others have blazed new trails inspired by a newly aroused American spirit, a nationalism which was curiously absent in the earlier years.

The present version of TWENTIETH CENTURY MUSIC: How IT DEVELOPED, HOW TO LISTEN TO IT has been enlarged to include twenty-three chapters instead of the original eighteen. The chapter on polytonal and atonal ramifications has now become two chapters due to added material. "Jazz and American Music" grew to such proportions that I had to make a new chapter dealing with the younger American contemporaries who were born in the twentieth century, beginning with Aaron Copland. An entirely new section is Chapter 18, "Music as Affected by the War," made up of material from newspapers, personal interviews, and articles in the magazine *Modern Music,* for permission to quote from which I am indebted to its editor, Minna Lederman. Another addition is Chapter 22 on Latin American composers. The postlude is much expanded to discuss the development made in radio, phonograph, and motion pictures.

And again I send forth this revision with the hope that it may fulfill its mission of helping listeners—in classrooms, concert halls, and over the radio—to understand better, and, therefore, to appreciate more, the contemporary trends in music.

M.B.

New York
January, 1947

CONTENTS

PRELUDE

PART I: LOOKING BACKWARD

INTERLUDE

PART II: LOOKING FORWARD

PRELUDE

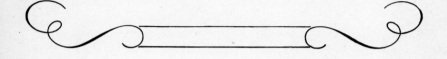

CHAPTER I

THE ART OF LISTENING: YESTERDAY AND TODAY

THE person whose listening experience is bounded on the south by Bach and Handel and on the north by Wagner and Brahms, will have to cover considerable ground to reach present-day frontiers. To thrust the contemporary, dissonant, apparently chaotic music upon such an auditor would probably create disagreeable impressions and rebellious reactions. The road must be taken gradually and the new country crossed by easy stages. Then it will be discovered that we are not in a musical no man's land, but have passed through rapidly changing scenery which, however, forms a continuous trail blazed by twentieth century pioneers. "No one can promise that the scenery will be appreciated along the way. Traveling is neither in a stage-coach, a victoria, nor by bicycle, but by automobile or airplane. An airplane consciousness is an indispensable adjunct for the appreciation and understanding of twentieth century art." (*Music through the Ages* by Marion Bauer and Ethel Peyser.)

What do you hear when you listen to music? Are you a heart-listener, a head-listener, or merely a foot-listener? In other words, does music appeal to your emotions, your intellect, or does it arouse in you only a response to rhythm?

Those who have not been trained to concentrate actually hear a very small proportion of the music to which they listen. They get the outer crust of the rhythmic and melodic outlines, with a harmonic background unconsciously included. Many of them "know nothing about music but know what they like." No problem is presented in compositions to which the listener is accustomed, nor in unfamiliar works written in familiar idioms. But what happens when the music steps

3

out of this sphere? He hears something intangible, incomprehensible, unpleasant. He grasps in vain for some familiar bit of rhythm, harmony, or melody. He is disturbed by something he neither understands nor likes. He makes up his mind that "modern" music is not for him and usually joins the army of those who decry or deride that which they fail to understand.

This army includes regiments of musicians who come to modern music with prejudices born of their early training. They cannot fit it to the traditions of the past, to the principles and rules with which they were taught to measure accepted masterpieces.

Most listeners, regarding present-day music as harmful to the continuance of a traditional lineage, dismiss it as the work of fanatics. By avoiding the discomfort of exploring unknown territory, they do not retard progress but only their individual development. The race of the swift and the battle of the strong continue, but they are out of the running and blame modern conditions instead of their own intolerance and short-sightedness.

We have experienced unbelievable development in radio, aeronautics, architecture, painting, and scientific research. Why should we not expect music to follow in the footsteps of its fellow arts and of invention? It is the usual story of the vision of the few, which is gradually tolerated, then generally accepted, and finally superseded by a new vision. The natural procedure is from the known to the unknown, and the right of way of the new is contested at every step. Opposition to innovation has made history.

We never profit by the experiences of the past. We do not seem to realize that we repeat what other ages have gone through, and never seem to understand the secrets the past would reveal. We are not inventors and innovators but merely pawns used by a force which is a composite of the accumulated needs, beliefs, desires, ambitions, inspirations, and inhibitions of each age. This gigantic force is the cause behind the ever-changing effects. Religion, politics, economics, social conditions, art, all act and react upon each other in response to this "spirit of the age," and in turn help to create it.

There have always been conservatives and radicals among composers, performers, and listeners. The old and the new have always been at swords' points. What an ideal balance would be reached if we could accept the novelty and admit the old also! Such a compromise is more possible for the interpreter and the listener than for the composer, who represents the active principle. The listener is passive; the interpreter in relation to the composer is passive, but active in relation to the listener. In other words, the composer is the brain center, the audience the extremities, and the interpreter, the nerve system. The contemporary composer naturally reflects the musical viewpoint of his age. He is a microcosmic ray, as it were, of its composite consciousness. The past supplies building material for the composer, but dwelling places for the listener and interpreter.

No matter how beautiful, how satisfactory, or how scientific the art of a period may be, we know that it encloses seeds of its fruition, and, at the same time, of its destruction. At the height of perfection, decay begins. The spirit of beauty caught in a net, subjected to a microscope, and preserved in alcohol becomes a museum specimen. Nor can art flourish in the strait jacket of standardization. And so we see throughout the centuries, three inevitable stages in every art epoch: youth, maturity, and decay. The fact that the epochs overlap creates friction. The new is seldom welcome; it breeds alarm and distrust. In time it proves its right to a place in the sun, becomes overconfident and arrogant, and, finally, after a life or death struggle, is supplanted by an upstart, a usurper. And the cycle begins again! "There is nothing new under the sun," however, and the new is the progeny of the old, inheriting sometimes its strength, or supplying a lack. It is the problem of Ibsen's *Master Builder*.

This ever-changing viewpoint causes the fundamental differences between classic, romantic, impressionistic, and neoclassic forms, which result in differences of structure and sound in each succeeding age. "Yet looking down the vista of crystallized points-of-view, from Palestrina to Hindemith, it is surprising to see how regularly, how unradically they develop. What to an outsider appears to be radical music, is frequently only a super-forceful gathering together of tendencies that have been quietly asserting themselves for years." ("The Genesis of a Musical View-Point," from *The Gamut,* October-November 1928, by Marion Bauer and Rose Heylbut Wollstein.)

Fortunately, we keep the best of the old through the interpreters and listeners, and the composer learns from the past and sometimes explores the "museum specimens," seizing upon anything which fits the needs of his day and adapting it to the technic and idiom of the period in which he lives. This fact may help to explain the present interest in the music of the eighteenth century, which has influenced twentieth century *neoclassicism* (pages 188-9). It may also account for the two divergent tendencies in today's musical creation: a radicalism which attempts to make a clean break with the past, and an enthusiastic delving into folk music and the spontaneous outpourings of early music forms. "Our musical viewpoint rests upon the twin foundation-blocks of Honegger, Hindemith, Varèse, Milhaud, Stravinsky, Copland, varieties of eruptive ... music; and the aged yet ageless forms of early English carols, Tudor songs, Negro Spirituals, French madrigals and rondeaus as they lived in Ronsard's day, chorales and motets of Sweelinck, and the fragile beauties of early instrumental music." ("The Genesis of a Musical View-Point.")

The changes which take place in musical taste and the differences of critical opinion concerning works of the past and the present keep the course of true listening from running smooth! Formerly it was believed that a work of art which received the stamp of approval would survive through the ages. But experience has demonstrated that no composer's immortality is inviolate, and although we give the title of *classics* to works which have been tried by many and have apparently stood the test of time, another disintegrating factor comes into consideration. Music, like architecture, clothes, and language, is subject to changes of style. These changes are due, not merely to whim, but to the needs, spiritual and aesthetic, of the generation. Taste in general swings back and forth from the classic spirit to the romantic.

The word *classic* is used in so many different connections: for works of any type that stand the test of time; classical (art music) versus popular (music of the people); the *Classical Era,* the eighteenth century including Karl Philipp Emanuel Bach, Haydn, Mozart, and Beethoven, during which period the sonata was the prevailing fashion, and the *Romantic Era,* the nineteenth century ushered in by Beethoven in his last years and including Schubert, Weber, Schumann, Chopin, Liszt, etc., in which the sonata was replaced by shorter forms and compositions with titles indicating mood.

The *classic spirit* and the *romantic spirit* is again a different use of the terms, an attempt to define which may help the listener to solve some of his problems. The *classic spirit* deals primarily with perfection of form and technic; is impersonal, intellectual, and abstract; is occupied with artistry and craftsmanship; and, to borrow Robert Haven Schauffler's words, it is the "architectonic, clarifying impulse." When carried too far, it tends to make a dynamic art static; to exaggerate the importance of outer realities at the sacrifice of the inner meaning; to be more interested in the vehicle of expression than in the expression per se; and to mistake self-imposed rules for fundamental laws.

The *romantic spirit* deals primarily with content and its significance; is personal, emotional, and programmatic; is occupied with invention and imagination; and, as Schauffler says, is "the adventurous, enriching" impulse. When carried too far, it tends to become oversentimental; to exaggerate the importance of the inner meaning at the sacrifice of concise form; to be more interested in self-expression than in artistic utterance, and to disintegrate the purity of the art.

We are accustomed to think of Haydn as a classicist and Schumann as a romanticist. Suppose we were to revaluate our terms and to consider Bach as a romanticist and Ravel as a classicist!

If an age is romantic in tendency, it will go back into the archives of the past and choose art works most closely allied to its point of view. If, on the other hand, the classic spirit predominates, it will pick out, from the past, works of entirely a different caliber. And according to the "spirit of the times" the new works will be fashioned.

This probably is the reason for the extraordinary upswing in the appreciation of Bach's compositions and our eager search for forgotten masterpieces. Our present-day composers are more classic than romantic in their tendencies, and more attuned to the classic spirit. Bach was a modest, retiring genius who worked not only because of a great inner urge but also because in a purely utilitarian way he had to supply cantatas for St. Thomas' Choir at Leipzig, or chamber music at Cöthen, or proper studies for his own children. What a surprise it would be to him to find himself a twentieth century box-office attraction!

On the other hand, we hear less Mendelssohn, Liszt, Schumann, and Chopin than formerly, and more Brahms. We apparently need to free ourselves from the intensely personal emotionalism in which the nineteenth century romanticists clothed their self-expression.

Even Wagner was no longer the divinely authorized music prophet to the young in prewar Germany, and one young Russian composer relegated him to the museum with the remark that his works were interesting only from a historical point of view as a means of studying the methods of the past. This seems drastic and almost the speech of a fanatic to those who still listen with joy to *Die Meistersinger, Tristan und Isolde,* and the *Ring.* Yet the composer who today would imitate Wagner would bring no pleasure to the cultivated musician. Wagner opened new vistas to his contemporaries but his speech, so perfect for him, was of his day, even though it was neither fully understood nor appreciated then. Our speech is terser, more abrupt, and cuts out unessentials, *suggesting* rather than *elaborating* details. We have learned to supply for ourselves what the musical autonomy of our era leaves to our imagination.

Today, Debussy's music is familiar, therefore it presents fewer problems than it did in 1905. This brings to mind a statement made to me some years ago by Iwan d'Archambeau, the violoncellist of the late Flonzaley Quartet: "To show you how the human faculties adjust themselves, I may say that when we first played the Ravel quartet it contained difficulties that appeared impossible to overcome until we tried the Hugo Wolf work. Then Ravel seemed simple; in turn, the difficulties of the Reger quartet simplified Wolf. And Schoenberg! Well, Schoenberg would make anything seem easy by comparison! With each work we have to learn a new technic of expression. After having studied the Schoenberg work as we did, we know the idiom in which it is written and another work from the same hand would be less difficult to get hold of. In the same way, the Debussy quartet meant the mastery of an entirely new technic for the instruments, but now we have learned Debussy's idiom."

No two people hear sound alike any more than they react alike emotionally. It is difficult to realize that so tangible a thing as tone has no actual borders, that it is not a question of pitch and intensity but of the recording power and nervous sensibility of the ear which hears it. Ears vary as much as eyes, and we should have terms to express an aural range comparable to myopic or presbyopic vision. It is almost impossible to make the non-musician believe that hearing can differ to any great degree in people none of whom is deaf. It is much the same as trying to explain color to one who is color-blind, or absolute pitch to one tone-deaf.

It would be interesting and instructive in trying to analyze reactions to contemporary music to measure the nervous sensibility in individual cases. Listeners can stand dissonance in different degrees, much as they can carry intoxicating drinks, electrical current, or physical pain. Some can bear very little discord and others can hear a great deal before a disturbing reaction is registered. At what point the sensation of pleasure is turned into pain, due to discordance or intensity of sound, would make an illuminating field for experimentation.

But we should have to take into consideration the fact that the ear is tremendously elastic in its powers of adjustment, and sounds which are at first disturbing may become so familiar, through our habit-forming propensities, that the pleasure-pain sensations are sub-ject to a wide scale of modification. And sounds which were painful, when once accepted and organized by the brain may become pleas-urable.

We are children of an age of great complexities not the least of which is modern harmony, but the public soon accustoms itself, unless it is enslaved by prejudices, to new combinations of tone. The fact that a child practicing on an instrument can repeatedly play the same false tone, without being disturbed by the dissonance, shows how rapidly the ear forms a habit for unusual combinations.

Can tone apart from form produce an emotional response as color does? Is it the juxtaposition with other tones that produces its effect on the sympathetic nervous system? Is it timbre or pitch or both which produces the reaction? Would tone separated from rhythm produce emotional reaction, providing that it were tone in the abstract, and not a cry of pain or the expression of some other mental state? What makes the appeal to the greatest number, melodic content or rhythmic outline?

The untutored listener responds to obvious rhythms (a foot-listener), the banality of which annoys the trained musician who seeks his satisfaction in melodic and harmonic complexities. Modern rhythms have, however, influenced modern tonal effects and vice versa. Rhythm represents the physical plane in music; melody, the emotional; and harmony, the intellectual. The perfect art work must be a well-balanced combination of all three. We can trace how the predominance of one or another of these elements has shaped the musical expression of different eras in the world's music.

To the listener we would recommend catholicity in taste, breadth of interest, and tolerance. Knowing more about music, its science and history, makes more intelligent audiences, but the idea that such knowledge takes away from the emotional pleasure to be derived from the art of listening is a fallacy.

In a little book on *Musical Taste and How to Form It,* M. D. Calvocoressi writes: "...You may incline to wonder why, since between the music that appeals to your own instinctive taste and the music on whose merits all the best judges agree there is more than enough to provide for a lifetime's enjoyment, you should wish or should be asked to trouble about contemporary works upon which doubt may exist." The author answers that "if great artists live in your time, you owe it to yourself and to them to acknowledge them." Also, appealing to the listener's more selfish instincts, he says, "If things worth enjoying exist, you naturally wish to enjoy them.... So that for your own sake, as well as for the sake of the artists who devote their life to creating fine music, it is essential that you should be prepared to appreciate today's music as well as yesterday's, and as much of it as is compatible with your own nature and the enlightenment which experience brings."

Music does not "progress," and in no sense can one call old music inferior to the new or vice versa. To achieve the art of good listening is to accept the old music for what it is, and likewise the new, each for its own virtues. Happy is he who can enjoy the Old and yet appreciate the New!

PART I: LOOKING BACKWARD

CHAPTER 2

PAST INNOVATIONS AND PREJUDICES

THE twentieth century listener with nineteenth century ears is prone to think that no other generation has had so difficult a problem of adjustment; but history points out his error. When the Chinese scale of five steps (pentatonic) was increased to seven, about 600 B.C., it was thought the final doom of music had been sounded! There have been periods in the history of music, however, in which the new seemed deliberately to break down the old, when time-honored rule was overthrown, and workers in the creative field of music were revolutionary rather than evolutionary. We are going through such a metamorphosis today. Composers, feeling that everything possible has been said in the diatonic scales, are experimenting with new and ultra-old scale formations. Melody, harmony, counterpoint, rhythm, and musical forms are being subjected to the same revision. The new musical terminology shows that transformations are taking place. What did the nineteenth century know of the whole tone scale, quarter tones, musical impressionism, atonality, polytonality, Scriabin's mystic chord, and dissonant counterpoint?

In the ninth century when plainsong had reached perfection, it required a high standard of performance and musical sensibility. The traditional interpretation of the chants was handed down orally, with a notation merely as an aid to memory. This notation, called *neumes,* was a series of signs derived from the Alexandrian Greeks to show the rising and falling of the singing voice in the chants without denoting definite pitch. But when the revolutionary innovation of part singing appeared, staff notation for indicating the exact pitch relationships became a necessity, and the tradition of the delicate nuances required by the neumes was lost.

"The tenth century was regarded by some historians as a period of decadence. Plainsong had reached the pinnacle of its possibilities, and the attempt to saddle it with rules and regulations to preserve it revealed its weaknesses and led, through striking innovations, to its passing. But out of the decadence of one period rises the phœnix of a new art. The ninth century lack of fixed notation and rhythms led to the tenth century search, which developed into mensural and polyphonic composition. But with them the art of the chant passed." (*Music through the Ages,* by Marion Bauer and Ethel Peyser.)

When some unknown theorist introduced the innovation of drawing a red line across the page to indicate F of the bass clef and wrote the neumes above and below it, he opened the way for the further innovations of Hucbald (840-930) and Guido d'Arezzo (995-1050), who is credited with having invented the four-line staff and the syllables of the *sol-fa* system.

It is almost unbelievable that *ars organum* held sway for three centuries! This first attempt at harmonization resulted in adding a second melody running parallel to the *cantus firmus* (fixed song or subject) at a distance of a fifth or a fourth. This music sounds almost impossible to our ears, but later I will point out a return of its use in the twentieth century. In addition to the simple organum composed of the *vox principalis* and the *vox organalis*—the principal voice and the organating or organizing (accompanying) voice—a composite organum developed of three or four voices, resulting from the doubling in octaves of the two parts. From the tenth century on, however, experiments were made by giving greater freedom to the organizing voice, allowing it to remain stationary for several syllables or leading it in contrary motion to the principal voice. This use of contrary motion became the "new organum" and developed into *discant.* In the *Oxford History of Music* H. E. Wooldridge said that this method of discant "was the subject of a continuous effort extending apparently from the beginning of the twelfth century to the second half of the thirteenth, and carried on both in France and England."

The right-of-way of *ars antiqua* (organum and discant) was disputed in the fourteenth century by the *ars nova* (counterpoint). The protest of Jacobus de Liége, until recently attributed to Jean de Muris, against the "moderns" sounds startlingly familiar! "There are singers who have the impudence to sing," he wrote, "and to compose discant when they know absolutely nothing of the nature of consonance . . . it is no more than if a stone thrown by chance should hit the mark. . . . They mutilate, curtail, and corrupt the song; and if by good luck they light on a concord, such is their ignorance that they at once proceed to a discord. Alas! What grief! And some endeavor to cover their defects by saying that the new method of discant uses new consonances. They offend the intelligence and the senses of all who know their faults; for when they should give delight they produce only dejection." He deplores the "modern divergence from the theory and practice of Franco and his school, . . . innovations in notation, exaggerated sentiment in discant, the excessive use of discords and the abandonment of the old *organum* and *conductus* in favor of motet and cantilena." (Grove's *Dictionary of Music and Musicians.*)

And this statement of Jacobus twentieth century "moderns" should take to heart: "Some moderns consider those who do not cultivate the new art to be uncultured, uneducated, unlearned, and ignorant; and they look upon the old art as barbarous, irrational, but the new as exquisite and rational." One of the "moderns" against whom Jacobus leveled his shafts was Philippe de Vitry (c. 1285-1361), French poet, theorist, and composer. This revolutionist wrote a treatise called *Ars Nova* in which he gave an exact picture of the case of *ars antiqua* versus *ars nova*. It was a period of reaction against the old. No doubt the rich secular music of the Troubadours had much to do with the revolt against the rigid discipline and mathematical regulations of the church music. It resulted in greater harmonic and rhythmic freedom, and, going to the opposite extreme, in a positive ban against the use of consecutive fifths and octaves, the basic principle of organum. This ruling may have been brought about by composers who were sick and tired of the limitations of the old order, and it is only now, six centuries later, that composers have broken away from the power of an arbitrary rule which seemed to be a fundamental law. But harmony manuals still forbid consecutive fifths and octaves!

Probably the greatest master of the fourteenth century was Guillaume de Machaut (c. 1300-1377), the first to use music definitely as an art expression. Although he was recognized as a leading poet, until recently his music was regarded as primitive and unschooled. Many of his extant manuscripts illustrate the innovations of the *ars nova:* sacred and secular compositions; secular music as an art product; the first mass in four vocal parts; instrumental preludes and postludes alternating with the vocal passages; lays, motets, rondels, ballads, and *chansons balladées* as the forms in current use; and manuscripts in which only one line carried the text, in French or Latin, showing that the other parts were played by instruments. This means that Machaut was either the inventor or an innovator in the use of instrumental accompaniments, and that he was one of the first serious composers to write for solo voice.

Martin Luther (1483-1546), who recognized that music was a power in the lives of the people, brought back the early Christian custom of congregational singing by adapting appropriate words in the vernacular to worthy folk tunes. By introducing folk song into hymnody, he made the reform a people's movement, reconciled secular and sacred music, created the German *chorale,* the cornerstone of the new harmonic system, and gave a foundation upon which the art of Bach and his predecessors was built. This influence was not restricted to vocal compositions but was particularly active in developing the music for the organ. "The hymns were harmonized in four parts. They were usually sung in unison with the accompaniment of the organ or a group of instruments. This great change, or revolt, broke the backbone of polyphonic music, freed the spirit of the people, and first brought into use modern scales (major and minor as we know them)." (From *How Music Grew,* by Marion Bauer and Ethel Peyser.)

The next important change in musical thought may be dated approximately at 1600, and was the reaction of the Italian Renaissance on music. The *Camerata,* a group of composers, poets, singers, and amateurs, banded together in Florence at the home of Count Bardi, with the intention of creating a dramatic form modeled on the Greek drama. In attempting to bring to life the melodic declamation of the Greeks, they succeeded in creating a new *stilo rappresentativo,* or recitative. The primary object was not the creation of opera, which actually happened, but the use of music to heighten the effect of poetry. Opera was an accidental by-product!

The accomplishments of Jacopo Peri, Giulio Caccini, Emilio Cavalieri, Luca Marenzio, Vincenzo Galilei, Jacopo Corsi, Laura Guidiccioni, Ottavio Rinuccini, Strozzi, and Count Bardi, members of the

Camerata, are well known. These liberals and moderns were not in accord with the "Goths," as Galilei called the contrapuntalists, and they actually broke their power. The Camerata began their crude attempts about fifteen years before the turn of the century. In 1600, when Maria de' Medici was married to Henry IV of France, Peri and Rinuccini were commissioned to write a work, and the opera *Euridice* was the result. At its first performance, members of the Camerata played the harpsichord, three *chitarrone* (large guitars), viola da gamba (precursor of the violoncello), theorbo (double lute), and three flutes, which constituted the orchestra. Works in which the subjects were mythical became opera. Biblical stories, sung and acted in the oratory of the churches, became oratorio.

In 1570, Jean Antoine de Baif established in Paris L'Académie Française de Musique et de Poésie. Its members, poets and musicians, attempted to write music that should express poetry and should first and foremost *adhere to its meter*. After much experimentation and a long struggle to shake off the shackles of circumscribed plainsong, measured music—music with time designation and bars—was invented. They wrote madrigals, which they arranged for single voices with one or more instruments. While the Italians developed the recitative, the French were evolving a rich rhythmic song called *musique mesurée à l'antique* (music in ancient meter). Jacques Mauduit and Claude Le Jeune were members of this group.

As in the case with every innovation, the Camerata was not as revolutionary as it seemed, and the direction was pointed, at least as far as the music is concerned, by three writers of madrigals: Marenzio, Gesualdo, and Monteverdi. Few more interesting figures exist in music than Don Carlos Gesualdo, Prince of Venosa (1560-1613), audacious innovator. So revolutionary was he, in fact, that the value of his compositions was not recognized until the twentieth century made a new estimate of his position in the musical world. In 1926 Cecil Gray and Philip Heseltine published an interesting study of him as murderer and musician, in which Mr. Heseltine said: "After three centuries he [Gesualdo] is seen to hold a proud place in the distinguished company of those great men whose music was the crowning glory of the Renaissance.... He is by no means an isolated person of eccentric genius but rather the fine flower of a school of daringly imaginative experimental composers." The second half of the sixteenth century was a period of tentative experiments aimed to break up the old order of polyphonic tradition. "Viewing music as a whole," Mr. Heseltine wrote, "the contributions of experimental composers may be regarded as sketch-books and notes, insignificant in themselves but of the utmost value to the man of genius who is able to develop the resources which these but suggest, and to make use of them as a means of expression. Now Gesualdo was just such a man."

Gesualdo wrote one hundred and forty-seven madrigals, which were widely sung, and the first set was published in 1594. His "modernism" showed itself in his extraordinary use of chromaticism, as his music was based on a twelve note scale, and not the customary church modes nor the encroaching major and minor diatonic harmony. Mr. Heseltine stated: "In many ways the music of the early twentieth century is akin to that of the early seventeenth. Realism, impressionism, tone-painting, experiments in sound for sound's sake were then, as now, preoccupations of many composers." Gesualdo went to Ferrara, which was a center of art toward the close of the century, and at his court Torquato Tasso was an intimate, supplying Gesualdo with forty or more poems. Gesualdo, in addition to his harmonic daring, was dramatically expressive.

The use of the solo voice in sixteenth century art music had been introduced as a novelty, although the Troubadours had sung their verses to the accompaniment of the lute several centuries earlier. John Dowland wrote songs and accompaniments in England, and Claudio Monteverdi (1567-1643) wrote madrigals which, though modern and harsh to the ears of his contemporaries, were definite experiments in harmonic combinations and expressive music. Monteverdi is regarded as the originator of the modern style because he united the best points of the polyphonic school with those of the new monodic, and added an element of drama to the madrigal. When, at the age of forty, he turned to opera writing, it was with a fully matured and modernistic technic which he had learned from his dramatic madrigals. In the struggle against counterpoint he became aware that new riches had to be brought to music to replace what polyphony had supplied. These new riches included the importance he gave to the orchestra, using tone color to heighten the expressive power of music, and studying the individual traits of instruments; the invention of the tremolo and pizzicato; his turning the sixteenth century madrigal ino the seventeenth century *cantata da camera;* and the composing of several operas which put the seal of artistic achievement upon the tentative experiments of the Camerata.

As was the case in the fourteenth century when *ars antiqua* was forced to give way to *ars nova,* in the sixteenth century *La nuove musiche,* as Caccini called his *canzone* in *stilo arioso* (songs in the style of the aria), was making its way to the detriment of the Golden Age of polyphony of which Palestrina and Orlando di Lasso, both of whom died in 1594, were the last great composers. The sixteenth century ultramodernists had their detractors too. In 1600 and 1603 Artusi, a monk, musician, and theoretician, wrote on the *Imperfections of Modern Music,* setting himself up as the defender of the threatened tradition and deploring in no uncertain terms music's decadence. "He complained that the new composers [Gesualdo and Monteverdi] were interested only in pleasing the senses and not in satisfying the intellect. He denounced the conceit of these artists who questioned the right of way instead of following the road traveled by the masters." (Freely translated from *Monteverdi* by Henri Prunières.)

"Though I am glad to hear of a new manner of composition," Artusi wrote, "it would be more edifying to find in these madrigals reasonable *passagi,* but these kinds of air-castles and chimeras deserve the severest reproof." Again he said, "You hear a medley of sounds, a variety of parts, a rumble of harmonies that are intolerable to the ear ... with all the best will in the world, how can the mind see light in this chaos?"

In the preface of his fifth book of madrigals Monteverdi parried Artusi's shafts by stating that his works were not written haphazardly, but that another system of harmony existed besides the ancient theorist Zarlino's, and that the modern composer, in his use of dissonance and consonance, followed other rules than those dictated by the masters of the past. Monteverdi complained that the past composers were occupied exclusively with the architecture and the treatment of the voices rather than the resources of art. They wrote "pure music," but the moderns sought, above all, to translate in an expressive and live manner the sentiments suggested by the words. The first sacrificed the poetic text to the harmony; the second sought to make harmony the servant of the words. Monteverdi knew the old rules, and claimed, if he infringed them, that it was done deliberately. Prunières in his

Monteverdi, from which I am translating freely, says: "It would be impossible to say in a more distinguished, dignified manner that he [Monteverdi] was not the ignorant one, knowing perfectly both the old and the new methods of music, but it was the pedant Artusi who would not admit the eternal renewal of artistic forms."

CHAPTER 3

THE BEGINNINGS OF THE MODERN ERA: BACH AND EIGHTEENTH CENTURY DEVELOPMENTS

IT has often been remarked that the seventeenth century produced no great composers and still it was a period of revolutionary developments in music. "That age of turmoil and yet of swift progress," Charles Sanford Terry calls it in *Bach: The Historical Approach*. "... A pulsing century of rapid, organized growth, perfected and crowned by the absorptive genius of Bach!"

From the Camerata to Bach, innumerable innovations succeeded in breaking down time-honored traditions. Johann Sebastian Bach (1685-1750) welded together the heterogeneous tendencies which had been growing for almost a century and bound them into such a homogeneous unity that the year of his birth is regarded as the beginning of the era of modern music. Handel and Domenico Scarlatti were born the same year, while Jean Philippe Rameau was born shortly before them. Scarlatti and Rameau were the "modernists" of Italy and France.

The experiments of the Camerata, resulting in opera, oratorio, and ballet, opened new homophonic paths.

Although every type of musical instrument was known to the ancients, and seeds planted centuries before had taken root in the sixteenth century, instrumental music had not developed into an *art* until the seventeenth. The potentialities of instruments, used merely as accessory to the voices, were disclosed and developed, and early types of keyed, wind, and stringed instruments were improved. The little town of Cremona became the center of the violin industry and the Amati, Stradivari, and Guarneri families transformed the antiquated chest of viols into violins, violas, and violoncellos the perfection of which has never been equaled.

New instruments produced performers, composers, and new types of composition. Italy created a school of violin virtuosi, continuing the ascendancy it had won in the musical world during the age of vocal polyphony. Thanks to the Renaissance and the Reformation, these seventeenth century composers were enabled to draw on the resources of both sacred and secular music, and to acquire greater technical freedom from the folk dance and perfection of form and style from the madrigal and motet. The violin sonatas of Torelli, Vitali, Corelli, and Vivaldi were examples of ultramodernism of that age.

The harpsichord and clavichord became the important keyboard instruments of the seventeenth century. In England, Thomas Morley, William Byrd, John Bull, Weelkes, Wilbye and Orlando Gibbons wrote Fancies "fit for Voyces or Viols," pavans, and galliards in the early years of the century. Many of the famous printed collections of vocal and instrumental music belong to this period. Later John Blow and Henry Purcell added a postscript to the fame of the Golden Age of English music. In France the art of the clavecin (harpsichord) was highly cultivated, and Lully, the Couperin family, Chambonnières, and others helped to create its literature. In Italy keyboard music reached its climax in the next century with Domenico Scarlatti (1685-1757).

George Dyson in *The Progress of Music* writes: "The young Scarlatti was undoubtedly the most emancipated of them all. His style, both of playing and writing, was that of a specialist. He used the harpsichord, not as an instrument for reproducing other kinds of music, but as a means of expression individual and complete in itself. Compared with his contemporaries, Bach and Handel, his technic is remarkably modern. He believed, as he put it, in using all his ten fingers. He also learnt to leap about on the instrument in a way which was at that time as novel as it was effective. His art is that of the solo-performer who specializes in the peculiar resources of a chosen instrument. As he also had a delightful musical fancy, his pieces have remained perennially fresh and engaging."

While German clavier compositions were numerous, the true contribution of that nation to the seventeenth century was its organists and organ works. Jan Sweelinck (1562-1621), the last of the great Netherlanders, was the founder of the school of organists which culminated with Bach. His pupils came from all over the musical world, including Italians, French, and Germans. Italy had Giovanni Gabrieli (1557-1612) and Girolamo Frescobaldi (1583-1643), and their German pupils snatched the palm of supremacy from Italy. The fruits of Luther's propaganda, the Protestant Church service and the chorale, gave Germany the impetus to become the leading musical force of the eighteenth and nineteenth centuries. The roster of famous German organists includes Froberger (1616-1667), a pupil of Frescobaldi; Heinrich Schütz (1585-1672), a pupil of Gabrieli and father of German oratorio and cantata; Johann Heinrich Schein (1586-1630); Samuel Scheidt (1587-1654); Johann Pachelbel (1653-1706); J. A. Reinken (1623-1722), a Dutch organist who became a potent influence in Germany; the Swede, Dietrich Buxtehude (1637-1707), who introduced a series of concerts called *Abendmusiken*. Reinken and Buxtehude had a direct influence on young Johann Sebastian.

Incited to experiments by the new instruments and the interest in soloists, the composers produced new musical forms. One of the most important of these was the *suite*, a collection of pieces which had developed from the folk dances of the different countries such as the *allemande* (of German origin), the courante or *corrente* (French or Italian), the saraband (Spanish or Moorish), and the *gigue* (Italian); the gavotte and minuet (French), the *chaconne* (probably Spanish), etc. In the different countries the suite was called by various names: *ordres, leçons,* partita, *sonata da camera.*

The Italians developed two kinds of sonata: the *sonata da camera* (chamber sonata), which was not a sonata in our understanding of the form but was more allied to the suite; and the *sonata da chiesa* (church sonata), which was developed from the madrigals when they were played instead of sung. Realizing that the instruments, especially the new and improved variety, were capable of feats impossible for voices, the composers took advantage of their greater technical possibilities and created an instrumental technic and instrumental forms. The church sonatas played for religious services were dignified and abstract, showing embryonic traces of the later sonata form structure and definite themes.

The works of Bach illustrate which forms had been invented during the seventeenth century, for he is a perfect example of the evolutionary, rather than the revolutionary type. He gathered together all the innovations of the generation preceding his birth and preserved them for the future through the force of his genius. His predecessors were the apprentices; Bach, the master. His compositions include suites, partitas, inventions, sonatas of the early type, concerti grossi, overtures, chorales, organ chorale-preludes, toccatas and fantasias, preludes and fugues, sacred and secular cantatas, the Passions according to St. John and St. Matthew, and the B minor Mass, an ancient form which he infused with new life and highly developed detail. He composed for church choir and organ, chamber music groups and solo instruments, harpsichord and clavichord, using instruments in his orchestra which are obsolete. He drew his material from the musical literature and assimilated the styles of the composers of the Netherlands, Italy, France, England, and Germany, but stamped them with his own overpowering individuality.

When the Italian composers introduced monody in 1600, they broke the power of counterpoint and quite unconsciously set up the science of harmony in its place. With the new harmonic system the church modes were gradually displaced by the diatonic (major and minor) scales, and the chromatic scale came into freer use. The polyphonic music, contrapuntally conceived, established definite harmonic conventions which gradually led to the recognition of the harmonic system above that of the contrapuntal. "Bach, for example, was the master of a contrapuntal technique never surpassed either before or since, but he was also heir to harmonic and tonal traditions which could bear the weight of a high imaginative freedom." (George Dyson in Grove's *Dictionary of Music and Musicians,* article: "Harmony.")

A. H. Fox-Strangways in the article on "Scale" in Grove's *Dictionary* claims that in the Handel-Bach period "a good deal of major is really Mixolydian and a good deal of minor is really Dorian." (For ecclesiastical or church modes see page 109, also *Music through the Ages,* page 47, and *How Music Grew,* page 74. The Mixolydian scale is the scale of g without an f sharp, and the Dorian is found by playing the white keys from d to its octave.)

Fox-Strangways also says, "The classical period—say, from the *B minor Mass* (Bach) to the *Deutsches Requiem* (Brahms)—definitely fixed major and minor."

Although Bach was admittedly not an innovator so far as form was concerned, he was tremendously interested in the problem of equal tempering. "The old keyboard instruments could not be played in all keys, as the fifths and thirds were tuned absolutely, that is, according to the mathematical divisions of the string. In their own key the intervals were perfect, but were out of tune in relation to the other keys. It was expedient to find a relative tuning so as to 'temper' them sufficiently to be practicable.... In 1691, a treatise on *Musical Temperament* by Andreas Werkmeister was published. His solution was to divide the octave into twelve equal half-steps. Bach was the first composer to demonstrate its feasibility in his *Well-tempered Clavichord*, Preludes and Fugues in the twenty-four major and minor keys." (*Music through the Ages*, Bauer and Peyser.) C. H. H. Parry in his biography *Johann Sebastian Bach* points out that Bach's adoption of the name *Well-tempered Clavichord* "was a public and deliberate recognition of a radical change in the construction of European scales, of such pre-eminent importance that it is no exaggeration to say that without it modern musical art would have been absolutely impossible. It need not be supposed that Bach was answerable for the acceptance of the new scale system. That was bound to come for the simple reason that the art could not get on without it....

"But whatever had happened earlier, it was inevitable that, directly instrumental music began to develop, the scale system hitherto in use should require modification. In the old style of unaccompanied choral music there were hardly any modulations at all.... When instrumental music came to be cultivated, the fact that instruments could take many intervals which were not natural to voices unaccompanied soon made a larger number of accidentals desirable, and the increase of accidentals led to a wider range of keys. And thus it was that musicians began to realize the difficulties of tuning."

Bach's championing the cause of equal temperament places him in the foremost ranks of progressive musicians of his time, and Parry calls the first series of preludes and fugues of the *Wohltemperirtes Clavier* (*Well-tempered Clavichord*) "one of the most epoch-making productions in the whole range of the art of music."

Another innovation for which Bach is directly responsible is a completely radical reform of fingering without which piano playing could not have advanced to a virtuoso stage. The early players of keyboard instruments had used flat fingers without the thumb, passing the second and the third over each other and employing the fourth and fifth only occasionally. Bach taught his children to curve their fingers and to use the thumb. In his *Clavier-Büchlein (Little Clavier Book)* written for his nine-year-old son Wilhelm Friedemann, Bach indicated the fingering by numerals showing the use of the thumb which he passed *under* the fingers instead of *over* as was the custom when the thumb was used at all. Bach's fingering thus anticipated that of pianoforte players, and his ideas in many directions were carried on and developed by his son Karl Philipp Emanuel, who was considered the greatest authority of the eighteenth century on clavier playing. He said of his father, "Living in an epoch in which there came about gradually a most remarkable change in musical taste, he found it necessary to think out for himself a much more thorough use of the fingers, and especially of the thumb."

At the same time François Couperin (1668-1733), organist and clavecinist, was experimenting in France, and acquired fame by his *Méthode: L'Art de toucher le clavecin (Method: The Art of Playing the Clavecin)*. Bach was interested in Couperin's innovations but worked out his own independently, as Couperin's method was not published until after Bach's experiments had been made. Couperin's theories of performing and of composing became a background for Bach's sons, as well as for Haydn, Mozart, and Beethoven.

The bridge between the beginnings of opera and its classic period was in the work of Alessandro Scarlatti (1659-1725), father of Domenico, in Italy, and of George Frederic Handel (1685-1759) in Germany and England. Earlier, Jean Baptiste Lully (1631 or 2–1687) had become the czar of music in France and was famed as an opera composer. He and Jean Philippe Rameau (1683-1764) formed a French style. Rameau was the butt of the War of the Buffoons (1752), which was actually a controversy between the French type of opera and the Italian *opera buffa*. Italian opera has always been a power in the musical world and has influenced, and even thwarted, the development of opera in other countries. Handel, Johann Christian Bach, Gluck, and even Mozart show effects of its power. England and Russia performed Italian opera almost to the exclusion of any other, including native works. The strength of Italian opera has been tested but not broken even by the Wagner regime, and today opera is still trying to find a way of escape from the insidious power of Italian opera traditions (Chapter 19).

In recounting innovations, Rameau's books on the science of harmony take important rank. In 1722 he published his treatise, concentrating principles which had been vaguely understood and employed for a century or more. The French historian and critic Fétis said that it laid the foundation for a philosophical science of harmony. "His discovery of the inversion of chords was a stroke of genius, and led to very important results." (Grove's *Dictionary*.) Many of his statements are still used as harmonic principles.

Handel's true contribution was not in the opera field but in that of oratorio. *The Messiah* still holds its place and has been the model for hundreds of lesser works. Along with many other eighteenth century works which have been pulled off the shelves and dusted, Handel's concerti grossi, many of his instrumental compositions, and some of his operas have been revived. In a list of ten famous musicians of that day, arranged in the order of their supposed genius, Handel's name is second, and Bach's seventh!

Johann Sebastian Bach summed up the past. He represented the conservative spirit of the eighteenth century; his sons were the radicals. Bach the father closed the baroque era; the sons explored new pathways, which led to the classic era. The father was renowned as an organist but comparatively unknown as a composer; the sons spread the fame of the Bach name in Italy and England and won the reputation of having greater talent than the father.

Karl Philipp Emanuel Bach (1714-1788), clavier accompanist to Frederick the Great, was known as "the Berlin Bach." He was regarded as one of the greatest musicians of his generation, and was interested in perfecting a homophonic style and in developing the new technic of composition. He is regarded as the inventor of the classic sonata, as he and other composers of his day, including his brothers Wilhelm Friedemann and Johann Christian, Hasse, Galluppi, Thomas Arne, and Paradies, experimented with sonata form. Emanuel Bach was a pioneer and a precursor of Beethoven, who adapted many of his methods to his own needs, and of Schubert as a writer of art songs. His treatises on the study of the *True Art of Clavier Playing* was the basis for the modern pianoforte technic, carried forward later by Clementi, Cramer, Czerny, Hummel, Moscheles, and Liszt.

Johann Christian Bach (1735-1782) wrote operas which are compared to his friend Mozart's for melodic charm and expressive instrumentation. Like Handel, he went to Italy and later to England, where he was associated with the King's Theater in the Haymarket and was known as "John Bach, the Saxon Professor." His friends were Garrick, Sheridan, Sir Joshua Reynolds, and Gainsborough. He was greatly interested in an invention, the new pianoforte, and he was one of the first composers to write "for the harpsichord or the pianoforte."

For centuries music was confined to the church and the court. The people had their music in the open streets or wherever they foregathered. But concerts, for which the public paid admission, were novelties in the eighteenth century, and, indeed, were to change the condition of the musician by giving him more social and economic freedom than he had known when he was employed in a noble's household. In addition to playing an instrument in a group, or singing, he often performed menial duties and was dressed in livery. Even Haydn was little more than a lackey, and Mozart left the court of Hieronymus, the Archbishop of Salzburg, because the Prince-Bishop ordered him to eat with the servants, and on a previous occasion Mozart had been forbidden the main doorway of the palace. Beethoven was the first composer who was invited to sit "above the salt." (A great saltcellar was used as a social boundary. From feudal times, at banquets, the gentry sat above and the common folk below the salt.)

In 1768 John Christian, "the English Bach," and another German, Carl Friedrich Abel, established a series in London known as the Bach-Abel concerts. The first public concerts in London of which there was any record were those of John Banister in 1673, continued by Thomas Britton, a coal dealer, lover of music, and friend of Handel. Buxtehude's organ concerts, the annual *Abendmusiken,* established at Lübeck in 1673, marked an innovation, for never before had music been played in the church outside of services, merely for pleasure. The Academy of Ancient Music "for the study and practice of vocal and instrumental music" was founded (1710) in London, by Dr. J. C. Pepusch. The Madrigal Society, which is still in existence, was founded in 1741.

About 1700 in many university towns of Germany, Switzerland, and Sweden the concerts of the *collegia musica* were begun. Sebastian Bach was a conductor of such an organization in Leipzig, and Emanuel Bach founded a branch in the University of Frankfort, where he was a student.

The first public concerts in Paris were the *Concerts spirituels,* established in 1725 by Philidor to give music to the people on the many religious holidays when the opera house was closed. Such an organization, where sacred cantatas, symphonies, and sonatas were played by an orchestra and virtuosi, created a sensation abroad and led to orchestras being formed in other European centers.

"Germany was the cradle of the symphony," says Paul Landormy in his *History of Music.* "... In the eighteenth century Germany was a land greatly divided in the political sense, portioned out among a crowd of petty sovereigns who were not rich, and who barely managed to provide for the upkeep of their courts. ... Yet, if put to it, they could support the expense of simple orchestra concerts." Their orchestras were supplied with players through an institution known in Germany as "the poor scholars," the pupils who were given free education with the condition of "learning the musician's trade and assisting at the concerts organized by the cities and the courts."

Where opera absorbed the public interest, orchestras developed more slowly, but Vienna had both. In 1750 the Musical Academies were established in imitation of the *Concerts spirituels.* These were the first public concerts in Vienna.

The "haphazard collections of palace officials" were gradually supplanted by professional orchestras in Dresden, Munich, Stuttgart, Rome, Venice, Paris, London, Darmstadt, Hamburg, Berlin, and in Leipzig where the "grand concerts," given in the Clothiers' Hall, became the famous *Gewandhaus* concerts. The most famous orchestra of forty to fifty professionals was founded at Mannheim (1767-77) under Christian Cannabich's direction. A group of composers, orchestral players, and conductors developed the symphony, which was actually Emanuel Bach's sonata form for full orchestra. In spite of the fact that there is not a composer of first rank among them, they created an orchestral style and tradition and were responsible for the transition in methods of orchestration which took place after Bach and Handel, making possible the work of Haydn and Mozart. This *Mannheim School* included Johann and Karl Stamitz, Franz X. Richter, Ernst Eichner, Giovanni Battista Toeschi, Ignaz Holzbauer, and others. Telemann was in Hamburg, Doles in Leipzig, Graun in Berlin, Graupner in Darmstadt, Gossec in Paris, Sammartini in Milan. Among the early symphonists were Boccherini, one of the first writers of string quartets; the sons of Bach; and Karl Ditters von Dittersdorf.

"Composers were given a new medium for which to develop new forms, a new system of dynamics was evolved which was to revolutionize musical interpretation, and the conductor, no longer an animated metronome, became a controlling force.... The same evolution which turned composers from polyphonic forms to the sonata and symphony created modern orchestration." (*Music through the Ages.*)

Christoph Willibald Gluck (1714-1787) is an extraordinary example of a conformist who turned radical. His early operas were in the prevailing Italian style, but after much traveling, hearing Handel operas in London and Rameau's in Paris, and visiting Hamburg, Dresden, and Vienna, where he came in touch with the new ideas of instrumentation, his musical convictions underwent a complete change. "Instruments ought to be employed," he said, "not according to the dexterity of the players, but according to the dramatic propriety of their tone." In 1762 he wrote his first epoch-making opera, *Orpheus and Euridice,* with Calsabigi as librettist. *Alceste,* which followed, was heartily disliked. The audience found that it was not amusing! *Orpheus* and *Alceste* formed the cornerstones of modern music drama, which was carried to heights by Mozart, Wagner, and Debussy. Gluck and Calsabigi succeeded in turning the tide from the superficial, decadent opera, in which the composers had been obliged to fit their inspiration to the outworn traditions and write according to the whims of the singers, to a new application of the principles of the Florentines carried on by Lully, Rameau, and Grétry.

In the Dedicatory Epistle to the Grand Duke of Tuscany which prefaces the score of *Alceste,* Gluck wrote a manifesto which has become famous as a picture of his times and a statement of his achievements in reforming "all those bad habits which sound reasoning and good taste have been struggling against in vain for so long."

The historic Gluck-Piccinni controversy was a war, not between the composers, but between their adherents, who pitted two unequally matched opponents against each other. Piccinni was a talented follower of the old *opera buffa* idea, and Gluck, the champion of the new. The two made settings of *Iphigénie en Tauride;* Gluck's version held the boards and won out against Piccinni's. The struggle for and against new musical ideas resulted in open warfare.

CHAPTER 4

THE CLASSICAL VIENNESE ERA AND THE
ROMANTIC MOVEMENT:
HAYDN, MOZART, BEETHOVEN, SCHUBERT,
SCHUMANN, CHOPIN

BY the time Joseph Haydn (1732-1809) entered the lists, the
Classical Era, with Vienna as its central field of action, was
well established. Haydn and Mozart infused with genius the
ideas of Emanuel Bach and the Mannheim symphonists, and gave
definition to the period which found its culmination in Beethoven.
That Haydn, Mozart, and Beethoven made the Austrian capital their
home has given the title of *Viennese period* to this most brilliant
musical era. "It is impossible to overestimate the importance of music
to the social and political changes which culminated in the decade of
Revolution," says W. H. Hadow. "They meant that the old régime
had been tried and found wanting; that the standard of taste was no
longer an aristocratic privilege; that the doors of the salon should
be thrown open, and that art should emerge into a larger and more
liberal atmosphere." (*The Viennese Period, Oxford History of Music.*)

Haydn was an ultramodernist in his day. When Albrechtsberger
accused Mozart of breaking rules, Haydn retorted: "What is the good
of such rules? Art is free, and should be fettered by no such mechanical
regulations. The educated ear is the sole authority on all these questions, and I think I have as much right to lay down the law as any
one." He gave concrete form and sanction to the sonata, string quartet,
and the symphony. "It was from Haydn," Mozart claimed, "that I first
learned the true way to compose quartets." Haydn was accused by his
detractors of being a mountebank and of trying to found a new school!
Among his definite innovations were: separating the opera sinfonia
from the concert symphony; making a definite distinction between
chamber and orchestral music; introducing a second theme in the

31

exposition of the sonata form; carrying the minuet over from the suite into the classical sonata, and making the rondo a dignified member of the sonata family. (See "Explanation of Musical Terms," page 415.)

Although Wolfgang Amadeus Mozart (1756-1791) wrote in all the forms used by Haydn, his innovations were principally in his contributions to the operatic repertory. He is regarded as the founder of German opera even though most of his operas were in Italian and were based on Italian tradition. Comparable to the Italian *opera buffa* and the French comic opera was the German *Singspiel.* Mozart put the stamp of the artist on this nationalistic opera of the people by the sheer power of his musical genius. He combined this national quality with the German's creation of symphonic music, the Italian's sense of melody, and declamation as used by Lully, Rameau, and Gluck. His tremendous musical invention displayed itself in his powers of characterization which surpassed those of any opera writer before him (and perhaps since!). He did not go to Greek mythology for his characters, as had most of the opera writers since the days of the Camerata up to Gluck, but to life or to the fantastic, thus opening the doors for Carl Maria von Weber and Richard Wagner—in other words, for *romanticism.*

In *The Limitations of Music* Eric Blom advances a fascinating theory in claiming that Mozart's early death may have been timely. "If we regard each number in the *Magic Flute* (his last opera) separately," the English critic reasons, "... we are often moved to wonder at their perfection, but still more struck by a curious and disconcerting strangeness, which is nothing else than the summer lightning of romanticism. It is positively disquieting to think that Mozart might have had ample time to turn into a romantic.... What it would have made of him, the greatest classicist of music, is unthinkable. There is in the *Magic Flute* a distant reaching-out towards Beethoven, towards Weber, towards Wagner even...."

The same thing may be said of the introduction to the C major string quartet, which on account of its chromatic treatment sounds more like Beethoven than like Mozart; and of the two last symphonies, the Jupiter and the G minor. As crystalline as these works seem today in structure and harmony, Mozart's contemporaries found the G minor very bold and advanced in style. And the originality of his instrumentation in *Die Entführung aus dem Serail* (*The Abduction from the Seraglio*) astonished his hearers.

George Dyson says that "Mozart was more sensitive to devices and subtleties of color than any musician then living." And he did much to advance the use of expression marks to give the exact dynamic intentions of the composer. "Mozart's orchestra is of the eighteenth century, small in scale, but it is a delicately adjusted body of players in which all the details have an exact significance." Of Mozart's scoring of the G minor Symphony, Dyson says: "Within these modest bounds (seven wind instruments and the usual strings) there was more orchestral magic than had yet been dreamed of. Each wind player is a soloist. That was the most important reform of Haydn and his contemporaries." (*The Progress of Music.*)

Mozart taught the composers who came after him the subtleties of orchestration. Dyson calls Mozart's overtures, concertos, and symphonies "the finest flowers of the eighteenth century."

With Ludwig van Beethoven (1770-1827) the profile of music was completely changed. He came into the world a classicist and left it a romanticist. His genius was not the only factor in the change which took place. In fact, he was a tool of his age, or, more correctly, a channel through which the revolutionary spirit became musically articulate. With the American Revolution, the French Revolution, the rise and fall of Napoleon, and the War of 1812, unrest and change were rampant. The day of the individual had dawned, and no more independent thinker than Beethoven existed. He took his place with the seers of the age—Goethe, Schiller, Kant, Fichte, Humboldt, Haydn, and Mozart.

Beethoven's tremendous crescendo in creative power made him the perfect vehicle for expressing the "spirit of the age." As J. W. N. Sullivan said in *Beethoven: His Spiritual Development*, "Beethoven's music continually developed because it was the expression of an attitude towards life that had within it the possibility of indefinite growth." "In his realization of suffering and in his realization of the heroism of achievement," his attitude toward life was the essence of romanticism. Sullivan also says, "Few men have the capacity fully to realize suffering as one of the great structural lines of human life"; and "No artist ever lived whose work gives a greater impression of indomitable strength than we find in some of Beethoven's most characteristic movements."

Beethoven was an innovator in spite of himself. "The new and the original is born of itself without one's thinking of it," he said. His work divides itself into three clearly defined styles: First, the stage of imitativeness, in which he used the forms handed to him by his eighteenth century predecessors, was an out-and-out classicist, and made experiments in various instrumental combinations.

Second, the stage in which his individuality began to assert itself, marked by his own statement to his publishers concerning two sets of variations, op. 34 and 35 (1803): "Both are handled in an entirely new manner ... usually I hardly realize when my ideas are new, and hear of it first from others; but in this instance I can myself assure you that I have done nothing in the same manner before." In this period we find his poetic gift in its richest plenitude representing the activity of a vigorous, deeply emotional mind. The compositions include three piano concertos, the C minor, G major, and the Emperor; the three Rasoumoffsky quartets (op. 59); the Harp Quartet; the violin concerto; *Fidelio* with the four overtures; also the Egmont and Coriolanus overtures; the Kreutzer, the Waldstein, and the Appassionata sonatas, and the symphonies from the Eroica to the Eighth.

Third, the transcendent period which "rises from the active life to the contemplative; from the transfiguration of human joys and sorrows to the awe and rapture of the prophetic vision," says W. H. Hadow in his study of Beethoven (*Collected Essays*).

Perhaps the fact that he had completely lost touch with the outer world of sound drove him into the holy of holies, that sphere of inner hearing of which he was seer and prophet. The modernism and profundity of these last works made the critics say, "Poor man, he is deaf and cannot hear the terrible discords he is writing!" The third period may be said to have begun with his F minor string quartet, op. 95, known as the Serioso, and includes the B flat piano trio, op. 97; the last piano sonatas from op. 101 to op. 111 inclusive; the Ninth Symphony, and the last five string quartets, from op. 127 to 135, including the Great Fugue.

Of the last quartets Robert Haven Schauffler writes in *Beethoven: The Man Who Freed Music*: "The old quartet form did not suffice for the intense personalism of this music. So Beethoven invented new forms. In these the tempo changed more often and more capriciously than ever. The usual four movements grew to five—six—and even seven, as if in memory of the rococo *divertimento* and Suite. There was less strictness in the sonata-form movements. Their modeling was not so formally pronounced. The second subject sometimes burst in unprepared. The development grew shorter and more polyphonically intensive. . . . The most astonishing contrasts of naïve folk tunes with the music of philosophical reverie were forged in a whole by sheer sorcery. The voice-leading became wonderfully free and daring. In these quartets there are no neutral passages where the hearer may nod and recover. Every moment he must give all he has; for each note is packed with significance."

Schauffler justifies his title, *Beethoven: The Man Who Freed Music* by showing how one era of music was closed and another ushered in by the "versatile emancipator." "We have seen him," Schauffler says, "by sheer personal magnetism, force of will, and intensity of genius, liberate the art of music from the long-standing indignity of being carried on by lackeys. We have seen him establish the composer's vocation upon a professional basis. . . . The poor boy from Bonn was the first composer to attain the dignity of seeing his symphonies printed in score.

"We have seen Beethoven deliver the music of his day from the ignominious rôle of obsequious hanger-on of the fashionable world and make it a universal thing—a materialization of the utmost range of the human mind and spirit, omitting none of the peaks and abysses. We have followed this imperious figure as he emancipated personality in music, detonating in his scores such a profound charge of thought and passionate emotion that the world still vibrates with the shock. . . .

"He took Continental music from the salon to the concert hall; from the castle to the cottage, and made it the most democratic thing in the æsthetic world."

As the violin had been perfected in the seventeenth century and had led to many developments in music, so the instrumental invention of the eighteenth century was the pianoforte. During the second half of the century, interest was centered in manufacturing a keyboard instrument which would be adequate to the demands of the more expressive music which was coming rapidly into vogue. More dynamic variety, greater volume of tone, and powers of resistance were needed.

From the *gravicembalo col piano e forte* (the harpsichord which could be played gently and loudly) manufactured by Bartolommeo Cristofori (c. 1709) came the name pianoforte.

Through the rapid spread of the new instrument the virtuoso pianist developed, and a new type of showy salon music became so popular that it threatened not only to annihilate the classic composers but to vitiate good musical taste. Technical display was the aim of the composers, and Edward Dickinson said that "in many circles music reached the lowest stage of levity that it has known in modern times, and the agent of this travesty upon art was the piano." (*The Study of the History of Music.*)

The dynasty of the sonata was actually overthrown by this popular style of piano piece, and the short forms which were characteristic of the Romantic Era were introduced by the *étude*. At first it was intended merely as a mechanical drill, but it had many serious protagonists and became an art form when it reached Chopin and Liszt. Among the more important members of this school of virtuosity were Muzio Clementi (1752-1832), Jan Ladislav Dussek (1716-1812), John B. Cramer (1771-1858), who was also an important music publisher, Johann Hummel (1778-1837), John Field (1782-1837), Carl Czerny (1791-1857), Ignaz Moscheles (1794-1870), Kalkbrenner, Dreyschock, Henri Herz, Thalberg, and Carl Maria von Weber (1786-1826) in his piano works.

John Field was an interesting personality and an innovator. Of Irish birth, he was apprenticed to Clementi, who was a famous teacher and pianoforte manufacturer in London. Field went to Russia to demonstrate Clementi's piano, was one of the first great pianists, and introduced the short romantic piano piece in his nocturnes, the progenitors of Chopin's.

"I am different from all men I have seen. If I am not better, at least I am different," said Jean Jacques Rousseau, stating in a few words the essence of romanticism: man's consciousness of his own individuality, of his need to express his emotions, of his relation to other individuals, of his growing love for nature, of the changes that were taking place in the social life, of his revolt against the artificiality of eighteenth century conventionality, and his urge to express this awakened self-consciousness in literature and music. This was "Romanticism as opposed to Classicism—whose prescription of forms, regulation and tabulation in the arts had, up to this time, occupied men's minds in order to build something out of raw and improving materials. But as soon as these materials were firmly bound the bonds were broken, giving way to Romanticism. In this way Romanticism develops into its own classicism, and the art world grows newer and fresher on this continuous alternation.... Thus creative self-consciousness was born, which because of its too thorough permeation became, in time, its own destroyer.... Among thinkers, themselves seeking relief from old forms, were scores of poets, writers, scientists, philosophers, dramatists and composers: Jean Jacques Rousseau, Honoré de Balzac, Victor Hugo, Théophile Gautier, Berlioz, Schubert, Schumann, and Chopin." (*Music through the Ages.*)

The first great musical romanticist was Franz Schubert (1797-1828) whose real innovational contribution to music was the art song or *Lied* which became one of the accepted new forms. In it he blended the poem and the music perfectly and pointed the way for program music by his imitations of the sounds of nature in his accompaniments. While we appreciate the symphonies (the C major and the Unfinished), his chamber music, and compositions for piano, it still must be admitted that his genius was best expressed through the spontaneity and extraordinary originality of his six hundred or more songs.

Weber interests us as the connecting link between Mozart and Wagner. He established German romantic opera in which he introduced Teuton folklore and fantasy, and peasant life, thus sounding the first note of musical nationalism. Weber used the same type of literature for opera librettos as was popular in the poetry of the day. Nature was depicted successfully, and imagination and heart took the place of the vocal display and artificiality of the earlier conventional opera. He was the first to use the themes from the opera in the overture, and he gave greater importance to the orchestra in opera than any previous composer, again paving the way for Wagner. In his "Invitation to the Dance" he forestalled Liszt and Berlioz in writing program music. His operas *Der Freischütz* (*The Enchanted Archer*), *Euryanthe,* and *Oberon* are musical milestones.

Contemporary with Weber was a group in Italy whose influence upon the history of opera has been great. Among these, Gioacchino Rossini (1792-1868) whose *Barber of Seville* is a vital *opera buffa,* seems to be beckoning to some of the opera writers of our day.

Cecil Gray in *The History of Music* says that it is "perhaps the greatest of all comic operas without exception, and is as fresh and living at the present time as the day when it was written."

Another important name in opera innovation is Vincenzo Bellini (1801-1835), whose premature death may have robbed the world of many masterpieces. *La Sonnambula* (*The Sleep-Walker*), *Norma,* and *I Puritani* (*The Puritans*) are operas in the grand style, and Cecil Gray finds it only necessary to compare a typical melody from these works "with any melodies written before them to realize the enormous historic significance of the rôle played by Bellini in the idiomatic evolution of modern music." Gray considers Bellini "one of the most original composers in the whole history of music: owing little, if anything, to any predecessor, and exercising a most decisive and dominating influence on all who were to come after him."

Gaetano Donizetti (1797-1848), the third of the Italian opera composers of the early nineteenth century, has kept himself before the eyes of the public by his *Lucia di Lammermoor, L'Elisir d'amore* (*Elixir of Love*) and *Don Pasquale.* In Paris he wrote *La Fille du régiment* (*The Daughter of the Regiment*) and *La Favorita* (*The Favorite*).

Gasparo Spontini (1774-1851), an Italian who lived in Paris, composed in the tradition of the *opera seria* and yet pointed the way to French grand opera as the first writer of historic opera. He was the bridge between Gluck and Meyerbeer, influencing also Berlioz and Wagner. Somewhere I remember reading that a critic of his day said that if ever the time came when the operas of Spontini and Spohr would not be heard, it would be because the end of music had come. Spontini's *La Vestale,* revived at the Metropolitan in New York for Rosa Ponselle, is the only one of these to be heard today, and yet ... we still have music! Spohr, a famous violinist of his day, is an innovator in another direction—he was the first to conduct an orchestra, the London Philharmonic (1820), with baton and without the aid of a keyboard instrument.

Early in the century, during the days of the Empire and the Restoration, the French composers were famous for their *opéra comique,* at the same time when foreigners, such as Spontini and Meyerbeer, produced *grand opéra* in Paris. Giacomo Meyerbeer (1791-1864), German by birth, Italian by training, and French by adoption, was an opportunist. He has been accused of seeking success at the expense of sincerity, of pandering to the tastes of the public, of writing brilliant shoddy music; and yet it was the fault of the age which his music reflects, more than of the individual. His unusual gifts of orchestration which advanced the technic of instrumentation, his sense of the theater, his understanding of writing for the voice, his knowledge of how to build dramatic and musical climaxes, give him an important role in the dramatis personae of grand opera. In spite of his faults, Cecil Gray says, "all that was fruitful and enduring in Meyerbeer's art has been assimilated by others and has become public property." Among his successes, showing the development of the historic, romantic opera are *Robert le Diable, Les Huguenots, Le Prophète,* and *L'Africaine.* "Meyerbeer did not actually found a school," says Gray. "The Italian and German traditions which came together for a moment in his work eventually separated again, although they both continued to bear evident traces of their momentary confluence for some time, and attained two of their highest points in the art of Verdi and of Wagner respectively."

In Giuseppe Verdi (1813-1901) are summed up all the traditions of the Italian opera of the late eighteenth and early nineteenth centuries and the innovations of the nineteenth. Before 1851 he was the apprentice; after *Rigoletto, Il Trovatore,* and *La Traviata,* he was a master. He studied the traditions of French opera, Wagnerian orchestral methods, and modernized his style as was evident in *Aïda,* written at the command of the Khedive of Egypt for the opening of the Cairo Opera House (1871). Verdi is a rare example of a genius whose creative powers never waned, and his two last works, *Otello* and *Falstaff,* written when he was seventy-four and eighty respectively, are his greatest!

Cecil Gray finds in these two masterpieces a relationship to Cavalli and Monteverdi, "in which aria and recitative are so interpenetrated with each other and interfused as to form a homogeneous arioso style which is neither one nor the other. This fact lends additional force and significance to Verdi's often-quoted dictum *'Tornate all'antico e sara un progresso.'* " (To turn to the old is to be progressive.)

But to return to the German romanticists. The supreme musical exponent of the movement was Robert Schumann (1810-1856), "the most literary of composers," W. H. Hadow called him. "Literature and music were his artistic handmaidens, and his early acquaintance with German romantic literature influenced more definitely German romanticism in music. This resulted in his descriptive titles for his piano pieces; in his trying to recreate literary moods and to make musical characterizations and portraits of his friends. The short piece as introduced by Beethoven, Schubert, Mendelssohn, and the many minor composers of 'salon' music, was a perfect medium for Schumann's genius." (*Music through the Ages.*)

The literary vein which Schumann felt so deeply manifested itself in his musical journal, the *Neue Zeitschrift für Musik,* which was devoted to criticism and to the ideals and aims of the new romantic school. His literary style exhibited the exaggerations and sentimentality of the day, such as he had learned from Jean Paul Richter and E. T. A. Hoffmann. He created the impassioned Florestan and the poetic Eusebius, representatives of his own dual personality, and he peopled the magazine with many other children of his fancy, whom he named for his friends: Felix Meritis was Mendelssohn; Chiara was Clara Wieck; Estrella was Ernestine von Fricken; Jeanquirit was Stephen Heller. The characters, who appear also in his music, were members of an imaginary *Davidsbund,* or club of Davidites, who fought against the musical Philistines. It was a struggle of the new order against the old; of an ultramodern romanticism against a decadent classicism; of the youthful, subjective, and emotional against the artificial, insincere, and pedantic.

Among Schumann's "discoveries" were Chopin and Brahms, and he wrote to Clara in 1835 that "Mendelssohn is the most distinguished man I have ever met." Distinguished is the word which best describes Felix Mendelssohn-Bartholdy (1809-1847), his personality, his culture, his manner, and his music. He was a classical peg in a romantic hole! Although it must be admitted that the Overture to *Midsummer Night's Dream,* written when he was seventeen, is one of the finest examples of romanticism, for the most part his music leans toward the classic. "That Mendelssohn should have been a romanticist at all is a proof of the strength of the romantic tendency in his day," says Daniel Gregory Mason in *The Romantic Composers;* "he seemed born rather for the severest, purest, most uncompromising Classicism; and if he did, as a matter of fact, come to share the ideals of his age, it was in his own way and for his own ends. The crudities, the exaggerations, the morbid self-involution of the extreme phases of the movement, certainly never infected him." His cultivated taste directed him as a composer, as a landscape painter, and as the first to translate a Latin poem in its original meter, Terence's play *Andria,* which he offered for entrance into the University of Berlin.

The same impeccable taste was probably responsible for his great enthusiasm for Bach, and led him to revive the Passion according to St. Matthew a hundred years after its first performance in Leipzig. He was famous as the conductor of the *Gewandhaus* concerts at Leipzig, and he raised the standard of orchestral performances, played many classics, and helped the cause of music and contemporary composers unselfishly. He used the baton for conducting and treated the orchestra as an immense instrument upon which he played with feeling and style. He was one of the first to whom the term "interpreting conductor" could be applied, and his enemies called the Mendelssohn tradition the "elegant school" of conductors. He had an unusual knowledge of orchestration and was a pioneer in, and at the same time a master of, instrumental experiments and effects. His concert overtures, "Calm Seas and Prosperous Voyage" and "The Hebrides," were precursors of the tone poem of Berlioz and Liszt. By a curious coincidence his oratorios, *St. Paul* and *Elijah,* were performed in England with triumphant success comparable to that of his compatriot Handel a century earlier.

Frédéric Chopin (1810-1849) is doubtless the greatest composer for the piano the world has known. He recognized his medium and clung to it, after some early attempts at concertos and chamber music. From his own extraordinary gifts as a pianist his virtuosity in composition arose; to this he added a depth of emotion and sentiment which sounded a new note in music. His range of talent on the one end comes perilously close to the decadent salon music of his day, but on the other, he scales the heights of supersensitive, refined genius—"the boldest, proudest, poet-soul of his time," Schumann called him.

In spite of the fact that Chopin gave no descriptive titles to his compositions, his études, preludes, ballades, nocturnes, scherzos, impromptus, etc., epitomize the soul of romanticism, and he perfected the short piano piece as an art form, creating, with Liszt, a new type of piano playing in keeping with the demands of the romantic movement. He was the greatest innovator of his day in the technic of the piano, a supercraftsman and scrupulous artist. Bach, Mozart, Hummel, and Field influenced him, and he had as fastidious taste in his art as in his person. His experiments in the use of the damper pedal, of the singing tone and *tempo rubato,* of his chromatic and dissonant harmonies, foreshadowed impressionism. Debussy has often been called the twentieth century Chopin, or one might call Chopin the nineteenth century Debussy.

In an article in *La Revue musicale* (December, 1931) on *"Chopin et la musique contemporaine"* (Chopin and Contemporary Music), Stéphanie Lobaczewska said: "Without exaggeration, it may be affirmed that there is no daring in modern music, no evolution in the elements of music itself which were not prefigured in Chopin." The writer quotes André Coeuroy as saying: "Chopin in Poland seemed to be the first composer who felt instinctively the renovating value of national songs. Opposing to the foreign influences, the musical language proper to the race." "This is the first great lesson of Chopin," Mme. Lobaczewska continued, "to which the Moussorgskys, the Debussys, the Albenizs, Bartoks, Casellas listened. . . . And at home, *young Poland* follows the path indicated by Chopin. . . . He discovered in folklore the passions and the magic of the Past. And he took out of it, the emblem of a pure musical form. Here Chopin ceased to be a romantic to become the most daring of innovators."

The patriot imbued with the folk music of Poland and its national dances transformed the polonaise and mazurka into highly developed modern dance forms. It was his dream to "create tone poems having individuality." This he did. Zdislas Jachimecki in a recent study of Chopin's works states that "the new poetic forms, the new verbal creations of the works of Mickiewicz [Polish poet and intimate friend of Chopin] produced at this epoch, encouraged, even forced the young composer to open new paths for musical expression." Chopin was the first to give the title ballade to piano pieces, and two of them, the G minor and the F major, are based on poetic works of Mickiewicz. In these ballades the twentieth century sonata has its roots. The scherzos, too, are innovations, and have no relation to Beethoven's scherzos. Of the great F minor *Fantaisie,* op. 49, which might well be regarded as a prototype of the Liszt symphonic poem, Jachimecki writes: "This composition radiates a spirit completely modern and is a source of many of the means employed by the music produced from that day to this." The two sets of études, op. 10 and 25, are worthy of their place beside Bach's *Well-tempered Clavichord* and Beethoven's sonatas in the repertory of the professional pianist. In these Chopin definitely established a modern piano technic. The two piano sonatas have often been criticized as being weak in form, but Hugo Leichtentritt, a German critic and theoretician, contends that the extreme subtlety of their structure has not yet been measured, and that Chopin based them structurally on an intensive study of Beethoven's last works.

Chopin succeeded in his ambition "to create a new era in art." And as Arthur Ware Locke states in *Music and the Romantic Movement in France,* it "was the era of lyric poetry in music. The great development of lyric expression in the music of the first half of the nineteenth century, was the highest accomplishment of the musical romantic movement. In a broad sense the lyrical purpose of Chopin's and Schumann's works represents the substituting of the subjective for the objective point of view in musical composition, the emphasizing of individual feeling, and the sympathetic reflection in music of the changing moods of nature. Of all the music written under the influence of the romantic movement none has more permanent value than the lyrical compositions of Chopin."

CHAPTER 5

NINETEENTH CENTURY POINTS THE WAY:
PROGRAM MUSIC AND POSTROMANTICISTS

WHILE Schumann and Chopin were developing piano music along romantic lines, Hector Berlioz (1803-1869) and Franz Liszt (1811-1886) were increasing the possibilities of orchestral music and were strengthening the bond between music and the other arts through *program music,* of which they are illustrious exponents. They represent two distinct types, however, as Berlioz was concrete and objective in his use of program, and Liszt was psychological and subjective. Although it was Berlioz's intention to make the program a means and music the end, he translated, as it were, the incidents into music, adhering realistically to his story. In fact, he may well be regarded as the father of realism in music.

Liszt's methods were more suggestive and impressionistic. He allowed his mind to play on the program, giving full sweep to emotion and imagination, yet under the control of a technic. Berlioz's early years were not spent in music, and he lacked the discipline that Liszt had acquired as a prodigy pianist. At the same time, Berlioz was unhampered by tradition, because he did not know the past. Gluck and Beethoven were his guiding stars, and Lesueur, his teacher at the Paris Conservatoire, an original thinker and experimenter, encouraged his wayward pupil. Jean François Lesueur (1760-1837) must have been regarded as a rank infidel in the eighteenth century for his bold attempts to apply to church music Gluck's principle of making the music express the meaning of the word. Yet he deserves recognition as a precursor of romanticism, and his teachings come still closer to our day, as he recognized in the old Greek modes a "possible means of modern musical expression and the consequent tendency to combat any fixed conventions of harmonic style. This idea of harmonic freedom was inherited by his pupil, Berlioz...." (*Music and the Romantic Movement in France,* by Arthur Ware Locke.) Locke also states that to Lesueur "all music must be imitative, characteristic, and logical; it must have poetry, painting, and expressiveness, and finally it must have a descriptive program. Pure music did not exist for Lesueur ... he was one of the earliest theorists, if not the first, to state definitely the principle of the *idée fixe* and the *leitmotif,*" and he must have suggested their use to Berlioz.

The *Symphonie Fantastique,* a musical biography, shows Berlioz in full possession of Lesueur's theories. It is not mere coincidence that 1830, the year it was first heard in Paris, was the time when the Romantic revolution in the dramatic world broke out with Victor Hugo's *Hernani,* for which Berlioz, with Balzac, Théophile Gautier, Préault, and others, acted as claque.

Berlioz's position in the music world has never been settled. "Throughout his lifetime, from the very outset of his career even, his work never ceased to provoke the wildest enthusiasm on the one hand, and the most violent hostility on the other," says Cecil Gray (*The History of Music*). "To his admirers he is simply one of the very greatest of all composers who have ever lived; to his adversaries he is a less than second-rate figure, a mere scene-painter in sounds, with nothing save a gift for orchestration to commend him."

But no one questions his right as the great initiator of modern orchestration. Unlike the other composers of the romantic school, he knew nothing about the piano—in fact, he disliked it. Perhaps this was why he developed a technic for instrumentation comparable to Liszt's piano virtuosity. He knew the instruments, their capabilities and limitations, and he opened new avenues of tone color, discovered the relation between different emotions and instrumental timbres, and created a new orchestral language. Romain Rolland places him with Bach, Handel, Mozart, Beethoven, and Wagner for his studies and accomplishments in orchestration.

In his musical characterization and use of dramatic motives Berlioz "opened the way for Liszt and the modern program composers. He became thus the pioneer of that realistic movement which in our own day has assumed such prominence, providing, as early as 1830 ... the prototype of many modern masterpieces." (Daniel Gregory Mason, *The Romantic Composers*.)

Even though Liszt be regarded as a second-rate composer, undoubtedly the history of music reads differently for his having lived, and no one personality in music ever exerted a greater influence on his contemporaries. Spending most of his youth in France and being closely affiliated, through concertizing, with the music centers of Germany, Liszt was affected by the romantic movements in both countries. He is rightfully prophet and seer of the "music of the future." His long life spent as piano virtuoso (he was called the Wizard of the Piano); in teaching musicians from all over the world; in studying philosophy and literature with avidity; in composing in new styles and creating new forms; in preaching a new musical aesthetic, made him an international figure.

He was in Paris when Berlioz's *Symphonie Fantastique* startled its hearers. He was also a friend of Chopin and shares with him the reputation of having developed the new pianistic virtuosity. Later he became the great *Meister* and gave encouragement and performances to the ultramodernists who made a musical Mecca of Weimar because of his presence there. His followers banded together as the School of the Future and were fairly intolerant of those who preferred to remain on the outside. He recognized and encouraged the gifts of Richard Wagner, a colossal neophyte who had the genius to carry out and apply the theories of the high priest. James Huneker said that Wagner owed more to Liszt than money, sympathy, and a wife (Cosima was the daughter of Liszt and the Countess d'Agoult). Cecil Gray says, "... The extent to which Wagner was indebted to Liszt in the matter of both melody and harmony is seldom sufficiently emphasized."

Liszt was at once the victim of his magnetic personality and easy virtuosity which made him the petted darling of the salon from his piano-playing prodigy days, and of his intellectual curiosity and mystic tendencies which finally led him into the church as Abbé Liszt with minor orders. This duality of nature shows in his compositions. He was a master arranger of operatic fantasies, songs, and Gypsy folk music. Wagner, Bizet, Donizetti, Verdi, Schubert, all fell prey to his avaricious appetite for arranging other composers' music. Perhaps it is only fair to say that some of these are brilliant technical feats which show musical taste, while others reflect his time in the empty display of virtuosity, which has passed out of good taste and won for his works the unpleasant epithets of "tinsel," "dross," "vulgarity," etc. But he was also the inventor of new forms, and of a new orchestral technic, and the composer of the Faust Symphony, the B minor sonata, the Dante Symphony, many worthy pieces in the *Années de Pélérinage,* brilliant études, the two popular concertos for piano and orchestra, and the much imitated symphonic poems.

As an innovator of new forms and harmony, Liszt ranks high. He was a chromaticist, and many examples foreshadowing atonality may be found in his scores, Liszt's use of chromatic harmony, his rapid modulations, and the freedom of his melodic line were the result of the increasing desire to express a greater emotionalism in music. This same aim led to enriching experiments of his orchestral palette. He was the inventor of "theme transformation" or the cyclic use of themes, which has attracted many later composers.

Liszt very obviously was not the inventor of program music. It reared its head frequently during the past centuries, for example, in Jannequin's "Battle of Marignan," Daquin's "Cuckoo," Rameau's "La Poule," Kuhnau's Bible Sonatas, Beethoven's Pastorale Symphony, Schumann's *Carnaval,* Mendelssohn's Hebrides Overture, Weber's "Invitation to the Dance," etc. But the time was ripe to combine the arts of poetry and music, for instrumental music had reached such a degree of expressiveness that its composers, imbued with the spirit of romantic literature, felt impelled to tell stories in music. Liszt did, however, give the name *symphonic poem* to the form which the orchestral program music took. And he left as examples for Richard Strauss, Paul Dukas, Claude Debussy, and dozens of others, a group of twelve symphonic poems: *"Les Préludes," "Tasso," "Mazeppa," "Prometheus,"* etc.

To those who contend that absolute music is a higher type than program music, Liszt represents a destructive rather than a constructive force. It is the old discussion of the classic spirit versus the romantic. Regardless of its ultimate result, the symphonic poem is the keynote in the development of nineteenth century music, and no other form has exerted a greater influence on modern music. It leads logically to *impressionism.* The music of Brahms as a counter influence to program music will be discussed later.

The general advance in culture opened the way for composers to search, not only poetry, but history, science, fiction, legend, nature, and painting, for suggestive material which they might translate into their new tonal language. New discords came into use and a new system of harmony was making headway.

Beethoven had exhausted the potentialities of the classical sonata and had introduced new possibilities. Liszt innovated the one-movement sonata form in his B minor Piano Sonata and his concertos for piano and orchestra.

Because of the Hungarian Rhapsodies, which would better have been called Gypsy Rhapsodies, Liszt has been regarded as a nationalist. He was too cosmopolitan in his choice of creative material to be a nationalist, however. His role, rather, was a creator of national schools, as he encouraged different Europeans with whom he came in contact, to study the folk music of their countries, and he directed their efforts to found national schools. He was one of the first to discover Glinka, whom he called the prophet of Russian music, and he was always interested in the work of the Russians. He encouraged Grieg, Smetana, Albeniz, Sgambati, César Franck, and Camille Saint-Saëns. In *La Musique et les nations,* G. Jean-Aubry says: "The perspicacity of Liszt, his careful supervision of certain young people, his insatiable curiosity, his indefatigable apostolate throughout Europe made of him the awakener of the musical national conscience."

In Richard Wagner (1813-1883) we face the supreme romanticist. He attempted to solve the problem of romanticism through complete freedom of self-expression attained by a fusion of all the arts. Time has proved that his musical genius was more sound than his theory. To try to analyze his genius, to say of what his greatness consisted, to estimate his influence on a world sixty-four years after his death, is as difficult as to define Art, Music, the Absolute, or Divinity! "It is clear," Adolf Weissmann wrote in *The Problems of Modern Music,* "that Wagnerism, not as an idea, but through certain essential characteristics, has exercised a worldwide influence, which may be traced today to the remotest circles, not merely in reminiscent themes, but as unavoidable experience in form, color, and mood—Wagner's palette is recognizable in the most unlikely places where his spirit is otherwise entirely changed."

Wagner claimed to have learned his art from Beethoven, and yet he stated that the sonata form was obsolete, and set to work to develop his own form. This he found in the *music drama,* in which he combined within himself librettist, composer, and producer. And the greatest of these was the composer.

His unique genius carried opera beyond the reach of those who tried to follow in his path. Perhaps, if it were taken seriously today, his most potent influence might be his affirmation, in Weissmann's words, "that his own work should be sufficient proof to all contemporary and future composers that each new dramatic or imaginative idea could be and ought to be clothed in a new and suitable form." But instead of obeying the spirit of his message, too many of his adherents listened only to its letter, and pygmies tried to wield the battle ax of the giant.

But his orchestration, his rich harmonic web, his avoidance of formal phrases and of cadential interruptions, the long flowing melodic line, his treatment of the word to suggest the musical line, have opened the way for the twentieth century. His influence is found in modern chamber music, orchestral and program music even to the present day.

The *leitmotif,* which word he coined to mean "guiding" motive or theme, has had enormous effect on composition. In his hands, the leitmotif was developed symphonically with almost limitless variety and tone color, and indicated not only a character's mental attitude, but gesture and dynamics as well. These leitmotifs became a part of an orchestral pattern as a device of reminiscence and thought projection.

Wagner revolutionized the orchestra: he enlarged it, divided it into separate choirs, each complete in itself; he increased its sonority and power, showed the melodic possibilities of the brasses, and invented new bass brass instruments. The woodwinds, which had been improved as to intonation, tone quality, and technical facilities, became more significant. He showed what could be done by dividing the strings into many parts. Anton Bruckner (1824-1896) aimed to graft the Wagner melodic and harmonic system and orchestration on to the classic forms of symphony and church music. Gustav Mahler (1860-1911) profited by his knowledge of Wagner's orchestra, as did also Richard Strauss and many lesser composers.

Wagner and Berlioz were both excellent conductors. Wagner made of the orchestra the perfect medium for the modern composer; he also introduced a new type known as the "personality" conductor—

"that is to say," said Weissmann, "the conductor's personality was to inform the whole body of orchestral sound, to give it soul, and thus to reach and compel the imagination of his audience." "Personality" conductors are still the vogue.

Wagner's reforms in opera were aimed mainly against the artificialities of the Italian and French schools. He began as a disciple of Weber, to whom his early operas owe much, and he studied Gluck's theories. "The voice is now subservient to the plot, drama and feeling. No arias as arias are used, few choruses, and when they are, they become part of the action. The predominating solo voice sings in the older *arioso* style in which the lyric and dramatic unite, less dry than the recitative and more elastic than the outworn form. He abandoned the folk tune and its type for epic declamation. He achieved an orchestral-vocal polyphony, difficult of contemporary assimilation, yet digestible to adherents then and now." (*Music through the Ages,* Bauer and Peyser.)

Wagner's librettos were written in what Ernest Newman calls a "telegraphic style," avoiding the weaknesses of the old librettos which distorted musical form. He was not writing opera, but drama in music, demanding that the music convey the story. Although Weber and Gluck held similar theories, Wagner had greater imagination, more heroic subject matter, richer symbolic significance, and greater skill in developing the orchestra. "His subjects were akin in grandeur to the Greek dramatists," says Ethel Peyser, my collaborator, "who, like Wagner, made grist of the breadth and scope of their nobility which impelled an investiture of lofty ideas."

Tristan und Isolde is still the greatest music drama to most of us. It is too long, judged from present-day standards of terseness and the elimination of unessentials, but the music expresses a wealth of emotional ecstasy and such perfect balance between the composer's intentions and his results that it remains the apotheosis of nineteenth century romanticism. I believe it is not too much to claim that *Tristan und Isolde* has influenced more works than any other score extant.

Die Meistersinger von Nürnberg, the greatest comic opera ever written, bears out his theory that the subject matter must dictate the form in which the music is cast. "In this, Wagner has his opportunity to flay, by means of music, habits of entrenched ideas. It was his fight against his detractors, the struggle between classicism and romanticism, his defense of the new against the old, and his plea for spontaneity instead of prescribed artificialities." (Ethel Peyser.)

Ernest Newman says that "like Bach and Beethoven, Wagner closes a period."

Healthy competition is as natural to art as to any other branch of human endeavor, and so we find Johannes Brahms (1833-1897) brandishing his sword as defender of *absolute music* against the onslaught of the promoters of *program music*—Berlioz, Liszt, and Wagner. Not that Brahms was aware of any active warfare; in fact, the battle was fought between the partisans of the two sides. Those who favored Wagner disapproved of Brahms, and vice versa. Why they could not see that the romantic and the classic viewpoints were complementary instead of antagonistic, and that both are necessary for complete art expression, remains an unsolved riddle.

No better example of the successful combination of the classic and the romantic elements in the work of one man can be found than in Brahms's compositions. He took Beethoven and Bach as his platform deliberately and consciously, and yet he was a child of his day and was influenced by Schubert, Mendelssohn, and particularly Schumann. His North German inheritance and his early training in the classics drew him instinctively to the more severe framework of sonata form. Perhaps stirred by Schumann's manifestos in the *Neue Zeitschrift,* he seemed to feel that he was the chosen successor of Beethoven, and he believed it to be his sacred duty to rescue music from the blind alley of romanticism into which it had been led, and to conduct it back to the highway of classicism. He invented no new forms, but adapted Beethoven's structures to the deeper emotionalism and the enriched harmonic and rhythmic materials of his day. This is apparent in his chamber music and his symphonies. On the contrary, his songs, directly inherited from Schubert and Schumann; his choral works; his folk song arrangements which reveal his peasant soul; his susceptibility to Gypsy music and to the popular Viennese waltz rhythms; and his piano pieces, only two or three of which are programmatic, reveal the individual manner in which romanticism claimed this great nineteenth century neoclassicist.

Brahms's F minor sonata for piano, op. 5, is a revealing example of his early leanings to romanticism. Here is the romantic sonata in free form with a program suggested by a poetic quotation from Sternau which introduces the slow movement.

The program idea is found in his piano pieces, the Edward Ballade, op. 10, no. 1, and the Intermezzo op. 117, no. 1, which carries the quotation *"Schlaf sanft"* ("Sleep softly").

Although Brahms, like Beethoven, adopted Vienna as his home, he never really adjusted himself to the Viennese atmosphere. He remained a transplanted North German. Perhaps the sunnier temperament of the Viennese discovered in the enigmatical outsider an austerity, his reputation for which has been dispelled only in the light of later developments. "Somberness," "reserve," "reactionary spirit" are some of the characteristics for which Brahms's music has been criticized. A genial, humorous, kindhearted, self-cultured Brahms seemed to hide behind a social nonconformist, an austere exterior, a caustic satirical manner, an intolerance of any insincerity, pose, or lack of artistic integrity according to his Olympian standards. All this was probably a defense mechanism, a screen protecting him from intrusion. Even as his remaining a bachelor in the face of several serious love episodes with Clara Schumann, Agathe von Siebold, etc., was engendered by his fear of losing his precious freedom without which he could not have composed.

A real Brahms cult has existed for years which showed first in much imitation of his style and methods by young composers in Germany, England, and even America at the close of the nineteenth and beginning of the twentieth century. This cult has gradually been transferred from the composers to the performers and listeners (page 5) and is, very obviously, a protest against the ultramodern experiments which present unpleasant problems to many. A method of playing safe! On the other hand, Brahms no longer needs to be the object of a cult. As Clive Bell expresses it, he has passed from being part of a movement into the great tradition.

When Brahms played his first piano concerto (the D minor, op. 15) in Leipzig in 1859, he wrote to Joachim that it had been "a brilliant and decided failure." It was hissed because Leipzig was the hotbed of two factions, the adherents of Beethoven and Mendelssohn, and the followers of Liszt, and he did not appear to belong to either faction. Brahms antagonized the "Weimarites" the following year by signing, with several of his friends, a manifesto against the *School of the Future* because of its statement that the most prominent musicians were in accord with its aims and that the compositions of the leaders of the new school were recognized for their artistic value. In Vienna, a few years later, he was again the victim of the antagonism of the Wagner enthusiasts, and was pitted against Anton Bruckner and Hugo Wolf. The Viennese regard Bruckner as Schubert's direct descendant, and Brahms as an intruder. Bruckner's nine symphonies are long and repetitious but are the work of a sincere and unsophis-. ticated person to whom composing is a religion. Adolf Weissmann, a Viennese, admits that Brahms, "more than any other, achieved a definite and original style. Though apparently reactionary, he was by no means opposed to the modern spirit.

"In this matter Bruckner was very different. Wagnerians used to represent Brahms and Bruckner as opposites, and although the modern conductor and the modern concert-program have effected a kind of reconciliation, the feud between their followers secretly persists. Bruckner is to the Brucknerians a holy mystery which only the initiated dare approach." (*Problems of Modern Music.*)

Hugo Wolf (1860-1903) was so much of a Wagnerite that when he was a music critic in Vienna he wrote with bitterness against Brahms. Wolf's fame rests entirely on his songs, but these stamp him a genius. Wolf was consciously a modernist, although he displayed a gift comparable to that other Viennese, Schubert. His object was to apply to song writing Wagner's theories of reinterpreting the poet's ideas in music and of using the leitmotif. He lost himself completely in the excitement and almost hypnotic state of inspiration which the poems induced in him. He finally became insane. His accompaniments are still models to the modern composer, and are veritable tone poems, creating mood and musicianly background.

A younger romantic symphonist was Gustav Mahler (1860-1911), director of the Imperial Opera in Vienna, conductor of the New York Philharmonic Society (1909-1911), and composer of ten symphonies, the last unfinished. He was a man of almost fanatical enthusiasm, which showed itself in his love for the Wagner music dramas, which he conducted superlatively; in his passion for perfection on the opera stage and in the orchestra pit; and in his constant struggle to compose works of great length and wide scope while exhausting himself with his official duties. He aimed to create a new type of symphony based on Bruckner's form, but where Bruckner was simple and direct, Mahler was turbulent and complex. Mahler tried to express in symphonic form the emotionalism of Wagner and his great love of nature, blending his extraordinary knowledge of the orchestra with overwhelming subjective emotion and the desire to bend music to the solution of the problems of the universe. He was torn between the immensities offered by modern music and by his tendency to imitate those composers whom he revered. Weissmann said: "Mahler's symphonic work is psychologically important, as the revelation of a distraught soul; and musically important, as exhibiting a blend of the most primitive with the most modern in music. As a musician, Mahler looks to the past; as a psychological type, he looks to the future; he is more creative in the latter than in the former rôle, stronger where he appears weaker, but most certainly he was never born to become a classic."

He is called the "song-symphonist," for song is the seed out of which his works grow. Although he never wrote opera, his experience as opera conductor shows itself in his use of voices and in the sense of the dramatic one finds in his symphonies. His greatest work, critics agree, is *"Das Lied von der Erde"* (Song of the Earth), a song sequence with symphonic interludes on Hans Bethge's poems, "Chinese Flute." "Rightly understood," Weissmann wrote, "this work is a true reconciliation between homophony and polyphony; it attains harmonic freedom and realizes the aspirations of the modern spirit."

Mahler's place as a composer has not yet been settled. Like Bruckner, he has his ardent adherents and his detractors who point out his weaknesses and find the symphonies too long and musically too involved. His direct influence, however, has been in the impetus his orchestral scores have given to such composers as Richard Strauss and Arnold Schoenberg, and more recently to Dmitri Shostakovich.

Regarded from the neoclassicism of the present day, Max Reger (1873-1916) is the bridge over which nineteenth century neoclassicism has traveled. He is often called the modern Bach as he had an amazing contrapuntal technic based on Bach's principles, more chromatic than Bach but still grounded in a nineteenth century tonality. He used the Bach forms of prelude, fugue, chorale prelude, suite, toccata, fantasie, etc. He could also imitate Brahms's style in piano and chamber music, and wrote some songs in the tradition of the German *Lied,* which show traces of Hugo Wolf. Like Brahms, he was a master of the variation form.

Peter Ilyitch Tchaikovsky (1840-1893), in spite of his use of Russian folk tunes and his geographical position, was not consciously a Russian nationalist. He built his art not on his native folk music as did the *Russian Five* (page 59), but on the traditions of German post-romanticism. His six symphonies, which he admitted were programmatic, and his concertos for piano and for violin, show him as a *romantic symphonist,* while his tone poems are modeled on Liszt's as to form and program. As we said in *Music through the Ages,* "he spoke Liszt's language with a decided Russian accent." "The Tempest," "Romeo and Juliet," the Manfred Symphony, and "Francesca da Rimini" are his representative tone poems. An innovation in his charming Nutcracker Suite was his introduction of the celesta as an orchestral instrument. His nationalism is best represented by his operas, of which *Eugen Oniegin* after Pushkin, and *Pique Dame* (*Queen of Spades*) are the best known. Tchaikovsky's characteristics are displayed in his brooding melancholy, religious sentiment, deep-rooted emotions, charm of melody, long phrases, keen orchestral sense, instinctive feeling for tone color, and insistence on long pedal points.

In many discussions with Mme. Nadejda von Meck, his patroness whom he never met outside of letters, he states that from his standpoint every kind of music is program music, and that a mere play with sounds is a long way from being music. (Stravinsky notwithstanding!) A composer's inspiration is subjective or objective. Subjective music, like lyric poetry, expresses the personal feelings of joy or sorrow of its creator. Here a program is unnecessary and even impossible. "But it is otherwise when the musician in reading a poetic work, or at the sight of a beautiful landscape, is inspired to interpret musically the subject which fills him with such ecstasy. In this case a program is indispensable.... At any rate, from my standpoint, both kinds of music have a right to exist, and I do not understand the people who will admit the legitimacy of only one of them." And here we have a clear statement of what program music is.

Again he told Sergei Tanéieff, who succeeded Tchaikovsky as teacher at Nicholas Rubinstein's Conservatory at Moscow, that he did not see why it should be considered a fault that a symphony was program music. He then confesses: "At bottom, my symphony [the

Fourth] is an imitation of Beethoven's fifth symphony; that is to say, I imitated not its musical content, but its fundamental idea. What do you think—has the fifth symphony a program? Not only has it a program, but there cannot even be the slightest difference as to what the symphony purports to express." To Mme. von Meck he told what the program is: "This is Fate, that momentous power which hinders the desire for happiness from attaining its aim ... a power which, like Damocles' sword, always hangs overhead, which continually poisons the soul. This power is inevitable and unconquerable. There remains nothing but to submit to it and lament in vain." His is the morbid hopelessness which culminated in the Pathetic Symphony (the Sixth).

As Beethoven opened his symphony with the famous four notes, g-g-g-eb, so Tchaikovsky opens the Fourth with his *fate* motive:

The most famous English composer during this period of post-romanticism has been Sir Edward Elgar (1857-1934) who wrote orchestral and choral works from 1891 to 1904 which have given him a respected place in the musical world. He had particular skill in instrumentation and choral writing, as is shown in two symphonies, a violin concerto, the Enigma Variations, and his oratorios, *The Dream of Gerontius, The Apostles,* and *The Kingdom.*

In the United States the nineteenth century trends were evidenced by a group of Boston composers, George Chadwick (1854-1931), Arthur Foote (1853-1937), Horatio Parker (1863-1919), Mrs. H. H. A. Beach (1867-1944); also in Edgar Stillman Kelley (1857-1944), Ethelbert Nevin (1862-1901), not a symphonist but a writer of songs and piano music which enjoyed a vogue, Henry Holden Huss (1862), Henry K. Hadley (1871-1937), Rubin Goldmark (1872-1936), and others.

Edward MacDowell (1861-1908) is recognized as our greatest romanticist and poet-composer. The true spirit of romanticism which renews itself through a sincere love for music, for nature, and an appreciation of the other arts was MacDowell's. His Irish-Scotch inheritance, American birth and schooling, German and French musical training, his absorption of nineteenth century aesthetics, and his love of Norse legends stamped his individuality. Although his two piano concertos, his piano suites, and tone poems for orchestra flavor of the Liszt school, he was primarily a composer for piano, for which he formulated an individual style. His sonatas, the Tragica, the Eroica, the Norse, and the Keltic, have literary programs and are written in a free romantic form in which he has used theme transformations. In MacDowell's happy use of the short piano forms he has often been compared to Grieg. In their impersonal aloofness, and objective descriptiveness, MacDowell caught the first reflections of impressionism, which he enclosed within the pages of his *Sea Pieces, Woodland Sketches, Fireside Tales, New England Idylls,* and songs. "The Eagle," "To a Water Lily," "Out of the Depths," are only a few exquisite results of a tone poet's imagination.

In his early years he was an innovator, and W. F. Apthorp, much taken with the charm and earnest sincerity of the young composer, regretted that he could make nothing out of his music; he could not understand his idiom! The MacDowell Colony at his summer home in Peterboro, New Hampshire, stands as a tribute to his ideals and life purpose of perpetuating art by bringing the workers in all the arts into closer understanding of each others' aims and aspirations.

CHAPTER 6

NATIONALISM BASED ON FOLK MUSIC:
RUSSIA, CZECHOSLOVAKIA, HUNGARY, NORWAY,
ENGLAND, SPAIN, AMERICA

IS it not amazing that although every country had given unconscious expression in melody to its racial feelings, character, and
interests, until the nineteenth century, folk music was not recognized as a means for the development of a national art?

Liszt was evidently not only the Wizard of the Piano, but also the
conjurer of the genii of nationalism. For it was he who pointed out
to his apprentices from all countries, the vitality and serviceability of
the materials of their own environment, showing them that in the spontaneous music of a nation may be found the germ of its developed art.

He did not invent the idea of an art based on folk music, but he
was sufficiently sensitized to feel the contemporary currents of thought,
and to be the medium through which they were communicated
(page 48). Chopin, too, felt the call of his native Poland with its
picturesque songs and dance rhythms—felt it the more keenly because
of the political disaster which had overtaken it. Before the advent of
the Napoleonic wars, the national spirit was dormant and a universal
musical language satisfied the nations. When the countries became
more aware of political separateness, however, national thought developed and with it a national art consciousness.

An unconscious nationalism, an automatic reflection of a people's
peculiarities, psychology, social customs, and aesthetics, has always
existed. In the twentieth century, the two types of nationalism have been
blended: the folk elements, based on folk and popular music and influenced by the rhythmic and melodic elements of the language, have
become assimilated to the point of being used unconsciously, and the

58

elements which constitute the *soul of a people* have been subjected to conscious study and analysis.

The history of Russian music is the record of the awakening of a national art consciousness. It was less difficult for Russia to be the first to develop nationalism because it had no musical art traditions of its own. Before the nineteenth century, Russia imported opera from Italy and concerts from Germany; early in the century, French opera flourished and Boieldieu, the composer of French *opéra comique,* spent some time, and John Field, the Irish pianist and composer, won fame there. A Venetian, Catterino Cavos (1776-1840), however, was the first composer to use Russian folklore and national subjects. *A Life for the Tsar* (1836) by Michael Ivanovitch Glinka (1803-1857) recorded the birth of Russian opera and musical nationalism. *Russlan and Ludmilla,* based on a poem by Pushkin, which Glinka built on native folk music, followed.

In addition to the folk songs and dances from pagan times, the Russians' unaccompanied religious music gave the composers another rich and untapped source upon which to draw; the Russian church had remained democratic throughout the centuries, as its priests were always close to the people. The music was not an art product as in the Western church, but was closer to folk song than that of any other Christian ritual, with the exception of Luther's chorale. The music of the church and of the people reacted upon each other, for the old ecclesiastical modes of the early Christian church retained by the Russians appear in the folk songs.

When Russian national feeling was awakened by the Napoleonic invasion, the revolt against classicism in literature took on the nature of a reversion to folklore. The movement headed by Pushkin included Dostoievsky, Gogol, and Turgenieff in literature; Ostrovsky in the drama; Stassoff and Mihailovsky in criticism; and Glinka, Alexander Sergeivich Dargomijsky (1813-1869), and Alexander Seroff (1820-1871), a Russian Wagnerite, in music. They were followed by the *Russian Five:* Mily Balakireff (1837-1910), Alexander Borodin (1834-1887), César Cui (1835-1918), Nikolai Rimski-Korsakov (1844-1908), and Modest Moussorgsky (1839-1881).

Balakireff, the originator of the movement, was the only trained musician of the Five, and was destined, according to Glinka's belief, to carry on the campaign of Russian musical nationalism. His colorful score "Tamara" is exotic and brilliant and has had a wide influence on his colleagues and followers, and *"Islamey"* is a brilliant example of what the Russian Five donated to the piano literature of their day. César Cui, Balakireff's first convert, the son of a French officer under Napoleon, was an authority on military science, and was a self-elected press agent for the group. Borodin was a gifted amateur, an army surgeon, an experimental chemist, a writer of scientific treatises, a philanthropist and educator. He wrote *Prince Igor,* which reflects a barbaric and oriental color due perhaps to the fact that he was the son of a prince of the Caucasus. He combined the glamour of Asia with the knowledge gained from a Western European technic, as he came under the influence of Liszt in Weimar. This shows to advantage in his symphonies and string quartets. His lovely songs are sensitive and refined.

Rimski-Korsakov was a naval officer and a musical amateur, but he studied with such thoroughness that he became not only an authority but one of the most important masters in the twentieth century school of orchestration which numbers among its adherents his pupils Stravinsky, Prokofieff, and Miaskovsky. He has left tangible proof of his valuable ideas in his *Treatise of Orchestration,* one of the most important methods since Berlioz published his *Orchestration.* In his book *Music of Our Day* Lazare Saminsky paints a sympathetic portrait of the man whose influence has been so great on the music of the twentieth century: "I knew but one image of him: a giant of northern sagas with the wide eye of a benevolent sorcerer, a tenderly passionate and delicate artist—aristocrat, religiously in love with the freshest, airiest walk in art.

"The world at large has created a popular image of Rimski-Korsakov in conformity with the naked orientalism of *Schéhérazade* and *Chant Hindou....* For that matter did the world at large, who had had an inkling of the real Rimski-Korsakov in *Coq d'or,* sense all the import and historical consequence of this work? Do we realize that both Stravinsky and Prokofiev are *hardly possible* without this source and forerunner of both, their grotesque and their technique?"

Rimski's influence on Moussorgsky has been the subject of much discussion pro and con. Moussorgsky, the greatest of the group, in fact, one of the most original geniuses of the nineteenth century, was misjudged, or at least his ability was miscalculated by Rimski, who was his devoted friend and teacher. Rimski had all the technical refinements which intensive study of European methods had given him. He recognized his colleague's originality and talent, but the inherent strength of Moussorgsky's naturalism, he regarded as a diamond in the rough, and he felt a conscientious obligation to polish it in accordance with contemporary fashion. Many characteristics which later were recognized as crude strength and as Moussorgsky's complete rejection of all European influence, Rimski changed as mistakes in harmony, counterpoint, and form due to the rapidity and carelessness with which he put down his ideas. In the famous opera *Boris Godounoff* (or *Godunov*), for instance, Moussorgsky's consecutive fifths, which were forbidden by the laws of harmony, disturbed him. In many pages he conventionalized Moussorgsky's rhythms. One of the most patent examples is in the great opening chorus, where the irregular rhythms in alternating five-four and three-four meter have been simplified to straight two-four time. Something is lost in this shift of primary accents. In some instances, it is true, Rimski improved on Moussorgsky, especially in the orchestration, of which Rimski was a master. But after comparing the scores, Olin Downes wrote in the *New York Times,* June 23, 1930, "As for sheer knowledge of orchestration, Rimsky-Korsakoff's expertness as compared with Moussorgsky's technical equipment is the difference between the knowledge of master and pupil. Unfortunately the pupil's genius was greater than the master's, wherefore the master has often frustrated the purpose of the pupil when he had a sincere and honorable intention to help him." Mr. Downes went to Russia to see the original version of *Boris.* "The career of this work, in its own land," he wrote, "has a curious and inescapable analogy to the course of Russian history. It slept on shelves for about fifty years in the form in which Moussorgsky conceived it. In this form it did not see the light of day until the consummation of the revolution. Until then it existed for the public only in an emasculated form acceptable to the imperial theaters of 1874, and after that in a conventionalized and still incomplete version of Rimsky-Korsakoff. Now *Boris Godounoff* in its completeness and authenticity has been given to the world by the régime which overthrew the dynasty.... The music of *Boris* as a whole is far superior, far more dramatically truthful and modern in texture in Moussourg-sky's original version than in the Rimsky-Korsakoff's editing."

In opposition to occidental tendencies, Moussorgsky, a decided "Slavophile," discovered and glorified what Arthur Lourié calls the Scythian element in Russian music, "in which the archaic and Asiatic atmosphere circulates magically in Moussorgskian work, and to the ancient call of which no youth ever listened more keenly than did Claude Debussy." (*La Revue musicale,* July-August 1931.) Rimski, in Lourié's idea, occupied a position halfway between occidentalism and Scythianism. Slavophile in his inspiration and often in the choice of his sonorities, he remained attached to the traditions of the German school accepting the ideas of the postromanticists.

Moussorgsky alone was an opposing voice in this new Russian-European academicism, but he sounded the note of realism which was not heard distinctly until the twentieth century was at hand. Then Moussorgsky was hailed as having introduced a new manner of writing, new forms and new tonal material.

Moussorgsky was closer to Dargomijsky than to any of his own group, and brought to life the older composer's passionate search for "truth in Art." Of Dargomijsky's setting in opera form of Pushkin's version of the story of Don Juan, *The Stone Guest,* Cecil Gray says in *The History of Music* that it "represents the logical conclusion and best exemplification of his dramatic ideals, and a more striking contrast to Wagnerian music-drama could hardly be found. ... The whole work consists entirely of recitative with a strictly subordinated orchestral accompaniment possessing no independent existence or musical interest of its own. Both in this respect and in the extensive employment throughout the latter half of the work of the whole-tone scale, Dargomijsky's opera constitutes a remarkable anticipation of the *Pelléas et Mélisande* of Debussy...."

Of Rimski-Korsakov's use of the augmented chord (f-a-c♯, and d♭-f-a) we have a sample in the "Procession of the Marvels of the Sea" from *Sadko:*

In a following passage the bass reveals this whole tone scale:

So the assertion that the Russians gave Debussy the idea for his use of the whole tone scale is well founded (page 128).

Moussorgsky adapted the folk music freely to his own needs, and tried to characterize the people in his operas by stark realism. The democratic spirit which dominates Russia today was awakened by the emancipation of the serfs following Alexander II's accession, and the artists, moved to deep compassion for the people, preached the doctrine of throwing aside social and artistic conventions. "Make art the handmaiden of humanity. Seek not for beauty but for truth," they said. "Go to the people. Hold out the hand of fellowship to the liberated masses and learn from them the true purpose of life." (Grove's *Dictionary*.)

No one answered the call with more thoroughness than Moussorgsky. He studied the peasants; he became a psychologist, using music to delineate all phases of their lives. He was a musical portrait painter, working in strong colors; a powerful draftsman, loving his subjects and yet picturing them with pitiless honesty. In his operas, *Boris, Kovanshchina, The Marriage Broker,* and the fragments of the *Fair of Sorotchinsk;* in his songs, the "Peasant's Cradle Song," the "Village Idiot's Love Song," the cycle *In the Nursery,* and *Songs and Dances of Death;* in his extraordinary piano composition, "Pictures from an Exhibition," we receive as vivid an impression of Russian types and character as in the writings of Dostoievsky, Tolstoi, or Tchekov.

The "Pictures from an Exhibition," written as a memorial to his friend Victor Hartmann, a painter, describing in music ten of his pictures, is an important signpost pointing toward realistic impressionism.

Bedrich Smetana (1824-1884) was the founder of the national school of Bohemian or Czechoslovak music. He was distinctly a follower of Liszt as his six symphonic poems entitled *Mein Vaterland* (*My Country*) attest. They are programmatic and nationalistic. The second of the group, *"Vltava"* (Moldau) is named for the river which flows through Prague. There is also one called *"Vysehrad"* which describes realistically a national fortress at Prague. He recognized the need for building a school of music from the peasant tunes of Bohemia "to cut her cornerstone from her own quarries," he said. He made use of the polka, the Czech national dance, and in *The Bartered Bride* (*Die verkaufte Braut*) created a masterpiece which has given him a unique position among the writers of national music. Without being based on actual folk songs, it exhales an atmosphere typically Czech. W. H. Hadow wrote in his essay on Dvořák (*Studies in Modern Music*), "Neither Chopin nor Grieg have quite the same powerful material significance.... He [Smetana] made his art a wonderful stimulus to the national rebirth.... His works ... are the best medium for a Czech to become conscious of his national character."

Following in his footsteps was Antonin Dvořák (1842-1907), who, however, was a traveler and was more of a cosmopolitan than Smetana. He visited England and wrote works for English festivals. He spent three years in America, unhappy, homesick years, but he showed our composers how to use our own heretofore neglected material through his New World Symphony and his string quartet based on Negro themes. While he taught at the National Conservatory in New York, he met H. T. Burleigh, Negro composer and singer, who showed the Bohemian nationalist some of the spirituals which, through his own arrangements, Burleigh has since helped to make famous. It has been stated that some of Dvořák's simple themes which sound like Negro songs are really of Bohemian origin, and the idea of naming the symphony "From the New World" was suggested to the composer after it was completed. Be that as it may, it has had a stimulating influence, and the pseudo spiritual, "Going Home," adapted from the largo of the symphony, has enjoyed a popular vogue.

A nineteenth century Czechoslovak who came into fame in the twentieth century was Leos Janacek (1854-1928), with whom the modern spirit was introduced. He was a Moravian and devoted his life to studying Moravian folk music and trying to establish a national school. He is called the Czechoslovak Moussorgsky, and his influence on the contemporary school has been great. He has been its inspiration and model. Although he was an old man before he gained recognition, his place is with the new nationalists of the period after the First World War, and his contribution to opera will be discussed later (Chapter 19).

Closely allied to Czechoslovakia is Hungary, of which country Liszt was a native. It would have been much closer to the truth had Liszt called his rhapsodies *Gypsy* instead of Hungarian, for it has been conclusively proven by Béla Bartók and Zoltan Kodaly that much of the music regarded as Magyar or Hungarian is really Gypsy. Liszt, Brahms, Haydn, and even Bach, were influenced by the Gypsy-Magyar music. Bartók and Kodaly and his wife were pioneers in investigating Hungarian music, and they made clear the difference between it and the Gypsy tunes, many of which are popular art songs rather than folk songs. The so-called Gypsy Rondo by Haydn is really a wrong translation of *Rondo all 'Ongarese,* and Brahms's Hungarian Dances are Gypsy.

"Probably no other folk music is so dependent on language as is the Hungarian. The syllables and their accent are the bases of the rhythm which is fundamentally dance music. ... But unlike Gypsy music, the Hungarian folk tunes are undecorated, strongly syncopated, and abounding in amazing rhythm.

"Besides the old or native music, Hungary has a new style typical of the music of the old régime but different from any other folk music. Bartók thinks that this is the only nation that has ever been able to graft a new folk song on the old and still retain ancient character and characteristics.

"The Hungarian song is based to a large extent on the Dorian mode and on the Æolian and modern major tonalities. The Mixolydian is fairly frequent but the Phrygian and modern minor less so." (*Music through the Ages.*)

Bartók made thousands of phonograph records of Hungarian songs and brought them within reach of the schoolchildren, thus stimulating the nationalistic spirit. Much of this was done at the end of the nineteenth century. He also made collections of Balkan and Turkish folk music. His works, impregnated with this folk study, will be discussed later (pages 246-7).

In 1870, Edvard Grieg (1843-1907) met Liszt in Rome. Liszt encouraged the younger composer to study the folk music of his native Norway, and no one made better use of a conscious nationalism. Temperamentally he was fitted to be the chosen leader of a national school, for he had the poetic imagination and the love of folklore added to technical training which he acquired in Germany. No composer has been more deeply inspired by the forces of nature than Grieg. The elf finds materialization in his music. Rikard Nordraak did much to encourage Grieg's study of their folk songs as a means of national musical art development, and together they "abjured the Gade-Mendelssohn insipid and diluted Scandinavianism" and founded a society for the exploitation of the Northern School. From 1867 to 1880 Grieg was the conductor of a musical union in Christiania (Oslo) which he founded with Nordraak.

His curious characteristic fifths have a peasant-like harshness suggested, no doubt, by the little fiddle used by the country people in accompanying their dances. Dr. Eaglefield Hull found that Grieg's harmonic method "gives him a place with Moussorgsky and Debussy amongst the great harmonic initiators." The characteristic rhythms and melodic line have their origin in folk tune also.

The wave of interest in folk music which swept over Europe, by the end of the nineteenth century, had reached as far west as England and Spain. S. Baring-Gould investigated the rich folk music of Devon and Cornwall, and Cecil Sharp carried on research in England and America, discovering tunes of Anglo-Saxon origin brought over three hundred years ago and lost in the mountains of Kentucky and Tennessee. The Folk-Song Society of England was founded in 1898, and the influence of English nationalism is plainly discernible in the works of several twentieth century composers, such as Granville Bantock (1868-1946), Ralph Vaughan Williams (1872), and Gustav Holst (1874-1934).

Eaglefield Hull wrote that Vaughan Williams's Englishry is "derived from a deep love of English country life, a lifelong study of her folksong and dance, and a strong turn in favor of English contrapuntal style." Through study with Maurice Ravel the Englishman found his way in the use of medieval modes which the impressionistic composers were advocating. His melodic line shows the influence of folk song and his harmonic scheme that of impressionism. He uses the common chord, but the basis is often the twelve tone scale (pages 111-2).

J. B. Trend in the Introduction to his book *Manuel de Falla and Spanish Music* writes that when the change which occurred at the end of the nineteenth century is referred to as a renaissance, it is not a *rebirth* but a *getting down to facts.* "The facts of musical experience have to be excavated and exposed to view before any rebirth can take place; indeed, 'rebirth' is the last stage in the process, for it must be preceded by the reform which comes from a study of the facts. . . . The recent musical renaissance in various countries has been brought about by adventurous exploration. By getting down to the facts and exposing to view once more the musical traditions of those countries, it is free in spirit,—a protest against any form of dictatorship whether Latin or German. It is free no less in England, where culture is a bridge between the Latin and the Teutonic, than it is in Spain, which, deeply Romanized as it was, owes many of its peculiarities to the fact that it too was a bridge for seven hundred years between a Latin civilization and the civilization of Islam."

Felipe Pedrell (1841-1922) was the Spanish musician who gathered material on which the composers have constructed a new Spanish school. He collected the traditional songs from all Spain, and made valuable researches into the archives of Spanish music which had a rich heritage of church music (the Mozarabic chant), of music for the lute, and Gypsy music.

He impressed on his pupils, one of the most famous of whom was Manuel de Falla (1876-1946), the need of an unbroken tradition in any music the characteristic of which is national, a tradition derived not only from the folk song and from primitive music, but also from the masterpieces of the past, in which are reflected the genius of the race, its customs and temperament.

Outsiders recognize certain rhythms as Spanish, although others, just as characteristic, have not been identified as such. Trend discusses "the Spanish idiom" at length and states that the type was established in Europe by Bizet's *Carmen,* Lalo's Capriccio, Moszkowski's duets, and by Chabrier's *"España."* It can be found as early as the seventeenth century, is traceable in the street music, in the popular church music, and even to the songs of the shepherds in the dramatic entertainments of Juan del Enzina from the end of the fifteenth century. Manuel Garcia, the famous singer and founder of a family of singers, introduced the popular eighteenth century *tonadillas* to the rest of Europe and America. Although Andalusian song and rhythms are the best known and are considered the most characteristic, the music of Spain can be divided into four groups: the Basque, the music of Biscay and Navarre, irregular in rhythm with the jota as the characteristic dance; from Galicia and Castille, with gay, bright, strongly marked rhythms, such as the bolero and *seguidilla;* from Andalusia, the flamenco and the *cante hondo* (or *jondo*) which Raoul Laparra, the composer of the opera *Habañera,* considered as the bases of the future Spanish school; and from Catalonia, whose somber music is less Spanish in character because of its proximity to the outside world.

Francisco Barbieri (1823-1894) and Frederico Olmeda (1865-1909) shared with Pedrell the honor of demonstrating to the modern Spanish composers the possibilities of their national music.

In *L'Essor de la musique espagnole du XX*e *siècle,* Henri Collet writes: "The marvelous sadness of the gitano-andalusian song (*cante jondo*) which retains the power of its magical oriental scales, should not blind us to the point of making us disdain the more modest treasures of the folklore of other regions."

The Arabian modes have filtered into the Spanish folk songs, and Laparra discovered in some of the Basque dances the pure Arabian scale: d, e♭, f♯, g, a, b♭, c♯, d. In Castille, the *Marianas* show the effect of Arab or Hebrew scales. In general the tonality is Gregorian, and in the anthologies of Pedrell and Olmeda, Collet points out many examples of Dorian and Phrygian modes. "Almost all the Castillian songs, for example, come from a liturgical source, Gregorian or 'Mozarabic,' that is Gothic-Spanish.... They developed in the glorious epoch of the Crusaders and knew how to resist later the artistic influence of the Renaissance."

Rhythmically we find Spanish music related to our American popular music in its use of syncopation. This is not as strange as it may seem, for both have similar foundations. The tango, African in origin, became the habanera in Spain and has been adopted by our musicians. Many of the South American dances have found their way into Spain and vice versa: the early explorers probably carried characteristic music to the colonies in the new world. Julien Tiersot states that Bizet took his famous Habanera in *Carmen* from a song by a South American composer, Yradier. (*Musical Quarterly,* October 1927.)

The folk music of Spain has swayed foreign as well as native composers. Debussy and Ravel felt its insidious fascination and in turn they influenced the Spanish composers, Albeniz and Falla, for example, who added the charm of impressionism to that of their own Spanish idiom.

Enrique Granados (1867-1916) wrote two books of *Goyescas* in which he practically created a Spanish piano music style which he introduced to the outside world. Named for the great Spanish painter Goya, these piano pieces were developed into an opera based on scenes from the Goya pictures, which was produced at the Metropolitan in New York (1916). By arranging Domenico Scarlatti's sonatas he reminded the world of the Italian's residence in Spain and of his influence in creating a Spanish style in keyboard music. Granados also wrote four books of Spanish dances based on eighteenth century *tonadillas*.

Isaak Albeniz (1860-1909) was a Spanish nationalist of high merit and importance. He was an internationalist in acquiring knowledge, as he studied in Madrid, Paris, and Germany, where he, too, came under the influence of Liszt. In Paris, later, after studying with d'Indy and meeting Fauré and Debussy, he combined the nationalistic tendencies with impressionism and became an important figure as a bridge between the nineteenth century investigators of folk music and the twentieth century Spanish composers. His twelve piano pieces, *Iberia,* show the result of this liaison between Spain and France. Of one of these, *"El Albaicin,"* Debussy wrote, "Without exactly reproducing popular themes, it is by some one who has drunk them in, listened to them just to the point of making them so much a part of his music that it is impossible to perceive the line of demarcation."

The discovery that there is an American nationalism belongs chronologically to the twentieth century, but forces have been at work for almost three centuries which gradually are crystallizing into American music—not into one school but into various styles. Many have accepted the half-truth that we have no folk music, therefore can have no national school. We not only have a folk music but it is today a source of valuable research, and much of it is being unearthed. Folk music is not the only basis of our nationalism, however. We must bear in mind the composite character of our American civilization and culture in which are amalgamated the standards, ideals, habits and customs of practically every nation in the world. Yet the stamp "made in America" is recognizable the world over. We have been sung to sleep to the folk songs of our parents and grandparents, most of them of foreign birth; before 1914 we studied with foreign teachers at home and went abroad for further work with European masters. At heart we are a nation of pioneers, and that spirit of fearlessness, bravado, and energy, the vitally essential spark of Americanism, is gradually finding its way into our music. Heretofore, our composers, through ignorance of technical requirements, produced a music in folk style reflecting the heart of the people as did Stephen Foster, or they timidly imitated the methods and idioms of their European masters.

Many American-born composers completed their studies abroad, such as Charles Griffes, Aaron Copland, and others. Some composers born abroad have spent most of their lives here, such as Louis Gruenberg, Leo Ornstein, etc. Many Europeans came as mature artists—Charles Martin Loeffler, Ernest Bloch, Carlos Salzedo, Percy Grainger, Lazare Saminsky, Bernard Wagenaar, etc., planting old-world ideals, methods, and standards in American musical soil. The Hitler regime brought us Europe's greatest, including Schoenberg, Stravinsky, Hindemith, Bartók, Milhaud, etc. A few never studied abroad, such as Arthur Foote, Carl Ruggles, Charles Ives, Harold Morris. Even the American-born composers have the strains, often mixed, of European blood. Whether self-consciously American or unconsciously so, slowly and surely we are evolving an art which could be that of no other country save America.

Besides the folk songs of the immigrating masses, we have pure English folk tunes in the Kentucky and Tennessee mountains, also in Vermont. Cecil Sharp, the British folk song specialist, found that the Cavalier and the Puritan song of three centuries ago has flourished undisturbed and almost unadulterated in the out-of-the-way corners of this country. The lumberjack songs of Maine, the cowboy songs of the plains, the mining-camp songs of '49, Spanish songs of Southern California, the French Creole songs of Louisiana, the music of the Indian and the Negro, and the "white spirituals" are folk songs even though we have watched some of them in the making. Many popular songs of Spaeth's "Read 'em and Weep" variety and familiar hymn tunes deserve to be included in this list. All this is as good material on which to base a national music as any country needs.

Few nations have had the opportunity to study primitive music at first hand as we have in the American Indian. Henry F. Gilbert, Arthur Farwell, Natalie Curtis Burlin, Harvey Worthington Loomis, Arthur Nevin, Charles Wakefield Cadman, and Frances Densmore have made the music of the red man the object of their research. The phonograph records and the bulletins issued by the Smithsonian Institution form an invaluable source of information concerning aboriginal music, opening for the archeologist a door which has for ages been practically closed to the European.

Indian themes have been used in art music by Edward MacDowell, Gilbert, Charles Griffes, Frederick Jacobi, besides Cadman, Lieurance, Homer Grunn, Charles S. Skilton, etc. But the red man is not *à la mode* for the moment, and has had to yield the palm of popularity to his black brother.

Jazz belongs definitely to the twentieth century, but its roots are imbedded in the earlier music of the Negro. Stephen Foster caught the spirit of the Negro and gave us incomparable songs which fit H. E. Krehbiel's definition of folk music as that which "has come into existence without the influence of conscious art, as a spontaneous utterance, filled with characteristic expression of the feelings of a people." (*Afro-American Folk-Songs.*) Thomas Rice, the father of "Negro Minstrels," instigated a purely American institution which had its effect on our popular music.

But the true folk song of the Negro is his *spiritual*, in which he pictures his life among the white people, his sorrows, his joys, all reflected through his religious impulses. His interpretations of the Bible stories applying them to his needs, his use of English, may bring a smile because of the naïveté expressed, but no one doubts the tragedy and sadness in the groping of the primitive African among alien customs while making heart-breaking adjustments. Of the spirituals, Krehbiel wrote: "They contain idioms which were transplanted hither from Africa, but as song they are the product of American institutions; of the social, political and geographical environment within which their creators were placed in America, of the influences ... and experiences which fell to their lot in America."

The spiritual has the characteristic Negro rhythm which is to be found in pure African music. James Weldon Johnson says that "In rhythms African music is beyond comparison with any other music

in the world"; also: "The musical genius of the African has not become so generally recognized as his genius in sculpture and design,
and yet it has had a wide influence on the music of the world." (*The
Book of American Negro Spirituals*.) "In form," he writes, "Spirituals
often run strictly parallel with African songs, incremental leading lines
and choral iteration." That is, they are antiphonal.

Today's jazz was yesterday's ragtime, cakewalk, and coon song.
Jazz and *ragtime* are indicative of a chronological change, for jazz is
a very sophisticated development of ragtime. It will be discussed later
in relation to its twentieth century standing (page 316).

Several historical factors had their influence on the development of
our music. The Puritans who settled in New England permitted only
"Spiritual Songs," and music as a trade was forbidden. There were
"singing schools," and sacred music was later encouraged, so that the
first music societies were choral groups. This early development resulted in a cultural school of music in the nineteenth century with
such worthy names in the roster of Boston composers as George W.
Chadwick, Arthur Foote, Horatio Parker, Mrs. H. H. A. Beach,
Frederick Converse, etc. We have had our romanticists, headed by
Edward MacDowell; and many composers, Rubin Goldmark, Henry
Holden Huss, Henry Hadley, Edgar Stillman Kelley, Daniel Gregory
Mason, Edward Burlingame Hill, David Stanley Smith, to mention
only a few, have upheld the dignity of American composition—pioneers
whose object was not primarily to create an American school but to
write good music as they had learned it through classic and romantic
channels.

From 1685, the birth date of Bach, until 1914, the cultured world
was under the domination of German music. Our orchestras, conductors, teachers, and performers were predominantly German. Not
only the United States, but England, France, and even Russia were
propagating music sired by German traditions and characteristics. The
influence of Franz Liszt on every country has been pointed out. It
reached even our shores. And Dvorák's visit to this country may have
done something to awaken our realization of a virginal folk music at
our threshold.

With the opening of the twentieth century, other ingredients were
leavening German romanticism, beginning with the realism of Richard
Strauss. French impressionism introduced a non-Teutonic mode of

thought. The Russians, Scriabin and particularly Stravinsky, were speaking in new tongues. Schoenberg in Vienna was beginning to awaken from the spell of Wagner and Strauss, and to question the inevitability of that domination.

Then World War I broke. Its effect on America was twofold. In throwing off the yoke of German supremacy, we sought for substitutes in the music of other countries, and were driven to develop our own resources. Our contemporary music reflects the results of this duality. Our composers understand and employ every modern European trick of technic, tonality, harmony, counterpoint, melody, instrumentation, rhythm, and form. And to this they have indisputably added that touch of individuality—a national consciousness. Louis Gruenberg, Emerson Whithorne, John Alden Carpenter, Harold Morris, Roger Sessions, all have this combination of sophisticated means and American spirit. Howard Hanson, John Powell, Leo Sowerby, Roy Harris, Carl Ruggles, Charles Ives, Arthur Shepherd, Virgil Thomson, Douglas Moore, Ernst Bacon, Robert Russell Bennett, Henry Cowell, writing music differing completely in method and individuality, also reflect an American spirit. A new group of composers, born in the twentieth century are carrying it on: Aaron Copland, Marc Blitzstein, Paul Creston, Samuel Barber, William Schuman, Norman Dello Joio, David Diamond, Leonard Bernstein, Robert McBride, Earl Robinson, etc. Just what constitutes this "spirit" is as difficult to define in music as in any other phase of life, yet today we recognize it as American.

CHAPTER 7

NATIONALISM IN FRANCE:
"LA SOCIETE NATIONALE DE MUSIQUE,"
CESAR FRANCK AND HIS FOLLOWERS

THE national consciousness in France was aroused not through a study of its folk music resources but was the result of a revolt against German musical domination, a gesture that arose from political events surrounding the Franco-Prussian War.

With the exception of Berlioz, who was unappreciated by his own people, French tradition had been hidden in so-called French opera represented by the works of Gluck, Rossini, and Meyerbeer. French composers were popular only as writers of light opera, and the Second Empire seemed apathetic to instrumental music and indifferent to any serious native music.

A few orchestras were in existence before 1870, and some concert organizations, but as Camille Saint-Saëns said, the few chamber music societies that existed were closed to all newcomers, and "in those times one had really to be devoid of all common sense to write music."

The development of music in France between the time of the Franco-Prussian War and World War I is almost without precedent.

To César Franck (1822-1890), a Belgian by birth who lived in Paris from his twelfth year, credit is due for having founded the modern French school concerning which Romain Rolland, who never hid his preference for German music, said in 1905, "French art is quietly taking the place of German art." (*L'art français, silencieusement, est en train de prendre la place de l'art allemand*.) Franck made his home the center of a group of pupils and sympathizers. There they heard each other's compositions, discussed musical problems, and received the kindly, constructive criticism of "*le bon père* Franck," as they called him. Unconsciously he nurtured the roots of the revolt out of which

74

grew the new regime which was to change the face of the entire musical world. He taught them a new respect for classic forms, for chamber and orchestral music, for the fearless statement of their own ideals—and individuality. And these ideals, in which they had faith and which they were willing to champion, were his.

Among his pupils were Vincent d'Indy (1851-1932), Ernest Chausson (1855-1899), Henri Duparc (1848-1933), Guy Ropartz (1864), Charles Bordes (1863-1909), Guillaume Lekeu (1870-1894), Alexis de Castillon (1838-1873), Gabriel Pierné (1863-1937), Augusta Holmès (1847-1903), Pierre de Breville (1861), and Henri Expert (1863).

"A new generation was growing up...," writes Romain Rolland (*Musicians of Today*). "A generation that was serious and thoughtful, that was more attracted by pure music than by the theater, that was filled with a burning desire to found a national art."

This desire was realized in the Société Nationale de Musique (National Music Society) which has been called the cradle and sanctuary of French art. The first concert in the Salle Pleyel, November 25, 1871, was the beginning of a chauvinism without which French music would certainly not have made the advances it has in mastery of technical means, the development of individuality, and the expression of a national art. It first created the new music and then forced the French people to listen to it, thus awakening an interest in native music, inducing greater appreciation for it, and developing in general finer musical taste. Practically all the representative works by native composers have been performed by the society, which took as its motto *Ars gallica*. The composers were inspired to write knowing that they had a stimulating outlet for performance.

Romain Bussine (1830-1899), professor of singing at the Paris Conservatory, was its president, and Camille Saint-Saëns (1835-1921) was vice-president. César Franck was one of its founders along with Ernest Guiraud, Jules Massenet, Gabriel Fauré, Henri Duparc, Théodore Dubois, Jules Garcin, and Claude Taffanel. Rolland said that "it possessed the rare merit of being able to anticipate public opinion by ten or eleven years, and in some ways it has formed the public mind and obliged it to honor those whom the Society had already recognized as great musicians."

For ten years Franck, d'Indy, and their adherents were in power, and after Saint-Saëns's resignation in 1886 Franck, though refusing the title, was head until his death, when d'Indy became its director. The resignation of Bussine and Saint-Saëns was caused by d'Indy's suggestion that foreign classics be included in the programs. This was probably due to d'Indy's interest in the church music of the past, which led to the founding with Charles Bordes and Alexandre Guilmant of the Schola Cantorum. Begun as a radical movement, as is so often the case with individuals and groups the society became too conservative for the younger generation, several members of which seceded in 1909 and formed the Société Musicale Indépendante (Independent Musical Society) with Gabriel Fauré as its first president.

César Franck himself might be offered as the best example of the results achieved by composers in France through the influence of the National Society. Franck was forty-nine when his trio for piano, violin and 'cello was played at the first concert. The bulk of his works, including those for which he is justly famed, was written after 1874, and many of them were performed by the society. He had worked alone, misunderstood, and unappreciated by his colleagues, the public, and the press, regarded by everyone, except his pupils and disciples, as an enemy to existing art standards. He was given a professorship at the Conservatory, not as a teacher of composition, as he was not trusted in that capacity, but on account of his reputation as a great organist. Since 1858 he had held the position at Ste. Clotilde, where Liszt visited him in 1866 and compared his organ playing and gift for improvisation to Bach's.

In many other ways this lovable, modest master, simple in faith, rich in knowledge, and unquestioning in the world's attitude toward his achievements, was like Bach. Many of his organ works show the Bach influence in his handling of polyphony and also in his use of seventeenth and eighteenth century forms, as for example in the *Prélude, Fugue, et Variation* for harmonium and piano (1873), and in his last work, three chorales, he elaborated on Bach's chorale form, adding a thoroughly individual harmonic scheme, daring in modulating innovations and introducing chromatic effects which pointed the way to the use of the twelve tone scale (page 111.) He had adapted to his own harmonic inventions the canon, fugue, and variation, which Bach used to perfection. In the two great works for piano, *Prélude, Chorale, et Fugue* (1884) and *Prélude, Aria, et Finale* (1886), the structure is obviously an enlargement of Bach's forms passed through the processes of classicism and romanticism. He was the neoclassicist of the nineteenth century. The fine religious exaltation and contemplative character of his music also are comparable to Bach.

Franck left several oratorios which show the mystic trend of his imagination. *Redemption* was given by Colonne at a *Concert spirituel* in 1873, but it was not a satisfactory performance, and his greatest work in this form, *Les Béatitudes* (1869-1879), was never heard in its entirety until three years after the master's death, when it was an overwhelming triumph!

Franck was a debtor to Beethoven as well as to Bach, as he adapted the sonata form to his own needs in his famous Symphony in D minor (1886); the F minor Quintet for piano and strings (1879); the A major Sonata for Violin and Piano (1886), made famous by Eugen Ysaye and Raoul Pugno; and the D major Quartet (1889).

The Ysaye Quartet played the last work at a concert of the Société Nationale a month before Franck met with the accident which led to his death. It had an unqualified success which brought forth the remark from the composer, who had almost completed the span of "three score years and ten"—"There, you see, the public is beginning to understand me!"

"He was the first composer of the French School to use adequately the great forms of symphonic and chamber music which had been worked out hitherto by the Germans...," said Walter R. Spalding (*Music: An Art and a Language*); and Vincent d'Indy wrote: "At his death César Franck left a legacy to his country in the form of a vigorous symphonic school, such as France had never before produced." (*César Franck: A Study,* translated by Rosa Newmarch.)

Franck also handled the variation form most significantly, as may be seen in his *Variations Symphoniques* for piano and orchestra (1885). Spalding finds his individual characteristics in this work, "melodic intensity, novel chromatic harmony and freedom of form combined with coherence." He compares the naturalness of the melodic variations with Bach's Passacaglia in C minor, and the general structure in the finale with Beethoven's Eroica Symphony. The variations, based on two themes, are very free in treatment, combining variation form with sonata form in an essentially novel manner.

In everything he did, Franck was an independent thinker and an innovator far in advance of his day. He opened the door for impressionism and for Fauré, Debussy, and Ravel. Today his melodic lines, regarded as perhaps too long, give his work a unity. They were a protest against the two- and four-measure phrases which had become one of the mannerisms of romanticism.

His use of chromaticism while occasionally reminding one of Wagner, is distinctly individual and provoked imitation. He established the *cyclical* form in using *generative motifs* in the different movements of the sonata, thus effecting a new conception of inter-movement relationship.

In Vincent d'Indy's *Cours de Composition,* he claimed that the entire violin sonata was based on these three *generative* themes:

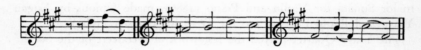

The form is completely free, as the first movement, while in sonata form, has no development; the third movement is a long free declamation called Recitative—Fantasia, in which he uses themes from the second and the fourth movements in an absolutely original manner; and the finale is a most ingenious dialogue in canon form between the violin and the piano.

The symphony, too, shows all sorts of freedom and individuality, beginning with a slow theme which is used again in rapid tempo. It is full of lovely melodic passages so characteristic of Franck. The second movement brings in the famous melody for English horn which made a Conservatory factotum say to d'Indy, "That, a symphony? ... But my dear sir, who ever heard of writing for the *cor anglais* in a symphony? Just mention a single symphony by Haydn or Beethoven introducing the *cor anglais*. There, well, you see—your Franck's music may be whatever you please, but it will certainly never be a symphony!"

In this offending movement Franck telescoped two movements into one, making the middle section a scherzo, and returning to the slow lyric part. The finale is cyclic in character, summarizing all that went before it. In it he also uses canon to emphasize the final theme.

To appreciate how advanced Franck was harmonically, I should recommend analyzing the close of the third movement of the violin sonata and of the third movement of the symphony. In both these he was an ultramodern of his time in his innovational use of cadence (Chapter 9).

Franck made use of augmented harmonies, which became the basis of the impressionistic musical language in Debussy's hands. In the chromatic movement of his voices he not only anticipated Debussy but opened the way for him. He certainly added many new tonal combinations to our musical vocabulary, thus making further steps possible.

The following example from the Symphony in D minor illustrates the remarkable freedom with which he traveled by means of chromatic progressions:

Symphony in D minor (1st movement)   César Franck

Although the talent of Saint-Saëns is overshadowed by that of Franck, his influence on the movement to regenerate French instrumental music should not be minimized. He was a classicist in a world of romanticists, and like Mendelssohn he worked to make the public and artists appreciate the classics. "From the historic point of view, Saint-Saëns is a notable figure," says Paul Landormy (*The History of Music*). "He undertook the musical education of France at the exact moment when Berlioz despaired of succeeding with the task, and he prepared the public for the great French school of symphonists which arose toward the end of the nineteenth century." He wrote symphonies and chamber music when no one else did so, and he lived to see his efforts overwhelmed by the full tide of impressionism.

Edouard Lalo (1823-1892) and Emmanuel Chabrier (1861-1894) were also members of the Société Nationale. Lalo's interest in chamber music was probably due to the fact that he played viola in a string quartet. Saint-Saëns, with a better schooled technic and a classic sense of form, did not have Lalo's buoyancy and rhythmic verve, so characteristic of French music. He it was who first showed the French composer how to make use of the Spanish rhythms and exotic mood which have been a source of inspiration to Chabrier, Debussy, Ravel, and others. He also opened the way for heightened orchestral color.

Chabrier, though not a pupil of Franck, was a member of the circle and was an important figure in the new movement. Edward Burlingame Hill (*Modern French Music*) calls him and Fauré "pioneers of progressive individuality" and says they may be termed the first modernists, "since their independent styles constitute an indubitable assertion of French traits." Of Chabrier's best known score, *"España,"* Hill says it "is Spain seen through a Frenchman's eyes, yet it is none the less a characteristic expression of such typical French traits as cheerfulness, enthusiasm, and striking humor. As such it is exceedingly important historically as the manifesto of a new spirit of independence, a return to an affirmation of the Gallic character and a rebuke to reactionary eclecticism. Chabrier did not acknowledge fetish worship in art. He did not feel impelled to write fugues, sonatas or symphonies. Music to him was primarily a means of subjective expression. Form and even style were of secondary importance, except as they helped him to attain his end. Herein lies Chabrier's significance as a pioneer of progress."

Like Debussy later, Chabrier was acquainted with the symbolist poets and the impressionist painters and evidently found the correlation of the arts stimulating to his creative imagination.

A serious menace to the development of French music was Lamoureux's great devotion to Wagner. He founded the concerts which after his death were continued by Chevillard. Although occasionally works by Lalo, d'Indy, and Chabrier were included, the programs were largely devoted to the Wagner music dramas in concert form, and a Wagner cult in Paris was fostered.

As an offset to the Wagner enthusiasm, a group of French musicians tried to awaken an interest in the pure French line of composers going back to the clavecinists, Couperin, Daquin, and to Rameau and Lully, the Italian-French opera composer of the seventeenth century. In this attempt to arouse the national consciousness, important educational institutions came into existence. In 1853 Niedermeyer opened a school to study the religious works of the masters of the fifteenth, sixteenth, and seventeenth centuries. Fauré, Messager, Gigout, and Expert were among its pupils, and Saint-Saëns was one of its teachers. As a result of this study of religious music, in 1892 Charles Bordes founded the Association des Chanteurs de Saint-Gervais, in which the revival was successfully realized.

In 1894, the *Schola Cantorum* was opened by Bordes, Guilmant, and d'Indy. Its aims were: To teach theory based on Gregorian music; to revive the church music of the Palestrinian period; to raise the standard of vocal and instrumental music in the Paris churches; and to perpetuate César Franck's teachings.

It has educated a number of famous French composers, given concerts of orchestral, choral, organ, and chamber music, revived Monteverdi and Rameau operas, and published anthologies of choral and organ music of the fifteenth to the eighteenth centuries, and important folk song collections. All of this has had, in the twentieth century, a tremendous influence on the more general study of musical history, entailing much valuable research and developing a real interest in musicology.

Vincent d'Indy (1851-1932), one of the most actively devoted of the Franck pupils, seemed in character and point-of-view like a reincarnation from the Middle Ages. His interests were rooted in the achievements of the early centuries, and yet his influences in his compositions were Franckian and Wagnerian. He used the cyclical idea in sonata form, according to his master's prescription, and his operas were built on the leitmotif idea and methods of Wagner's music dramas. Hill says: "He is one of the pioneers in the use of modal harmony for dramatic suggestion, an early experimenter in the whole-tone scale, and his treatment of dissonance, if at times almost acrid in its pungency, is free from reactionary suspicion and is always appropriate to his musical thought. . . . To fuse, as he has done, the spirit of classic forms with many elements of progress in expression, is no vain achievement. D'Indy is a valiant crusader in Art." (*Modern French Music*.)

Another important Franck pupil, whose career was cut short, was Ernest Chausson (1855-1899). He has left a *Poème* for violin; a symphony; a concerto for violin, piano, and string quartet; the *"Chanson Perpetuelle"* for voice and orchestra, and some chamber music, which attest to his unusual gifts and to the possibility of their further development had he lived beyond the time when, as Hill says, "he was acquiring self-confidence and a mastery over technical problems that justified ardent hopes for the future."

"After Lalo, Fauré and Chabrier," Jean-Aubry writes, "in the order of the years, it is Ernest Chausson who, the first of his generation, showed those musical qualities most fundamentally French and who felt most profoundly that support which letters and the plastic arts could furnish to music in the search for its national character." (*La Musique française d'aujourd'hui*.)

A fate similar to that of Edward MacDowell overtook Henri Duparc (1848-1933), a French composer and pupil of César Franck whom the master considered as one of the most gifted in his circle. To the musical world Duparc had been practically dead for forty-eight years, for in 1885 a nervous affliction robbed him of his ability to compose, and since that time he had lived in retirement in Switzerland hoping that his mental powers would be restored so that he might continue his career so ably begun. His music consists of a handful of songs, about a dozen in all, but each one bears the stamp of genius, and he stands as a song writer among the composers of France as Hugo Wolf does among the Austrians. He shares with Gabriel Fauré the honor of having put the French art song on the musical map. He chose for texts some of the same poets as Debussy—Baudelaire, Lahor, and Leconte de Lisle. *"L'Invitation au voyage"* (Invitation to a Voyage), *"Phydilé,"* *"Vie intérieure"* (The Inner Life), *La Vague et la cloche* (The Wave and the Diving Bell), *"Le Manoir de Rosamonde"* (Rosamond's Manor), *"Extase"* (Ecstasy), *"Lamento,"* *"Testament,"* and *"Soupir"* (Sigh) in their originality, *nostalgie,* melodic and harmonic beauty, charm and serious musicianship carry us to the very threshold of Debussy.

Roland-Manuel, the French critic, once said that it was a good thing

Gabriel Fauré (1845-1924) was not fully appreciated in foreign countries because he held the key to the secret of the spirit of French music. "It is to its credit," says André Coeuroy (*Panorama de la musique contemporaine*), "that the French school never allows itself to crystallize in one man. It is great also in that it is sufficiently individual and aristocratic to guard itself from the indiscretions of invaders.... Imitations of Wagner and of Franck are only mirages along the route that French music travels. It is in spite of Wagner and in spite of Franck that the works of Vincent d'Indy live and will live. That which saves the *Schola Cantorum* is its call to the voices of the race, d'Indy to the voices of Vivarais, Ropartz or Le Flem to the voices of Brittany, Canteloube to the voices of Auvergne, Déodat de Séverac to the voices of the Langue d'oc, Charles Bordes to the voices of the Basque country,—and it is also the call to the Gregorian Chant, the true French folksong, of which it is not difficult to discover the traces from Satie and Ravel to Poulenc or Milhaud. To have knotted again the thread of French music to the skein of medieval polyphony, is the best title to glory that the Schola has. To find a modern discipline in the past has been the effort our music has made for more than a half-century. To innovate in the tradition: a path essentially French."

And Coeuroy sees that this was the path taken by Fauré, the music prophet, "the firm and gentle precursor who in the face of the Wagnerian eruption created a harmonic language of tomorrow and, twenty years before Debussy, suggested the syntax of the new century. But, he created a grammar, and, above all, re-animated a spirit: the defunct spirit of the clavecinists and of the masters of the Renaissance." And in Fauré, the critic Louis Laloy says, the renaissance of modern French music began.

He was not a composer of great orchestral scores; his work was principally in the field of the art song, piano, and chamber music, and the greatest of these are the songs. As a reformer he desired to rid French music of antiquated formulas, "of descriptive intentions, of imitative harmonies, or metaphysical aims." In this he was a purist and a classicist.

The secret of his musical charm seems to be in his rare gift of melody, his extraordinary skill in modulation, and by means of his tone color in suggesting a mood, to illustrate a text in his songs, even as Debussy did later. He wrote almost one hundred songs in which he absolutely captured the French soul. *"Clair de lune"* (Moonlight), *"Nell," "Mandoline," "Au cimetière"* (In the Cemetery), *"Prison," "Les Berceaux"* (The Cradles), *"Les Roses d'Ispahan,"* and the song cycle to Verlaine's poems, *La Bonne chanson,* will serve to show his characteristics. He must be reckoned among the great song writers of the world.

He taught at the Niedermeyer School, where he was educated musically, and later at the Paris Conservatory, of which he became the director from 1905 to 1920. He was a member of the Société Nationale de Musique, president of the Société Musicale Indépendante, member of the Académie des Beaux Arts, and the year before his death was made president of the French branch of the International Society for Contemporary Music.

His pupils included Charles Koechlin, Maurice Ravel, Florent Schmitt, Georges Enesco, Roger-Ducasse, Louis Aubert, and Paul Ladmirault.

In describing the essentials necessary to French music, he inadvertently described his own characteristics: "Taste in clarity of thought, in the society and purity of form, sincerity, disdain for vulgar effect, in a word, all those virtues which might contribute to our art's completely finding its admirable personality and remaining forever that which it should be: essentially French." (*La Musique française moderne,* André Coeuroy. Freely translated by the author.)

CHAPTER 8

REALISM: RICHARD STRAUSS

R ICHARD STRAUSS'S (1864) place in this section of *Twen-tieth Century Music* is explained by the fact that he is the last of the great German romanticists, heir to the traditions of Wagner and Liszt, and of the French Berlioz, in direct line with Wolf and Mahler. Another reason for inclusion in Part I, Looking Backward, is that eight of his tone poems and all but twenty-four of his songs were composed before 1900. His operas, however, with the exception of the first, *Guntram,* belong to the twentieth century.

Strauss's father kept him strictly to the old masters. "You cannot appreciate Wagner and the moderns unless you pass through this grounding in the classics," is the son's verdict. This training, added to his inherent gifts, gave him a security of musical knowledge and prodigious technic rarely surpassed by any composer. In his treatment of program, he is a pioneer in musical realism, the seeds of which were planted by Berlioz and handed on to sprout in such exotic soil as that cultivated by Stravinsky and Honegger. "Where Liszt suggested a program, Strauss carried it to the *n*th power of realism. Where Richard Wagner proclaimed the doctrine that the symphonic poem as program music was unable to make itself understood without the aid of the stage, 'Richard II' upheld the symphonic poem as the means of ex-pressing practically any program." (*Music through the Ages,* Bauer and Peyser.) In "his avowed object of bringing music into direct rela-tion with daily life, and of developing its descriptive scope to such a pitch that it would be possible to depict a teaspoon in music," Cecil Gray tells us in *A Survey of Contemporary Music,* Strauss separates himself from the romanticists, "who sought to depict vague intangible moods and ideas rather than concrete realities, and are more attracted to the exotic, the strange, and the remote than to the commonplace actualities of everyday existence."

His Domestic Symphony (*Sinfonia Domestica*) carries this realism outside the bounds of artistry. The whirring of the windmills and the bleating of the sheep in "Don Quixote," and the introduction of the wind machine, amusing as they are, remind us only too forcibly that we are living in an age of materialism which has threatened to overpower idealism even in art.

After Strauss had been urged by Alexander Ritter "to the development of the poetic, the expressive in music," he wrote his first tone poem, *"Aus Italien"* (From Italy), which he says was the connecting link between the old and the new methods (1886-1887). He covers a wide variety of subjects and structural forms in these symphonic works, each of which raised a storm of controversial opinion upon its appearance. Frequent hearings have ironed out the difficulties, and Strauss's supremacy as a virtuoso composer and his genius in the handling of the orchestra are beyond cavil. He is absolute master of the mechanics of his art, although the occasional commonplaceness of his thematic material is curiously striking, and his effect often theatrical, as in *"Ein Heldenleben"* (A Hero's Life) and *"Tod und Verklärung"* (Death and Transfiguration).

"Till Eulenspiegel's lustige Streiche" (Till Eulenspiegel's Merry Pranks), in rondo form, is frequently called Strauss's masterpiece, and —dangerous as prophecies are—it will probably outlive his more grandiose and pompous scores. *"Also sprach Zarathustra"* (Thus Spake Zarathustra) has caused so much discussion that Strauss made the declaration, "I did not intend to write philosophical music or portray Nietzsche's great work musically. I meant to convey musically an idea of the development of the human race from its origin through the various phases of evolution, religious as well as scientific, up to Nietzsche's idea of the Superman." That's all! In spite of its length and weight it has pages of extraordinary beauty and profound musical thought. Strauss has used variation form in this as in his "Don Quixote," which like "Till Eulenspiegel," because of its tenderly humorous, sincere and human qualities, may outlive some of the more pretentious works.

He betrays the fact that he himself is the hero of *"Ein Helden-*

leben" by quoting from his own compositions. As in *Die Meistersinger* Wagner made a plea for justice in listening to the new, and in *Phoebus and Pan* Bach showed his resentment of the onslaught against the established standards of art as he saw them, so in *"Ein Heldenleben"* Strauss answered his numerous critics in noisy, raucously discordant music. And in this score, as in many others, he opened the way for the use of greater dissonance, which is one of the most characteristic features of twentieth century music. We can trace the result of his dissonances in those who have done their work since.

The opening phrase of "Don Juan" sounded as unreasonable to the ears of 1888 as does today's polytonality, which it suggests in its introduction of the dual tonalities of C and E.*

Allegro molto con brio   Don Juan, Richard Strauss, op. 20

(Peters Edition, copyright, 1904.)

The tremendous range of his melody, another characteristic of Strauss, is also shown.

Schoenberg's disjunct melodic line is certainly an exaggeration of Strauss's use of skips, nonchordal tones, and accidentals in general. From "Till Eulenspiegel" we quote in illustration the opening phrase and Till's appearance:*

Till Eulenspiegel's Merry Pranks, Richard Strauss, op. 28

(Peters Edition, copyright, 1904.)

* With the authorization of the publisher, C. F. Peters.

The extremely long range, rhythmic variety, wide dissonant skips, especially of sevenths and ninths, which the composers of today have adopted, the rapid modulation, the vigor and braggadocio of the opening measures of *"Ein Heldenleben"* are typically Straussian:

A Hero's Life, Richard Strauss, op. 40

(Copyright, 1899, F. E. C. Leuckart.)

The form is that of the first movement of a symphony painted on a huge canvas.†

One of the earmarks of the restlessness of our age is shown in our rhythmic groupings. We came out of the no bar era in the sixteenth century, then we experienced what Daniel Gregory Mason calls "the Tyranny of the Bar Line." We were bound by four-measure phrases and eight-measure periods dictated by the cadence. Polyphony allowed

* A whole tone scale.

† With special permission of Messrs. F. E. C. Leuckart, Leipzig, publishers of Richard Strauss's Op. 40, *Ein Heldenleben.*

greater freedom. Although Schumann was a prey to the checkerboard design of unbroken series of four measures, still he lapsed frequently and shifted his rhythms without changing the bar line. Brahms used this means of varying the meter, as for example in the Second Symphony in D major, in the first movement:

A twentieth century composer would probably have written the first measure in ¾, as it is, followed by a measure in ²/₄, one in ¾, one in ¼, and the rest as it stands. Or else he might have barred it, ⁵/₄, ⁷/₄, and as it stands.

Strauss has given a very interesting example in the following from "Till Eulenspiegel":

(Peters Edition, copyright, 1904.)

The rhythmic design of seven notes (marked with a brace) is heard three times, the first note of the group falling on a different beat of the measure each time, and the third time the note marked is shorter in value to conform to the ⁶/₈ frame of the last three measures. If we were to escape the "tyranny of the bar line," this passage might be written thus:

Another interesting example of a shift in rhythmic design of the same group of notes is to be found in the opening phrase played by the bassoon in Stravinsky's *Le Sacre du Printemps* (*The Rite of Spring*):

Le Sacre du Printemps   Igor Stravinsky
Lento

(Russicher Musik Verlag, copyright, 1921, Berlin.)

The Strauss of the songs continues the line begun by Schubert, followed by Schumann, Brahms, and Wolf. In many of these, romanticism, artistry, sincerity, and technical mastery combine. The emotionalism, tenderness, and fearlessness of youth were gradually exchanged for the domination of the orchestra in which Strauss found his true strength. He enlarged even the Wagner orchestra, and while he used it in masses of tone color as Wagner had, he also studied the characteristics of the individual instrument and taught the twentieth century composer the possibilities of an orchestral polyphony in which was woven a richer and more complex color web than ever had been dreamed of. In Strauss's orchestra the body was supplied by the woodwinds instead of the strings, and he multiplied the division of the strings, begun by Wagner, so that the maze of harmony created an impressionistic color. Weissmann found that the orchestra had a limiting effect on Strauss's imagination, "limiting, because much of the energy which might have gone to creative imagination was diverted to serve purely orchestral ends."

Strauss exhibits no fondness for nature unless we except his weak Alpine Symphony. He was rather the composer of civilization—he stood by "the restless, mechanical and commercial civilization of the opening twentieth century," Dr. Eaglefield Hull said.

Strauss's evolution from the classicist to the romanticist and realist led him from a study of Mozart, which has influenced him deeply all his life, to an equally close analysis of Liszt and Berlioz, both of whom had a more direct effect on him than Wagner. After twelve or fifteen years devoted to the tone poem, Strauss succumbed to the lure of the stage, and as an opera writer he is second only to Wagner. After the first failure, *Guntram* (1892-93), in which he tried to use Wagner's tools, he wrote *Feuersnot;* "a work of genius," Weissmann calls it, stating that "in this opera Strauss finds himself, and sets up a type of operatic art that rivals Wagner. Emotionalism is cut out and primitive eroticism is defended with the cheerful impudence of a guttersnipe."

Why Strauss sought erotic subjects such as *Salome* and *Electra* when he was, and is, obviously not of an erotic temperament has been a subject for much debate. Perhaps he believed that the orchestral technic he had at his command was better suited to attack the modern problem of impressionistic eroticism when the eroticism was external and objective, instead of subjective and a part of his mentality. In this way he was playing upon the subject and not having it use him. He has been accused of having chosen Oscar Wilde's *Salome* with his eye on the commercial value of a sensational work. It has passages of unforgettable beauty, and intensely vital moments. Throughout, Strauss has condensed melodic line and rhythm, and by using means which in 1906 were ultramodern he has combined dissonance and an exotic timbre with telling effect.

Electra (1909) is a symphonic poem with stage setting and vocal *obbligati* handled with such mastery of orchestra and merciless realism that the hearer is magnetized by the stupendous tasks allotted to singers, orchestra, and conductor, as well as by the musical effect, extraordinary melodic line, dramatic sense, and genius. Here we see how much Strauss has influenced the generation of composers follow-

ing him. He has condensed the four-hour music drama into the one-
act opera which he has handed on to his artistic descendants.

Der Rosenkavalier (1911) was Richard Strauss's *Meistersinger;* that
is, it is his comic opera written with all the tools of grand opera.
Strauss's old love for Mozart dictated much of the treatment, but it is
a Mozart crossed with *Die Meistersinger* and the Viennese waltz. It
has had success in Europe and America, and its characters created by
Hugo von Hofmannstahl (who was also librettist of *Electra,* taken
from Sophocles' version) have become personalities—Baron Ochs, the
Marshalin, and Octavian—even as Eva, Walther, and Beckmesser. In
his treatment of the Viennese waltz with dissonant harmonization
Strauss has achieved a piquancy and charm not quickly forgotten. The
motive of the Silver Rose * has trapped many a twentieth century
composer into imitating it:

Der Rosenkavalier, Richard Strauss

This can be explained as chords built on the twelve tone scale
(page 111).

Der Rosenkavalier may be said to have closed Strauss's career as a
successful composer. With the exception of *Ariadne auf Naxos* (1912,
revised 1916), his later works have not won public favor. The ballet
Josefs-Legende (1914), and the opera *Die Frau ohne Schatten* (1919,
The Woman without Shadows), have not been given in New York;
Die egyptische Hélène (1927) was not a success at the Metropolitan
Opera House, which gave it its world's première; the Alpine Sym-
phony and the ballet *Schlagobers* (*Whipped Cream*) seem to have the
outer shell of his orchestral skill but with nothing to say. The Alpine
Symphony is long, elaborate, and oversentimental, while *Whipped*

* Published with authorization of Mr. Adolph Fürstner (copyright, 1910, Adolph
Fürstner, Berlin W.).

Cream is much technical ado about nothing. *The Woman without Shadows,* that is, the childless woman, is written in most serious vein to a mystical and symbolic libretto by von Hofmannstahl. Some consider it a masterpiece too far ahead of its time to be a success, and others find weaknesses mercilessly revealed.

Ariadne auf Naxos, based on Molière's *Le bourgeois gentilhomme,* in spite of weaknesses in the libretto is full of sparkle, humor, and charm, with skilled condensation of material and an effectively reduced orchestra requiring only thirty-five players. It has another claim to our attention in the fact that Strauss shows again the influence Mozart has always exerted over him, and this time it has produced a pioneer work in neoclassic style, which fits in with the spirit of its day.

Throughout his career Strauss has carried on the double role of composer and conductor. He has conducted his own works notably, but he has the reputation of being a greater interpreter of Mozart both in opera and concert. So he has always been in direct touch with the classic spirit.

Before 1914 Richard Strauss was the great ultramodernist of the orchestral concert halls of the world. His realistic ideas, dissonant harmonies and noisy instrumental climaxes were misunderstood, were regarded as cerebral examples of virtuosity. During the period of World War I his scores were not played by the Allied nations. But in those few years a curious thing happened—Richard Strauss's works came back fully established as classics!

His latest operas include *Arabella* (1933, the last libretto by von Hofmannstahl); *Die schweigsame Frau* (1935, with a libretto by Stefan Zweig based on Ben Jonson's *The Silent Woman*); *Intermezzo* (1925, for which he wrote his own libretto); *Friedenstag* (*Day of Peace*), and *Daphne,* both of which were on librettos by Joseph Gregor and were produced in 1938; *Die Liebe der Danae* (*The Love of the Danae*), also on a Gregor libretto, the première of which was prohibited by Goebbels in 1944; and his last opera, *Capriccio,* on a text by Strauss and Clemens Kraus, the conductor who directed its first performance in Munich. "*Metamorphosen*," for twenty-three strings, was written in 1945.

INTERLUDE

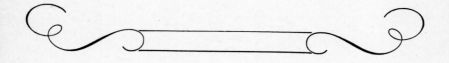

BREAKING DOWN ESTABLISHED RULES: NEW SCALES, MELODIES, CHORDS, HARMONIC RESOURCES, RHYTHMS, ETC.*

THE uninitiated listener seeks in vain for familiar landmarks in this new tonal country which, so far, has been explored principally by those imbued with the pioneer spirit. Melody, harmony, rhythm, form, have changed. There is nothing to guide him; nothing shows him whether he is on the right path. He has new problems to solve. He tries to fit what he hears to that which he has learned to accept as musical gospel. If the old is right, the new must be wrong because it breaks all the rules—apparently. He must learn the truth of Ferruccio Busoni's statement, "There is nothing properly modern—only things which have come into being earlier or later; longer in bloom, or sooner withered. The Modern and the Old have always been." (*A New Aesthetic of Music.*)

If we apply these words in considering new scale formations, we shall find that there are practically no new scales. So-called "modern" scales are for the most part new interpretations or readjustments of age-old conventions. And here the listener may question, "How about the whole tone scale?"

The Chinese have a legend which gives to their bamboo instruments the honor of being responsible for the formation of their scale. Lyng-lun was commissioned to systematize the confused array of sounds which constituted Chinese music. He cut a bamboo and on blowing into it produced a tone in unison with his voice and with the sound of the waves of the river Hoang-ho. Lyng-lun decided that this was the fundamental sound of nature from which all other tones

* The author recommends that the appendix, Explanation of Musical Terms, be read in conjunction with this chapter.

97

were derived. In answer to his musing, the magic bird Foung-hoang appeared with its mate and sang the same tone emitted by the bamboo, the human voice, and the river. Then all nature ceased in order to listen to the song of the magic birds. As they sang, Lyng-lun cut his bamboos and tuned them to the notes of the birds, six sung by the male and six by the female. These twelve tones are called *lüs*. When Lyng-lun had bound his bamboo pipes together, he had an instrument similar to the Greek Pan pipes on which he played a chromatic scale. The odd tones sung by the male were "positive and perfect"; the even tones sung by the female were "negative and imperfect."

This supplies the two series of whole tone scales. Each of the twelve degrees may be the starting point of a scale which repeats the tones in whole tone succession of one or the other of the two series.

The Chinese used the twelve degrees not as a chromatic scale, as we do, but as the starting point of pentatonic scales of twelve differing pitches. The most familiar form of the scale of five tones lacks the fourth and the seventh degrees.

Another explanation of the two series of whole tone scales may be arrived at through the progression of the circle of keys in ascending fifths: F C G D A E B F♯ C♯ G♯ D♯ A♯.

Or in descending fifths: E A D G C F B♭ E♭ A♭ D♭ G♭ C♭.

(NOTE: The scale positions were chosen merely with regard to the practical placement on the staff to avoid leger lines and double sharps and flats.)

It is also claimed that the whole tone scale is evolved from the series of overtones or partials from a given fundamental. As a ray of white light is the combination of its primary colors, so any single tone is the summation of a fundamental and its overtones. Many are under the impression that our major scale is a *natural scale,* but it is simply a man-made convention which has dominated our music for about three hundred years. If one could fasten the term natural scale to any musical sounds, it would be to the group of tones generated by a fundamental tone and known as the *natural harmonic series.* It is sometimes called the *scale of nature,* but just as often it is regarded as a chord—the *chord of nature.* In *New Musical Resources* Henry Cowell suggests that the overtone series is a scale in its upper reaches and a harmony in its lower reaches.

The sympathetic vibrations released by sounding a fundamental tone are not accidental, but follow a law which causes them to occur in regular and orderly succession. The human ear distinguishes compound sounds, co-vibrations in varying proportions (page 8). The mixture and proportion of the upper partials affects the *quality* of sound. When they are harmonic, that is, within the range of the harmonic series, the sounds produced are "musical." When the tones have upper partials lying outside the range of the harmonic series, they are not regarded as musical tones, although they may be used for purposes of music. Bells, triangles, and cymbals produce such "tinkling" or "clinking" sounds. Various types of drums with stretched membranes also have "inharmonic upper partials." The presence of very high upper partials produces almost unbearable noise, such as the grating of a rusty hinge, of the wheels on a steel rail, the scratch of a knife on a plate or of a piece of chalk on a blackboard.

The fact that the history of music has developed along the line of the *natural harmonic series* makes it seem plausible that the composers of the twentieth century have reached the stage of the higher overtones (from 7 upwards), and consciously or unconsciously are using them as the bases of their experiments in dissonant melody and harmony.

Pythagoras is acknowledged as the discoverer of the vibrational relationships of tones. By means of a monochord, he demonstrated that when a string was divided into two equal parts, each segment produced a tone one octave higher than that produced by the entire string.

One-third the length sounded the interval of a fifth above the octave. One-fourth of the string produced the second octave from the fundamental. The Greeks seemed to be indifferent to the interval of a third (page 107). Historically, the earliest musicians were monodic, that is, they were unaware of the art of combining tones of different pitch, therefore they are symbolized by the fundamental tone of the harmonic series. They sang melodies but used no harmony. When men and women, or men and boys, sang together, their voices produced the octave, 1 and 2 of the harmonic series. This covers the plainsong period as well as the Greek magadizing and the music of the ancient nations and primitive peoples.

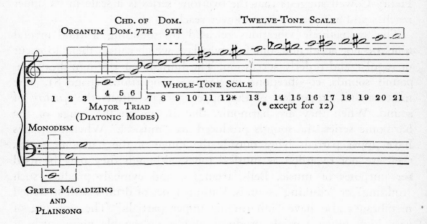

In *The Musician's Arithmetic* Max F. Meyer says: " 'The discovery of the octave' is undoubtedly the greatest event which ever took place or ever could have taken place in the history of 'musical civilization.' It is almost comparable in revolutionary importance to the discovery of fire in the history of general human civilization."

Organum, which lasted three centuries, was based on the 2nd, 3rd, and 4th overtones. When the interval of the third was introduced into music, the major triad appeared (4, 5, and 6 of the series). For many centuries we have been ruled by this chord and its inversions (upper partials 3, 4, 5, and 5, 6, 8). The overtones 6, 7, 9 produced the minor triad, and 4, 5, 6, 7 the dominant seventh chord which was regarded as a dissonant chord; and special rules, which our harmony students are still taught, were made for preparing and resolving the dissonant seventh. The first three octaves of upper partials dominated the period in which the diatonic major and minor modes superseded the ecclesiastical modes. The addition of the 9th overtone brings music up to the period of Wagner and César Franck.

Franck's well-known sonata for violin and piano opens with a dominant ninth chord, which seemed heretical to the listeners of 1886.

Sonata for Violin and Piano
Allegretto ben moderato
César Franck
Scheme

The twentieth century was ushered in with Debussy's experiments in the whole tone scale (upper partials 7, 8, 9, 10, 11, and 13). Scriabin evolved his *mystic chord* which registers overtones 8, 11, 14, 10, 13, and 9 (page 177). And Schoenberg raised the chromatic scale to primary estate by making it the basis of *atonality* (pages 210-1). It is found between overtone 11 and its octave, 22.

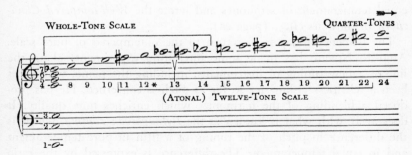

WHOLE-TONE SCALE   QUARTER-TONES

8   9   10 11 12* 13   14   15   16   17   18   19   20   21   22   24

(ATONAL) TWELVE-TONE SCALE

As the number of vibrations increases, it is obvious that the intervals become smaller than semitones and we see evolutionary, if not practical, reasons for *microtones,* quarter ones, third tones, eighths, sixteenths, etc. History has shown the fallacy, however, of stating that innovations are impractical!

The slight deviations in pitch due to equal temperament have not been mentioned. The important point in the above discussion is the relation of the new to the old, and the possible explanation of the new along the lines of the *natural harmonic series*. "Historically known human society employed *only three tempered scales*," says Professor Meyer in *The Musician's Arithmetic,* "the widespread twelve-tone scale, the tempered seven-tone scale of the Siamese, and the tempered five-tone scale of the Javanese. . . ." (page 128).

Until early medieval times the chief system in vogue was the Pythagorean, which sacrificed the accuracy of the major third in order to preserve that of the perfect fifth. It required twenty-seven tones to the octave. *Meantone temperament* was devised in order that instruments with fixed notes might be tuned on a more practical system.

"It must be remembered that medieval music was modal, and that composers did not require a large number of keynotes, since modulation and transposition were both kept within very small limits. Consequently it was thought better to preserve pure intonation, as far as possible, in the keys most commonly used, thereby sacrificing it in the unusual keys, even to the extent of making it impossible to use such keys at all." (*Acoustics for Musicians,* Percy C. Buck, page 95.) The system was called the meantone temperament because the major third was tuned "true," and the minor was a "meantone" compromise. This was the system in use when Bach championed the cause of the equal temperament of semitones and wrote the *Well-tempered Clavichord* to show its effect (page 25).

The tendency today is to return to the untempered or pure scale. Augusto Novaro has made some interesting experiments along the line of a new tuning of instruments, including the piano, which has been a relentless taskmaster so far as pitch is concerned. He has produced a blending of the harmonics which enriches tone quality. It does away with what is known as the *Pythagorean comma,* which is the difference in pitch of the tuning of a fifth in pure temperament and in equal temperament. The difference is expressed by the ratio 74:73.

Perhaps at this point a clearer understanding of the meaning of *consonance* and *dissonance* is necessary. As we speak of dissonance today—dissonant harmony, dissonant counterpoint, and dissonance in general—we give the term wider significance than it had in its earlier, and still recognized, theoretical usage. Consonant intervals, we are told, are those which are satisfying to the ear and do not need to be resolved; dissonant intervals are not satisfactory until they are resolved.

In the *Encyclopédie de la musique et dictionnaire du conservatoire* Paul Rougnon analyzes the etymology of the two words: *cum* (Latin), with; *sonare* (Latin), to sound: to sound with. "A consonance is the effect of two or more tones sounded together and uniting in a manner pleasant to the ear." *Dis* (Greek) double; *sonare* (Latin), to sound. "The exact meaning of this term is *to sound twice,* and designates the effect produced by two sounds which seem to repulse each other and give to the ear the impression of two distinct sounds, although struck together."

The difficulty with Rougnon's definition of consonance, from the twentieth century point of view, is its limiting statement concerning its "manner pleasant to the ear." As to their pleasantness or unpleasantness, consonance and dissonance are purely relative terms, for what is unpleasantly dissonant to one listener is pleasantly concordant to another. Rougnon further says, "One should not confound *dissonance* with *discord*. A dissonance is less satisfying to the ear than a consonance; but it is perfectly analyzable, musically speaking. On the contrary, a *discord* defies analysis and is in consequence antimusical." "What is discord?" Carl Engel asks in "Harking Back and Looking Forward" (*Musical Quarterly,* January 1928), and wisely answers, "An irritation of the aural mechanism which results in a greater tension of our auditory nerves."

With our growing experience of listening to unusual harmonic combinations, much that was regarded as discordant has become merely dissonant because it can be analyzed according to present day methods of tonal and chordal structure. This is true not only of our generation but was equally the case when the third was introduced into harmonic combination seven or eight centuries ago. These same "antimusical" chords and melodies defy analysis when they are measured by the rules of a former musical syntax because our musical language has been undergoing drastic changes in the last fifty years.

We have been taught for centuries that the unisons (primes), octaves, fifths, and fourths, are intervals of perfect consonance; major and minor thirds and sixths, of imperfect consonance; and all seconds, sevenths, and augmented and diminished intervals are dissonant. In terms of the acousticians the minor second is the "roughest" or harshest interval within the octave; the minor seventh next; then the major seventh, major second, diminished fifth, and augmented fourth.

According to the physical properties of tone, these classifications are correct, but our ears are so trained (or blunted) through familiarity with dissonance that it is impossible to make consonance and pleasantness, or dissonance and unpleasantness, synonymous. We need new terms to keep pace with such names as *polytonality* and *atonality*.

In *A Theory of Evolving Tonality* Joseph Yasser writes: "The fact itself of opposition of consonances and dissonances is, of course, largely a psychological phenomenon, since such opposition does not exist objectively. Acoustics gives us one *continuous* series of harmonic combinations gradually increasing in harshness but it cannot point to a perfectly objective and convincing indication according to which certain combinations are to be considered as consonances and the others as dissonances." (Footnote, page 235.)

Acousticians tell us that smoothness or roughness of a tone is due to the number and volume of the beats. These beats are occasioned by the fact that no two tones travel at the same vibrational rate, and the roughness occurs because the vibration of the two tones interfere with each other. The number of beats per second is equal to the difference between the two rates of vibration.

Yasser says, "The reaction of a musical ear to this or that number and volume of beats and, consequently, to the harshness they produce, changes with the development of musical art." Then he calls attention to Helmholtz's statement in *Sensations of Tone* that objectively no sharp line can be drawn between consonances and dissonances because the boundary that separates them changes its place as *tonal systems* change in the course of evolution. Therefore it is not the harmonic combination which decides where consonance ends and dissonance begins, but it depends on the "entire construction of the tonal system used at a given period."

The existence of this book is due to the fact that we have experienced in the twentieth century a change of *tonal system,* and, as has been the case each time, it has created chaos. And, as has also happened in the past, the new tonal system and the old have traveled along side by side with plenty of friends and foes rallying to one or the other standard, and a number of pacifists willing to accept the best of the new without casting out the best of the old.

To sum up:

CONSONANCE IS:	DISSONANCE IS:
unity	multiplicity
resolution	unresolved
finality	incomplete
restful	restless
answer	question
attraction	repulsion
satisfying	unsatisfying

Tonal systems are not disposed of easily. In fact, they are not disposed of at all. They are absorbed, reconstructed, revolutionized, superseded, but not destroyed. Actually there have been surprisingly few in the last three or four thousand years and they have been changed only by means of a slow evolutionary process. Even though seemingly drastic changes have taken place, the undermining of an ancient system must go on for a long time before the outward effects are manifested as innovations. Two important factors in tonal systems have been scale formations and the tempering of intervals.

The general classification into *pentatonic* or five tones, *diatonic* or seven tones, and *chromatic* or twelve tones to the octave, shows the evolutionary character of scales. "We should not lose sight of the fact," says Joseph Yasser in the first chapter of *A Theory of Evolving Tonality,* "that a genuine musical scale (or tonality, in a more fundamental sense) is, in a way, an organic phenomenon, a materialized product of our inmost psychic functions, which, like everything else live and organic, is bound to grow, to expand, to evolve continuously. It is essentially an *evolving,* not a *static* phenomenon."

The pentatonic, which may be found by playing the black keys on a piano, was doubtless a universal scale, not belonging to any one nation or race, but marking a stage in the evolution of man's musical consciousness. It is the scale of primitive man and of early civilizations. The Chinese and Japanese have clung to it throughout the centuries; it is familiar to us through many characteristic Scotch and Irish folk songs; traces of the pentatonic are to be found in the music of the American Indians and Eskimos, as well as in that of African and Australian aborigines. "In Europe particularly," Joseph Yasser wrote in *The Future of Tonality,* a supplement to *Modern Music* (November-December 1930), "despite the difficulty of obtaining authentic information, the pentatonic scale is now known to have been used in Scandinavia, the British Isles (strongest evidences), Northern France (Brittany), Germany (Nithart's *Minnegesänge*), a good many parts of Russia (European and Asiatic), some parts of Finland, Rumania, Bulgaria, and possibly Spain....Even the old Gregorian chants are not devoid of pentatonic elements. Ancient Greece (one of their sources, besides Hebrew cantillations, which are also full of 'pentatonisms') experienced at one time the practical use of the pentatonic scale (eighth century B.C. according to Plutarch), in spite of the parallel existence of heptatonic and other scales in her musical theory."

The pentatonic scale is the basis of Yasser's new theory of scale evolution in which this early form of five steps is named the *infra-diatonic*. He calls it the "5 + 2" scale, indicating that the half steps, which occur between the third and fourth, and seventh and eighth degrees of our major scale, were used as auxiliary steps gradually developing into our major scale, which he calls the "7 + 5," a combination of seven diatonic and five chromatic degrees. He explains the search for the smaller division of the half step by his theory of the *supra-diatonic* scale which, according to the laws of evolution, seems to be the direction in which music is traveling. The supra-diatonic is the "12 + 7" scale, based on the twelve tone scale, definitely established by Schoenberg, Ravel, Scriabin, and many others, with a further division of the half step into auxiliary steps of smaller dimensions. This "12 + 7" scale is one of many attempts to explain and justify the use of the *quarter tone*. The Greeks employed it in their *enharmonic* scales, and the Orientals use it constantly (Chapter 17).

The Chinese did away with the fourth and the seventh degrees because they created problems. They claimed that these steps "were as useless in music as an extra finger would be on each hand." In *La Lyre d'Apollon,* by Ernest E. Britt, the author calls this suppression of the intervals, "radical means, but barbarous; a surgical operation which upset the equilibrium of the harmonic functions and crystallized Chinese music into this pentatonic form without half-steps."

The interval called the tritone (three whole steps, f-g-a-b), formed by the presence of the fourth and the seventh in the scale, has always been a source of anxiety. In the Middle Ages it was considered an evil spirit, the *diabolus in musica*. The six tone scale, or the hexachordal system, was the result of Guido d'Arezzo's attempt to avoid the tritone. When melody was influenced by the introduction of harmony, it was found that "the instinct of the troubadours, the minstrels and the minnesingers, not contaminated by scholasticism, proved by songs freely inspired that the relationship of the tritone had nothing subversive and resolved itself naturally by the mutual attractions of the semitones *si* to *ut* and *fa* to *mi*" (E. E. Britt). Or the seventh to the eighth degree and the fourth to the third.

The diatonic scale has had a long and checkered career. It owes its development to the fact that the Persians, Egyptians, Hindus and Greeks built their scales on the principle of a fourth (the tetrachord).

"To the realignments of the Greek tetrachord via the church modes of the Middle Ages, we owe our own diatonic scales. *'Tetrachord'* means 'four strings,' and relates to the basic principle of the Greek music system. The two outer tones, which measured a perfect fourth in our nomenclature, were fixed, and the intermediate tones were movable." (*Music through the Ages*, Bauer and Peyser, page 35.)

Aristoxenos, a Greek musician and theoretician of the fourth century B.C., stated that there were three genera, or classes, of tetrachords:

> *diatonic:* a-g-f-e, a-g-f♯-e, a-g♯-f♯-e;
> *chromatic:* a-f♯-f-e, a-g♯-g-e, a-g♯-f-e;
> *enharmonic:* a-f-f-e, a-a-f-e, a-a-f♯-e.
> ¼ tone ¼ tone ¼ tone

Evidently the enharmonic genus gave a sensuousness and richness to Greek song which we are incapable of understanding or appreciating. The Orientals have retained the use of intervals smaller than the semitone, but apparently the Occidentals have lost the keen ears necessary for their adoption. Will we again cultivate the ability to hear them in the near future? This is one of the questions suggested by present day tendencies.

Combining two tetrachords in conjunct or disjunct method (that is, by overlapping or separating the tetrachords) gives the various species which we know as Phrygian, Dorian, Lydian, Mixolydian, Hypodorian, etc. The Dorian species had a "modal life," according to Gustave Reese in *Music in the Middle Ages,* while the other six species are different aspects of the Dorian mode. Both Greek and Hebrew music have been influenced by the Egyptian, and in a volume on the historical development of *Jewish Music* A. Z. Idelsohn expresses the opinion that Egyptian music did not die out with its religion, because "some of the best human expressions in it were taken over by Israel and Greece." Jewish music retains its Semitic-Oriental characteristics, according to Idelsohn, and reflects the spiritual life and struggle of the race. It has the modal form of Semitic, Altaic, or Hindu music; that is, it is composed of short music figures or tonal groups within a certain scale similar to the Hindu *ragas.* "The composer operates with the material of these traditional folk motives within a certain mode for his creations. . . . Sixteen of these modes are most widely known throughout the Near East." Jewish music has the ornamentation of Oriental music; it is unrhythmical, narrative or recitative in style; its tonality is based on the quarter tone system and has twenty-four steps to the octave; the folk tunes are usually tetrachordal or pentachordal in range; there is no harmony, it is monodic.

Of the four chief scales found in Jewish music, two correspond to the Greek Phrygian and Dorian, although we have no way of knowing whether the tempering, which differs from ours, was similar to that of the Greeks. The third scale is almost identical with our major scale (the Greek Lydian); and the fourth is a fascinating combination of a tetrachord with the characteristic Oriental augmented second (d-e♭-f♯-g) and the Phrygian (a-b-c-d).

Idelsohn says, "Whether or not Jewish music, in its *origin,* was based on or even affected by a quarter-tone system, we have not sufficient data to prove or disprove. . . . In the Orient the Jews sing in those scales, using the quarter-tone steps of their neighbors, while the Jews of the Occident employ the same scales with steps of semitone system."

The Bible was chanted, according to tradition, in a cantillation or singing tone for which different modes were used for different parts of the text. The ancient Pentateuch mode was the Dorian scale; the mode of the Prophets was the Phrygian; the mode of Job is the Ionian or a modified Lydian, approaching our major scale. There were also modes for different types of prayers. These intonations were handed down orally from generation to generation, and attempts were made

to preserve them by indicating the rise and fall of the voice which later
developed into a musical notation with Greek letters to help the teacher
or leader. It is very clear that the early Christian church, composed
of Romans who inherited the Greek traditions and of Hebrews who
had their own, founded the music on the Jewish chant, using the
familiar modes which were similar to those of the Greeks. In some
way the names of the Greek modes were handed down to the Christian
fathers incorrectly so that the Dorian and Phrygian were exchanged,
because the order of the Greek octave species was completely reversed.
   There are eight ecclesiastical or church modes:

AUTHENTIC SCALES OR MODES   PLAGAL SCALES OR MODES

  I. Dorian: II. Hypodorian:
     d e͡f g a b͡c d   a b͡c d e͡f g a

 III. Phrygian: IV. Hypophrygian:
     e͡f g a b͡c d e   b͡c d e͡f g a b

  V. Lydian: VI. Hypolydian:
     f g a b͡c d e͡f   c d e͡f g a b͡c

 VII. Mixolydian: VIII. Hypomixolydian:
     g a b͡c d e͡f g   d e͡f g a b͡c d

   The Gregorian plainsong is the bridge between the music of the
ancient civilization and that of the modern. As long as music was
predominantly vocal and polyphonic, the modes served the purposes
of the composers. With the encroachment of harmony, however, they
gradually settled down into the familiar system of major and minor
scales in which the eight or more ecclesiastical modes were reduced
to two. Equal temperament had its share in making all keys equal,
and in increasing the possibilities of modulation, and thanks to the
freer use of the chromatic intervals (Yasser's "7 + 5" scale), the
musical language was composed of twelve major and twelve minor
scales, or fifteen if we include the three enharmonic scales. Although
our major scales remained tetrachordal—made up of two similar disjunct tetrachords: c-d-ef g-a-bc—the *triad* or three-voiced chord became
the unit of measurement. Key relationship was governed by the circle
of fifths, and chords by a circle of thirds.

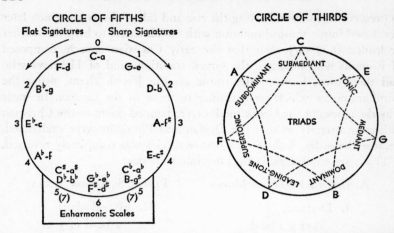

In the circle of fifths, we have a table of key signatures for all major and minor keys. In the circle of thirds we see the possibilities of building triads, chords of the seventh, chords of the ninth, chords of the eleventh, and chords of the thirteenth, thus:

TRIAD   CHORD   CHORD   CHORD   CHORD
        OF THE 7TH   OF THE 11TH
              OF THE 9TH   OF THE 13TH

When we consider that chords similar to these in scope may be built on each degree of the scale (major and minor), that they may be inverted (the arrangement of the intervals shifted), and that through our use of chromatic or auxiliary steps they may be altered in dozens of ways, we recognize that we have a very wide musical vocabulary.

After centuries of chord building in thirds, Schoenberg suggested building them in fourths—c-f-b♭-e♭. His experiments have resulted in a new tonal system which will be discussed in a later chapter (page 217).

This example from Schoenberg's opera *Erwartung* * shows the har-

* This citation from the monodrama *Erwartung* (*Waiting*), op. 17, by Arnold Schoenberg, is used with permission of the original editor, Universal-Edition, A.G., Vienna (copyright, 1922).

monic effect of chords built in fourths. Analyzing the fragment from the standpoint of a new tonal system is much less confusing and less complicated than trying to force it into the mold of an earlier system:

Erwartung   Arnold Schoenberg

etc.

(Universal Edition)

Wagner made use of chromaticism more than any composer before him, but his harmonic scheme could still be analyzed as belonging to the "7 + 5" scale. His basis was diatonic and the chromaticism was auxiliary. C. H. Kitson says, in *The Evolution of Harmony,* "Dvořák began with the premise that all the notes of the chromatic scale were equally related." Kitson also speaks of "the formation of new scalic systems from a fusion of the diatonic and chromatic formulæ."

As the use of chromaticism, following the line of the natural harmonic series, grew more frequent in the works of late nineteenth and early twentieth century composers, the diatonic outlines became fainter and the chromatic scale has gradually become established as the basis of a new tonal system. As a fundamental scale it is known as the twelve tone, or "duodecuple" scale, and is also the scale of *atonality* (Chapter 15).

In the diatonic scales each degree is the root either of a major or of a minor triad; in the twelve tone scale each degree may be the root of both a major and a minor triad, thus:

etc.

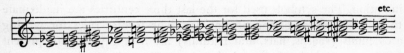

This immediately increases the colors of our tonal palette and makes it feasible to analyze the following passage from Debussy's prelude, *"Les Sons et les parfums tournent dans l'air du soir,"* according to the semitonal system, treated not as a modification of the diatonic mode but itself as a definite mode, in which each tone is the root of a triad:

(Durand et Cie., copyright, 1910)

To attempt to explain this and the following example according to the rules of diatonic harmony creates unnecessary complications and the breaking of time-honored rules. But a new tonal system creates its own rules.

When the listener considers that each chord has its own related chords and modulating powers, he begins to realize the wider scope of this twelve tone scale. Of its relation to atonality, I shall speak later.

Although there is no doubt in the minds of twentieth century composers that new tonal systems have been established, we are painfully aware that notation has not kept pace with other musical reforms. Notation is merely a convenient means of indicating the composer's intention. The symbols used for the last three centuries are inadequate to meet the needs of the present day. The former rules for writing accidentals (sharps, flats, and naturals) are as antiquated for present music as are those of diatonic harmony. Since the twelve tone scale has come of age, each degree of that scale needs its own name in order to establish its identity and independent function. The semitone between c and d, for example, is no longer dependent on those diatonic degrees to be known as a lighter shade of c or a darker shade of d (using the word chromatic in its true etymological derivation from *chromos,* color) but it has signed its declaration of independence! The existing notation is awkward, disconcerting, and inadequate for atonality and polytonality, or for any melodic line or harmonic progression in the twelve tone scale.

One musician of the nineteenth century vintage argued that the whole tone scale was illogical because it could not be notated according to existing rules. A clear case of putting the cart before the horse! The scale has an entity, but its notation is unsatisfactory because of the limitations of the system. The instinct of the artist always has preceded the scientific justification. Debussy, himself, notated the whole tone scale in many different ways to suit either his own convenience or the demands of the key signature, apparently. In his prelude *"Voiles"* he wrote it: a♭-b♭-c-d-e-f♯g♯. In *"Reflets dans l'eau"* we find it: g-a-c♭-d♭-e♭-f-g, etc. In *"Mouvement,"* the third of the group of *Images,* he changed the spelling of the scale, using enharmonic notation: c-d-e-f♯-g♯-a♯, a♭-b♭-c-d-e-f♯, etc.

In its evolutionary travels, harmony used as units of measurement, first the fifth (and its inversion, the fourth), then the third (with its inversion, the sixth). The third and sixth dominated counterpoint just as the fifth and the fourth had dominated organum, and the third was the basis of chord building. A recent tendency is to use the second and the seventh, and augmented and diminished intervals as the point of departure for the new polyphony (dissonant counterpoint) and for building chords. To which statement these few measures of a hornpipe from a suite for piano by Richard Donovan and published in the *New Music Quarterly* (April 1933) will testify:

(New Music Quarterly, copyrighted, 1933.)

"Of all the wonders of all the arts, surely harmony in music is the most wonderful," says Ernest Newman ("The Elastic Language" in *A Musical Motley*). "It may be that some day each of the other arts will be brought to a standstill from the sheer impossibility of putting to new uses the material that in the course of many centuries will have been manipulated in every conceivable manner. . . . But to musical novelty no man can see an end, because the language of music is not a fixed but a fluid one." And he speaks of "harmony as a language that, instead of remaining fixed, as a spoken language becomes after a certain time, is infinitely elastic both in its vocabulary and in the combinations of that vocabulary." Newman claims that harmony cannot be taught because of its elasticity. Who has not had the experience of learning all the "don'ts" of textbook harmony and then finding them in the works of reputed composers, or turning composer oneself and having to write not because of the rules of theory but in spite of them?

The value of the discipline and the historic background one gains from theoretical studies cannot be denied. It is obvious, however, that it is just as impossible for the theorists to keep up with the composers as it is for the composers to be ruled by the theorists. A new tonal system must be subjected to a period of experimentation before it can become established; it must be established before the theorists can study it scientifically, and it takes a long time before the new idea, established by the composer and explained by the scientist, reaches the classroom or the public.

Occasionally composer and theorist is one person, as is the case with Schoenberg. Today many of the composers are working quite consciously along new lines. There must be many who are unconscious innovators, but the trend is toward a definite search for new musical resources. This is the case not only with the composer but with many scientifically minded musicians who are giving their earnest attention to the problems of contemporary music. The listener, too, must be aware that not only tonal systems and musical forms have changed but the taste of a former day also is subject to change. Sincere study of the problem reveals that it is legitimate and logical. Time will be the final judge in this case as in many others, and the chaff will be sifted from the wheat.

Newman, in speaking of past treatises on harmony, says: "If the use of harmony as a language had been in any way dependent on a knowledge on the composers' part of the nature of the material they were manipulating, music could never have been written. . . . Theory has always failed utterly to explain the practice of its own day. The seventeenth and eighteenth century composers who were also theorists were constantly using chords rightly and accounting for them wrongly."

The prevalent theory that melody came first and harmony was evolved from it is challenged by Newman. "It could be argued with equal, perhaps superior, force that melody has been evolved from unconscious harmony: that is to say, man did not first invent a scale and then discover how to make harmonies from it, but a subconscious feeling for harmony—a feeling it may have taken thousands of years to develop—guided him in the construction of the scale. Nothing in the whole history of the subject is more remarkable than the way in which the unconscious instincts of men have guided them to the truth of harmony where the reasoning of the theorists would have led them away from it."

The harmonic resources of the twentieth century are probably the richest and most varied the composer has ever dealt with. There seems to be no limit in possible tonal combinations, and he has freed himself so completely from the tyranny of textbook rules that nothing seems impossible or incorrect. In fact, we are in danger of accepting much that should be rejected. In the last analysis we say that Good Taste must be our criterion, but even that worthy has been subject to so many and such violent reversals of opinion recently that he no longer is permitted to rule despotically, but meekly says, "It wasn't done in my youth." As is the case in every epoch of change such as our own, the pure ore is mixed with much dross; sincerity and insincerity are frequently caught playing each other's rôles; the ability to create sensational effect is often mistaken for a gift for invention. It is a time when our young students should apply themselves to acquiring complete mastery of past methods (not merely those of the nineteenth century, however) in order to acquire a twentieth century technic. We can no longer start where the last composer left off, but rather where the first one began! We must know the possibilities of the pentatonic scale and how to harmonize it. Debussy, Ravel, Stravinsky, and many others have used it. Organum has lifted its head again, not, as in its day, as the only means of harmonization, but as one way of giving an individual touch (page 140). Many are interested in the results obtained from an intimate study of Gregorian music and the golden age of polyphony. They are not copying the styles of Palestrina, Vittoria, William Byrd, or Marenzio, but they are mastering them in order to allow them to direct their usage of twentieth century resources, pointing, perhaps, to a renaissance of choral music. The primitive in all phases of art is influencing creative workers, and music of aborigines presents suggestive rhythms and melodic patterns. Folk music is subject to earnest research and in some countries is affecting the contemporary style of composition. Bach has been a beacon light to many and is heard with deeper appreciation than ever before. The eighteenth century is closer to us than the nineteenth for the moment. The only things the young composers will not tolerate seem to be the mannerisms and the formulas of the romanticists (even as the romanticists rebelled against the classicists!). In spite of the fact that the younger composers have turned away from impressionism, or think they have, they are using many of its tools. They are also forging new works out of the materials that Schoenberg, Stravinsky, Alban Berg, Ravel, Milhaud, Honegger, Hindemith, etc., have prepared for them.

Dissonance is the point of departure for twentieth century harmony. Where our musical forefathers built on consonance, we study the affinities and repulsions of dissonant combinations. We are more interested in harmonic progressions than in resolutions, because *progression* implies a fluidic or dynamic state where *resolution* is immobile or static.

As an example of how old material may be renovated to sound new, I offer the following:

a. A good old-fashioned diatonic harmony exercise which any first-year student could solve:

b. The same exercise doctored up by means of altered chords (raising or lowering parts of the chord by means of accidentals):

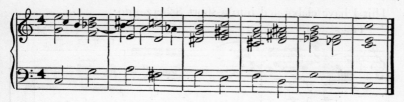

c. An elaboration of b into a short Prelude:

Allegretto moderato   M.B.*

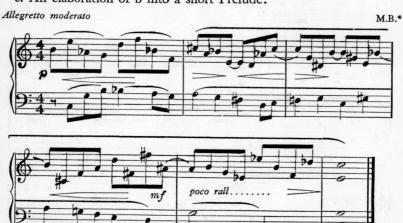

* All the material in this book is covered by copyright.

Here is a progression of dissonant chords (sevenths, ninths, elevenths, and thirteenths) built in thirds based on the twelve tone scale:

This I have elaborated into a short Scherzando:

In previous times *dominant* and *tonic* represented movement and repose. This resulted in the cadence, which became tyrannical and controlled the length of the phrase, the rhythmic impulse, the shape of the melodic design, and the structure of the composition. "Oh, those interminable cadences!" was the criticism a music student made of a recently revived Handel opera.

The typical cadence which has ruled music during the harmonic era is formed of the three primary chords, tonic (I), subdominant (IV), and dominant (V); that is, the triads found on the first, fourth, and fifth degrees of the major or minor scale. Some of the familiar cadences are V, I; IV, I; IV, V, I; $I\,^6_4$*, V, I, in scores of possible positions and arrangements, including also substitute chords: the supertonic (II) in place of the subdominant; the submediant (VI) in place of the tonic; the mediant (III) or the chord on the leading tone (VII) in place of the dominant, etc. The cadence is to music what punctuation is to poetry.

Evolution has done its work as thoroughly in the use of the cadence as in other branches of the science of music. Here are a few examples of how the cadence has been affected by the changes which have taken place in scales and chords in the twentieth century. Still recognizing the dominant and tonic idea of movement and repose, the composers have in many cases used arbitrary chords as the points of movement and repose.

Maurice Ravel terminates the first movement of his Sonatine (copyright, 1905, A. Durand et Fils, Paris) thus:

---

* $I\,^6_4$ is the second inversion of the tonic chord.

The last measures of Louis Gruenberg's "Syncopep," op. 25, no. 4, from *Jazzberries* (quoted with permission of the original editor, Universal-Edition, A.G. Vienna, copyright, 1925), are as follows:

Prélude, op. 74, no. 5 by Alexandre Scriabin ends thus:

The closing cadence of Ernest Bloch's *"Incertitude"* from *Five Sketches in Sepia* (copyright, 1924, G. Schirmer, Inc.) is:

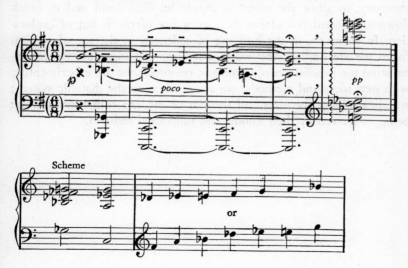

Toccata, op. 21, no. 3, from *Four Piano Pieces* (copyright, 1930, Cos Cob Press) by Marion Bauer ends with the following chords:

Scheme

We might successfully sum up the new music as an attempt to escape the obvious, to avoid timeworn combinations, to elide the unnecessary, to allow the mind to supply implied detail and to break down established boundaries in a spirit not of revolt but of exploration. In harmony, in the building of cadences, in the use of musical forms we are finding new ways of treating old material; we are exhausting the possibilities of chromatic resources; we are experimenting with new ideas and methods; we are revaluating the diatonic system; we are studying the aims and theories of modern composers and are being influenced by their idioms and individual technics.

PART II: LOOKING FORWARD

CHAPTER 10

IMPRESSIONISTIC METHODS—DEBUSSY AND HIS INFLUENCE

IMPRESSIONISM as developed by Claude Achille Debussy (1862-1918) was one of the strongest factors in the creation of a different and non-Teutonic mode of thought in music. It was the result of a nature in revolt. First, as a pupil at the Conservatory he would rail against the rules of harmony to his fellow students. Why must dissonant chords be resolved? Why were the consecutive fifths and octaves forbidden? Why was parallel movement in the voice parts forbidden? He would improvise curious chord successions in which augmented intervals and chords of the ninth, eleventh, and thirteenth —all unresolved and traveling in the same direction—hurt reactionary ears which had accepted the traditional teachings without question. Achille, as he was called, was regarded as an impossible and dangerous revolutionary! He taunted them with "What are you so shocked about? Can't you listen to chords without wanting to know their status and their destination? Where do they come from? Whither are they going? What does it matter? Listen; that's enough. If you can't make head or tail of it, go and tell M. le Directeur that I am ruining your ears." (*Claude Debussy: Life and Works* by Leon Vallas.)

His teacher, Guiraud, seemed to understand him and was interested in his eccentric notions, although he counseled him to curb his wild experiments if he wished to win the Prix de Rome. Debussy worked out logical reasons in his own mind for his tonal idiosyncrasies in all kinds of unusual scale combinations and modulations, and in a wider variety of rhythmic figures as well as new harmonic and melodic patterns.

He won the Prix de Rome in 1884 with his cantata *L'Enfant*

prodigue, and again his natural tendency to revolt against anything which was orthodox and static led him to leave the Villa Medici at Rome before the allotted three years were up. Like his famous predecessor in revolt, Berlioz, he plotted constantly how he could return to Paris, and did not write all of the compositions which were, according to custom, to have been sent back to Paris from Rome. *"Printemps,"* inspired by Botticelli's *"Primavera,"* for orchestra and humming chorus, such as Debussy used later in *"Sirènes"* (the third of the *Nocturnes*), was sent from Rome and shocked some of the judges. *"La Damoiselle élue"* to Rossetti's translated text, was written in Paris, as was the *Fantaisie* for piano and orchestra which was not heard in public until after his death. In 1890 he was to have had the Festival concert given to the winners of the Prix de Rome, but again there was trouble. Debussy was stubborn and refused to write the traditional overture he was supposed to have composed in Rome; he was furious because they would not include *"Printemps"* on the program. There was no Debussy concert!

His one object now seemed to be to compose in contradiction to everything he had been taught at the Conservatory, to express his own artistic ideals in as beautiful a manner as possible, and to perfect his style. He was a lover of everything exquisite and individual. He cut away from his musical colleagues and, seeking congeniality among artists in other lines, was drawn into a circle of young symbolist poets and impressionist painters who met at Stéphane Mallarmé's and in cafés. Among his acquaintances were Paul Verlaine, Henri de Regnier, Maurice Vaucaire, Pierre Louÿs, André Gide, Whistler, Monet, Renoir, Sisley, Manet, Pissarro, Degas, and Jacques-Emile Blanche.

Vallas quotes this statement made by Debussy's musical colleague Paul Dukas: "Verlaine, Mallarmé and Laforgue used to provide us with new sounds and sonorities. They cast a light on words such as had never been seen before; they used methods that were unknown to the poets that had preceded them; they made their verbal material yield subtle and powerful effects hitherto undreamt of. Above all, they conceived their poetry or prose like musicians, they tended it with the care of musicians, and, like musicians, too, they sought to express their ideas in corresponding sound values. It was the writers, not the musicians, who exercised the strongest influence on Debussy." (*Claude Debussy: Life and Works.*)

At this time Debussy was an ardent Wagnerite. "All that Wagner could teach him of the potency of dissonance, of structural freedom and elasticity, of harmonic daring, Debussy eagerly learned and applied, as a foundation to his own intricately reasoned though spontaneous art," says Lawrence Gilman in his Guide to *Pelléas et Mélisande.* "Yet Wagner would have gasped alike at the novelty and the exquisite art of *Pelléas et Mélisande,* of the *Nocturnes,* even of the comparatively early *Prélude à l'après-midi d'un faune;* for this is music of a kind which may, indeed, have been dreamed of, but which certainly had never found its way upon paper, before Debussy quietly recorded it in his scores." That Debussy turned away from Wagner after his second visit to Bayreuth in 1889 meant that he disagreed with his aesthetic philosophies and his theater more than he did with the music. But with characteristic perverseness he denied Wagner and wrote criticisms against him while still being unconsciously under his influence.

The term *impressionism* was first applied in derision to the works of a group of painters after Claude Monet had exhibited a picture in 1867 which he called *"Impression: Soleil levant"* (Rising Sun). The study of the effect of light and atmosphere on color made by Edouard Manet led to the *plein-air* movement. The emotional reaction of what the eye beheld caused the painters to question, to reason, to create a new technic. Monet succeeded "in fixing the fugitive changes of nature," and a choice had to be made between what the eye saw and what the mind perceived. A new correlation between the arts was effected in which the word, the musical sound, color, and line were bent to the will of the writers, musicians, and painters in a new interpretation of beauty; in a freedom from confining regulations; in an attempt to avoid direct representation and to substitute the artist's impression; in a blending of the arts that would break down the boundaries that separated them and would reveal their mystery.

In all probability impressionism would have come into music had Debussy never composed, because music usually follows the aesthetic directions which the sister arts take. But in searching for escape from the dogmatism of conservative methods, he found among these symbolists, impressionists, and realists the exact counterpart in painting and literature of what he was trying to create in music. He was an impressionist temperamentally before he had written any impressionistic music. It satisfied his intuitions and artistic desires. He was merely the tool of a world-thought which was of greater import than the individual who reflected it.

And so Debussy created a style comparable to the impressionism of the painters and the symbolism of the poets, applying their technic to the world of sound, trying to suggest in tone intangible, abstract mental images induced by a thought, an emotion, a perfume, a color, a poem, a scene, any definite object, suppressing unnecessary detail, and reproducing not the reality but the *emotion* evoked by the reality. This is impressionism.

There were other contributing factors in Debussy's development of an impressionistic technic aside from the suggestions he adopted from his artistic confreres. He had studied piano as a child with a pupil of Chopin, and he sensed the Polish-French composer's characteristics as few of his contemporaries did; the technic of his piano compositions often recalls Chopin. When a very young boy, he went to Russia as pianist for Mme. von Meck, Tchaikovsky's patroness. It is not at all certain that he heard the music of Moussorgsky at that time, but apparently he came in contact with the Russian folk music and some songs of Borodin. However, the seed was planted, and when he later read the score of *Boris Godounoff,* he found in its extraordinary musical independence food for thought which led him into a deeper study of his own resources and musical means. That Debussy may have heard the whole tone scale in Russia has been suggested (page 63), but it is more probable that the realization of its possibilities came to him at the Paris Exposition in 1889 when he spent hours listening to the strange exotic music of the Javanese gamelang (orchestra), the tonality of which was a near whole-tone scale. At the exposition, too, he heard other exotic music based on pentatonic scales, of which he made good use. At the Conservatory he was in Franck's class in improvisation, and he knew the works of Chabrier, who like himself was a friend of the contemporary writers and painters. He was not deaf to the melodic influence of Massenet, and Duparc's songs must have brought out a note of sympathy.

While in Rome he had occasion to hear Gregorian music, which impressed him so deeply that he made a study of medieval church modes, which he revived with new freedom and effective imagination. He also made use of a style approximating organum.

Another strong influence in Debussy's development was his conviction that French composers should throw off the yoke of Teutonic domination and recapture the line created by Rameau, Couperin, and the French clavecinists. He said that no matter how much the French appreciated the music of Beethoven, Schumann, and Wagner, a slavish imitation of their styles was grafting a Teutonic branch on to a Gallic tree, with hybrid results. He wrote in his last years in a neo-classic style, desiring (in a group of six sonatas only three of which he completed) to return to the classic style of the seventeenth and early eighteenth centuries. He frequently imitated the structure, title, and spirit of the French clavecinists.

This composite style of Debussy is found in his exquisite songs, his piano compositions, his opera *Pelléas et Mélisande,* and his orchestral scores, which include *"Prélude à l'après-midi d'un faune"* (Prelude to the Afternoon of a Faun) on a poem by Mallarmé; three *Nocturnes: "Nuages"* (Clouds), *"Fêtes"* (Festivals) and *"Sirènes"* (Sirens); *"La Mer"* (The Sea), and three *Images: "Gigues tristes"* (Sad Gigues), "Iberia," and *"Rondes de Printemps"* (Rounds of Spring).

His songs, of which there are over thirty, are on texts by Baudelaire, Verlaine, Debussy (*Proses lyriques*), Pierre Louÿs, Mallarmé, and by the early French poets François Villon, Charles d'Orléans, and Tristan l'Hermitte.

He wrote a few chamber music works. The most famous is the String Quartet in G minor, which has been a model for many twentieth century composers.

Debussy's artistic rating in 1901 is thus set forth by Leon Vallas in his volume *Claude Debussy: Life and Works:* "Debussy ... was a favorite with writers, painters, and some few musicians, but he was ignored by the general public and detested by reactionary artists who condemned, anathematized, and excommunicated him. We must also allow for his spirit of contradiction, his love of mockery, his attitude of boyish impertinence towards all established reputations, and all those personal elements which prompted him to exaggerate his opinions.... The majority of musicians were strongly influenced by Wagner and Franck, and thus unintentionally, and even unconsciously, they came under the dominion of German art. Whilst devoting themselves with passionate ardor to the renewal of national art, that *Ars gallica* whose triumphs were celebrated at the *Société Nationale,* they were actually receiving their strongest impetus, directly or indirectly from Germany. These almost unconscious tendencies aroused in Debussy a lively and aggressive hostility to labored intricacy of style, exaggerated sentimentality, and all adherence to false traditions. He urged the return to a simpler, more discreet type of art, more in keeping with the character of the French nation and with its past history."

The appearance of Debussy's setting of Maeterlinck's drama *Pelléas et Mélisande* at the Opéra Comique in 1902, after ten years of work, was epoch-making. It created opposing impressions. Most of the critics tore it to shreds, and others saw in it the beginning of a new era. The general public was disappointed, but it was aroused to curiosity and the work was kept in the repertory. Jean Périer, Mary Garden, Jeanne Gerville-Réache, and Hector Dufranne created the roles, as they did at the Manhattan Opera House in New York in 1908. It shook the traditional foundations of opera as had no work since *Tristan und Isolde*. "It was 'revolutionary' in extreme if one remembered Wagner and Strauss. And yet, Debussy succeeded in doing what Wagner tried to do: in writing an opera in which text, action, and music should be a blended perfection; in orchestrating so that the word should not be covered by the music; in eliminating all vocal melody in the form of arias, duets or concerted numbers with almost no orchestral thematic development. The sincerity with which Debussy sought to engulf his individuality in that of the personalities of the drama, and his intense desire to separate himself from the artificialities of the theater relate him to Gluck as an innovator." (*Music through the Ages,* Bauer and Peyser.)

Of his opera Debussy himself said: "...I have tried to obey a law of beauty which appears to be singularly ignored in dealing with dramatic music.... I do not pretend to have discovered everything in *Pelléas;* but I have tried to trace a path that others may follow, broadening it with individual discoveries which will, perhaps, free dramatic music from the heavy yoke under which it has existed for so long." (*Claude Debussy: Life and Works* by Leon Vallas.)

In 1911 Debussy produced *Le Martyre de Saint Sebastien* (*The Martyrdom of Saint Sebastian*) for chorus and orchestra to Gabriele d'Annunzio's play. In spite of the profound beauty of the music, in which a different style is apparent, the work has never achieved success. Perhaps, as Beethoven said of his quartets, it is music for a later age.

We hear constantly of "impressionistic methods," and yet the problem of what they involve is not easily solved. We are agreed that Debussy was the first to make these "methods" into a musical language with newly adjusted rules available for composers in many countries who must be regarded not so much as his imitators as his followers, eager to explore the paths he deliberately opened.

Perhaps our first step should be an attempt to show how impressionists broke away from the accepted use of chord combinations within a given tonality or key. For example, in Debussy's fourth *prélude,* from the first book of twelve, *"Les Sons et les parfums tournent dans l'air du soir"* (Sounds and Perfumes Stir in the Evening Air), the key is A major, but in every measure chords are introduced which do not belong to the scale:

"... Les sons et les parfums tournent
dans l'air du soir."—Ch. Baudelaire

Modéré   Claude Debussy

(Durand et Cie., copyright, 1910.)

The American impressionist Charles Griffes opened thus the first of his four *Roman Sketches* (op. 7), "The White Peacock," which carries the signature of four sharps, making use of a chord of the dominant ninth, preceded by a combination which sounds suspiciously bitonal (in two keys):

The White Peacock
Languidamente e molto rubato

Charles T. Griffes

una corda

(G. Schirmer, Inc., copyright, 1917.)

After twelve measures comes a theme which looks as though it might be in C major with a few accidentals, but it does not remain in that tonality long:

etc.

(G. Schirmer, Inc., copyright, 1917.)

In Maurice Ravel's *Valses nobles et sentimentales* he wrote as the opening of the fourth waltz the following measures, ambiguous so far as key is concerned, and suggesting polytonality (page 231):

Valses nobles et sentimentales: IV
Assez animé   Maurice Ravel

(Durand et Cie., copyright, 1911.)

Sometimes, often in fact, the chords are no longer triads (the common chord of three voices) but are sevenths or ninths, as is the case in Ravel's *"Jeux d'eau"* (The Fountain):

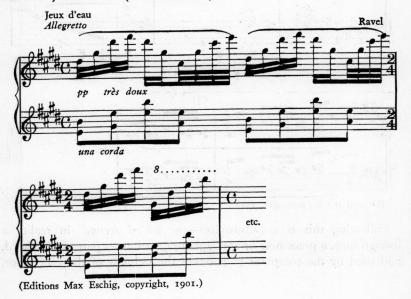

(Editions Max Eschig, copyright, 1901.)

The chordal scheme of the first phrase is as follows:

Although the key signature of Debussy's *"Feuilles mortes"* (Dead Leaves), the second *prélude* of the second book, indicates C sharp minor, the first two chords are ninths with no apparent connection with the key. The fourth and fifth measures show Debussy's love of mixing different unrelated triads in succession, as he has an F sharp major chord, an augmented on F natural, and an A minor triad following each other in a rhythmic design:

(Durand et Cie., copyright, 1913.)

Following this is a Debussyism—the *added second*—in reality a foreign tone, a grace note or appoggiatura, written as part of the chord, and used by the composer to enhance the richness of the tone color.

Feuilles mortes   Debussy

An obvious example of the added second is found in Debussy's "Jimbo's Lullaby" from *Children's Corner,* that set of delightful pieces which he wrote for his little daughter who outlived him only a year.

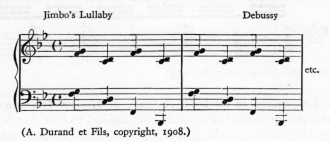

Jimbo's Lullaby   Debussy

(A. Durand et Fils, copyright, 1908.)

In the accompaniment to "Golliwogg's Cakewalk" from the same set, Debussy uses the same device. It can be found on the last page of the third of the *Images,* called *"Mouvement";* there he uses it in a passage of the whole tone scale.

Later the appoggiatura included not only single tones but complete chords, as in the following measures from a manuscript of mine:

Quietude   Marion Bauer *

*All the material used in this book is covered by copyright.

This leads logically to the combining of two or more keys, which is *polytonality* (Chapter 16).

An interesting example of the dissonant effect of an appoggiatura is found in Ravel's *"Oiseaux tristes"* from *Miroirs,* a set of five impressionistic pieces for piano published in 1906.

Oiseaux tristes   Ravel

(Editions Max Eschig, copyright, 1905)

René Lenormand in his book *A Study of Modern Harmony,* calls g natural the appoggiatura according to classical technic, but it seems more reasonable to call the g sharp a dissonant after-beat, with the same explanation for each chord following.

It will be remembered that Chopin made use of a dissonant appoggiatura in his Etude in F major, op. 25. The effect is bitingly modern!

And the first measures of Ravel's *Valses nobles et sentimentales* are too charming to be omitted:

Valses nobles et sentimentales   Ravel
modéré-très franc

etc.

(Durand et Cie., copyright, 1911.)

As though in defiance of the pedants who forbade parallel movement of the voices, Debussy used that device almost more than any other—similar motion by fifths, octaves, triads, sevenths, ninths, etc. Modern theorists sometimes apply the term "impressionistic method" to this particular type of chordal treatment, which has been copied by practically all the composers of this century. It must not be believed that Debussy was the first to use consecutive chord sequence, but he was the first to make it a mannerism.

The Ravel quotation from *"Oiseaux tristes"* is an example of parallel motion in all the voices in which the composer also made use of the twelve-tone-scale triad harmonization (page 111).

Repetition of a chord formation on different fundamental tones is known as *gliding chords*. This sequence of ninths from Ravel's *"Pavane pour une Infante défunte"* (Pavan for a Dead Infanta) has been adopted by composers of popular music and is a characteristic example:

Pavane pour une Infante défunte   Ravel

(Copyright 1899.)

Here is an example from Debussy's "Minstrels," the last *prélude* of the first book:

Minstrels   Debussy

(Durand et Cie., copyright, 1910.)

Like the Ravel citation, it is harmonized in the twelve tone scale. In this example from *"Reflets dans l'eau"* (Reflections in the Water)

the sequence is not based on perfect triads but on thirteenths or sevenths according to the enharmonic reading of the chords:

(A. Durand et Fils, copyright, 1905.)

This from *"Jardins sous la pluie"* (Gardens in the Rain), based on triads, has the same principle of gliding chords:

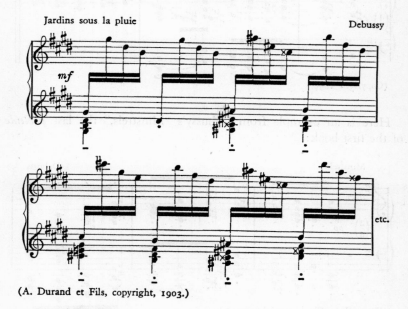

(A. Durand et Fils, copyright, 1903.)

And particularly effective is Ravel's use of ninths and sevenths in the following measure from *"Jeux d'eau,"* and how fascinatingly dissonant is the last chord of the eleventh, created by holding b sharp:

Jeux d'eau   Ravel

The fourth measure of Charles Griffes' "The White Peacock" shows
with what delicacy of effect he had absorbed impressionistic methods:

The White Peacock   Griffes   (scheme)

(G. Schirmer, Inc., copyright, 1917.)

Another phase of these impressionistic methods is the "escaped"
chord. It is comparable to the traditional pedal point except that the
newer form is often a chord instead of one or two notes, and the effect
is as though the dissonant chord or group of chords had escaped
from the established harmony or tonality suggested by the sustained
chord.

The beginning of Debussy's "General Lavine—Eccentric" from the
second book of *préludes* is an example. The C major tonality is established (although the third of the chord is missing) and the dissonant
triads from the twelve tone scale are "escaped" chords:

General Lavine . . . eccentric   Debussy

(Durand et Cie., copyright, 1913.)

The close of *"Reflets dans l'eau"* shows escaped tones against sustained chords.

"La Cathédrale engloutie" (The Engulfed Cathedral) opens with "escaped" chords, but our interest is more concerned with the curious formation of the chords, without thirds, giving rise to intervals of fourths, fifths, and octaves. This is *organum*, an extinct volcano as we had supposed, in eruption after a thousand years of inactivity (page 116).

Here is a sample of ninth century organum:

Organum (IXth Century)

And one of twentieth century organum (*"La Cathédrale engloutie"*):

La Cathédrale engloutie   Debussy

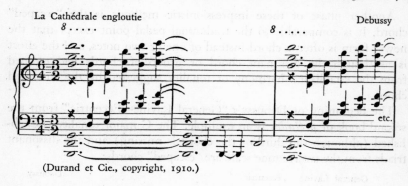

(Durand et Cie., copyright, 1910.)

In the next quotation, by Zoltan Kodaly, the Hungarian composer, we see organum in which the third is included but the peculiarity of the effect is enhanced by the sequence of chords in their third position (second inversion), which formerly we were cautioned to employ rarely and with restrictions. Its use in this "Epitaph" from opus 11 (*Sept pièces pour le piano*) is characteristically of the twentieth century:

Épitaphe   Zoltan Kodaly

(With permission of the original editor, Universal-Edition, A.G., Vienna, copyright, 1921.)

Kodaly harmonized this in still another way which we shall examine later.

The use of the whole tone scale is associated in our minds with Debussy, and we can find hundreds of citations in his works. The most patent example, however, is *"Voiles,"* * the second *prélude* of the first book, which is written entirely in the whole tone scale with the exception of one section of six measures in the pentatonic scale. Here Debussy does some interesting harmonizing, using only the degrees of the pentatonic scale for his chord formations of fifths and fourths:

* The French word *Voiles* might be translated "Veils" or "Sails," and to many, "Veils" expresses perfectly the spirit of the composition. Alfred Cortot has unconsciously created dissension in our camp by giving the following analysis of its mood in his essay on Debussy in *French Piano Music:* "Boats lie at anchor in the shining port. Their sails flutter idly, and on the breeze which stirs them sweeps the flight of a white wing over the crooning sea towards the horizon bright with the setting sun." I do not know whether this explanation is Cortot's or Debussy's.

Both the accompanying figure (a) and the melody (b) are in whole tone:

(Durand et Cie., copyright, 1910.)

He harmonizes the melody by means of augmented triads, but he also shows how the tones of the scale may be arranged in chords:

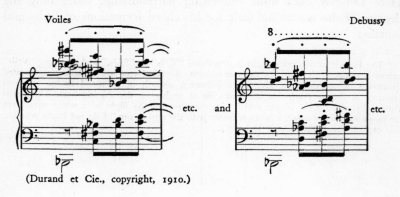

(Durand et Cie., copyright, 1910.)

And this is a delimiting process in the whole tone scale that has given it a much wider vogue with greater potentialities for development than would ever have been possible if used merely as a melodic medium harmonized constantly as a triad (augmented). It has opened the door to much of the harmony that has evolved since Debussy. Arranging the whole tone scale as a chord in thirds, which helps to solve the problem of how to notate it, and then constructing chords ad lib, we present these few out of countless possible combinations:

This chord can be transposed a half step, and all the resulting combinations, added to these, make a much wider palette of color.

As can easily be seen, combining these two whole tone scales or chords produces the twelve tone or duodecuple scale, with all sorts of possible extradiatonic chord formations (page 217) which we will discuss later. (See Horace Alden Miller's *New Harmonic Devices,* page 107.)

Debussy's use of exotic subjects with consequent exotic mood and harmony is still another means he cultivated for developing tone color. If he acquired the whole tone scale and use of chords of the ninth, as is claimed, from the Javanese gamelang, that in itself is exotic. In *"Pagodes"* he uses at least six patterns based on the pentatonic scale, interweaving them in such a manner as to make the effect completely Chinese, and by means of rhythmic variety in the patterns taking away any feeling of monotony.

Here is one of the themes, which sounds as though it might have come from authentic ceremonial music:

This pattern, which accompanied the theme, suddenly becomes a subject for canonical or imitational treatment, thus:

He harmonizes the accompanying figure thus:

(A. Durand et Fils, copyright, 1903)

Debussy uses the pentatonic scale with entirely different results in *"La Fille aux cheveux de lin"* (The Girl with the Flaxen Hair), in the first book of *préludes,* when he celebrates in song a sweet Scotch lassie. He also uses it occasionally just for color without any exotic intention, as in *"Voiles"* (page 141) and in *"Reflets dans l'eau"*:

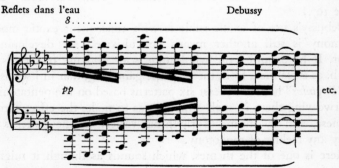

(A. Durand et Fils, copyright, 1905)

A charming exoticism in which Debussy has indulged with extraordinary success is his use of the Spanish idiom. Manuel de Falla, the Spanish composer, wrote (*La Revue musicale,* December 1920) that

Debussy composed Spanish music not by using authentic tunes but by *feeling* them, by realizing the foundation on which they rest and conveying the essence of them in music all his own.

J. B. Trend, in commenting on Falla's article ("Manuel de Falla and Spanish Music"), says: "Debussy's Andalucía was an Andalucía of dreams . . . ; and to Debussy, Falla must have seemed like a visitor from his own dream-land. But if Debussy heard from Falla that his dreams had in a sense come true, Falla must have felt that he himself was, as it were, part of Debussy's dream. . . . Many of Debussy's works created a marvelous atmosphere of poetry and suggestion; to Falla these came with the force of an *evocación* of his own country and its music and all his later work . . . may be regarded as an effort to convey this poetry and suggestiveness with the conviction of one who knows that dreams can sometimes come true. So far he had been expressing the letter of Andaluz music; he began now to realize how Debussy had managed to convey the spirit."

Debussy had direct influence on Albeniz, and, perhaps one might say, indirect influence on Falla, whose first compositions date from the year of Albeniz's death.

Falla finds in *"La Soirée dans Grenade"* by Debussy the real musical Andalucía. "The vague wandering melody is not really *cante hondo,* but a poetical suggestion of it, an *evocación." "La Puerta del Vino"* from the second book of *préludes* was the result of Debussy's having received a postcard from Falla from Granada, picturing the gate known by that name. The rhythm of the habanera, or tango, was used by Debussy in both these works.

In *"La Puerta del Vino"* the distant thunder of polytonality is distinctly heard in the introduction and then in the first enunciation of the theme with its ancient modal feeling and Oriental scale. The effect of polytonality, or several tonalities employed simultaneously, is achieved by using the D flat chord as a pedal or organ point, the complete chord not being heard until the nineteenth and twentieth measures.

La Puerta del Vino
a.   Debussy

etc.

(Durand et Cie, copyright, 1913)

The polymodal feeling continues, and Debussy uses the triad harmonization of the twelve tone scale, bringing back the first part,
though not with exact repetition. *"La Sérénade interrompue"* from the
first book of *préludes* is another Spanish picture. The second of three
orchestral *Images,* "Iberia," is also Spanish in character, and again
Manuel de Falla praised it, also stating that Debussy "had a considerable and decisive influence on young Spanish composers, especially on
Albeniz, to whom he demonstrated the art of utilizing merely the
fundamental elements of popular music, instead of following the usual
method of employing authentic folk-tunes."

Considering that Maurice Ravel (1875-1937) was born in the French
Basque country, Ciboure, Basses-Pyrénées, it is natural that he too
should have found the Spanish rhythms and melodies intriguing. The
"Pavane pour une Infante défunte" is a dance, bearing a seventeenth

century title, for the death of a Spanish infanta. In his piano work *Miroirs*, the clown's serenade *"Alborada del Gracioso,"* is Spanish. For orchestra he wrote a *Rhapsodie Espagnole* which includes a *"Prélude à la nuit—Malagueña—Habañera"* and *"Feria"* (Feast). His Habanera, which is often played as a violin number, was written originally for voice as a vocalise without words. His *opéra buffe, L'Heure espagnole* (*Spanish Time*) is amusingly Spanish and yet only a Frenchman could have the tact and humor to present it to the public without offense. More recently he wrote the Bolero.

Ravel also used the exotic Chinese mood successfully in his *"Laideronette, Impératrice des Pagodes"* from *Ma Mère l'Oye* (*Mother Goose*), which he wrote as a piano suite for four hands and then made into an orchestral ballet.

It is often claimed that Ravel was an imitator of Debussy. The two had the same artistic environment, yet their compositions reveal fundamental differences in style and methods of working. Ravel was rhythmically more incisive than Debussy, and his form was more traditional, while the older composer, in his struggle for freedom, created his own, deliberately avoiding the form either of classic or romantic composers. Ravel, with an experimenter's curiosity, shifted his style and technic to fit the individual problem of each composition —and he loved problems.

This curiosity led him away from impressionism into experiments with neoclassicism, polyharmony, and polytonality. An influence as strong as Debussy's was that of Erik Satie, whose *Sarabandes* and *Gymnopédies* scandalized the students at the Paris Conservatory when Ravel played them. Chabrier also was an influence. Where Debussy reflected something of Chopin's piano style, Ravel was closer to Liszt in the brilliancy of his virtuosity, as for example in *"Ondine,"* the first of three pieces called *Gaspard de la nuit*. Debussy was an exceptional pianist—Ravel was not. Debussy instituted a delicate individual style of instrumentation far from the massive orchestration of Wagner and Strauss. With Debussy each instrument was practically a solo one. Ravel, perhaps taking suggestions from his brother musician, developed into one of the greatest orchestrators of his day. The ballet *Daphnis et Chloë*, which reflects Debussy's impressionism, is exquisitely written for orchestra. *"La Valse, poème chorégraphique"* represents the study Ravel had made of the Strauss waltz, picturing an imperial Viennese court in 1855, and handled with a sophisticated, modern technic. The Bolero, too, was a study in instrumental effects, while *"Tzigane"* was an attempt (at the request of Yelly d'Aranyi, Hungarian violinist) to model a modern work for violin after Liszt's Hungarian Rhapsodies.

All through Ravel's career he had leanings toward a classic idiom, as may be seen from his Sonatine (1905) and *Le Tombeau de Couperin* (1914-17), a collection of dance forms in imitation of the seventeenth century but with a distinctly individual and modern technic. He wrote two piano concertos, the first showing both neoclassic and jazz influences; the second, for left hand alone, was written for the one-armed pianist, Paul Wittgenstein.

His earliest songs, on texts of Clément Marot, the sixteenth century poet, reflects his interest in the French classic period. *Schéhérazade,* consisting of *"Asie," "La Flute enchantée,"* and *"L'Indifférent,"* again shows his interest in the exotic. *Histoires naturelles* on texts by Renard are unique in charm, fantasy, and in the touch of irony always present in Ravel's humor. Songs in a later style, *Chansons madécasses* for voice and chamber music accompaniment, were written as a commission from Mrs. Elizabeth Sprague Coolidge.

Both Debussy and Ravel made use of the medieval modes as a means of procuring the effect of a classic style, and they understood how to combine the modal effect with modern technic in pleasing fashion.

In the first movement of the Sonatine, Ravel has used a natural minor (f♯, g♯, a, b, c♯, d, e, f♯), and the opening phrase is in the Hypoaeolian mode. Yet he has not flinched at the use of sevenths and ninths, alongside of modal cadences. In the *Menuet,* a most graceful movement, his bass moves in consecutive fifths without offense, and within hearing distance is a modal cadence with chords of the ninth:

Sonatine   Ravel

(A. Durand et Fils, copyright, 1905)

In 1918, Ravel, who had served in the war, wrote as a tribute to his comrades fallen in battle the *Tombeau de Couperin*. Particularly striking is his harmonization by means of chords of the seventh, ninth, and eleventh in place of common triads. Yet he creates a modal feeling by means of the cadences, as for example in the *Forlane:*

Le Tombeau de Couperin (Forlane)   Ravel
Allegretto

(Durand et Cie, copyright, 1918)

(scheme)

7th   7th   11th   9th   11th   11th   11th   11th

In a collection of simple piano pieces by Gabriel Grovlez, *L'Almanach aux images,* dated 1911, the composer caught the modal spirit in *"La Sarabande; Chanson du chasseur,"* in which he used a major scale with the fourth degree sharped (d, e, f♯, g♯, etc.); *"Le Pastour,"* in which the pentatonic scale reminds one of the pipes of Pan; and in *"Petites litanies de Jésus,"* which is both liturgical and impressionistic.

In Debussy's *"Hommage à Rameau"* the opening phrase might be called a twentieth century plainsong. It is in Hypoaeolian mode:

Hommage à Rameau

Debussy

(left hand an octave lower)

(A. Durand et Fils, copyright, 1905)

In one of my early songs, "Red Man's Requiem," I wrote a Dorian accompaniment (D minor with no b flat):

Red Man's Requiem

Marion Bauer

etc.

(The Arthur P. Schmidt Co., copyright, 1912)

And in a later one, "I Love the Night," I used the Lydian mode (f to f without b flat):

I Love the Night

Marion Bauer

I— love   the night,   that in long vi-o-let shroud

etc.

(G. Schirmer, Inc., copyright, 1924)

From quite a different source—twentieth century England—Arthur Bliss combines effective modal melody with a measure of whole tone scale in "Rout," a work for chamber orchestra and soprano in which the singer has meaningless syllables to sing in place of words:

Rout *
Allegro risoluto (violins)   Arthur Bliss

* From Curwen Edition 90726. By permission of Messrs. J. Curwen & Sons, Ltd.,
24 Berners St., London W. I.

A composer for whom France has great respect and admiration is
Paul Dukas (1865-1935). He was best known by his symphonic scherzo
on Goethe's tale of the "Sorcerer's Apprentice" (*L'Apprenti sorcier*)
which is regarded as one of the most important scores of French impressionistic music. His opera *Ariane et Barbe Bleue* on a text of
Maeterlinck is second only to *Pelléas et Mélisande* in French opera
of the twentieth century. It has something of the same elusive charm
and shows his sterling musicianship. Among other operatic works
which have received recognition in France, besides these two and
Ravel's *L'Heure espagnole*, are Fauré's *Pénélope*, Ropartz's *Le Pays*,
De Séverac's *Cœur du moulin*, and Albert Roussel's ballet, *Padmavati*.
Albert Roussel (1869-1937) "remains in touch with youth," said Henry
Prunières, the erudite editor of *La Revue musicale*. "He adapts himself
extraordinarily to the new generation and stays young with the young."
He was a student at the Schola Cantorum, and as a naval officer visited

the Orient. Both influences were apparent in his earlier works. Later, however, he showed new polytonal tendencies in neoclassic style.

Florent Schmitt (1870) is a master of orchestration and was one of the first to write ballet in the modern fashion in *La Tragédie de Salomé*. His quintet for piano and string quartet is regarded as one of the important French chamber music works.

Charles Koechlin (1867), Albéric Magnard (1865-1914), Erik Satie (1866-1926) of whom we will speak later, Déodat de Séverac (1873-1921), André Caplet (1878-1925), Louis Aubert (1877), Paul Ladmirault (1877), Jacques Pillois (1875-1935) who spent his last years in America, Roger-Ducasse (1873), Philippe Gaubert (1879-1941), Gabriel Pierné (1863-1937), and Gabriel Grovlez (1879-1944) are a few of the older generation of composers who have been influenced by the forces in vogue at the close of the nineteenth and beginning of the twentieth centuries. They show the truth of Jean-Aubry's statement made in 1916 (*La Musique française d'aujourd'hui*): "It is undeniable, even for those who are least informed concerning things musical, that the attention paid to music has never been as great in France as at the present moment, even taking into consideration what happened in the sixteenth century, or in the second half of the eighteenth."

IMPRESSIONISM AND THE TWENTIETH CENTURY RENAISSANCE: ENGLAND, POLAND, HUNGARY, SPAIN, ITALY, AMERICA, ETC.

THE Impressionist School, as it developed, was a direct cause of the renaissance which occupied the attention of practically the entire musical world. Debussy not only created a new method of composition, but he aroused the composers in other countries to artistic stocktaking. If some have been accused of imitating him, it was the sincerest form of flattery, and without that intense emotional and intellectual interest in the new language the many innovations which followed could hardly have taken place. He was not only an impressionist, but in the same way that Beethoven the classicist embodied the germs of romanticism, and Schumann, those of impressionism, Debussy gave promise of a new futurism or realism which has since manifested itself as neoclassicism with polytonality, atonality, linear counterpoint, and an investigation of quarter tones as by-products.

When the twentieth century opened, impressionism was the acute problem of the day, rapidly crystallizing in form, with recognizable earmarks. So in speaking of the impressionists of other nationalities we refer to a definite type or variation of type.

In England, Cyril Scott (1879) was one of the first impressionists, a *mystic impressionist* he might be called, thus sharing a title with Scriabin. While he was not unaffected by Debussy, other influences united in forming his style, which a few years ago sounded so strange and forced that he was subjected to attacks from critics, public, and colleagues. One friend who always understood and appreciated, not only his music, but the point of view which led to that angle of self-expression, was Percy Grainger, himself an important innovator in the use of harmony and in studying and using folk material wherever he has found it, in his native Australia, in Denmark and Norway, and today in the United States. When the two were students in Germany, Scott became interested in the writings of Stefan George, a symbolist poet who has also attracted Arnold Schoenberg, and in the paintings of the mystic Melchior Lechter. Like Scriabin, Scott has been a serious student of occultism—of Eastern mysticism, which perhaps accounts for a peculiar exoticism in his work. He sought to escape from the commonplace, and he evolved daring harmonic plans in which he used chords harmonized in fourths (page 217). His impressionism is well defined in such compositions as "Rikki-tikki-tavi and the Snake" from his *Jungle Book Impressions,* and "Elephant Dance," in which he shows an uncommon delight in expressing humor in music. His piano sonata is a work of fine proportions and was thoroughly modern when he wrote it (1908-10). He has been hurt by being best known through some of his least representative compositions, which today sound obvious and sentimental.

In Frederick Delius (1863-1934), England had an original composer whose delicacy and charm produce an individuality which is hard to catalogue. His work is impressionistic and is based on a chromaticism which he worked out apart from French models, although he lived on French soil for many years. Dr. Hull said: "The art of Delius looks backward and not forward. It belongs to the evening of a great period. It is resplendent with the iridescent chromatic rays and aureoles which sometimes appear immediately after sunset. He is the last great representative of Impressionism, itself the close of the great Romantic period in music." (*Music: Classical, Romantic and Modern.*)

There is in England a group of song writers whose songs are largely impressionistic; this includes Rutland Boughton, Cecil Armstrong Gibbs, Peter Warlock (d. 1932), Herbert Howells, John Ireland, Norman O'Neill (1875-1934), Norman Peterkin, Roger Quilter, Martin Shaw, and Gerard Williams. In addition there are composers some of whom represent nationalistic tendencies, like Granville Bantock, Ralph Vaughan Williams, and Gustav Holst, who wrote orchestral music such as "The Planets," but also contributed to a revival of choral music with his *Vedic Hymns* and his "Hymns to Jesus."

In an early song cycle, *On Wenlock Edge,* for voice, piano, and string quartet, Vaughan Williams showed the influence of French impressionism, which in later compositions he amalgamated with an English nationalism (page 66). His London Symphony is characteristically national in spirit, although it shows impressionistic methods in harmonization and in the creation of moods. It is curious that British composers have been more attracted to Walt Whitman than Americans. Vaughan Williams set "Toward the Unknown Region" and for the choral sections of his Sea Symphony used Whitman texts. And Delius wrote a beautiful work, "Sea Drift," with Whitman words, for voice and orchestra.

John Ireland (1879) and Frank Bridge (1879-1941) were influenced by impressionism and yet their works have an element easily recognized as English. Arnold Bax (1883), of Irish extraction, expresses a sensitive, poetic nature in impressionistic music, although he writes also in extended sonata and symphonic forms. Lord Berners (Gerald Tyrwhitt, 1883) uses all the twentieth century technical equipment in his music, which has been influenced more by Stravinsky than by Debussy. He has an extraordinary humor which finds amusing expression in his compositions, such as his "Funeral March for a Pet Canary," etc.

Arthur Bliss (1891) came into the field when impressionism was already on the wane. His first works were daringly modern and in experimental style, such as "Madame Toy," "Rout," and "Conversations." His present tendencies toward modern romanticism are shown in a more recent piano concerto.

Eugene Goossens (1893), a gifted Englishman of Belgian extraction who is now a citizen of this country, was for some years the conductor of the Cincinnati Orchestra. He did some excellent work in impressionistic vein in his early period. His *Kaleidoscopes, Nature Studies, Gargoyles,* and *Ships* for piano show unusual talent. More recently he has progressed with the times and has become neoclassic, although in real achievement he has not surpassed his earlier efforts. In 1947 he left America for a post in Australia.

Poldowski, which is the pen name of Lady Dean Paul, who died in London in 1932, was of Polish birth but her works reflected French impressionism. She wrote some fine songs.

Another Pole, who spent much of his life in Paris drinking at the fountain of impressionism, was Karol Szymanowski (1882-1937). While his works for piano, voice, orchestra, and chamber music are impressionistic, he later wrote a Stabat Mater which is very impressive and displays a profound emotional style and a mature technic. He was president of the Polish section of the International Society for Contemporary Music in Warsaw, where he had been interested in recreating the spirit of Poland in music without going into its folk music.

In Hungary the two men who have done remarkable research work in folk music are Béla Bartók and Zoltan Kodaly (page 65). Of the two, Bartók was the more ultramodern in his composing methods, while Kodaly has combined his study of Magyar folk music with modern European methods and has written some beautiful impressionistic piano music, besides a comic opera of national interest, *Hary Janos*. His *Psalmus Hungaricus* is a more modern expression, and, like Szymanowski's Stabat Mater, shows the new tendency toward a revival of interest in choral music.

Ernst von Dohnanyi (1877) is a Hungarian pianist and conductor, whose music shows the influence of Brahms.

In Spain the combination of national characteristics and Debussy's influence has been remarked in the work of Albeniz and Manuel de Falla. Falla's early opera *La Vida breve,* the ballets *El Amor brujo* and *The Three Cornered Hat,* and "Nights in the Gardens of Spain" for orchestra are distinctly impressionistic in technic. With the ballet *El Retablo de Maese Pedro* (*The Picture of Master Pedro,* or more precisely, *The Puppet Show of Master Pedro*) he came into a more modern technic, which became pure neoclassicism in the Harpsichord Concerto, composed for Mme. Wanda Landowska, the Polish harpsichordist, who has put effort and enthusiasm into bringing back that art of another age. The civil war sent Falla to Argentina, where he remained until his death.

The musical renaissance in Italy brought to the fore several gifted composers who made chamber music and the orchestra their goal, although they included opera in their attainments. Ildebrando Pizzetti (1880), more dominated by classicism than by impressionism, has done important work in modern music drama. Ottorino Respighi (1879-1936) in his Roman trilogy, *Pines, Fountains,* and *Festivals of Rome,* was more realistic than impressionistic, and his style was more influenced by Strauss than by impressionism.

G. Francesco Malipiero (1882) reflects the spirit of innovation and his works are strongly individual and original. In impressionistic style are two early orchestral works, *"Pause del silenzio"* and *"Ditirambo tragico."* He threw over past models in an attempt to find his own language and means of expressing only essentials. He made the short motive the center of his musical thought, and his endeavor to find a new melodic form took him out of the class of impressionists into that of the later innovators. He lived in Paris for a time, and in J. & W. Chester's *Miniature Essay* on Malipiero, Guido M. Gatti says that "instead of being powerfully influenced by any master or school— although temporarily assimilating those tendencies with which he was most in sympathy—he soon began to strike out a path for himself." He covered his tracks by destroying the works which would doubtless have reflected the influence of impressionism.

After a study of Italian traditions—Cavalli, Monteverdi, and Cavalieri —he expressed his protest against the sentimentalities and insincerities of the late nineteenth century operas by a series of experiments of revolutionary character and lofty ideals. *Sette Canzoni,* which is really seven acted songs, is, according to Gatti "a perfect vindication of the composer's principles." In his setting of Goldoni's *"Le Baruffe chiozzotte"* Malipiero used a *recitativo parlato* in place of song, the orchestra giving the necessary musical background. He also went back to the pre-Monteverdian opera, to the mystery play, in a work of moving simplicity based on the life of St. Francis of Assisi. His composition for string quartet, *"Rispetti e strambotti,"* which won the Coolidge prize in 1920, is a collection of musical "epigrams and aphorisms" strung together without any reference to previous tradition in quartet writing. He is today a neoclassicist.

Alfredo Casella (1883-1947) of Italian birth and French training, was thoroughly impregnated with Debussy's principles and methods. As a pianist and a conductor he visited many lands, including America, and returned to Italy with the intention of aiding in building up a new school of composition. He was an innovator and a clever propagandist. In 1917 he founded the Italian Society of Modern Music, and worked valiantly in its cause. His most impressionistic score was "War Films." His versatility made him turn from impressionism to neoclassicism, and he plied the trade of polytonality and atonality thoroughly. His *Pupazetti* for piano are humorous, and his orchestra work *"Elegia eroica"* shows technical mastery. He was influenced not only by Debussy but by Mahler, Stravinsky, and Schoenberg. He had a facile technic which easily changed from one style to another. With his Sinfonia (1926) he turned to a study of old Italian instrumental forms. In his ballet *La Giara* he showed unusual charm and ability in handling a folk type in which he had left the path of dissonance which he traveled so easily.

Among the older Russians the romantic spirit seems never to have gone the way of impressionism, unless we except Vladimir Rebikoff (1866-1920), who was one of the first to experiment in new tonalities, old modes, and in freedom of form. The line of Tchaikovsky and Rubinstein was carried on by Alexander Glazounoff (1865-1936), Alexander Gretchaninoff (1864), who came to America as a refugee, Nicholas Medtner (1879), Serge Rachmaninoff (1873-1943), Paul Juon (1872-1940), and Nicholas Tcherepnin (1873-1945). Rachmaninoff, who became an American citizen, was a great pianist and an accomplished composer of piano works, five piano concertos, symphonies, and tone poems, the best known of which was inspired by Böcklin's painting "The Island of the Dead."

Richard Strauss's realistic methods counteracted any influence that impressionism might have had in Germany. In fact, it could hardly be expected that impressionism would find sympathetic reaction in the German temperament. Of the same generation as Strauss, Hans Pfitzner (1869), one of the leading composers, devoted most of his work to opera and conducting. Weissmann calls Pfitzner's musical legend "Palestrina" a "considerable intellectual and ethical achievement, the high-water mark of a career in which strength of purpose has predominated over an artistic talent by no means trifling ... it is a last example of successful Wagnerism." But Pfitzner is a reactionary of mixed qualities—"of the romantic, the aesthetic, the poet, the student, the musician and the schoolmaster."

Franz Schreker (1878-1934) was an able and inspiring teacher to many of the younger Germans and Austrians, "leading his pupils away from the beaten track of tradition to face present day problems," Adolf Weissmann wrote (*Problems of Modern Music*), "yet leaving them free to follow or reject his own precepts." Opera is his most successful means of expression, in which Weissmann found "a most interesting and effective amalgam of Wagner, Puccini and Impressionism, with a Viennese tang."

The title of "first impressionist in America" may well be placed at Charles Martin Loeffler's door, as he is the bridge between French and American impressionism. An Alsatian born (1861-1935), he was drawn to Paris, where he drank in the same atmosphere, congenial to his natural affinity for things French, as Debussy. He, however, had had the experience of a childhood spent in Russia; youth in Hungary; violin study in Berlin with Joachim, and then a return to Paris. At the age of twenty he came to the United States, where he became viola player in the Boston Symphony Orchestra. There the young musician was a new voice among Germans who played German music and taught German methods. What he had assimilated in Europe, he reproduced in the music he wrote in Boston. That his impressionistic tendencies were not understood is natural. Also, that he remained aloof and quietly went his own musical way is characteristic of the man, to whom compromise was unknown. His music reflects his highly sensitized, refined fastidiousness, his culture, and his meticulous craftsmanship.

When Philip Hale wrote in 1895 that Loeffler "believes in tonal impressions rather than in thematic development," and that he "has delicate sentiment, the curiosity of the hunter after nuances, the love of the macabre, the cool fire that consumes and is more deadly than fierce, panting flame," he was giving a better picture of impressionism than he knew. Loeffler, a born impressionist, wrote as he felt; rarely duplicating a type, he paralleled the symbolist poets, or wrote under the influence of Gregorian plainsong, taking his subjects from Virgil to Yeats, with Maeterlinck included on the way. His best-known orchestra scores are *"La Mort de Tintagiles"* (The Death of Tintagiles) after Maeterlinck and "The Pagan Poem" after an eclogue of Virgil. His "Music for Four Stringed Instruments" is chamber music of a high order. Then there are two rhapsodies, *"L'Etang"* (The Pool) and *"La Cornemuse"* (The Bagpipe) for oboe, viola, and piano; several songs; *"Hora Mystica,"* a symphony for men's voices and orchestra, and his "Canticle to St. Francis," in both of which he reveals a mood of religious meditation expressed by his remarkable use of Gregorian song. He registered his Russian impressions in an orchestral work, "Memories of My Childhood."

The first American impressionist is John Alden Carpenter (1876) of Chicago. He started his career as a composer of songs distinctly influenced by French impressionism. And yet he exhibited an individuality, a culture, a refinement of technic and maturity of style in these early works, as he has in later compositions. His choice of texts shows his characteristics—Verlaine, Yeats, Lanier, Tagore, Barnes, Sassoon, and Wilde—and he has been entirely successful in picturing the moods presented by this international array. No one has translated the spirit of the *Gitanjali* more convincingly than Carpenter in "The Sleep That Flits on Baby's Eyes" and "When I Bring to You Colored Toys." The suggestion of Orientalism in his Chinese tone poems *Water Colors* is true impressionism. "In 'Adventures in a Perambulator' and the Concertino, however, we see signs of a new American impressionism. The orchestral suite describing the sensations and emotions of a baby wheeled about by its nurse is delicately humorous. The subtitles show an awakening desire in Carpenter to express American life." ("Impressionists in America," *Modern Music*, Marion Bauer, Jan.-Feb. 1927.)

The Concertino is one of the early experiments in using characteristically "made in America" melodies and syncopated rhythms. "A light-hearted conversation between piano and orchestra ... mostly of rhythms, American, Oriental and otherwise," Carpenter calls it. Skillful workmanship, native refinement, humor, mark this work of interesting cross rhythms, ⅝ measures, a waltz, and an impressionism more of America than of France.

"Krazy Kat," his jazz pantomime, based on George Herriman's newspaper comic strip, a most American Americanism, is impressionistic caricature, but in spite of its desire to be democratic and commonplace, its composer handles the harmonic twists and jazz rhythms with a skill that shows the deep-dyed musician and technician. Frankly experimental, it helped to develop a new style of "showing up" American life to ourselves without apologia, an expressionism or realism which has developed in the last decade.

Diaghileff, director of the Ballet Russe, requested Carpenter to write a ballet of American everyday life. Diaghileff did not produce *Skyscrapers,* but the Metropolitan Opera Company did, in 1926. Here is Carpenter at the acme of this new-found American realism, in which jazz and popular melodies rub shoulders with ultramodern dissonance. The suave, elegant gentleman, temporarily lost, came back with a composition for piano and orchestra, "Patterns," which he played in

1932 with the Boston Symphony Orchestra under Serge Koussevitzky. The work shows that Carpenter, who has gone through interesting metamorphoses, has put his house in order for the new neoromanticism which is rapidly becoming a reality. Other works in this later style include "Sea Drift"; *"Danza,"* a violin concerto; and a symphony.

Percy Grainger (1882), who played the first performance of Carpenter's Concertino in Chicago, has been discussed as a musical folk-lorist. His work in that direction and as a student of primitive music is invaluable. He has, at the same time, developed a unique style in composing which is modern in effect, and is also related to impressionism or perhaps to realism. He has caught the secret of presenting the everyday tune (a Britisher would probably call it a "homely" tune) with a charm and decorative harmonization which has created a style distinctly his own. He has influenced the harmonic treatment of other composers, as for example Leo Sowerby in one phase of his development, his treatment of folk music.

Grainger's harmonies are acrid, dissonant, yet rich and satisfying; his rhythms are full of complicated cross-groupings; he has long been an experimenter with the timbres and possibilities of instruments in unusual combinations; his music is full of vitality and energy. He is an inveterate innovator.

To include Louis Gruenberg (1884) as an American impressionist is to discuss merely one angle of his work, but the compositions of an earlier period show how deeply imbedded in impressionism those early years were. From his studies with Busoni in Vienna came an influence of Richard Strauss and a not altogether somnolent love for Wagner. Another phase definitely visible in his early work is a love for the sensuous richness and warmth of Oriental harmony and melody. In the tone poems "The Enchanted Isle" and "From Hills of Dream," and his symphony, which the Boston Symphony Orchestra played in 1932, Gruenberg is an impressionist and a dyed-in-the-wool romanticist, as he is also in his delightful opera *Jack and the Beanstalk,* which he wrote on a text by John Erskine (1930). Gruenberg the composer of music inspired by jazz, and culminating in the Jazz Suite, "Daniel Jazz," and "Creation," and the opera *Emperor Jones,* will be discussed later.

One of the most serious losses that American composition has suffered was in the death of Charles Tomlinson Griffes (1884-1920), who was one of the first to put into American piano music something of the elusive charm and color of French impressionism. While studying in good conservative fashion in Berlin, he heard someone practicing an unfamiliar composition which so impressed him that he went to the pianist's door to ask its name. It was Ravel's *"Jeux d'eau,"* and the pianist was Rudolph Ganz. It seems incredible that an incident seemingly of such trifling import could change a man's career. But Griffes, instead of being a concert pianist, as was his intention, became one of our foremost composers after discovering French impressionism. Norman Peterkin in the *Chesterian* wrote: "Like many of the young composers the world over, he was influenced by and temperamentally attracted to the methods and innovations of Debussy and Ravel and later to some of the advanced Russians. However, he was never enslaved by these influences, but was able to extract from them precisely those elements he needed to set free and express his own personality." In two songs to texts by Oscar Wilde, *"La Fuite de la lune"* (The Flight of the Moon) and "Symphony in Yellow," a new Griffes appeared.

His pieces for piano, *Three Tone Pictures:* "The Vale of Dreams," "The Night Winds," "The Lake at Evening"; Barcarolle; *"Notturno";* and the *Roman Sketches* suggested by poems of William Sharp, including "The White Peacock," "Nightfall," "The Fountain of the Acqua Paola," and "Clouds," give him a standing of being the most important American piano composer after MacDowell. Fiona MacLeod's verses attracted him, and some of his most serious and musicianly songs are "The Lament of Ian the Proud," "The Rose of the Night," and "Thy Dark Eyes to Mine."

His orchestral tone poem, "The Pleasure Dome of Kubla Khan," stands up remarkably and is without doubt one of the best American scores. His "Poem for Flute and Orchestra," written for and played by Georges Barrère; the string quartet on Indian themes; the ballet, *The Cairn of Koridwen,* in which he used a chamber orchestra, show his development. His *Sho-jo,* a Japanese ballet, and his *Japanese and Chinese Songs* based on authentic Oriental scales reveal his love for the exotic in music, which was nurtured by his interest in eastern folklore.

Had he lived, he would have gone along with the times, for his tendency was toward absolute music, breaking away from impressionism as his sole medium.

That he felt the ultramodern is shown by a reaching toward polytonality as may be seen by the following example from "Clouds," in
which the clash between tonalities creates dissonance:

Clouds from Roman Sketches   Charles T. Griffes

And a few measures later in the same work he wrote:

(G. Schirmer, Inc., copyright, 1917)

Does it not give a musical parallel of William Sharp's description
of the clouds "crumbling so slowly"?

He was at heart a shy, reticent person, with an eager interest in
his own and others' experiments, sincere and modest, and with a
student's love of work, without regard for public opinion.

The sonata for piano, written two years before his death, is a
neoclassic work of austere idiom and great musical integrity. He used
unusual arbitrary scale combinations, neither major, minor, nor modal,
out of which he built the melodies and took out all unnecessary chord
clusters writing horizontal (or polyphonic) music rather than vertical
(or harmonic). The following theme shows the scale, or mode, in
which it is written, for in this avoidance of accepted modes it is like
the music of Scriabin (page 175):

Sonata for Piano   Charles T. Griffes

(G. Schirmer, Inc., copyright, 1921)

Griffes wastes no unnecessary notes in the first movement, which is concise and clear as to form with the usual main themes, short development, and recapitulation. The starkness of his harmonies is illustrated by the second theme of the first movement, which begins:

Sonata for Piano   Griffes
b.

(G. Schirmer, Inc., 1921)

His amazing economy of means shows how completely Griffes had mastered the technic of modern composition.

The second movement, *molto tranquillo,* which enters without pause, reminds one of a plainsong chant in modern tonality:

Sonata for Piano   Griffes
c.

(G. Schirmer, Inc., 1921)

The accompaniment is an arpeggiated figure of a chord without a
third and polytonal in effect most of the time. As a contrast to this
stark, uncompromising music, the next pages are filled with passionate
beauty. The last movement, *allegro vivace,* opens with a contrapuntal
introduction in which this arbitrary scale combination is heard:

Sonata for Piano   Griffes
d.

(G. Schirmer, Inc., 1921)

which when harmonized gives this curious combination of two part
harmony:

e.

With a splendid feeling for balance, Griffes works up the finale into
a frenzied presto as though the restraint of the entire sonata were spent
in these last two pages of syncopated rhythms and full harmonies.

All these works tell of a great promise broken by his untimely
"Rendezvous with Death." With less than forty compositions to his
credit, Griffes left indelible traces on American music.

Edward Burlingame Hill (1872) is an impressionist, as he has ably
demonstrated in his orchestral poem "Lilacs" on Amy Lowell's verses,
and his symphonies in which the harmonic basis is impressionistic.
Hill was chairman of the division of music at Harvard.

Emerson Whithorne (1884) reflects in his early works European
associations. A set of vivid piano pieces, *New York Days and Nights,*
successful musical impressions of Times Square, Chinatown, the ferry-

boat, Greenwich Village, and the chimes of St. Patrick's, were composed with a consciousness not only of impressionistic methods but of later developments in polytonality and chord formations.

Whithorne wrote a ballet in collaboration with Irene Lewisohn, called *Sooner and Later,* which was produced at the Neighborhood Playhouse a year before Carpenter's *Skyscrapers* appeared. A similarity of ideas and methods is apparent, although the two works are differently treated. Both use an American subject modeled somewhat on the modern European ballet. "Saturday's Child," for voice and chamber orchestra, on a text by the Negro poet Countee Cullen, is a distinct addition to American music and one of Whithorne's best scores. He has a "Poem" for piano and orchestra, and "Fata Morgana," a symphonic poem. He has combined impressionistic and neoromantic moods in some of his excellent contributions to American chamber music, a piano quintet, a quartet, and a violin sonata.

Frederick Jacobi's sensitive and refined work shows leanings toward impressionism. He studied New Mexico Indian music, some of which material he used in a string quartet and an orchestral work. He has written choral works, "The Poet in the Desert," also "Two Assyrian Prayers" for soprano and orchestra, a Friday Evening Synagogue Service and other works showing a deeply religious nature, and more recently concertos for cello and for piano, chamber music, and an opera, *The Prodigal Son,* in which the new romanticism is apparent.

The composer of *The King's Henchman* and *Peter Ibbetson,* two American operas which have been performed at the Metropolitan Opera House in New York, is Deems Taylor (1885), whose natural mode of expression is impressionistic. His orchestral suite "Through the Looking Glass" and his charming music for the ballet in *The Beggar on Horseback* also reveal his bent for impressionism.

Ernest Bloch (1880), an American by choice, is Swiss born. He came to this country in 1916, with beneficial results both to himself and to those Americans who were his pupils. He returned for a short time to Switzerland. One of the most gifted composers of the twentieth century, he has written in many forms. In his symphony "Israel" he might be called the music prophet of the Hebrews, for he achieved a noble style in which he seemed to capture the tradition and spirit of the Old Testament. *"Schélomo,"* a Hebrew rhapsody for cello and orchestra; *"Trois poèmes juifs,"* "Two Psalms," a *Prélude* for soprano and orchestra, Psalm 22 for baritone, choral works and a movingly beautiful Sacred Service for the Synagogue, and pieces for violin were all influenced by his Jewish ancestry.

Roger Sessions, a pupil of Bloch, in an article written for *Modern Music* (Nov.-Dec. 1927) says: "The orientalism of the Jewish works shows itself in certain melodic and harmonic traits. The trumpet calls, for instance, with which they abound, give them a character at once barbaric and ritualistic. Actual Jewish melodies, on the other hand, occur but rarely and incidentally, and not as the result of a desire on Bloch's part to reproduce folklore. What he has done is to allow his imagination to play on the embodiment of a truly Jewish spirit in music, and in so doing he has created a style which is entirely personal."

That Bloch has an extraordinary gift for construction and complete technical mastery is evidenced in a group of masterpieces including his String Quartet in B minor, his suite for viola and piano which won the Coolidge prize (1919), the violin sonata, and his quintet for piano and string quartet, which deserves a place beside the Schumann, Brahms, and Franck quintets. A second string quartet (1946) and a violin concerto on Indian themes have added luster to his fame.

His Concerto Grosso is a modern version of a classic form written to show his pupils "how it should be done." It is a fascinating work which wears well.

His music for piano and quartet in impressionistic style is couched in a more modern idiom than that of Debussy. He is a more impulsive, impassioned individual and he could never be as detached and as impersonal as Debussy. His works abound in dissonances, and he speaks in a harmonic and rhythmic language which, however, always remains Bloch's true tongue. He seems to follow no vogue and to court no following.

His "America," in which he set himself the task of painting his emotional reaction to the land of his adoption, won a prize in 1930. Curiously enough, his very dissonant and free jazz section was the most convincing part of the work. Shortly after that he wrote a score called "Helvetia."

Sessions wisely says: "The newer music, so radically different from his own, owes then something very concrete to the culture which has gone into the making of Bloch. And if the effort of a different conception to assert itself has temporarily seemed to isolate him, to deprive him of adequate recognition, there can be no doubt that the adjustments of history will restore to him his true place among the artists who have spoken most commandingly the language of conscious emotion."

CHAPTER 12

SCRIABIN, THE MYSTIC IMPRESSIONIST

THE musical prophet of the Russian symbolists was Alexandre Scriabin (1871-1915), as Debussy was of the French. Scriabin the occultist—a Theosophist—was the motive power of Scriabin, the composer. He attempted an esoteric correlation of life and art, in which he conceived art as transforming life into joy.

Scriabin's music divides itself into three definite periods. First came the piano compositions of a poetic, refined "salon" type in which the hand of Chopin is distinctly visible, even in the Russian's use of the Pole's titles—*préludes,* mazurkas, études, etc. But in this imitative period a striking personality was emerging, in which many of the characteristics of the later Scriabin were in evidence. During this time he wrote four of his ten sonatas for piano, the *"Poème tragödie"* and *"Poème satanique,"* his first two symphonies, and the F sharp minor Piano Concerto.

In the second transitional period he wrote the "Divine Poem" (op. 43). According to Alfred J. Swan (*Music, 1900 to 1930*) the theme of the finale brought forth the statement from Scriabin: " 'For the first time I found *Light* in music, found this rapture, this soaring flight, this suffocation from joy.'.... But already before," Dr. Swan continues, "in the final pages of the *Fourth Sonata,* the *Poème,* op. 32, No. 2, the *Preludes* op. 37, No. 2, and op. 39, No. 1, he has found glaring, radiant light, such as had never been couched in sounds before... but in Scriabin it is of a dazzling white color."

The compositions of this period include those from op. 43, the "Divine Poem," to the Fifth Sonata, op. 53. In 1903, freed from an irksome teaching position at the Moscow Conservatory, his spirit found expression in forty works for piano and some for orchestra. He was always more at home in the idiom of his own instrument, and many find that his greatest works are not the symphonies, but his ten sonatas and some of his piano pieces, which number almost four hundred.

During this time Scriabin came in contact with French impressionism, and the idea of opening new harmonic paths thrilled him. "His search resulted in innovations which centered the eyes of the musical world upon him, gave him a place as a revolutionist and pioneer, and made him appear, for a time at least, as one of the standard bearers of the new music." (*Music through the Ages,* Bauer and Peyser.)

The third period includes *"Le Poème de l'extase"* (op. 54) for orchestra; "Prometheus: The Poem of Fire" (op. 60) for orchestra, piano, organ, choir, and color keyboard; *Études; Poèmes; Pièces; Préludes; Vers la Flamme* (op. 72), and five sonatas for piano.

This last was the transcendental period and was given over to the composing of cult music. The last years of his life and all the compositions from the "Poem of Ecstasy" on, were devoted to the preparation of a great *Mystery* which was to be the apotheosis of his art life. It was to have been an oratorio-opera, a high ritual, in which music, speech, gesture, scent, and color were to be united in expressing his religious beliefs. "The 'passive initiates' as he termed the audience, were to participate, and the purpose of the composition was to engender in the hearers that state of mind in which they might have a vision of the higher planes of consciousness we hope to call our own," says Katherine Ruth Heyman, who was a most sensitively initiated interpreter of Scriabin's music. (*The Relation of Ultramodern to Archaic Music.*)

All of the symphonies had esoteric meanings. The first is a hymn to art. The third, the "Divine Poem," is made up of three movements: *"Luttes,"* the struggle to free the spirit; *"Voluptés,"* the intoxication of sensual enjoyment; *"Jeu Divin,"* the Divine Play in which the spirit recognizes its power to overcome the phantoms of the physical self. The "Poem of Ecstasy" is the ecstasy of the spirit in creative activity. In the fifth symphony, "Prometheus," the composer approaches his ultimate aim of uniting sounds and colors. In it Miss Heyman observes "the spreading of those great wings on which he hoped to bear human-

ity upward and out over the borders of this fettered earth life.....
Scriabin always has wings; sometimes soaring, sometimes brooding,
but always wings."

As in the symphonies, so in all his works, two moods are in evidence, the satanic and the seraphic, and there was a constant fight
between the opposing forces in his nature. The ten sonatas tell the
story of Scriabin's musical and psychical development. The fourth
and fifth were written during what his friend and disciple, Leonid
Sabaneyeff, considered the culminating point of his life, when "he
felt an extraordinary wave of creative art and the compositions written
by him at this time bore the genuine impress of the musical previsions
of genius." "Mystical moods" controlled him, and particularly in the
last sonatas did he search for musical speech which should express
this exaltation. According to Dr. Hull, who wrote a definitive biography of Scriabin (*A Russian Tone Poet*), the seventh sonata is full
of the visions which he dreamed of attaining in the "super-music" of
the *Mystery*. "The sixth is more earthly, more human. The seventh is
Scriabin the mystic, the sixth Scriabin the artist. In the ninth sonata,
the element of Satanism reaches its height. He often wondered why
he had written it; for he recognized it as a falling away from grace,
and called it the *Black Mass*. In the tenth, the artist, and not the
mystic, again goes his way." (*Music: Classical, Romantic and Modern,*
by Eaglefield Hull.)

In Scriabin's music one finds a wealth of exquisite melody and
rich harmony. He developed so individual a harmonic style that one
cannot approximate an imitation without seeming to be a plagiarist.
Independently he freed himself from the shackles of tradition but
not entirely. His phrases are usually four measures long and his pieces
may often be analyzed by means of a rhythmic pattern which is repeated in different keys. Howbeit, the rhythmic designs are often
complicated and fascinatingly characteristic of Scriabin's individual
style. He used sonata form but not slavishly; in fact, his sonatas are
more in the structure of the romantic sonata than in the classic, and
like Liszt's B minor, often in one movement.

Scriabin's harmonies are vertical, rarely horizontal, although his
use of complicated figurations in the inner voices give it a feeling of
polyphony where no true polyphony exists. It is not difficult to trace
the problems Scriabin set for himself, rhythmical, modulatory, or har-

monic, in many of the short *préludes*. He did not break with ideas of
a central tonality or key until near the close of his career, although he
often used interesting tonal patterns out of the beaten track of either
diatonic or modal harmony.

As early as opus 11, No. 10, he wrote a *Prélude* in C sharp minor
in which he harmonized his tonic chord by adding a third below its
root, making it a chord of the seventh on the submediant or VI (sixth
degree) of the scale. In the same measure he was not satisfied to use
an ordinary subdominant (IV of the scale), so he altered it by raising
the root, thus

The altered chord in the first and third measures marked with an
asterisk is found innumerable times in Scriabin's early music—it is a
supertonic (II of the scale) seventh with the third raised.

In op. 11, No. 6, is one of the rare examples of a contrapuntal idea,
a *Prélude* in B minor which is a canon in the second. In the final
cadence the altered chord (supertonic seventh with the third raised)
appears.

In the fourth measure of the *Prélude* in B major, op. 27, No. 2, a
sequence of sevenths quite à la Debussy appears.

In the *Prélude* in F sharp minor, op. 31, No. 2, an uncommon chord
combination occurs:

Five altered chords appear: the first and third (marked with *) are supertonic ninths with third raised, followed by subdominant (IV of the scale) sevenths with the root raised, and the fifth is a dominant seventh with the fifth lowered.

In the little C major *Prélude,* op. 31, No. 4, Scriabin brings in several peculiar progressions, another form of harmonization of which he was fond:

Prélude
Lento

A. Scriabin, op. 31, No. 4
scheme

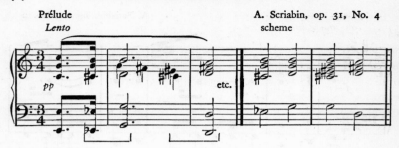

In the final cadence he gives a decided modal feeling:

Prélude

Scriabin
op. 31, No. 4

When one thinks of the Russian folk music with its modal background, it is strange that Scriabin used the old modes so little. In fact, his music is touched less than that of any other Russian by the folk song of his people.

Toward the end of the first period, although he still wrote in tonality, he used more and more dissonance, as for example in the F sharp major *Prélude,* op. 37, No. 2, which he opened with a chord belonging no longer to the type formed by thirds, but is distinctly built in superimposed fourths. In the repetitions of the phrase, Scriabin uses first another combination of fourths, then chords of the ninth, and other chords of fourths, thus:

CHD. IN 4THS   CHD. OF   CHD. OF   CHD. IN 4THS   CHD. IN 4THS
           THE 9TH   THE 9TH

SCRIABIN

SCRIABIN

From this time on Scriabin began using arbitrary scales and chords as his point of departure, often revealing his melodic or harmonic scheme at the close of the composition. One might liken his method to the use the Hindus make of the *ragas* or modes, tonal combinations in which different compositions are composed (page 108). For example, the C major *Poème,* op. 44, No. 2, uses this combination of tones:

The first part looks like the Phrygian mode; the second section is chromatic; and the last four notes form a cadence in which the neighboring tones of the dominant appear.

"*Feuillet d'album*," op. 45, No. 1, makes use of the following tones, in which a lowered sixth is conspicuous:

A. Scriabin, op. 45, No. 1

* Lowered sixth.

The *Prélude* (*Lugubre*) in A minor, op. 51, No. 2, is written in this interesting scale and cadence. Here Scriabin uses a natural minor scale with the fourth degree raised:

A. Scriabin, op. 51, No. 2

b.

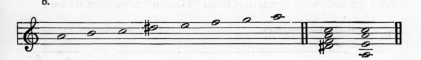

Scriabin gradually evolved a synthetic chord known as the *mystic* chord, out of which the entire score of "Prometheus" was constructed, as were many other of his compositions of the later years. It is composed of the 8th, 9th, 10th, 11th, 13th, and 14th overtones in the fundamental series of harmonics (page 101), the next step in tone evolution after Debussy's whole tone scale. Scriabin treated it as a chord built in fourths:

Schoenberg's chords of fourths (page 217) are based on perfect fourths, whereas Scriabin's fourths, from the lowest up, are augmented, diminished, augmented, perfect, and perfect. As a scale, it reads c-d-e-f♯-a-b♭. It differs from the whole tone scale only in the fact that the fifth step is a♮ (a natural) and not g♯ (g sharp). But Scriabin used it as a *chord* not as a *scale*. In *Modern Harmony* Dr. Hull shows the tonal combinations possible in triads, chords of the seventh, inversions, and new selections of tones.

"*Quasi Valse*," op. 47, gives a very good example, in a composition not technically complicated, of how Scriabin utilized the synthetic chord.

Quasi Valse   A. Scriabin, op. 47

And the following quotation from *"Masque"* illustrates its use:

Deux Poèmes (Masque)   A. Scriabin, op. 63, No. 1
Allegretto

The sixth and the seventh sonatas use the following chords as their master keys:

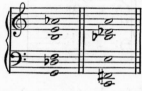

I am indebted to Miss Heyman for permission to reprint the following from her essay on Scriabin in her book *The Relation of Ultramodern to Archaic Music:* "In Russia there has been since ancient times a sect called *Khlisti,* and they have invocational chants, series of notes that represent the elements. ... Now whether Scriabin drew the motivs that he used in his *Eighth Sonata* from the Russian sect Khlisti, or from other shrines in which they had been conserved, I have no means of knowing; but there are just five short motivs used as the basis of his *Eighth Sonata,* and some of them are familiar as nature motivs taught me by an initiate in London, ... and if I am correct, these five short motivs are the runes, according to tradition given to Scriabin from one source or another, of the five elements."

Miss Heyman speaks of "the curious feeling of being out of doors" which the eighth sonata gives when properly played. And she also relates an experience which she shared with a friend at a performance of the "Poem of Ecstasy," that of listening with closed eyes and seeing during the ecstatic climax, "a sea of molten gold on which there floated a ship of violet light, immaterial, supernatural." When Miss Heyman played the tenth sonata for me, I was aware of brilliant flashes of light, like sparks, which Miss Heyman assured me was a frequent reaction. Apparently Scriabin attempted to work out such consonances on various planes, and tried to materialize his impressions in "Prometheus: The Poem of Fire," in which he co-ordinated, or, at least, made the essay to co-ordinate, sound and color.

In opus 65, a series of études, Scriabin was one of the first composers to use the intervals of the seventh and the ninth as a definite unit. In these compositions he made the fifth the unit of one, the seventh of another, and of still another, the ninth.

We often come across the augmented fourth or diminished fifth (c-f♯, c-g♭) used as a bass figure, standing in the relation of tonic and dominant, or chord of rest and chord of movement. Scriabin regarded the augmented fourth as cutting the octave exactly in half. Examples of its use are to be found in his *prélude* from one of his last compositions, op. 74, no. 5, in the fourth and fifth measures. He also used a contrivance which Schoenberg has made his own, stretching the octave to a ninth:

Scriabin was a mystic impressionist with his roots in romanticism. His vogue has apparently passed with both impressionism and romanticism, but I agree with Sabaneyeff, who says that he has profound faith in a "Scriabin renaissance." Some day he will be recognized as one of the great composers for the pianoforte. The enormous literature he left behind will be loved and played by a future generation as it is now by a few Scriabin "specialists." Present day pianists have neglected all but a few of his less significant works.

CHAPTER 13

SIBELIUS, SYMPHONIST AND NATIONALIST

JAN, or Jean, Sibelius (1865) is not alone Finland's greatest composer, but he is regarded by his countrymen as one of their national heroes. The government granted him a pension which made it possible for him to work at composition in spite of two wars and political upheavals.

His entire output shows greater unevenness than is usually found in the works of composers who have reached his heights. His early compositions reflect national feeling and idiom, traits which he retained in his symphonic writings. His songs and choral works number many of uncommon beauty, while his piano pieces are generally inferior, as is also much of the incidental music he wrote for the theater. Those who know Sibelius only as the composer of *"Valse triste,"* "Finlandia," and others of his weaker works, know him not at all, because it is almost inconceivable that those compositions could have been written by the composer of the Fourth Symphony or even the delightful incidental music to Strindberg's play *Swan White.* Thanks to Koussevitzky and Stokowski we have been able to get a fair estimate of Sibelius's value, for they made known many of the orchestral works.

"The roots of his art remain deep in his soil," says Olin Downes (*Great Modern Composers,* ed. Oscar Thompson), "and its origins stretch far back into the past of his people." *

Sibelius has always been a storm center of controversial opinions. Several English critics popularized him in the early part of the century, and gave him a place in the foremost ranks. Others found

* By permission, from *Great Modern Composers,* by Oscar Thompson, editor. Copyright, 1941, by Dodd Mead & Co., Inc.

him much overrated. One of the younger generation places him as "a romantic composer with his own personal way of saying things" (Aaron Copland in *Our New Music*). Copland continues, "Sibelius does not live in a twentieth century world. He is a hangover from the eighteen-nineties, and although his ruminations on life and man are fairly interesting and are expressed in a purely personal way, they are conclusions arrived at from old-fashioned premises, premises that no longer hold water in our time. . . . Sibelius is, by nature, a folk composer. Like a folk composer he writes his music out of a special landscape and out of a provincial imagination." *

Ernest Newman recommends that a study of Jan Sibelius's music should begin with his latest, his maturest works, for, he said in a *Sunday Times* of London, "it is in the later works that they [conductors and orchestras] will find the explanation of many a passage in the earliest works that by itself is far from clear; because while it *looks* like music of the usual kind it is in reality something quite different in meaning. It is no use in playing one of the broader lyrical melodies in his first two symphonies as if it were Tchaikovsky or Strauss; no use playing one of his passages of imitation as if it were merely bad Bach." Newman suggests that the secret of "what Sibelius is driving at" lies in the four last symphonies and in the tone poem for orchestra, "Tapiola," written at Walter Damrosch's request in 1926.

A frequent hearing of the Fourth Symphony in A minor has brought profound respect for the music and for its composer. Many consider it the greatest symphony of the twentieth century. In spite of its mood of gloomy tragedy and the elusiveness of its compact structure, it has a majesty and nobility of feeling which give it tremendous sweep.

Cecil Gray (*Sibelius*) says: "It is a landmark, not merely in his own development, but in the history of musical form, representing as it does the farthest point to which the principle of elimination of nonessentials has been pushed. There is not a superfluous note in the score from beginning to end, and hardly one that is not of thematic origin."

When Walter Damrosch presented it at a concert of the New York Symphony (1913), he apologized for its somberness and dissonance, stating that he felt obliged to have his patrons hear the latest experi-

* By permission, from *Our New Music*, by Aaron Copland, published by Whittlesey House. Copyright, 1941, by McGraw-Hill Book Co., Inc.

ments in musical composition regardless of whether he liked or disliked them! To some in the audience, at least, the Fourth Symphony was a great musical experience and revelation.

Sibelius has written seven symphonies. An eighth, commissioned by Koussevitzky, has never been released. Like Beethoven's, they come in pairs: a symphony in lighter mood is followed by one of darker hue. The First is somewhat derivative and romantic in type. Gray says: "It is in the same *genre* and tradition as the symphonies of Tchaikovsky, Glazounoff, Dvorak, and many similar composers, but it stands head and shoulders above all of them in thematic distinction and formal cohesion.... Sibelius, in fact, begins where they left off."

In the Second Symphony, Sibelius becomes an innovator in introducing, as Gray says, "an entirely new principle into symphonic form." In the first movement, Sibelius works with several thematic fragments of equal importance which he welds into unity in what is usually the development section. "Nothing in the entire literature of symphonic form is more remarkable," says Gray, "than the way in which Sibelius here presents a handful of seemingly disconnected and meaningless scraps of melody, and then breathes life into them, bringing them into organic relation with each other and causing them to grow in stature and significance with each successive appearance, like living things." The Third is serene in mood, as is the Fifth, a radiant sunny work. The Sixth is again an experiment in which the conventional sonata form is put aside for a freer type of procedure. There is no slow movement, and the scherzo has no trio. The Seventh Symphony is in one movement, with one chief subject and many shorter, fragmentary motives. "The *Seventh* shows him at the summit of his powers in respect to fecundity of invention and subtlety and intricacy of design," says Gray. "It is not merely a consummate masterpiece of formal construction, however, but also a work of great expressive beauty, of a lofty grandeur and dignity, a truly Olympian serenity and repose which are unique in modern music, and, for that matter, in modern art of any kind."

Sibelius as a national composer has been a subject of interest to many, and his "nationalism" has been misunderstood. "Finlandia," for example, is not filled with Finnish folk songs. In fact, he does not consciously use the folk idiom of his land in any of his music. Another misconception is the picture of Finland as a desolate wilderness inhabited by a primitive race, whereas in reality it is a highly civilized country of cultured people, up-to-date ideas, and important sociological, scientific, and artistic achievements. Therefore, the notion that Sibelius's music is of primitive nature is false.

It has a primeval quality, of the grandeur and austerity of the great forests, and the composer once wrote in a letter quoted in the program book of the Boston Symphony Orchestra (Nov. 17, 1932): "It is true I am a dreamer and a poet of nature. I love the mysterious sounds of the fields and forest, waters and mountains. . . . It pleases me greatly to be called an artist of nature, for nature has truly been the book of books for me. The voices of nature are the voices of God, and if an artist can give a mere echo of them in his creations, he is fully rewarded for all his efforts."

His nationalism is expressed in the following lines with which the composer prefaced "Tapiola":

> *"Wide-spread they stand, the Northland's dusky forests,*
> *Ancient, foreboding, brooding savage dreams;*
> *Within them dwells the forest's mighty god,*
> *And wood sprites in the gloom weave magic secrets."*

Another claim to national influences in Sibelius is the fact that many of his earlier works were based on the national epic, the *Kalevala*, compiled early in the nineteenth century from Finnish folk poetry and mythology. In this the characteristic love of nature and interest in magic are prevalent. His first musical epic is *"Kullervo,"* an unpublished symphony for soloists, chorus, and orchestra, based on the story of one of the chief characters in the *Kalevala*. Gray says it was "the first large-scale piece of music, based upon a national subject and set to words in the native language, which Finland could recognize as her own. With *Kullervo*, in fact, Finland became musically articulate."

The next work, an orchestral tone poem, *"En Saga,"* made Sibelius's name known in European countries. "The Swan of Tuonela," another of his famous scores, is one of four legends for orchestra again dealing with characters in the *Kalevala*. Another of the *Kalevala* legends, "Pohjola's Daughter," which Sibelius made into an orchestra work, he conducted at the Litchfield County Choral Union at Norfolk, Conn., when he visited this country in 1914. He was, at that time, made a Doctor of Music by Yale University. Several choral works such as "The Origin of Fire," "Luonnotar," "The Song of Väino," come from *Kalevala* legends.

Sibelius is over eighty years old, one of the world's most respected composers, having gone his own way, untouched by the atonal, polytonal, neoclassic, outside world, living in retirement near Helsingfors and speaking his own original language with a subtlety of meaning in which breathe vitality, conciseness, and beauty—an erudite, primeval, national modern.

CHAPTER 14

STRAVINSKY: THE MUSICAL BAROMETER

THE violently controversial opinions concerning the work of Igor Stravinsky (1882) are of signal importance because they show how long it took for his place in the musical universe to become definitely fixed, and how difficult it was to consider him with the necessary detachment for a final opinion. He has been a human barometer, recording the changes that have taken place in musical aesthetics in the twentieth century. It is useless either to hold him responsible for the change of front which is apparent in his style of composing, or to regret that he did not remain the realist-primitivist that he was in 1910. Another reason for controversy is that the musical public, as is its wont, pitted Stravinsky and Schoenberg against each other. Those who were followers of the one decried the other. It would seem, however, that Stravinsky, more than any other composer either of the present or the past, has been a channel through which have surged powerful forces, thrown out of their usual course by the chaotic upheavals the world has experienced. We cannot escape the truism that art reflects cosmic thought; Stravinsky, by a series of conditions outside his conscious control, was the proper medium for its musical expression.

He is by nature an innovator, an iconoclast, a realist, a non-sentimentalist. He was trained to be a lawyer, so he must have learned to think logically. Music came to him in childhood through hearing his father, an opera singer, and his friends, but he was not seriously trained in music until he was an adult, consequently he was free from many prejudices and pedantries that are formed unconsciously during early study years. He lived in Russia at a time when the renaissance of national thought was at its height, so that he was influenced by Moussorgsky's music and that of Rimski-Korsakov, who for a short time taught him; his imagination was stirred by the Russian literature and the stage, and he succumbed to the lure of primitive folklore.

After he had tried his hand at a few compositions, including a Tchaikovsky-like symphony, a song cycle with orchestral accompaniment, some piano études, and two orchestral works, "Fireworks" and *"Scherzo fantastique,"* in Paris he met Serge Diaghileff (or Diaghilev, 1872-1929), the impresario of the Ballet Russe. Again it would seem that outside forces were at work, for that meeting opened a new path to Stravinsky and changed the course of twentieth century music. Stravinsky's collaboration with Diaghileff in creating a new type of short ballet covered almost twenty years (1909-1928). The ballets for which he is most renowned are the earlier ones: *L'Oiseau de feu, Petrouchka, Le Sacre du printemps* and perhaps *Rossignol* and *Les Noces,* although this by no means completes the list.

Diaghileff "made" Stravinsky, but Stravinsky supplied him with sensational music with which to "carry on." Diaghileff also was responsible for the creation of a line of least resistance for the French composers, who followed the path opened by Stravinsky. Some of the *Group of Six* (page 236) wrote ballets for him, among which were *Le Train bleu* of Darius Milhaud, *Les Biches* by Poulenc, *Les Facheux, Pastorale,* and *Les Matelots* by Auric. Debussy composed *Jeux* and permitted a choreographic setting for *"L'Après-midi d'un faune";* Ravel wrote one of his loveliest orchestral scores, *Daphnis et Chloë;* Satie wrote *Parade, Jack in the Box,* and *Mercure;* Henri Sauguet, one of the younger Frenchmen, wrote *La Chatte;* Florent Schmitt's *La Tragédie de Salomé* was presented. Diaghileff stepped outside of France and ordered ballets from Richard Strauss (*Joseph's Legend*), Falla (*The Three-cornered Hat*), Prokofieff (*Chout, Le Pas d'acier,* and *Le Fils prodigue*), the Italian Rieti (*Barabau and Le Bal*), the English Lord Berners (*The Triumph of Neptune*) and Constant Lambert (*Romeo and Juliette*), Dukelsky, a Russian in New York (*Zephyr and Flora*), and a Russian in Paris, Nabokoff (*Ode*).

Milhaud wrote his charming *Création du monde,* and Honegger *The Skating Rink* for Borlin of the Swedish Ballet. Casella wrote *La Giara.* In fact the market was soon flooded with ballets that were far from masterpieces. Many of them were "occasional pieces" written carelessly and without form, workmanship, or inspiration, works which could not possibly have a lasting effect on music.

Stravinsky had a tremendous influence on the younger composers who were writing ballets. They imitated his harmonies, his rhythmic figures, his brutality and ugliness. The ultramodern tricks became obvious and obnoxious, as offensive as the worn-out banalities and supersentimentality of the pseudo romanticists. Experiments good and bad seemed more important than honest self-expression. The unrest and the undercurrent of discord and danger, which colored the prevailing state of mind in Europe before World War I, culminated in a work like Le Sacre du printemps. Debussy's imitators, copying not his strength, but degenerating into a pastel-shaded saccharinity, no longer expressed the feelings of the people. With the war came the need for strong colors, strong rhythms, violent contrasts, and brutal dissonance, and they rallied around the new standard-bearer, Stravinsky.

In the meantime, Stravinsky met a new situation in Paris. He had arrived there a conquering barbarian, musically speaking. But before long he fell under the spell of the unfamiliar culture, the outcome of a rich past of which Stravinsky knew little or nothing. As someone wittily remarked, he discovered the eighteenth century too late. Or perhaps, after finishing Le Sacre, a fatigued composer was looking for a new path where intellectual problems would replace the elemental emotionalism in which he had spent himself.

Soon Stravinsky's style changed, or rather he set about to develop a style. He called himself a "classicist, an objectivist, a constructive artist." And he wrote articles concerning his ideas on music in which he said that his Octuor for Wind Instruments was a musical object, and that the individual timbre of each wind instrument without nuances was reason enough for the music without looking for extraneous causes and emotions. "Sound for sound's sake" was his slogan. Then he became absorbed in the problem of "style." The nineteenth century had had no style because style was lost in what the composer had to say instead of how he said it. The case of classicism versus romanticism again! B. de Schloezer said in La Revue musicale (February 1929), "Because he felt the profound need of a style, of a super-individual armour, Stravinsky turned toward the masters of the eighteenth century." Realizing the impossibility of an artist's creating a style, especially if he is born into an age where everyone is individualistic and is obliged to exaggerate his peculiarities and to oppose them violently to others, nothing remained for him to do but to revive the forms of the past. "An attempt full of risk," says de Schloezer, "which seemed bound to fail, because this language which Stravinsky determined to resuscitate, was it not the product of a mental structure very different from our own? And would not the transportation of this style into the present amount merely to a stylization?" De Schloezer sees in the Octuor, *Oedipus Rex,* and *Apollon Musagetes,* the realization of Stravinsky's project, and certainly the new classicism, *neoclassicism,* has swept over the musical world.

The hour for this new classicism had struck. Stravinsky was not its originator, although he apparently had felt the undercurrents and was ostensibly its prophet. Debussy was conscious of its proximity and Ravel was by nature a classicist; Reger had heard its call; Strauss turned to it in *Ariadne auf Naxos* and in other works; Schoenberg, Hindemith, Milhaud, Honegger, Poulenc, Casella, Copland, Bartók, Prokofieff are only a few who are twentieth century classicists.

No one seemed to understand that Stravinsky, whose scores had reached perilous heights of sophistication impelled by an intellectual primitivism, had had a change of heart. *Pulcinella,* a ballet with singing, based on Pergolesi airs; Symphony for Wind Instruments, in memory of Debussy; the Concertino for string quartet (written for the Flonzaley Quartet); *Mavra,* a stage work reviving the *opéra-bouffe;* the "Octuor"; the concerto for piano, wind instruments, and percussion; a piano sonata and a *Sérénade en La* for piano followed each other in rapid succession, all in the new style—"the eighteenth century viewed from the standpoint of today," he said.

After Stravinsky's piano sonata was played at a concert of the League of Composers in New York, Lawrence Gilman wrote in the *Herald Tribune* (October 26, 1925): "Some men succumb to the Grape, some to 'the dreadful heart of Woman.' Stravinsky has succumbed to the Eighteenth Century. He sees himself, it is evident, as the initiator of a private Renaissance. Let others—Schoenberg and his like—concern themselves with the drastic subtleties of a new art. But he would reanimate the past.

"One night—it must have been soon after the War was over—Stravinsky went to sleep and dreamed that he was visited by Johann Sebastian, and Handel, and Scarlatti, and a delegation of their contemporaries, and that they dropped their mantles on his bed, saying to him with profound impressiveness and feeling, 'These, Igor, are for thee: wear them worthily!' Then Stravinsky, springing out of bed and throwing the score of *L'Oiseau de Feu* into the Lake of Geneva (which is fairly deep at Clarens) donned with a gesture of ineffable pride the mantle of Johann Sebastian—that was the one he chose; and now, garbed in his magical investiture, he would summon the dead years from their marmoreal sleep."

But in Gilman's opinion the "private Renaissance" did not pan out. "Was Stravinsky's dream a betrayal? Was it only an ancient dressing-gown of his own that he mistook for the shining mantle of the Eighteenth Century?"

"Stravinsky turned away from his own disgraceful past," Gilman continues, "so shameless in its pursuit of color and fantasy and sardonic wit. Brusquely he shut the door upon it so that he might not see the reproach in the eyes of his Firebird, and the pitiful spectacle of his Neanderthal adolescents weeping on each other's necks."

"The clock marks the hour, but what marks Eternity?" Walt Whitman asks. "Stravinsky wrote ballets which shook the foundations of the musical world and set the fashion for the young composers of every country. He caused a harmonic and orchestral upheaval in a day of revolution. *Polytonality, polyharmony, polyrhythms* (many different rhythms heard simultaneously), *multirhythms* (changes of time signatures in rapid succession), *atonality* (the absence of a central tonality), all are found in his scores." (*Music through the Ages*, Bauer and Peyser.)

In the transitional stage, when he denied emotion and romanticism as a possible principle of creative thought, the young, willy-nilly, followed him—into the eighteenth century—in the hope of finding a new simplicity. Could it be possible that he is headed for a *neoromanticism*? *Œdipus Rex, La Symphonie de Psaumes* (Symphony of Psalms), and later works, show indications of a warmer, more personal expression. As he approaches romanticism (not of the nineteenth century variety, however), he completes the circle of historical evolution in musical structure, although not in chronological order. He started as a postromanticist; next he was a postimpressionist, an ultramodern primitivist or effectivist; then came the classicist (neoclassic in its manifestation), and now he is on his way, as are many others, for it is in the air, to being a new type of romanticist. Withal he has genius.

In the early ballets, Stravinsky is a musical descendant of Moussorgsky and Rimski-Korsakov. From the former he inherits a crude fearlessness, and from the latter a mastery of orchestration and a mood such as in *Le Coq d'or* (Rimski). Moussorgsky was interested in the peasantry of his own day while Stravinsky was more concerned with primitive times, with pagan Russia. He drew on folk song and legend as did the Russian nationalists, but his musical delineation is comparable to the paintings of Gauguin, also of Matisse, Derain, and Picasso, who were among the painters of Diaghileff's staff. Coloristically he might be compared to Bakst, who was also one of Diaghileff's aids.

L'Oiseau de feu (1910) was the first ballet that Stravinsky wrote for Diaghileff. It was an Oriental tale based on a national fairy story. The theme of the Introduction is based on this tonal combination:

L'Oiseau de Feu (a)   Igor Stravinsky

In the "Round of the Princesses" we meet with folk material:

L'Oiseau de Feu (b)   Igor Stravinsky

Except in a folk song, it is rare that Stravinsky uses as long a melody.

In the "Infernal Dance of King Kastchei" we begin to find the Stravinsky who won his reputation for the use of syncopations and for incessant repetitions of rhythmic phrases. We meet the whole tone scale and the use of the augmented triad. The *Berceuse* is simple, direct, impressionistic and is one of the few examples of Stravinsky in a tender mood.

Another simple melody which is constantly reiterated is the theme of the finale:

From the vantage point of the present day the *Firebird* in its garb as a suite which the composer reorchestrated in 1919 seems mild and beautiful music. At the close Stravinsky uses a means of harmonization explained as "escaped" chords, or as the impressionistic method of harmonizing members of the twelve tone scale in parallel motion:

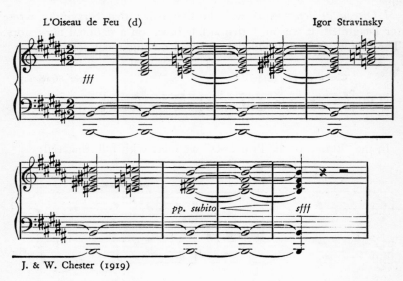

J. & W. Chester (1919)

Petrouchka (1911) was intended as a piece for piano and orchestra in which, according to André Schaeffner (*Stravinsky* in the series of *Maitres de la musique ancienne et moderne, Les Editions Rieder*),

Stravinsky intended to represent a dispute between the orchestra and the piano, a protest against the long-haired romanticist who had outlived his day. The piano solo was intended as a caricature of the concert style of a past generation! And the composer was indicating his intentions by ironically employing what might be termed *polyharmony,* the simultaneous use of complete chords from different keys. This differs from *polytonality* in the fact that the latter may be a combining of single melodies of differing tonalities rather than triads as we find them in this quotation from *Petrouchka:*

Petrouchka (a)   Igor Stravinsky

Edition Russe de Musique (1910-11)

From the fifth chord on, Stravinsky used the 6-4 chord of which I spoke before (pages 140-1).

When Diaghileff heard the sketches of the new work it was immediately commandeered for a ballet, and the poet-pianist was turned into a puppet brought to life by the Charlatan. The puppets, Petrouchka, the Moor, and the Ballerina, are of secondary importance to the extraordinary picture of Russian peasant life. The scene at the fair is masterly.

In the Russian Dance, Stravinsky uses commonplace polyharmonies put together with appropriate simplicity of means and vulgarity of effect:

Petrouchka (b)   (c)   Igor Stravinsky

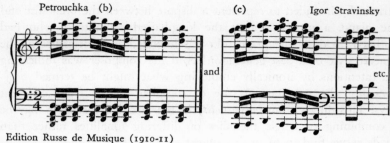

and

etc.

Edition Russe de Musique (1910-11)

Another amusing effect for two clarinets in which Stravinsky uses
bitonality (two different tonalities, C major and G flat major) follows:

Petrouchka (d)   Igor Stravinsky

etc.

Edition Russe de Musique (1910-11)

Here is music which throbs with human life—vital, passionate,
exuberant. It is a picture of the masses not the classes, and he presents it impersonally, as he does all his work—realistic, essentially
Russian, at times vulgar, sensual, cruel; again humorous, gay, almost
hysterical; tragic, violent, morbid, but never sentimental. Today
Petrouchka is regarded by many as Stravinsky's greatest masterpiece,
although when it comes to a decision *Le Sacre du printemps* would
probably receive the most votes.

Le Sacre du printemps (*The Rite of Spring,* 1913) is a picture of
pre-Christian Russia when pagan rites such as were found among
all primitive peoples were in order. Two ideas are exposed in the
choreography and music: the pagan belief in the holiness of spring
as the expression of the creative impulse, and the sacrifice of a con-
secrated one, a maiden. The music is in two parts; the theme of the
introduction has been quoted (page 90). It is scored for bassoon in
a high, unnatural register. It is derived from a folk melody, and it

resembles one used by Moussorgsky in "Night on the Bald Mountain" and also in *The Fair of Sorotchinsk*.

In the "Harbingers of Spring" appears that extraordinary and incessant rhythmic figure in which the accents re-enforced with eight horns come in most unexpected parts of the phrase, and the chord is an eleventh, f♭, a♭, c♭, e♭, g, b♭, d♭. The "Dances of the Adolescents" has this simple melody as its theme:

Le Sacre du Printemps (a)   Igor Stravinsky

etc.

Edition Russe de Musique
(Russicher Musik-Verlag, Berlin, copyright, 1921)

But what Stravinsky does with it is far from simple! The "Play of the Rapt" is followed by a dance entitled "Spring Rounds." The introduction is an excellent example of *multirhythmic* music on account of the rapid changes of time signature:

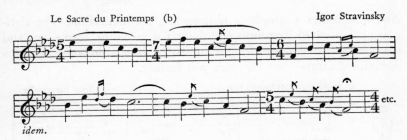

Le Sacre du Printemps (b)   Igor Stravinsky

idem.

This is followed by one of the most poignant parts of the entire work. It is based on this motive:

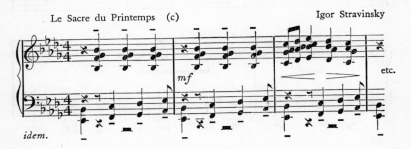

Le Sacre du Printemps (c)   Igor Stravinsky

etc.

idem.

In "Games of the Rival Tribes" meters change rapidly. The Sage of the Tribe enters to a processional, and the "Dance of the Earth" closes the first half with tumult and clash of dissonances. The second part opens with "Pagan Night." Here Stravinsky achieves a mood of gloom, mystery, and oppressive beauty. "Mystical Circles of the Adolescents" is based on this melody, harmonized with harsh polytonal effects:

Le Sacre du Printemps (d)   Igor Stravinsky

idem.

And then comes a sample of ultramodern harmonization: The clarinets play in parallel sevenths and the violas in ninths, then oboes and bassoons in octaves, and violins in sixths; later trombones sound a diminished octave—but I'll spare you further.

Le Sacre du Printemps (e)   Igor Stravinsky

idem.

The score becomes more and more tense, and more and more dissonant in the "Glorification of the Elected One," in the "Evocation of the Ancestors," "A Ritual for the Ancestors," and finally, the "Sacrificial Dance of the Chosen One" who must dance herself to death.

Stravinsky overstepped himself in indicating time signatures in this section for practically every measure changes $\frac{3}{16}$, $\frac{5}{16}$, $\frac{3}{16}$, $\frac{4}{16}$, $\frac{5}{16}$, $\frac{3}{16}$, $\frac{4}{16}$, etc., and all one can do is to trace rhythmic patterns which are comparatively distinct and repetitious.

The first performance created an unprecedented scene—the pent-up emotions which had been brewing against "modernism" broke with a force of antagonism that prevented the dancers from hearing the orchestra. And a year later when it was given in concert form, the protest was so deafening that Debussy, who was present, begged the audience to allow the performance to be completed. "Whether or not the work is a thing to be treasured," Lawrence Gilman wrote in the notes of a Philharmonic-Symphony program in 1930, "each hearer will decide for himself. But at least it teaches us again the inexhaustible responsiveness of music to new ways of apprehending life, new adventures of the imagination, new conceptions of sensibility and truth and beauty."

America did not hear the *Sacre* in ballet form until April, 1930, when the League of Composers presented it in collaboration with the Philadelphia Orchestra Association under the direction of Leopold Stokowski, although Pierre Monteux, who conducted the original ballet performance for Diaghileff, Koussevitzky, and Stokowski had played it in concert.

The opera *Rossignol,* based on a story of Hans Christian Andersen, has had a checkered career. Stravinsky began it in 1909 but finished it only in 1914, when it was performed by the Ballet Russe. He rewrote it in 1917 as an orchestral work under the title of *"Le Chant du Rossignol"* (The Song of the Nightingale). The music reflects his earlier and later periods, with something of Debussy and also of Rimski-Korsakov's *Coq d'or. Rossignol, L'Oiseau de feu,* and *Petrouchka* have been in the repertory of the Metropolitan Opera Company.

This very interesting example of a pentatonic harmonization in four parts occurs in *Rossignol:*

Le Chant du Rossignol   (a)   Stravinsky

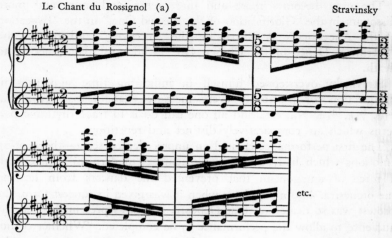

Edition Russe de Musique (1917)

In these same measures Stravinsky supplies an accompaniment which makes an excellent polyrhythmic illustration. Against the above rhythm he opposes a ⅜ meter, although it is notated in the same meters as above:

Le Chant du Rossignol   (b)   Igor Stravinsky

Harps

Celli and double basses
Edition Russe de Musique (1917)

Les Noces (*Russian Wedding*) is a cantata with dances. Soloists and choruses are in the orchestral pit with four pianos and percussion. The percussion includes four timpani, one xylophone and bell, tambourine, triangle and cymbals, side drum, snare drum, bass drum, and small cymbals. The melodies are taken from folk music, but again they are accompanied with dissonance, and the rhythmic element sets the patterns for the melodic. The strong beats, coming in at irregular intervals, create very complicated rhythms. There are many repetitions of rhythmic figures, melodic themes, chord sequences. The pianos are used as percussion instruments.

The text describes four scenes from the primitive marriage customs of Russian peasant life. Stravinsky avowedly shunned beauty of sound or aesthetic values and wished to make *Les Noces* an exhibition of craftsmanship. And yet it has a curious power and inherent strength which call out a response to its tragedy even when it is humorous. Stravinsky began it in 1914, finished it in 1917, but changed the instrumentation four times, until in 1923 it arrived at its present stage. The text, compiled by the composer from popular sources, preserves the tang of the peasantry. It was presented in America for the first time by the League of Composers and Leopold Stokowski in 1929.

"In spite of its folk basis," we say in *Music through the Ages,* "it is the most abstruse of all Stravinsky's ballets, and marks a turning point toward simplification, toward the eighteenth century musical forms and *neoclassicism.*"

Pulcinella is the first ballet after Stravinsky's "change of heart," but he had written the three pieces for string quartet; *Pribaoutki* (Pleasant Songs) for voice and eight instruments; *"Berceuses du Chat"* (Lullabies of a Cat) for a woman's voice and three clarinets; Five Easy Pieces for piano, four hands; *Renard,* a burlesque chamber opera based on popular Russian tales, commissioned by the Princess Edmond de Polignac; an Etude for Pianola; *L'Histoire du soldat,* a second chamber music opera; "Ragtime" for eleven instruments; the "Piano Rag-Music"; and Three Pieces for Clarinet Solo which Stravinsky wrote after hearing a homesick colored jazz player of an American orchestra in a London café trying to comfort himself with his clarinet in a corner.

The first war was responsible for Stravinsky's turning away from the great orchestra and developing the art of the chamber orchestra. *L'Histoire du soldat* (*The Story of the Soldier*) calls for a Narrator, who tells the story of the Soldier returning from the wars and meeting a stranger who is the Devil. The dancers are the Soldier, the Devil, and the Princess, and the work is accompanied by a chamber group of eight pieces. It is probably the first of Stravinsky's works through which two streams of influence—Bach and Handel, and jazz—seem to flow. This incongruous combination appears in the piano Sonata and the Concerto for piano, wind instruments, and percussion; also in the *Capriccio* for piano and orchestra and in the violin concerto. These works show a definite turning from subjectivism, and a strong trend toward what might be called the *neobaroque,* with an emphasis on the constructive side of the art, and a leaning toward traits of the late baroque of the eighteenth century in the importance of the melodic line, the use of polyphony, and the adoption of the preclassical sonata form.

His treatment of percussion, the tympani particularly, in *L'Histoire du soldat* is interesting and novel, for it becomes a part of the polyphonic line, and its effect is decidedly exciting. Stravinsky showed his extraordinary technic of instrumentation in the colossal effects he attained with such slender means.

Perhaps in using the melodies of Pergolesi for *Pulcinella,* Stravinsky realized that he would be brought face to face with the necessity for harmonic and formal simplification, but his personality still dominates the score.

Mavra, an *opéra bouffe* on a book by Pushkin, was a direct attempt to imitate the style of the early nineteenth century opera. It is dedicated to the memories of Pushkin, Glinka, and Tchaikovsky. One reason for its lack of success may have been that the public had not yet accustomed itself to the idea that the *enfant terrible* of music was trying to be a good boy. Somehow the public has never quite reconciled itself to the fact that Stravinsky of *Le Sacre* and *L'Histoire du soldat* is gone forever; or at least, so he says.

Many of the works of this time seem to have been experiments and self-imposed discipline in the development of a new style. The master was willing to become the apprentice again in order to reach another stage of mastery. *Oedipus Rex* would indicate such a psychology. Stravinsky calls it an opera-oratorio. The Greek play by Sophocles, arranged as a libretto by the composer and Jean Cocteau, was translated from French into Latin by J. Danièlou. No longer in transition, Stravinsky had perfected a new language as gripping and individual as was *Le Sacre,* but more profound and less dissonant. The amazing facility with which he previously startled the musical world was there, but it had matured and he exercised control in the use of limitless

means. Still detached and impersonal, he told a tragic and horrible
tale by means of a narrator, soloists, and a chorus of male voices, and
for the first time since 1914 used a complete orchestra.

The League of Composers and the Philadelphia Orchestra Association presented the first stage performance in America (1931) after
Koussevitzky had given a concert performance with the Boston Symphony Orchestra. Leopold Stokowski, conductor of the stage production, wrote as a foreword in the program:

"When art expresses ideas and emotions that are fundamental, it
knows no limit of period or country. The music of Stravinsky's
Oedipus-Rex is in places markedly Russian, as for instance the melodic
and rhythmic design of the phrases sung by the shepherd and the
messenger after the announcement of the death of Polybus. In other
places the feeling of Greek tragedy inspires the music of Stravinsky,
as for example the broad sweeping strokes of the melodic line of
Creon's speech, or the frenetic agitation of the chorus near the end.
But in general the music is detached from national characteristics—
nonrealistic, abstract. It is dark, archaic, somber in color, while in form
it is one long line of ever increasing ominous tension. Both Sophocles
and Stravinsky accept completely the primitive superstitious ideas on
which the tragedy is based. To the modern mind the fact that Oedipus
is unconscious that he kills his father and marries his mother would
destroy the tragic conflict. But seen from a universal angle this becomes the symbol of all human action leading to pain and death
through ignorance. So through new forms Stravinsky expresses eternal
ideas."

To carry out Stravinsky's directions that the actors were to be "as
immovable as columns and should appear and disappear by means of
a mechanical process," it was given with giant puppets designed by
Robert Edmond Jones who expressed his idea of "a space of shadow-
darkness-distance—great archaic figures moving half-seen, in a world
of dreams.... Music, mystery, a reminder of the old, forbidden,
terrible secret hidden in the depths of our thought— ... In its present
form it is only a hint of the awe and beauty that may one day be
evoked in the theater by the use of these heroic archetypal figures."

After *Oedipus Rex*, Stravinsky filled a commission he received from
Mrs. Elizabeth Sprague Coolidge for a chamber ballet, for the opening

of the concert hall of the new wing which had been built through her financial aid at the Congressional Library in Washington, D. C., for the annual Festivals of Chamber Music. He wrote *Apollon Musagetes*, the truly neoclassic result of an attempt to write a work in which there should be "no contrast, no intrigue, even in the instruments themselves," and he took his figures from the classic days of the white tarlatan ballets, and borrowed the variation forms and dancing steps from the eighteenth century ballet.

The Symphony of Psalms is closely related to *Oedipus Rex* in its *neobaroque* treatment of melody, its musical idiom, its employment of chorus and large orchestra, in the starkness of its harmonies, its characteristic rhythms, intensity of mood, maturity, and seriousness. It is a choral symphony with an orchestra of cellos and basses, flutes, oboes, trumpets, horns, and pianos, based on selections from the Psalms, written in 1930 at the request of Koussevitzky for the fiftieth anniversary of the founding of the Boston Symphony Orchestra.

World War II proved a disturbing factor in Stravinsky's life. In 1934 he had become a French citizen. In 1939 he visited America, gave a series of lectures at Harvard, and the next year applied for American citizenship. He has made California his home.

A work written during the Paris days (1934) was *Persephone,* music for a ballet for Ida Rubinstein on a poem by André Gide. It is called a melodrama, as the score includes a narrator in addition to a chorus and orchestra. It was conducted in America by the composer at a performance by the Boston Symphony Orchestra.

In 1935, in Paris, Stravinsky played his concerto for two pianos with his son Svietoslav Suleima, a brilliant, complex work in which sonorities are strongly contrasted in the four movements. Eight years later (1943-44) he used the same medium for a sonata for two pianos. Here the composer shows a marked change in style in a shorter, simpler, more gracious work. While both are typical of Stravinsky, the concerto is definitely reminiscent of the late baroque and the sonata of the classical sonata. Here we find a simplified style, showing the composer's characteristic economy. In the first movement he employs sonata form with a concise exposition, short development section, recapitulation, and coda. The sonata opens with this diatonic theme with a bitonal appearance of tonic and dominant in F major:

Sonata for Two Pianos
Igor Stravinsky
1943-44
Moderato ♩ = 63

Piano I

Moderato ♩ = 63

Piano II

(Copyright, 1945, by Chappell & Co. Inc., N.Y. Associated Music Publishers, Inc.)

The lyrical second theme in C major is accompanied by an ostinato figure in the dominant, while the second piano plays an innocuous and simple counterpoint:

Stravinsky

leggiero
(Copyright, 1945, Chappell & Co. Inc., N.Y. Associated Music Pub. Inc.)

The development is extremely simple and polytonal.

The second movement has four variations on a slow, stark diatonic theme which is heard three times and is strictly contrapuntal. In the opening statement a second voice enters as a canon in inversion:

The first two variations are melodic, accompanied by a rhythmic figure throughout; the third is contrapuntal, and the fourth is a short restatement of the theme.

The finale is a short three-part form with polytonal tension, in which one finds real Stravinskian wit and vigor.

These illustrations are an excellent example of what Nicolas Slonimsky calls *pan-diatonicism,* that is, the use of the diatonic scale as the basic tonal material, without, however, the harmonic restrictions of an earlier age. Pan-diatonicism is a bitonal or polytonal consolidation of diatonic harmony. The *Harvard Dictionary of Music* says that *"pan-diatonicism* might be considered as the 'diatonic' counterpart of atonality which applies the same principle of 'harmonically unrestricted combination' to the chromatic scale." It is "a reaction against the 'pan-chromaticism' of the late 19th century." Slonimsky states that it is a favorite technique of neoclassicism.

Another work that recalls the style of the concerto grosso is the Dumbarton Oaks Concerto in E flat for sixteen instruments (1938). Written specially for Stravinsky's American tour in 1937 was *Le Jeu de Cartes* (*Card Party*), "a ballet in three deals."

One of the first compositions in what might be called his American period was the Symphony in C for the golden jubilee season of the Chicago Symphony Orchestra. In neoclassic style, reflecting something of Haydn and Mozart, it still has the individuality, rhythmic vitality, and ingenuity of Stravinsky, and shows his love of moving on to new problems with each score.

"Circus Polka," which is frequently programmed, was written originally for a band and was commissioned, incredible as it may seem, by Ringling Bros. and Barnum and Bailey Circus, and was presented in Madison Square Garden, New York, in 1942. In 1944 a commission came from Billy Rose for a ballet, portions of which were used in his show *Seven Lively Arts*. It is heard on orchestral programs as *"Scènes de ballet,"* in which the music in eleven parts is patterned after the forms of the classical dance. Stravinsky also wrote a longish work for small orchestra called *"Danses concertantes"* which is a sort of caricature of the ballet music of the last century.

In these recent "American" works Stravinsky shows more and more a tendency to neoromanticism. This new romantic feeling is particularly evidenced in a Hollywood composition, "Four Norwegian Moods," based on Norwegian folk tunes which he states that he uses only as "a rhythmic and melodic base," and the word "mood" simply "indicates a form or manner of style" and "must not be interpreted as *impression* or *frame of mind.*"

As *Oedipus Rex* and the Symphony of Psalms were the culminating point of his *neoclassical,* or Paris period, so Stravinsky has reached another peak in his *neoromantic,* or American period with his *Ode* (1943) and his Symphony in Three Movements (1946).

The *Ode,* dedicated to the memory of Serge Koussevitzky's wife, Natalie, was composed for the Koussevitzky Music Foundation. It is a chant in three parts: "Eulogy," a song with sustained melody and accompaniment in fugal treatment; "Eclogue," "a piece in lively mood," Stravinsky stated for the Boston Symphony Orchestra program notes, "a kind of *concert champêtre,*" suggesting out-of-door music, an idea cherished by Natalie Koussevitzky and brilliantly materialized at Tanglewood by her husband; and "Epitaph," an inscription, which closes the "memorial triptych" serenely. It finds Stravinsky in a gracious, gentle mood.

The symphony is dedicated to the Philharmonic Symphony Society of New York "as an homage and appreciation" of his twenty years' association with it. "This Symphony has no program," he stated, "nor is it a specific expression of any given occasion; it would be futile to seek these in my work. But during the process of creation in this our arduous time of sharp and shifting events, of despair and hope, of continual torments, of tension and, at last, cessation and relief, it may be that all those repercussions have left traces in the Symphony. It is not I to judge." (From *Notes on the Program* of the Philharmonic-Symphony Society of New York, Jan. 24-25, 1946, by Robert Bagar and Louis Biancolli.)

The symphony is not in traditional form, but Ingolf Dahl, Stravinsky's friend and associate, points out in the Philharmonic program notes that it is "another example of that additive construction, for the invention of which Stravinsky is justly famous and which has proved so influential on the younger composer. It is a formal principle which conceives of music as the succession of clearly outlined blocks, or planes, which are unified and related through the continuity of a steadily and logically evolving organic force. This, of course, is the exact opposite of classical and romantic symphonic thought, just as the comparable additive principle of romanesque architecture is differentiated from the interlacing connectivity of the gothic or baroque."

For the first time in a generation, Stravinsky has returned to a type of harmonization that reminds one of *Le Sacre du printemps.* This has created a warmth and color that were not present in much of the music of the purely neoclassic style. Neither does one find any of the irony and wit, so characteristic of much of Stravinsky's moods.

"His knowledge of instrumentation is dazzling! And his system of dynamic effects has been worked out with incredible ingenuity and scientific application. Each instrument plays according to the nature of its possibilities as to timbre, pitch, volume, and dynamic range. Each musician plays practically a solo. He has often eliminated the strings completely as being too sentimental and possibly because they do not fit into the theory of dynamics. He has taught the twentieth century the value and possibilities of the small chamber music groups. All in all he has been an astounding and, at the same time, a dangerous influence on present-day composers." (*Music through the Ages.*)

CHAPTER 15

SCHOENBERG AND HIS INNOVATIONS: ATONALITY AND TWELVE TONE TECHNIC

ARNOLD SCHOENBERG (1874) started his composing career as a postromanticist. His earliest work was written without benefit of pedagogy, and the little instruction he had, he received later from Alexander Zemlinsky, who became his brother-in-law. Zemlinsky told a friend in 1902 that he could teach Schoenberg no more. "He knows more than I do now, and what he does not know, he feels. He has a brilliant intellect and an inquiring mind. And he has the greatest amount of sincerity." He also said that Schoenberg had had to paste together two sheets of manuscript paper in order to hold his elaborate orchestration. The composition was "Pelleas and Melisande," a tone poem on Maeterlinck's drama.

In addition to the characteristics enumerated by Zemlinsky, Schoenberg had a restless spirit, great physical vitality, intellectual curiosity, and a devotion to art which bordered on fanaticism.

Today the early works seem reactionary, pointing to extraordinary talent and strong influences of Wagner, Brahms, Mahler, and Strauss. Long before he had set out on a path of experimental invention, however, they were regarded as radical. "Schoenberg's youthful works appeared just at a time when artists lived in the comfortable possession of all the equipment at their disposal," says Egon Wellesz in a study of his teacher, *Arnold Schoenberg*. "They regarded as a disturbing factor all that was bold, austere, or unusual; and they sought with all the means in their power to stifle it. Nowadays, when it is considered good form to be revolutionary, and when Schoenberg has opened up a way for a new development in music, it is so easy to forget what had been accomplished between 1900 and 1910, and how much the present young generation owes to the pioneers."

Schoenberg was introduced to the public with a string quartet which remained unpublished. Before 1900 he had written some very beautiful songs in direct line with the traditional *Lied,* although showing a strong individuality and unusual gifts, which aroused antagonistic demonstrations; and the beautiful sextet, *"Verklärte Nacht"* (Illumined Night, op. 4), in which the composer used the form of the orchestral tone poem for a small group of strings.

In 1900 he began the *Gurre-Lieder,* which was not completely orchestrated until ten years later. The work suffered from not being performed immediately. In New York when it was heard in 1932, it sounded old-fashioned from the present standards, and yet it was a marvelous score for a young man of twenty-six to have achieved. Its quotations from Wagner, too, were disturbing, blinding many to the innovations of orchestration, and the rare beauty of certain passages such as the song of Tove. The work, a cantata on poems by Jens Peter Jacobsen, calls for a tremendous orchestra, soloists, narrator, and chorus, and is decidedly romantic.

Next came "Pelleas and Melisande," op. 6; Eight Songs, op. 6; the first string quartet (in D minor), op. 7, which takes almost an hour to perform, and is modeled on Beethoven's last quartets; Six Songs with Orchestra, op. 8; the Chamber Symphony, op. 9; and the second string quartet (in F sharp minor), op. 10, in which, in the last two movements, he included settings for soprano of poems by Stefan George. The first performance of the quartet, which today is recognized as a beautiful composition though it suggests the Schoenberg who was soon to burst forth with new theories, was the occasion of wild scenes of laughter, whistling, and hissing.

In 1909, his famous opus 11, *Drei Klavierstücke* (Three Piano Pieces) appeared. This was the first of a series of compositions in which Schoenberg made a complete break with the past, provoking world-wide dissension and criticism. Two songs, op. 14, and fifteen songs, *Das Buch der hängenden Gärten* (*The Book of the Hanging Gardens*), op. 15, by Stefan George; Five Orchestral Pieces, op. 16; a monodrama, *Erwartung* (*Waiting*), op. 17, an opera for solo voice (page 218); the opera *Die glückliche Hand* (*The Hand of Fate*), op. 18; Six Short Piano Pieces, op. 19; *"Herzgewächse"* (Flowers of My

Heart), op. 20, a song with celesta, harp, and flute accompaniment; and *Pierrot Lunaire,* op. 21, belong to the same period.

"Genius learns only from itself; talent chiefly from others. Genius learns from nature, from its own nature; talent learns from art," said Schoenberg in 1911. And again when his George songs and opus 11 were first performed he stated in the program: "In the *George Lieder* I have succeeded for the first time in approaching an ideal of expression and form that had hovered before me for years. Hitherto I had not sufficient strength and sureness to realize that ideal. Now, however, that I have definitely started on my journey, I may confess to having broken off the bonds of a bygone æsthetic; and if I am striving towards a goal that seems to me to be certain, nevertheless I already feel the opposition that I shall have to overcome.... I am following an inner compulsion that is stronger than education, and am obeying a law that is natural to me, and therefore stronger than my artistic training." (Quoted from *Arnold Schoenberg* by Egon Wellesz.)

Schoenberg enlarged the scope of his artistic horizon by being also a painter, and, like Debussy, was influenced by impressionist painters and symbolist writers. His paintings brought him to the attention of Wassily Kandinsky, the postimpressionist painter of Munich, who was a member of a group of painters, poets, musicians, critics, dramatists whose aim was "the expression of the *soul* of nature and humanity." Schoenberg thus worked out the philosophy of *expressionism* in his music.

Kandinsky claimed that Schoenberg was not working from a material standpoint but was seeking that inner spirit without which no great art could be evolved. "To those who are not accustomed to it the inner beauty appears as ugliness," says Kandinsky (*The Art of Spiritual Harmony,* by Wassily Kandinsky, translated with an introduction by M. T. H. Sadler), "because humanity in general inclines to the outer and knows nothing of the inner. Almost alone in severing himself from conventional beauty is the Austrian composer, Arnold Schoenberg."

Kandinsky considered that Schoenberg realized "that the greatest freedom of all, the freedom of an unfettered art, can never be absolute. Every age achieves a certain measure of this freedom, but beyond the boundaries of its freedom the mightiest genius can never go. But the measure of freedom of each age must be constantly enlarged. Schoenberg is endeavouring to make complete use of his freedom and has already discovered gold mines of new beauty in his search for spiritual harmony. His music leads us into a realm where musical experience is a matter not of the ear but of the soul alone—and from this point begins the music of the future."

Even though we are conscious that the true spiritual meaning of art and of life has been forcing itself upon us, we are living in a very material age, and we have come to the pass where the two elements— the material and the spiritual—are warring. In fact, many of the problems of Stravinsky's and of Schoenberg's art attest to the fight that has been going on in the field of aesthetics.

Schoenberg's "change of heart," his search for a way out from mere technical skill, invention, and the demands of the aesthetics of his youth, are expressed in a sentence from his *Harmonielehre* (*Treatise of Harmony*), completed in 1911: "Every combination of notes, every advance is possible, but I am beginning to feel that there are also definite rules and conditions which incline me to the use of this or that dissonance." And, true to type, he set about finding a scientific explanation for the "inner beauty" his intuition had forced him to heed.

Thus evolved an *atonal* style—a new melodic, harmonic, structural, and rhythmic order. His melody moves by skips and leaps; for consonant tone masses he substitutes the juxtaposition of dissonant sounds which he worked out scientifically, if arbitrarily; in place of the long phrases he uses short arabesques of rhythmic patterns; and sonata form is exchanged for a terse telegraphic style in which he has carried the elimination of unessentials to the extreme of omitting elements which to many seem essential. Schoenberg differs from innovators of the past in that they built consciously on the past, whereas he attempted to break consciously with all traditions and to substitute a new and logical foundation on which to base *absolute* music in what Weissmann calls "a ruthless search for truth and truthful expression." As Schoenberg gets further away from his early romanticism, he attains this state of absolutism, or expressionism, which, in his case, is a phase of neo-classicism.

Atonality, the term which has been given to Schoenberg's type of music, has aroused heated discussion. Webster's Dictionary defines tonality as the principle of key in music, or the character which a composition has by virtue of the relationship of all its tones and chords to the keynote of the whole. Atonality means literally "without tonality."

By substituting twelve independent centers with new tonal and chordal relationships, Schoenberg has removed what he considers the limitations of having one tone center, in favor of "pan-tonality."

"To decide between the claims of tonality and those of atonality has become a matter of feeling, or rather of conviction, quite apart from considerations of fact," Schoenberg said at a lecture in Paris before the Ecole de Musique. "Music depends not only upon acoustics but upon logic and upon those particular laws which result from the combinations of tone and tune. ... Tonality, tending to render harmonic facts perceptible and to correlate them, is therefore not an end but a means. If it is at all possible to achieve unity and terseness without resorting to tonality, tonality ceases to be needful.

"Its relinquishment, it is true, implies a corresponding relinquishment of the structural process founded upon the very principle of tonality; and therefore early examples of *works written by means of twelve notes between which no relationship exists other than their relation to one another* were necessarily very brief." The italicized phrase is preferred by Schoenberg to the term *atonality*.

"It is likely that, for a time at least, consonant chords will have to disappear from music if the tonal principle is eliminated—not for physical reasons, but for reasons of economy," Schoenberg stated. "A tonal consonance asserts its claims on everything that follows it—and regressively on all that came before. Hence consonant chords tend to occupy an excessive amount of room, and might disturb the balance proper to the new scheme—unless some way is eventually found either of satisfying or of suppressing the requirements of such chords."

Schoenberg said that he was convinced that a time will come when audiences will find dissonances natural, and the harmonic phenomena resulting from the dissonances quite intelligible. (Condensed from an article in the *Musical Times* of London.)

A partial analysis of the first of the Three Piano Pieces, op. 11,* may make the attempted explanation of Schoenberg's principles more understandable. The piece opens with a three-measure melodic phrase, a pattern chosen from the twelve tone scale.

* (These citations from *Drei Klavierstuecke*, op. 11, no. 1, by Arnold Schoenberg, appear with permission of the original editor, Universal-Edition, A.G., Vienna, copyright, 1910.)

Drei Klavierstuecke

Arnold Schoenberg
op. 11, No. 1

(a)

(Universal Edition, copyright, 1910)

This we find repeated, but never in exactly the same way, as, for example, in measures 9-11:

(b)

idem

And measures 16-18:

(c)

idem

And measures 53-56:

(d)

etc.

idem

And the final cadence is obviously based on the same pattern.

The next pattern, one measure long, begins on the second beat of the fourth measure, and, with very slight rhythmic variation, is repeated twice. It must be considered as the cadence of the first phrase:

In these examples we find several methods of varying a motive as explained by Adolph Weiss, who was a student in Schoenberg's master class at the Berlin State Academy of Fine Arts ("The Lyceum of Schoenberg" in *Modern Music,* March-April 1932). Schoenberg seeks co-ordination, or relation of parts to the whole, through the subdivision of a germ-cell which for him is a single motive. "The forms of variation which the motive undergoes might be called musical mitosis," says Mr. Weiss, and he tabulates the methods of varying a motive thus:

(1) changing the intervals or notes and holding the rhythms; (a) and (b)
(2) changing the rhythm and using the same tones or intervals; (b) and (c), (e), (f), and (g)
(3) simultaneous combinations of both these methods; (a) and (d)
(4) inversion;
(5) elongation;

(6) contraction;

(7) elision (of one or more notes);

(8) interpolation (of one or more notes);

(9) the crab-form (*motus cancrizans,* repeating the motive backwards).

"Schoenberg uses them to build not only the complete thematic material but all other parts of the composition as well—secondary voices, accompaniments, harmonies, etc...."

A trick which Schoenberg uses often, and which we find in opus 11, no. 1, might be described as pulling the intervals out of their sockets! That is, he stretches them beyond the limits of an octave, making a truly naïve motive sound complicated, as for example:

Reduced to a common fraction, as it were, the notes under the bracket would read:

And the next measure treated in the same manner would be:

In fact, he uses the condensed form of the design (b) as an inner voice pattern later in the piece.

The middle section is based on the first pattern and also uses the above stretching exercises:

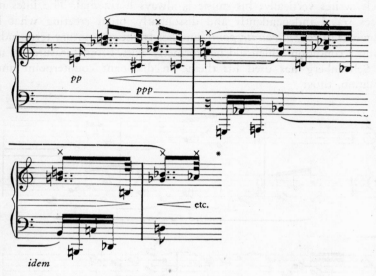

idem

* The crosses mark the original melody.

Inverted to intervals within the octave the figure becomes:

The fortieth measure, which looks most formidable with its leaps of
ninths in both hands, may be reduced in a similar manner.

As you may have noticed, the basic principle of this piece is not
melody and accompaniment, but is contrapuntal in effect. Schoenberg
rarely writes vertically; his music is always horizontal. The lines or
voices travel independently and dissonantly, often creating what is
known as *dissonant counterpoint,* another twentieth century term indicating a condition which did not formerly exist. From measures 25 to
32, Schoenberg has used his theme in dissonant counterpoint and
imitation, thus:

(Universal Edition, copyright, 1910)

As a teacher, Schoenberg is unexpectedly conservative, that is, he
carries his pupils along the line music has traveled. His *Harmonielehre*
is a book of musical aesthetics as well as a treatise of harmony. Dr.
Wellesz speaks at great length concerning the *Harmonielehre* and
Schoenberg's teaching. Wellesz gives us the master's definition of consonance and dissonance: "He defines consonance as the closer and
simpler relation with the ground-note (fundamental tone), and dissonance as the more remote and more complicated. Thus he holds by a
graduated distinction between consonance and dissonance. The con-

sonances turn out to be the first over-tones; the nearer they are to the ground-note the more productive they are. The more remote the over-tones, the less they can be made to fit in with a combination of sounds, and the more they need resolution."

Schoenberg found a gap in the harmony, in chords in thirds. He suggested building them in fourths because he found the fourths more uniform for chord building than the thirds. He used them in "Pelleas and Melisande" and in the Chamber Symphony.

It will be noticed that these chords of perfect fourths contain twelve tones and that they can be reduced to these scales:

The chord may consist of three, four, five, six, up to twelve voices, used in almost limitless combinations. That the time was ripe for *chords in fourths* may be seen from the innumerable examples which can be quoted from the works of Satie, Ravel, Debussy, Scott, Hindemith, Casella, Milhaud, Honegger, Copland, Harris, etc.

Schoenberg opened new paths with their use but he soon developed away from them into the "law" of the twelve tone scale, of which the chord in fourths is only a small and unimportant factor.

An excellent example of his use of the twelve tone series, with his characteristic wide intervallic leaps, may be seen in this melodic (instrumental) line from the monodrama *Erwartung:* *

(Universal Edition, copyright, 1922)

The phrase marked by the brace forms the pattern of ten tones out of the twelve. The second brace marks an exact repetition of tones in a different rhythmic arrangement.

In the third of his Five Orchestral Pieces, one of the most mysteriously beautiful of all his scores, we find this free chord sequence:

* This citation from the monodrama *Erwartung,* op. 17, by Arnold Schoenberg, is used with permission of the original editor, Universal-Edition, A.G., Vienna (copyright, 1922).

Of his use of the *twelve tone series,* Adolph Weiss writes: "The twelve tone series is a definite arrangement of all tones of the chromatic scale in a set order. It is applied in all the forms of variation, har- monically or contrapuntally, horizontally or vertically, to the construc- tion of every detail of a twelve-tone composition." It is the material out of which the theme is made, and "the series may be divided or sub-divided into smaller groups of related motives, and any group may be joined to any other to form new combinations. . . . It is an outgrowth of the aesthetic and logical implication of the chromatic system, which has the chromatic scale as its foundation, in contra-distinction to the diatonic, which uses major, minor and other modes. Its possibilities are unlimited, first, because the choice of the series (which takes the place of the key, scale, or tonality) is arbitrary; second, because chordal construction is not restricted to building up by thirds, fourths, or fifths, etc.; and third, because the greatest 'freedom' in co-ordination is left to the taste and discretion of the composer."

Pierrot Lunaire is probably the most frequently performed of Schoen- berg's scores (if one excepts *"Verklärte Nacht"*). The music is still Schoenbergian in extreme, although it was written in 1912. It reveals great technical facility, contrapuntal dexterity, daring harmonic treat- ment, a touch of the old romanticism, moments of transcendent beauty, alongside of acrid harmonic and melodic effects.

The voice "neither sung nor spoken" is a reaching out for an effect that I remember hearing in the performance at the Neighborhood Playhouse of Charles Griffes's posthumous work, *Salut au Monde,* in which Walt Whitman's lines were intoned by the chorus, without using an exact pitch, each voice finding its natural pitch. The result was a marvelous wealth of tone color, of a harmonious dissonance welded together by rhythmic definiteness. It obviously was the effect Schoen- berg sought in *Pierrot Lunaire* and in other choral works—an experi- ment, a new tone medium, without a background of tradition.

The quality of the voice harmonizes well with the instruments de- manded by the score—piano, violin, viola, clarinet, flute (and piccolo), bass clarinet, and cello. The text, "Thrice Seven Poems," is from the French of Albert Giraud, translated into German by Otto Erich Hartle- ben, and into English by Charles Henry Meltzer. It represents the relentless battle between the ideal and the real, between the spiritual and the material. "Moonlight" is a symbol of ideality or spirituality, and the first seven poems—the Poet Drunk with Moonlight—represents the idealism of youth: Pierrot the Dandy of Bergamo, who "whitens his face in a marvelous way with just one fantastical moon-ray"; the pallid maiden washing her linen in the moonlight; and the seventh poem, "the dying, melancholy moon," in which the fight for materialism, "some unrelenting love ... wasting with desire," has already begun.

In the second group of poems, Pierrot sinks to the depths of materialism and crime; night is black and moonless, he falls into bad company, laughs at religion, becomes a thief, and his heart bleeds from his own degradation; he sees in a body hanging from the gibbet a symbol of his own crimes; then in a dream "the moon, a keen and shining sword," beheads him and he cries in despair,

> "Cruel crosses are the verses
> Bleeding poets dumbly fashion. ..."

In the third group, Pierrot, wearied with sin, and with senses jaded, gradually seeks idealism again; he finds "a tiny speck of moonlight faintly gleaming on his inky shoulder," and try as he might to get rid of it, the ray of idealism sticks. He starts homeward with a moonbeam as his rudder, and the cycle ends with his complete resurrection. (This analysis of the text of *Pierrot Lunaire* is drawn from an article by the author which appeared in the *Musical Times and Herald,* London.)

The songs are composed for different combinations of instruments, for instance: the first, "Moonstruck," is for flute, piano, violin, and cello; the third, "Dandy," for piccolo, clarinet, and piano; the seventh, "The Sick Moon," for flute alone; the eighth, "Night," for bass clarinet, cello, and piano, etc.

Schoenberg has displayed his extraordinary knowledge of musical form in his use of traditional forms, as for example, "Night" is a passacaglia; the seventeenth, "Parody," is first a canon, and then an inverted canon. "The Moon-Spot" (No. 18) is a famous example of the crab-canon (*motus cancrizans*), in which there is a double canon between the piccolo and clarinet, and the violin and cello. These advance to the tenth measure and from that spot the entire music in every part is played backwards to the beginning. To show how the crab moves, I have quoted three measures of the clarinet theme as it appears at the point of reversal in the score:

Pierrot Lunaire   Arnold Schoenberg, op. 21

Clar. in B♭

(with permission of the original editor,
Universal-Edition, A.G. Vienna, copyright, 1914)

Verily, this is a case where the music sounds just as well backwards as forwards!

Dr. Wellesz tells us that at the same time the piano plays a three-part fugue based on the theme of the canon between piccolo and clarinet in notes of double value (augmentation). He compares it for skill to the work of Bach in his great study of the *Art of the Fugue.*

The "Serenade" is a solo for cello with piano accompaniment and always the *Sprechstimme,* of course. It is a fascinating example of Schoenberg's use of chords, for here the harmonic principle prevails, with vertical music as a result.

Serenade from Pierrot Lunaire   Arnold Schoenberg
Sehr lansamer Walzer   op. 21

(with permission of the original editor,
Universal-Edition, A.G. Vienna, copyright, 1914)

These five-voiced chords are chosen from the twelve tone series, and
are built in fourths or thirds, or fourths and thirds, as best suited
Schoenberg's intentions for melodic movement. It is a slow waltz, and
although I have quoted only the piano accompaniment, the "Serenade"
has been used as a number for cello solo.

In building chords, Schoenberg does not double voices, as was customary in former harmonic systems based on triads. It is also noticeable
how much we need a reform of notation when we see how often
Schoenberg is forced to use accidentals in order to make his meaning
clear (page 113). His feeling for cadence is shown in this sixteen-

measure period of three phrases, with the modern use of the half cadence and the full stop.

As Schoenberg advanced in exploiting his theories by applying them to his own compositions, he used what might be called a contrapuntal harmony. Schoenberg says on this subject: "The mutual saturation of these two principles, harmony and counterpoint, is so complete, their distinction or separation so incomplete, that every result derived from voice-leading may be a harmony, and every harmony may have its foundation in voice-leading. Apparently we are turning to *a new era of the polyphonic style,* and chords will be the result of voice-leading, justified through melodic content alone. Some day we shall recognize in the harmonies of the most modern writers today the laws of the older periods, only in a broader and more universal application." (Quoted from "The Lyceum of Schoenberg" by Adolph Weiss, *Modern Music,* March-April 1932.)

This "new era of the polyphonic style" culminated for Schoenberg in the twelve tone technic, frequently called the *twelve tone system.* In a letter to Nicolas Slonimsky, which appears in *Music since 1900,* Schoenberg stated that his aim was to base the structure of his music *"consciously* on a unifying idea, which produced not only all the other ideas but regulated also their accompaniment and the chords, the 'harmonies.' " After the piano pieces, op. 23, and the Serenade, he became conscious of the real meaning of his aim: "unity and regularity," which unconsciously had led him in this direction. Thus the intervals of the chromatic scale became the basis of a motivic idea, or "tone complex" which developed into one of the most important innovations of the twentieth century.

In Schoenberg's hands the basis of a composition is a single pattern, a series or a "row" of twelve tones in arbitrary arrangement. The row is a "prime" and the intervals are used in the order in which they appear in the row, although they may be subjected to many variations and combinations, such as changes of register, enharmonic spelling, inversions of the original series, and a myriad of rhythmic designs which give multiplicity to the melodic and harmonic structure of a composition. Schoenberg transposes the entire series or "row" starting from any of the other eleven degrees of the chromatic scale. Other forms of the series are arrived at by *inversion,* that is, changing all ascending intervals to corresponding descending intervals, and vice versa; by *retrogression,* reading the series backward; and by *retrograde inversion,* by reading the inversion backward.

In Ernst Krenek's Twelve Little Piano Pieces, he presents the series or "germ cell" as he names it, as follows:

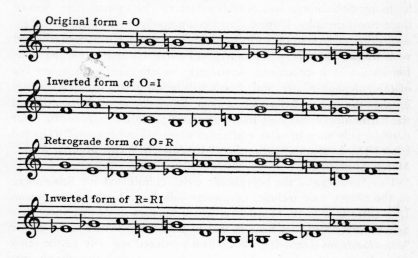

These he uses in the pieces, as, for example, in the first:

Dancing Toys   Ernst Krenek, Op. 83

(G. Schirmer, Inc., copyright 1939)

With his working out of the twelve tone technic, Schoenberg may be said to have entered the third period of his creative activities. Dr. Wellesz places the date at 1920; the Piano pieces (op. 23 and 25) were followed by a Serenade in which the movements are March, Minuet, Variations, "Sonnet," "Dance Scene," *"Song without Words,"* and

Finale, showing the neoclassic return to old dance forms. The Serenade is written for clarinet, bass clarinet, mandolin, guitar, violin, viola, cello, and in the "Sonnet" a base baritone voice is added. Later came the Wind Quintet, op. 26; the third string quartet, op. 30; variations for orchestra; music for a film production; *Von Heute auf Morgen* (*From One Day to Another*), an opera based on the twelve tone series.

Arnold Schoenberg was one of the first musicians to leave Germany when Hitler became dictator. He arrived in America in October 1933. He eventually made his home in Pasadena, California, where, in 1944, his seventieth birthday was celebrated. He has been teaching many American pupils since 1933.

Schoenberg's "American" period shows definite changes in style, perhaps as a result of his new environment. One of the first of these works, Suite for String Orchestra, however, is not in twelve tone technic. Written for schools and colleges, it shows his amazing command of a diatonic contrapuntal technic. The violin concerto, op. 36, and the fourth string quartet, op. 37, on the other hand, are definitely in an advanced state in his use of the tone-row in a long and sustained composition. There is also a sensitive balance of form displayed, and individual character in each new work. Obviously Schoenberg, in searching to replace classical tonality, has developed another system, based on interrelationship, which finds its ultimate expression in the piano concerto, op. 42 (1944).

The first eight measures show the tone-row.

Concerto for Piano and Orchestra   Arnold Schoenberg, Op. 42

(G. Schirmer, Inc., copyright 1944)

This is followed by a transposed retrograde inversion, the theme in retrograde, and the transposed inversion of the original form, making a long melodic line of thirty-nine measures.

It is beyond the scope of this book to offer a fuller analysis of the concerto. Such an analysis may be found in the *Musical Quarterly* of October 1944, in an article "On the Spontaneity of Schoenberg's Music," by Heinrich Jalowetz. "What is here revealed," Jalowetz writes, "—a genuine formative imagination applied to the creation of sound, structure, and musical character; the intensity and subtlety of all musical relationships down to the last detail; and that stylistic uniformity of language which stems from a deeply rooted personal world of expression and ideas—all this is brought into evidence in spite of the restrictions imposed by the rules of the technic."

Other works are the Second Chamber Symphony, begun in 1906 but completed recently; Variations for Band, and "Ode to Napoleon." The Variations, op. 43-A (1943), scored originally for band, was rescored for orchestra as op. 43-B. The full title is Theme and Variations for Orchestra in G minor. The surprising information that the work is in G minor shows that Schoenberg lapsed temporarily from atonality, as he did in the Suite for String Orchestra. This work is also traditional in style and rich in polyphonic treatment.

Schoenberg's acknowledgment of the world condition was made in his setting of Byron's "Ode to Napoleon" (1942), a gesture against tyranny and dictatorship. He gives the words to a speaker, whose part is written on one line, thus prescribing rhythm and phrasing, and a blending with orchestra, but it does not indicate so much direction for pitch as does the *Sprechstimme* in *Pierrot Lunaire.*

Although it is composed in the twelve tone technic, the listener is conscious only of a work of unusual inspiration and beauty, in which the speaking voice is effectively blended with the orchestral texture. A complete analysis was made by Kurt List in *Modern Music* for March-April 1944.

As a composer, as the writer of the *Harmonielehre,* as a teacher, Schoenberg has had influence not only on his pupils and on composers, but on music in general. By his disciples Schoenberg is worshiped and revered. His great intellect and his accepted martyrdom of being misunderstood and unappreciated are keys to his character of unflinching honesty and stubborn fanaticism. As a pioneer he has opened new paths, but where they will lead has not yet been completely answered.

One of the results of Schoenberg's experiments before 1920 was the new conception of tonality which occupied the period between 1920 and 1930, and has influenced all the elements of music: melody, harmony, form, instrumentation, and rhythm itself. Many different currents are being developed simultaneously, and evolution in music has never traveled so fast. *Simplification* is the watchword, and while Schoenberg has not seemed to simplify music, the younger men may find their way along the paths he has opened by means of his revolutionary ideas.

Among Austrian composers whose training was received from Schoenberg were Alban Berg (1885-1935), Anton Webern (1883-1945), Egon Wellesz (1885), Paul Pisk (1893), and Karl Horwitz (1884-1925). Berg and Webern are the most important of Schoenberg's disciples. Berg was the link between the postromanticism of Vienna and the new departure as developed by Schoenberg, his master. Berg showed the influence of Wagner and of Bruckner, but to a greater extent of Gustav Mahler. Impressionism, too, had its hand in the first phase of his development. When he came in touch with Schoenberg in 1904, the association brought to maturity his unique and unusual talent.

Berg was a slow worker and his compositions are numerically few. He laid stress on form, and his strong romantic bent, which shows in a definite lyricism, is not lost in his employment of atonal methods. He came before the public through his opera *Wozzeck* (page 297), although he had already written Seven Early Songs (1907) and the Piano Sonata, op. 1 (1908). A string quartet, op. 3, is the first work to pave the way for emancipation from traditional tonality. This freedom is found in Three Orchestral Pieces, op. 6, his first composition for large orchestra, and the form is that of a suite. To this period belong Four Pieces for Clarinet and Piano, and Five Songs with Orchestral Accompaniment (after postcard texts by Peter Altenberg). Following *Wozzeck,* he wrote a chamber concerto for violin, piano, and thirteen woodwinds (1925) on the occasion of Schoenberg's fiftieth birthday. The first theme is constructed from letters in the names of Schoenberg, Webern, and Berg that appear in the musical alphabet. One of Berg's finest and most expressive works is the Lyric Suite (1926) for string quartet in six movements. The concert aria, *"Der Wein" (Wine),* on texts from Baudelaire translated into German by Stefan George, is in twelve tone technic used more strictly than it was in the Lyric Suite.

At the time of his death, Berg was completing his opera *Lulu,* the text from two plays by Frank Wedekind. While it has never been performed in this country, a group of symphonic pieces from the opera, arranged by the composer, were presented here by Serge Koussevitzky (page 298). Berg did not hesitate to break away from the twelve tone technic when he saw fit. The theme of the variations in the *Lulu* suite is a street song, for example, and in his last great contribution to music, the violin concerto written for an American violinist, Louis Krasner, he brings in a folk song and a Bach chorale.

The violin concerto was inspired as a memorial to a young friend, Manon Gropius, the daughter of Mahler's widow, Alma Werfel. The composing of this concerto brings to mind Mozart and the Requiem, for the twentieth century Austrian survived this work only by a few months, and it became a memorial to himself.

Anton von Webern's compositions are of an intimate chamber-music type in which he followed Schoenberg's precepts. He condensed form and intensity of expression into works of miniature length. He used the twelve tone series, as Berg did. His works include a passacaglia, op. 1, which is an exception to his usual concentrated style; Five Movements for string quartet, op. 5; Six Pieces for orchestra, op. 6; songs; a string trio, and a chamber symphony, op. 12, written for the League of Composers.

Other works include Bagatelles for String Quartet, op. 9; Orchestral Pieces, op. 10; Cello Pieces, op. 11; *Klavierlieder,* op. 12, which are an attempt at simplicity and show expressive power; Chamber Songs, op. 14, settings of poems by Trakl. These were followed by a group of religious work to Latin texts which include Five Sacred Songs for voice and five solo instruments, op. 15; and two vocal cycles: Three Songs for voice, E flat clarinet and guitar, op. 18, and Two Choruses with chamber music accompaniment to Goethe texts. In these last, Webern approached twelve tone technic. In an article, "Berg and Webern—Schoenberg's Heirs" in *Modern Music* (Jan.-Feb. 1931), Theodor Wiesengrund-Adorno wrote of Webern: "The composer . . . faces the problem of preserving his own freed style—that dispenses with any superficiality of composition, recognizes no sequence, and especially no rhythmic repetition—against the demands of the twelve-tone technic. . . . He has filled out the gap between the independent and the twelve-tone method of procedure which Schoenberg's dialectic creates."

Webern returned to a work in large dimensions with a two-movement string trio, op. 20, which Wiesengrund-Adorno calls "one of the mas-

terpieces of modern music, a counterpart in many respects to Berg's
Lyric Suite."

Webern was interested, as were also Erwin Stein and Paul Pisk, in
symphony concerts for the workingman, which he conducted before
the Nazi regime. He also conducted an amateur choral society, performing, among other works, Mahler and Schoenberg choral compositions.

With communications again established with Vienna, we learn of
the tragic death of Webern in September 1945, as the result of a shot
fired while he was standing at the door of his son-in-law's home near
Salzburg. He was working on his first long composition, an oratorio.
He had just been made president of the newly revived Austrian section
of the I.S.C.M. (International Society for Contemporary Music). His
death is regarded as a great loss to the rebuilding of music in Vienna.

Paul Pisk, pianist, composer, and conductor, is now an American
citizen, who teaches in a Southern California college.

Egon Wellesz is a recognized authority on Byzantine music. He is
the author of a two-volume work, *The New Instrumentation,* and his
compositions have been devoted to opera and ballet, with his interests
centered on Greek subjects. World War II caused him to leave Vienna
and to establish himself in England.

At the time that Arnold Schoenberg was developing his twelve tone
technic in Vienna, another Viennese, Josef Matthias Hauer (1883) was
also working on the problem of utilizing the chromatic scale as a basis
for atonal music. There is, however, little relationship between the
working out of Schoenberg's "tone-row" and Hauer's "tropes." Hauer
derived his system from Goethe's *Farbenlehre* (Method of Colors),
the *International Cyclopedia of Music and Musicians* tells us. He
divides the chromatic scale into two groups of six tones in forty-four
different arrangements called *tropes.* Dr. Karl Eschman in his valuable
book, *Changing Forms in Modern Music,* goes into a detailed analysis
of the workings of Hauer's system. Hauer has written many compositions using the tropes in four different styles, which Eschman states as:
"Simple twelve-note melody and homophonic accompaniment; notes
sustained, suggesting a first step toward counterpoint; polyphonic
style; and static tropes (divided in vertical planes)," called by Hauer,
"obstinate" counterpoint, "because the voices are independently minded,

angular or 'linear.' " This type is the closest to Schoenberg's use of the series.

In the spring 1946 issue of *Modern Music,* Alfred Schlee writes from Vienna, Hauer's "development has been in a straight line and he has built his system with uncompromising consistency. His method of arranging the twelve tones, fundamentally different from the composition technique of Webern and Schoenberg, involves a deliberate turning away from purely musical ideas. Hauer denies the existence of an 'art.' He classes the discovery of the twelve-tone series with the discovery of the orbits of the stars. . . . In recent years he has composed pieces with twenty-four tones. These are examples of his final system which, according to what he has written, may be expanded at will. The twelve-tone series becomes an intellectual game, which Hauer is convinced will at some future date assume the role that chess has today. With his white Vandyke he looks like a Don Quixote, and when he talks the fire of genius shines in his eyes."

CHAPTER 16

POLYTONAL AND ATONAL RAMIFICATIONS:
NEOCLASSICISM, MILHAUD, HONEGGER, BARTOK, SPANIARDS, POLES, ETC.

POLYTONALITY is just what the term implies—many tonalities—that is, the simultaneous use of different tonalities (page 210). When only two keys are heard, it is frequently called *bitonal.* Another variant is *polymelodic,* which implies several melodies woven together either dissonantly or consonantly. The term *poly-harmony* has been explained (page 193) as the juxtaposition of two or more chords. These may be the combination of dissonant keys or closely related keys. By an analysis of the natural harmonic series (page 100) many polychordal combinations may be explained:

As the study of a polychordal system is new, it is still very much in the experimental stage. Henry Cowell suggests combining three triads fifths apart, as C, G, and F played simultaneously; thirds apart, C, E, and A; then seconds apart, C, D, and B. Using both major and minor chords, this would give a wide variety of polychords without including chromatic steps.

Darius Milhaud, in an article in *La Revue musicale* ("*Polytonalité et Atonalité,*" February 1923) gives a very simple recipe of taking the chord of C major and superposing each of the eleven other major triads. Every chord can be expressed in four different ways:

> major + major (c e g + d f♯ a)
> minor + major (c e♭ g + d f♯ a)
> major + minor (c e g + d f a)
> minor + minor (c e♭ g + d f a)

231

And this repeated on eleven different chromatic steps, and the
chords written in inversions. With three keys, this would produce
fifty-five combinations.

A truly lovely example of music composed on this basis is Debussy's
"Brouillards," the first *prélude* in the second book, published in 1913.
The sixth and seventh measures show his system:

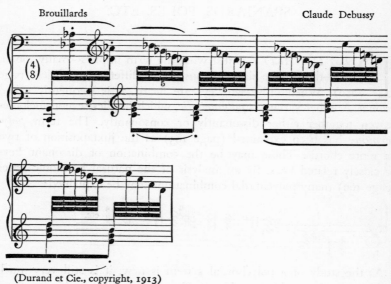

(Durand et Cie., copyright, 1913)

And here is another bitonal passage:

(Durand et Cie., copyright, 1913)

The following passage from Ravel's *Valses nobles et sentimentales,* no. 7, shows that the idea of bitonality was in the air in 1911, waiting to be picked up by Darius Milhaud and colleagues of his decade. Here the prevailing tonalities are F major in the left hand and E major in the right:

Valses Nobles et Sentimentales   Maurice Ravel

(Durand et Cie., copyright, 1911)

This is not only bitonal (and in the fourth and eighth measures, tritonal), but it is also birhythmic, the right hand playing 6/8 meter against the three quarter notes of the left.

René Lenormand analyzes this passage in his *Study of Modern Harmony* as an example of unresolved appoggiaturas, and bases the whole thing on the chord f-a-c-d (F major with sixth added). This is doubtless one explanation, but in view of later developments, it is more logical to think of it bitonally.

Many theorists contend that there is no such thing as a new harmonic system, and they explain every modern combination through the old laws by countless alterations, appoggiaturas, foreign tones, etc. But why not take the short cut? Why put new wine into old bottles?

In Alfredo Casella's *Onze pièces enfantines* (Eleven Pieces for Children) he makes rather obvious use of bitonality in the *Preludio:*

Preludio   Alfredo Casella

etc.

(Universal Edition, copyright, 1921)

It looks as though the composer had forgotten to indicate sharps for the left hand!

Polytonality is distinctly a French product; in fact, Milhaud is often regarded as its inventor. This is hardly the case, as it reared its head before the advent of Milhaud. He, however, established its usage and stamped it with his personality, just as we connect atonality with Schoenberg.

Milhaud stated in the article in *La Revue musicale* that a little two-voiced canon by Bach, which he quoted, presents the idea of bitonality. If the two parts were read separately one is in D minor and the other in A minor. This of course is something of what the French would call *une blague,* as the parts are planned to sound consonant when played together. Still, by misapplying the rules of seventeenth and eighteenth century counterpoint a new system might be evolved.

Milhaud also quotes a bagatelle by Béla Bartók which is much more to the point. The violin part is written with the signature of four sharps and is in the key of C sharp minor, and the cello part is in four flats and is in F minor. Serge Prokofieff wrote *"Sarcasmes"* with different key signatures in the two staves.

Erik Satie (1866-1926) was as much an instigator of polytonal effect as Milhaud. He used it in his compositions, which might be designated as musical cartoons. The world at large never knew whether Satie was laughing at or with them. But he was called the "father of humor in modern music," and he helped to form a musical creed among the younger composers, the *Group of Six*—Honegger, Milhaud,

Poulenc, Auric, Germaine Tailleferre, and Durey—and a still younger group of four, L'Ecole d'Arceuil, named after the place where Satie lived. These included Sauguet, Cliquet-Pleyel, Jacob, and Delvincourt. The American composer Virgil Thomson is an ardent Satie disciple.

Satie was a friend of Sâr Peladan, the founder of a mystical order of painters, La Rose-Croix, for which he wrote incidental music to a drama by Peladan. In this, *"Le Fils des étoiles"* (The Son of the Stars), he has anticipated the general employment of chords in fourths and polyharmony by such chords as these, picked at random from the score:

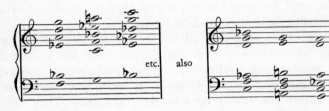

At forty he became a student at the Schola Cantorum, and after that he seemed to bend all his efforts in the direction of humor in music. One suspects that behind the humorous titles of his pieces there lurks the intention of breaking down a phase of sentimentality which he found in impressionism and the imitators of Debussy, and of wanting to rid music of the incubus of scholasticism. Some of the titles were *"Pièces en forme de poire"* (*poire*—pear—in French is an equivalent of our slang term "lemon!"), *"Veritables préludes flasques"* (composed for a dog!), *"Croquis et agaceries d'un gros Bonhomme de bois"* (Sketches and Annoyances of a Wooden Man), *"Aperçus désagréables"* (the disagreeable impressions being Pastoral, Choral, Fugue!), etc.

He and Jean Cocteau were friends, and at Cocteau's instigation he wrote the ballets *Parade* and *Mercure*. André Coeuroy says that Satie brought "the music-hall spirit" and American jazz into modern society. "For Satie the esthetic of the music-hall became a tyranny without results. For the young musicians, it was a powerful reaction which they understood must be used but not abused. The usage which the best of them have made of the idea up to now proves its excellence and the intelligence of putting it to work." (*Panorama de la musique contemporaine.*)

Satie's most serious composition, *Socrate,* is a symphonic drama with voice adapted for the stage from the dialogues of Plato.

After World War I the type of impressionistic music which had been the vogue in Paris no longer satisfied the musicians of a tragedy-drenched country. The revolt against Debussy did not last, for, after all, had he not opened their eyes to many new possibilities in music, possibilities they had not yet had the chance to try out? But their instinct to find their own way and to try experiments on their own account led to new developments in French music. Besides which, Stravinsky had come to Paris with Diaghileff. So music expressed the need for strong colors, strong rhythms, violent contrasts, brutal dissonance, caricature, and no sentiment.

The Group of Six were not affiliated by any common ideal or aim. They were not a school as were the Russian Five, but it happened that they were young, enthusiastic, gifted, and radical; interested, at the instigation of Satie and Cocteau, in breaking down the reign of impressionism and setting up a musical democracy. They did not remain together long; in fact, they hardly functioned as a group. Each of them wrote part of a ballet to a scenario by Jean Cocteau, called *Les Mariés de la Tour Eiffel* (*The Couples at the Eiffel Tower*). The outstanding talents of the group were Arthur Honegger (1892) and Darius Milhaud (1892). Francis Poulenc (1899) and Georges Auric (1899) remained more closely associated, writing somewhat in the same light style and producing works of charm rather than of importance, reflecting the Satie influence. Auric wrote some popular music. Mlle. Tailleferre wrote a charming impressionistic ballet, *Marchand d'oiseaux* (*The Bird Merchant*), pieces for two pianos, *"Jeux de plein-air"* (Outdoor Games), which she has orchestrated, chamber music, and a piano concerto. During World War II she came to America. Louis Durey dropped out of the picture.

Darius Milhaud writes with tremendous facility and has tried many branches of composition: theater, orchestra, chamber music, piano, and song. His first work was a lyric opera on a text by Francis Jammes, *La Brebis égarée* (*The Lost Sheep*), which shows the earmarks of impressionism. He has written a number of stage works on texts by Jean Cocteau and Paul Claudel, including *Le Boeuf sur le Toit* (*The "Nothing Doing" Bar,* the name of a famous Paris restaurant), *L'Homme et son désir* (*Man and His Desire*), *Protée* (*Proteus*), an

Orestes trilogy, *Les Malheurs d'Orphée* (*The Sorrows of Orpheus*), *Le pauvre matelot* (*The Poor Sailor*), and *Christophe Colomb,* his most pretentious opera (page 304).

As a young man he was an attaché in the French legation at Rio Janeiro. In a set of piano pieces, *Saudades do Brasil* (*Souvenirs of Brazil*), he combined experiments in polytonality with the South American rhythms, which fascinated him.

In the following measures from "Corcovado" we find the tango rhythm and the keys of D major (right hand) and G major (left hand):

VII—Corcovado from Saudades do Brazil   Darius Milhaud

(Editions Max Eschig, copyright, 1922)

The polytonal combinations change rapidly, thus creating variety of tonal color.

"Tijuca" opens with the combined tonalities of A major and A minor, and the harmonizing chord is built in fifths:

VIII—Tijuca   Darius Milhaud

(Editions Max Eschig, copyright, 1922)

"Sumare" is harmonized in the right hand in chords in fourths. The left hand (also a chord in fourths) is an example of a mannerism frequently used by polytonalists, an ostinato (or continuous) rhythmic figure over which the composer weaves dissonant harmonies:

IX—Sumare   Darius Milhaud

a. *Léger*

(Editions Max Eschig, copyright, 1922)

Measures 24-43 show Milhaud's use of polychords rather than poly-tonality, as in the following (measures 28 to 31):

(Editions Max Eschig, copyright, 1922)

"Laranjeiras" uses chords harmonized in fifths instead of fourths, another modern form of chord building:

XI—Laranjeiras   Darius Milhaud
Alerte

(Editions Max Eschig, copyright, 1922)

In a work for two pianos, "Sun Splendor," I have used chords in fourths and in fifths:

Sun Splendor   Marion Bauer, op. 19

When two or three melodies in different keys and rhythms travel independently side by side, Milhaud admits that these polytonal means result in atonal effect.

It was a logical step from the dance rhythms of South America to jazz—and Milhaud was an easy convert. The beginning of the jazz phase was *Le Boeuf sur le Toit,* a cinema-symphony on South American airs which aroused a storm of criticism. Because of its aggressive dissonance, jazz and tango rhythms, the vulgarity of some of the melodies, and its daring novelty, Milhaud was called an impostor and a sensationalist. He wanted to write one long work using the rhythmic, melodic, and instrumental elements of jazz, and *La Création du monde (The Creation of the World)* resulted. This Negro ballet on a sketch by Blaise Cendrars, written in 1923, a year before Gershwin's "Rhapsody in Blue," was produced by the Swedish Ballet in Europe and America. It is a curious combination of Bach and jazz, a form of *plaisantrie* in which Stravinsky also indulged (page 317). "Jazz, after that, never interested me at all," Milhaud said, "but from it a rhythmic freedom remained."

In spite of polytonality, the extreme dissonance of which has been much softened in the later phase of his development, Milhaud shows a definite lyricism, and a strongly romantic strain which leans more and more to a neoromanticism. This typically French love of melody shows in some of his fourteen string quartets, many of his songs, including *Les Poèmes juifs* (*The Jewish poems*), *Le Voyage d'été* (*The Summer Journey*), a group of songs composed in 1939; the *Album of Mme. Bovary,* piano pieces from his music for the film, *Mme. Bovary,* and a group of piano pieces, *The Household Muse* (*La Muse ménagère,* 1945).

Like Schoenberg and Stravinsky, Darius Milhaud makes his home in California, but he is in the San Francisco region, and has been teaching composition at Mills College, Oakland. He arrived in this country in July 1940, bringing with him the symphony in four movements commissioned by Frederick Stock for the fiftieth anniversary of the Chicago Symphony Orchestra. It was composed in the midst of tragic and difficult events. His *"Cortège funèbre"* (Funeral Cortege) was written in May 1940, and it expresses according to Milhaud, "the feelings we all had in France at this terrible period."

Other recent works include a violin concerto; a *Concertino de printemps* (Spring Concertino) for violin, viola, and cello; *La Fantaisie pastorale* (Pastoral Fantasy) for piano and orchestra; *La Suite provençale,* on popular folk airs of the eighteenth century; and *Suite française,* written for band and first played in 1945. Milhaud wrote it with high school bands in mind. He said that the youth of the nation "need music of their time, not too difficult to perform, but, nevertheless keeping the characteristic idiom of the composer." He made an orchestral arrangement of the suite, the five parts of which are named after French provinces, "the very ones in which the American and Allied armies fought together with the French underground for the liberation of my country," he said: "Normandy, Brittany, Ile-de-France (of which Paris is the center), Alsace-Lorraine, and Provence." He used some folk tunes of these provinces.

Arthur Honegger created a sensation with several of his scores, such as *Le Roi David* (*King David*) and "Pacific 231," and his opera *Judith.* He and Milhaud were friends and colleagues at the Paris Conservatory and although he was one of the Group of Six, he never subscribed to the aesthetics which Cocteau tried to outline for *les nouveaux Jeunes* (the new Youth) as Erik Satie called them. He himself explained that the name was applied by Henri Collet, critic of the *Comoedia,* who went to Milhaud's home to make the acquaintance of the young musicians. There he met the six, and in an article he prematurely compared them to the Russian Five. This was in 1919. A year later Honegger stated his aesthetic principles to Paul Landormy, critic of *La Victoire,* in these words: "I attach great importance to musical architecture, which I should never want to see sacrificed for reasons of a literary or pictorial order. My model is Bach. . . . I do not seek, as do certain anti-impressionists, the return to harmonic simplicity. I find on the contrary that we should use the harmonic materials created by the school which preceded us, but in a different way—as the base of lines and rhythms." (Translated from a pamphlet on Honegger by the gifted French critic and composer Roland-Manuel.)

His works prove his statements. His early essays in chamber music show a mastery of polyphonic technic. Of a string quartet and five sonatas, the best is the one for cello and piano. His dramatic psalm, *Le Roi David,* served to prove how far he was from agreeing with Cocteau's manifesto of the aims of *Les Six* published in *Le Coq et l'Arlequin.*

Honegger is at his best in dramatic work where he handles a large canvas—orchestra, chorus, and soloists. He was given a commission by the theater at Mézières in Switzerland, to write incidental music for a poem by René Morax which was to be staged. It represented David as shepherd, captain, chieftain, king, and, finally, prophet. In less than two months Honegger composed twenty-eight canticles, psalms, songs, cortèges, marches, fanfares, and the dance before the Ark of the Covenant. He caught the barbaric spirit of the oriental tribes of Israel in a remarkable fashion, and his work, *Le Roi David,* afterwards remodeled into an oratorio with a narrator telling the story, remains one of the foremost examples of French art after Debussy. *Judith* was first written as incidental music to a work by Morax and afterwards turned into an opera. While the role of Judith is important, about two-thirds of the score is devoted to choruses, in which Honegger again showed his mastery in writing on a Biblical subject in choral style.

Roland-Manuel finds that the mimed symphony *Horace Victorieux* is more characteristic of the personality of the composer. It "marks the complete emancipation of Honegger's talent. With this athletic symphony, our musician becomes plainly conscious of his power. We see his distinct reactions to the methods of writing which the imitators of Stravinsky have brought into fashion."

For orchestra, Honegger is best known by his entertaining "Pacific 231," in which he celebrates his love from boyhood for the power and perfection of the locomotive. Incidentally, it is descriptive realism, but it also shows an extraordinary talent for orchestration, rhythmic design, and the gradual building of an overpowering climax. It is a better composition than the orchestral work "Rugby."

In the concertino for piano and orchestra he approaches more nearly the dictates of neoclassicism, and here, too, in the finale he pays his respects to jazz.

In 1939 Honegger completed a dramatic legend, *Nicolas de Flue,* for the National Swiss Exposition, but the war prevented its performance as a popular and patriotic *Festspiel.* The text is by Denis de Rougemont, based on the career of a Swiss hero of the fifteenth century. The music is simple, for the most part, and popular in character. Honegger shows his usual skill in writing for chorus. In 1941 he wrote a symphony for strings which won high praise at the first postwar international music festival, "Spring 1946 in Prague."

In 1947, when he visited New York, Charles Münch, the French conductor, performed a new symphony by Honegger. It created a profound impression.

Another work, *Jeanne d'Arc au bucher (Joan of Arc at the Stake)* on a text by Paul Claudel, was dedicated to Ida Rubinstein who spoke the leading rôle in prewar performances. There are both speaking parts and singing rôles, a mixed adult chorus and a children's chorus, and orchestra. Honegger composed a cantata, *Libération de Paris,* text by Bernard Zimmer, which had a performance when the French capital was freed.

A musical tragedy by Honegger on a text by Jean Cocteau, *Antigone,* (1924-27) was one of the first operas to be given at the Paris Opéra after the liberation. Honegger is at present professor of composition at the Ecole Normale de Musique in Paris.

"Honegger is a thorough workman with an immense technic, an admirable sense for form and a musical nature," we say in *Music through the Ages.* "He is temperamentally drawn to Schoenberg rather than to Stravinsky, whom he regards as an extremist and therefore a dangerous influence. He disapproves of the various attempts to go back to Gounod, Rossini, Liszt, but he admits that two Cantatas by Bach, which he heard when he was fourteen years old, drove him 'back to Bach' and decided him to become a composer."

Among Honegger's earlier pupils were Marcel Delannoy and Jean Rivier. They did not copy his composing methods, but got from him a large conception of musical architecture.

Jacques Ibert (1890) wrote an orchestral suite, *"Escales,"* which is frequently programmed. He is well known for his piano piece *"Le petit âne blanc"* (The Little White Donkey) although he has more important compositions, including songs, chamber music, and stage works. He was director of the French Academy in Rome and was named in 1945 as a possible director of the Opéra.

Henri Sauguet (1901) wrote an opera, *Chartreuse de Parme,* which was played at the Paris Opéra in 1939. "His music showed rare and attractive qualities," says Auric. "Without once trying to shock or surprise, these amiable compositions, delicate, and of a keen and ingenious wit, happily carried on in one of the better veins of our national art." In 1944 Sauguet's opera *La Gageure imprévue* (*The Improvised Wager*) was an immediate success.

Olivier Messiaen (1908), a pupil of Paul Dukas and an organist, seems to be the "white hope" of French music. His is a serious talent, mystic and religious in character. One of the works, *Les Visions de l'Amen* (Visions of the Amen, 1943), is a distinct enrichment of two-piano literature. It is a sevenfold amen: Amen of the Creation, "Let there be light, And there was light"; Amen of the stars, of the planet Saturn; Amen of the Agony of Jesus; Amen of Desire; Amen of the angels, of the saints, of the songs of birds; Amen of the Judgment; Amen of the Consummation. He began to compose at the age of seven. He became organist at La Trinité in 1939, and in 1936 he helped to found the group *Jeune France.* With him were André Jolivet, Daniel Lesur, and Yves Baudrier.

Messiaen's purpose, thinks John Cage, "is to express lofty sentiments in the most direct manner possible, rather than to evoke in any way the 'classical' tradition of music." In an article, "The East in the West," in *Modern Music,* Spring 1946, Mr. Cage writes that Messiaen's music, "like a changeable silk, shows now aspects of the Orient, now of the medieval world, and now of twentieth-century impressionism." Mr. Cage finds an emphasis on harmony in his music that is "not medieval nor Oriental but baroque. Messiaen's use of inverted scales and rhythmic structures and his nonthematic procedure (the medieval subject or ground, expressed either melodically or rhythmically, being used instead) account for the congruity between his music and its avowedly spiritual program."

He has written a book, *Technique de mon langage musical* (*The Technic of My Musical Language,* 1944), in which he shows that his inspiration comes from Gregorian chant, from Hindu music, particularly its rhythm, from Debussy's *Pelléas et Mélisande,* and from the songs of birds! He quotes Dukas as having counseled, "Listen to the birds, they are the great master!" He also classifies Debussy's chords with the added notes, and a list of chord progressions chosen at random and which seem to have no end.

Koussevitzky performed Messiaen's symphonic poem *"Les Offrandes oubliées"* (Forgotten Offerings). Among his recent works are *"Les Corps glorieux"* (Glorious Bodies, 1939) for organ, *"Quatuor pour la fin du temps"* (Quartet for the End of Time) for violin, clarinet, cello, and piano (1940-41, at which time he was a prisoner of war), *Trois petites liturgies de la Présence Divine* (*Three Little Liturgies of the Divine Presence*) for choir of women's voices, celesta, vibraphone, Martinot waves (*onde,* an instrument not unlike the theremin), piano, battery, and string orchestra (1944), and *Vingt regards sur l'Enfant Jésus* (*Twenty Glimpses of the Infant Jesus,* 1944) for piano.

Another pupil of Paul Dukas and of Louis Aubert, Henry Barraud (1900) was introduced as a composer by Pierre Monteux. Barraud is a conductor and critic also. In 1939 he finished composing his piano concerto on the very day that he was called out as a reserve lieutenant. Later he escaped from the Germans and reached the "free zone" of France. Finally he joined the resistance in Paris and worked secretly for the liberation of the French National Radio. Several of his works are a testimony of this tragic period. The piano concerto unconsciously echoes the period between "Munich" and the beginning of the war in the tension and violence of its style. *"L'Offrande à une ombre"* (Offering to a Spirit) is in memory of a friend and fellow composer, Maurice Jaubert, killed by the Germans in 1940. *Le Mystère des saints innocents* (*The Mystery of the Innocent Saints*) is an oratorio on a text by Péguy, dedicated to the memory of his brother, hero of the

Free French movement, shot by the Gestapo in 1944. And *Le Diable à la kermesse* (*The Devil at the Kermis*), a ballet written during the occupation, is "a kind of reaction against the sorrows and trials of the period."

NEOCLASSICISM covers a multitude of styles. To include under that head the trivialities and mannered works of Poulenc and Auric, the later Stravinsky compositions, Schoenberg's abstractions, Prokofieff's Classical Symphony, Bartók's work, which was influenced by his folk music research, Hindemith's masterly counterpoint, Casella's manufacture, and the artificial style of many who should be romanticists, shows the elasticity of the term. And yet, generalizations may be made which fit most types of neoclassicism. Classicism was characterized by a tonal center, a chord, a scale, a mode; romanticism indulged in tonality plus modulation; the characteristic progressions of postromanticism (Wagner) were chromatic; the next step was the polytonal and atonal combination of neoclassicism. Romanticism broke up the long line and developed movements of the sonata into shorter forms and four-measure phrases; neoclassicism has reduced form to the development of one- or two-measure patterns often based on rhythmic design. Almost all neoclassicists believe that they are simplifying music. Many of the compositions seem like ephemeral experiments, trivial in content and in effect. But there is no denying the fact that the psychology of the age has produced its own music.

In 1927 Stravinsky wrote in *The Gamut,* "There is much talk nowadays of a reversion to classicism, and works believed to have been composed under the influence of so-called classical models are labeled neoclassic.

"It is difficult for me to say whether this classification is correct or not.... I fear that the bulk of the public, and also the critics, are content with recording superficial impressions created by the use of certain technical devices which were current in so-called classical music.

"The use of such devices is insufficient to constitute the real neoclassicism, for classicism itself was characterized, not in the least by its technical processes, which, then as now, were themselves subject to modification from period to period, but rather by its constructive values.

"...If those who label as neoclassic the works belonging to the latest tendency in music mean by that label that they detect in them a wholesome return to the formal idea, the only basis of music, well and good. But I should like to know, in each particular instance, whether they are not mistaken."

Béla Bartók was one of the most innovational composers of the twentieth century. He used his discoveries in Hungarian peasant music as the basis on which to build a forceful, elemental idiom. His harmonies, although original and dissonant, are based on ancient modes and a Magyar pentatonic scale, and he worked with utmost economy of means. Hugo Leichtentritt in *Modern Music* (March-April 1929) said that to understand Bartók's music better, "we must realize that it is his purpose to revivify the already exhausted, over-refined, music of Europe with a transfusion of new blood from the peasant music of Hungary...."

Bartók's earliest preoccupation was with the pseudo-Hungarian style of Liszt. Brahms, Strauss, and even Debussy were influences. In 1905 he began his own researches in the folk music of Hungary. He uncovered Slovakian, Hungarian, and Rumanian folk songs, spending forty years in scientific research. He made studies also of North African Arab, Turkish, Serbian, and Bulgarian folk songs.

After his death in 1945 a fellow countryman, Otto Gombosi, wrote in the *Musical Quarterly*, January 1946, "His [Bartók's] long preoccupation with folksongs shows a double aspect. On the one hand, he created a harmonic idiom, a new musical language, out of the intrinsic qualities and possibilities of the folksong. On the other, his melodic world became saturated with the style of folksong, its basic elements and forms. Gradually a new style developed that was highly personal while at the same time unromantic in its collective background. Bartók's folksong arrangements are his acknowledgment of his indebtedness to Nature for freeing his wings and, at the same time, the composer's workshop, in which every step of his stylistic development was planned, tried, and carried out."

The fact that this folk music differed fundamentally from that of western Europe was the main source of the individuality of Bartók's style. "The surprising eruption of the primacy of melody, the constructive use of elemental rhythmic forces, the utmost expansion of the concept of tonality, and last but not least the uninhibited power of emotion and the intensity of vision are Bartók's main contributions to new music," Dr. Gombosi writes.

Bartók has a long list of compositions, including many for piano, voice, orchestra, and chamber music. The early period closed with "Allegro Barbaro" for piano and the one-act opera *Prince Bluebeard's Castle* (1911). Two sonatas for violin and piano, piano concertos, rhapsodies, and many folk song arrangements fill in the second period. His six string quartets (from 1907 to 1940) are an important contribution to modern chamber music. His collection of pieces for piano, *Mikrokosmos* (1926-37) represents a unique addition to the teaching repertory in modern vein, a twentieth century *gradus ad Parnassum*, it has been called.

There are few records in music history comparable to that of Bartók's closing years. He came to America in 1940 as an exile through his own volition. He was sick, penniless, and broken in spirit, and yet in this last period some of his greatest composing was achieved, like an apotheosis of his life's work. In 1937 he composed a sonata for two pianos and percussion which he and his wife, Ditta Pasztory, played. A concerto for violin and orchestra and a concerto for two pianos and orchestra followed in quick succession. He also wrote for Benny Goodman "Contrasts" for violin, clarinet, and piano (1938), in which the American idiom is reflected. In 1939 he wrote a divertimento for string orchestra; the Sixth String Quartet dates from 1940; in 1943 he wrote a sonata for solo violin and a concerto for orchestra; and in 1945 a concerto for viola and orchestra. The concerto for orchestra was commissioned by the Koussevitzky Music Foundation in memory of Natalie Koussevitzky. Bartók described the work as "symphony-like" but stated that he had treated the single instruments or instrumental groups in a *concertant* or soloistic manner resembling the form of the concerto grosso. The work is neoclassic in effect in spite of the folk song influence in the treatment of the melodic line and the harmony.

Zoltan Kodaly is not as ultramodern as Bartók, although he has used ultramodern means. I quoted a few measures from Kodaly's "Epitaph," op. II (page 140) as an example of the modern use of organum. The same theme appears harmonized in chords in fourths in the right hand and chords of the seventh in the left which still flavor of "impressionistic methods." *

* With permission of the original editor, Universal Edition A.G., Vienna.

Épitaphe   Zoltan Kodaly, op. 11, No. 4

(Universal-Edition, copyright, 1921)

The pupils of Bartók and Kodaly include a number of talented Hungarians, such as Georg Kosa, Ladislau Lajtha, Alexander Jemnitz, Imre Weisshaus, Tibor Harsanyi in Paris, and Tibor Serly in America.

Among neoclassic works of interest is Manuel de Falla's Harpsichord Concerto, composed in 1926 for Wanda Landowska. It finds its sources in religious and popular Spanish music of the sixteenth and seventeenth centuries, and it has been defined as "an effort of rhythmic-tonal modernity." News from Argentina stated that Falla had finished the oratorio *Atlantis* just before his death (1946). The extensive work was begun many years ago in Spain. Friends from Argentina said that only about two-thirds of the orchestration was complete, however. It is to be hoped that enough indications were left for someone else to carry on the work of finishing it.

The civil war from 1936 to 1939 changed the face of Spanish music. The composers of the younger group were encouraged by the newly developed interest which had come into being in the twenties and thirties. The twentieth century composers studied at home and found a welcome for their new scores. Whether the composers who were driven into exile will ever again become a part of the Spanish scene is doubtful. But wherever they are, they are carrying on the ideals of the Spain from which they stemmed.

One of the most gifted of the younger school was Ernesto Halffter (1905), a pupil of Falla, who had his first compositions, Two Symphonic Sketches, played in public when he was only eighteen. His Sinfonietta in D won a national prize in 1925. It is neoclassic with considerable use of polytonality. In 1928 La Argentina, the famous dancer, produced in Paris, Halffter's one-act ballet, *Sonatina,* on a poem by that name. He has written a string quartet, a sonatina-fantasia for string quartet, three sonatas for piano, the Portuguese Rhapsody for piano and orchestra (1939), songs, and a four-act opera, *La Muerte de Carmen* (*The Death of Carmen*). He held the post of director of the National Conservatory of Seville from 1934 to 1936, when the civil war interrupted all activities. He lives in Lisbon, Portugal.

An older brother, Rodolfo Halffter (1900), is also a talented composer. Gilbert Chase, in *The Music of Spain,* says that "he began by showing Schoenbergian tendencies and, while he subsequently veered toward greater tonal clarity, he has retained a mordant and ironic quality reminiscent of Stravinsky's middle period." * In 1939 he was obliged to leave Spain because of his association with the musical activities of the Second Republic. After its downfall he went to Mexico, with the musical life of which country he has become associated.

In 1930 the two brothers were part of a young Madrid group which included Salvador Bacarisse (1898), Julián Bautista (1901), Juan José Mantecon (1896), Gustavo Pittaluga (1906), Fernando Remarcha (1898), and Rosa García Ascot, who settled in Mexico. Pittaluga defined the point of view of his associates, according to Mr. Chase, as having as its most significant feature that "it did not discuss the problem of nationalism or folklorism, with which musicians of the previous generation had been so largely preoccupied. Instead, Pittaluga insisted upon the necessity of writing 'authentic' music in an entirely non-ethnical sense, that is, music whose worth is to be measured solely by its *musical* qualities, without admixture of any literary, philosophical, or metaphysical associations. For the rest, 'no Romanticism, no chromaticism, no divagations—and no chords of the diminished seventh!' " In other words—a clear manifesto of neoclassicism.

Pittaluga had a performance in 1930 of his ballet *La Roméría de los cornudos* (*Pilgrimage of the Cuckolds*). He has written a light opera *Zarzuela antigua, El Loro* (*The Parrot*), the Military Concerto for violin and orchestra (1933), a Little Suite for ten instruments

* By permission, from *The Music of Spain,* by Gilbert Chase. Copyright, 1941, by W. W. Norton & Co., Inc.

(1933), *Six Spanish Dances* for piano (1936), and *"Capriccio alla romantica"* for piano and orchestra (1936). During the civil war Pittaluga was in Washington (1937-39) on the staff of the Spanish Embassy.

Gustavo Durán (1906) was associated with the Madrid group, and he wrote a ballet, *El Fandango,* performed by La Argentina. His compositions were destroyed in 1939 because of his distinguished service as commander of the Republican Army. He is now living in New York.

Enrique Casal Chapí, who was a musical director of opera in Madrid, wrote songs on poems by Lope de Vega which, Mr. Chase says, "reveal a clear and elegant style, authentically Spanish in the classical sense." He is the grandson of Ruperto Chapí, a composer of many light operas. He said that he believed "in writing Spanish music that comes from *within,* not from the use of folkloristic accessories." After having sought refuge in France, he settled in Santo Domingo (1940), where he is conductor of the orchestra in Cíudad Trujillo. In 1942 he conducted an overture of his composing.

Gilbert Chase records as one of the most talented of the younger composers outside of the Madrid group, Joaquin Rodrigo (1902), who is blind. In 1923 he composed a symphonic sketch, *"Juglares,"* and won a national prize for *Five Children's Pieces* for orchestra. Another of his symphonic poems is *"Per la flor de lliri blau"* (By the Flower of the Blue Lily), the only one of his major works based on folk material.

Several of the older Spanish composers were interested in the problem of music based on regional folk music. One of these is Oscar Esplá (1886), who spent a few years in study with Max Reger in Germany. In 1931 he was made director of the Madrid Conservatory, but during the civil war he went to Brussels.

Joaquin Turina (1882) was a student of Vincent d'Indy in Paris, an influence which is distinctly marked in his early chamber music. On Albeniz's advice he turned his attention to Andalusian music. He was a critic and an important influence in the music of Spain. He is a composer of charm rather than of greatness.

Federico Mompou (1893), although a Barcelonian by birth, has spent most of his adult years in Paris. He has written many piano pieces and songs in a style which he calls *primitivista,* the characteristics of which are an absence of bar lines, key signatures, and cadences.

The name of Conrado del Campo (1879), although not known outside of Spain, is found as teacher of many of the younger men. He has written seven string quartets and many large orchestral works, definitely romantic in character and Spanish in sentiment and flavor.

Serge Prokofieff (1891), easily second in renown to Stravinsky among the Russians who made their careers outside of Russia, is the author of an early neoclassic work, the Classical Symphony (1917). It is claimed that his idea in writing it "was to catch the spirit of Mozart and to put down that which, if he were living now, Mozart might put into his scores." This statement gives rise to controversial feelings as to what Mozart might have written had he been living in 1917! The Classical Symphony, however, is a delightful introduction to neoclassicism and has an insouciance quite characteristic of its composer. Prokofieff has traveled somewhat the same path as Stravinsky, having written ballets for Diaghileff, including *Chout* (*Buffoon*), *Le Pas d'acier* (*The Age of Steel*), and *Le Fils prodigue* (*The Prodigal Son*); an opera for Chicago, *The Love of the Three Oranges;* and an early orchestral work, Scythian Suite, which has something of the barbaric fascination of his chorus *"Sept! Ils sont Sept!"* (Seven! They are Seven!) written in 1915, to cuneiform incantations excavated in Mesopotamia.

Prokofieff differs from Stravinsky in being a concert pianist, and many of his works reveal that fact, as for example his five piano concertos, of which the third and fifth are particularly characteristic of his style. The Fifth Concerto has five movements, none in sonata form, but the developments are all very concise, and, according to his own confession, this and all his works are founded on melodies. He keeps the melodies that come to him in a notebook and when he begins a work of major proportions he usually has accumulated enough themes for half a dozen symphonies. The effect is distinctly neoclassic. His rhythmic verve and sense of satire are obvious elements of his composing gifts.

After many years spent in Paris, the United States, and European musical centers, Prokofieff returned to his native land and since about 1935 he has been one of the leading composers of Soviet Russia (page 281).

A Polish composer, who lived in Paris and more recently in California, and has written in neoclassic style, is Alexandre Tansman (1897). He combines a refined and sensitive musicality with modern technic and the artistic trends of the French capital. He has written five symphonies, two piano concertos, three string quartets, songs, piano pieces, and a lyric drama.

Karol Rathaus, a Pole who studied in Germany, wrote an opera, and piano, orchestral, and chamber music, before he came to the United States, of which country he is now a citizen. He is professor of music at Queen's College, Flushing, N.Y.

Jerzy Fitelberg (1900), the gifted son of Gregor Fitelberg, violinist and once conductor of the Warsaw-Philharmonic, shows unusual talent in chamber music in neoclassic style. His name has been made known to the American public by a concerto for orchestra and a violin concerto. Both father and son have become American citizens.

Another foreigner who made his early career in Paris, following it with a brilliant success in America, is the Czechoslovak Bohuslav Martinu (1890). His works reached this country in 1932 via the Coolidge Festival, and the following year he won the Elizabeth Sprague Coolidge prize in chamber music. André Coeuroy said that he is "one of the most happily endowed musicians not only of Czechoslovakia but of all contemporary Europe." He shows neoclassic tastes with which he has blended a neoromanticism. After a short period as music teacher in high school and violinist in the Czech Philharmonic, he went to Paris in 1923, where he became a friend of Albert Roussel, who advised him musically. Martinu is practically self-taught in composition. His neoclassic tendencies are shown in his chamber music and in a concerto grosso, which was almost a war casualty. He lost a copy of it in Paris, but on his arrival in New York, he found that George Szell had rescued a copy in Prague. It has had many performances in America.

Martinu has been a most prolific composer, and in the amount of work he has completed during his American sojourn since 1941 are four symphonies, the first a commission from the Koussevitzky Music Foundation; a violin concerto commissioned and played by Mischa Elman; the Madrigal-Sonata played at a concert of the League of Composers; a beautiful musical tribute, "Memorial to Lidice"; a *Concerto da Camera;* a sonata for cello and piano; a piano quartet into which he integrated Czech melodic material; a collection of six songs;

a concerto for two pianos and orchestra written for Luboshutz and Nemenoff; and many other works. His output also includes piano music, operas, ballets, many early concertos and orchestral works, cantatas and songs. Martinu has been invited by Prague to return to his native country.

Jaromir Weinberger (1896) is known as the composer of the comic opera *Schwanda: Der Dudelsackpfeiffer*. He came to America in 1939, since which time he has written variations on the tune "Under the Spreading Chestnut Tree," the Bohemian Rhapsody, and a Lincoln Symphony.

CHAPTER 17

POLYTONAL AND ATONAL RAMIFICATIONS (cont.): DISSONANT COUNTERPOINT, *Gebrauchsmusik,* QUARTER TONES, ETHER MUSIC, HINDEMITH, ENGLISH COMPOSERS, SCHILLINGER, ETC.

DISSONANT counterpoint is a direct outcome of the "back to Bach" movement. It is the result of linear or horizontal writing in an atonal or polytonal system and is neoclassic in so far as it is an imitation of classic forms of canon, imitation, and fugue. "Dissonant counterpoint" explains its exact function better than *linear counterpoint,* which term is found in the newer text books. Horace Alden Miller defines it in his *New Harmonic Devices* as: "An adaptation of the old tonal counterpoint to the altered demands of the new 'supertonal' harmony. Melodic lines combined in unorthodox counterpoint with atonal relations." The addicts of dissonant counterpoint claim that Bach broadened the possibilities of counterpoint in his day by a freer use of intervals which had been forbidden in the day of *strict* counterpoint, so as the harmonic bars have been let down to admit all sorts of melodic "strays," the new polyphony has done the same. In place of major and minor thirds and sixths and perfect intervals (the basis of classic counterpoint), the modern writer of counterpoint makes up his tonal vocabulary arbitrarily of augmented or diminished intervals, seconds, and sevenths, in fact, everything and anything that Bach would heartily have disapproved of.

For example, Richard Donovan wrote his prelude to a Suite for Piano with apparently just such rules governing his counterpoint:

Prelude   Richard Donovan

New Music Review (1933)

And here is the opening theme of Ernest Krenek's Piano Piece, op. 39, no. 1, in which the polytonal scheme is evident, as well as linear design:

(with permission of the original editor,
    Universal-Edition A.G., Vienna, copyright, 1926)

Paul Hindemith (1895) was the most prominent German composer of the interwar period, and certainly one of the most talented of his generation. The bulk of his creative work marks him as a leading spirit in neoclassicism, and he has turned his talent to account in many channels. He played violin professionally at thirteen; earned his living in cafés, cinemas, dance halls, operetta theaters and jazz bands; at twenty he was concertmaster of the Frankfort Opera; he founded the Amar Quartet of which he was violist, and from which he resigned in 1930; and he taught composition at the Berlin Hochschule from 1927 to 1937. In 1934 his music was condemned as antagonistic to the spirit of Nazi Germany, although he himself met the Aryan requirements. He was invited by the Turkish government to become an official adviser in reorganizing its musical life. In 1937 he visited America at the invitation of the Elizabeth Sprague Coolidge Foundation, and in 1939 he returned to the United States, where he became a citizen and is a faculty member of the Music School of Yale University.

Hindemith's intense musicianship first showed itself in the music of his German period, which includes four string quartets the most beautiful of which is op. 22; two string trios; the two song cycles, *Das Marienleben* (*Mary's Life*) and *Die Junge Magd* (*The Young Maid*), which have spiritual depths; a series of compositions in neoclassic vein and a wide range of instrumental combinations which he calls simply *Kammermusik* (Chamber Music); a number of sonatas for violin, viola, cello; a concerto for piano with chamber orchestra accompaniment; and operas, which will be discussed in Chapter 19. In this earlier music Hindemith has been a remarkable exponent of dissonant counterpoint and has written with plastic melodic lines.

Richard Strauss is supposed to have said to him, "Why do you write atonally? You do not have to, you have talent!"

Gebrauchsmusik is a recent movement in which Hindemith was a protagonist. It deals with the "sociological function of music," and has as a basic idea that music—good or bad—is futile if it cannot attract an audience. Hindemith and others realized that music was becoming more and more abstract and that it was necessary to give the young a type of music which would be of interest to them. The group also realized the importance for music's future of bringing the young Germans after World War I into its circle. So by means of his Film-Music Studio in connection with the Hochschule in Berlin, Hindemith gave the younger students and composers tasks in illustrating films with music, and he encouraged the Youth Movement in Germany to create a new and simpler music as well as to cultivate an appreciation for the old.

In the *Musical Quarterly* (October 1931) Willi Reich quotes, in an essay on Hindemith, a manifesto of the *Jugendbewegung* (Youth Movement) in which Hindemith had a hand: "The developments of the last decade have made it increasingly clear that the work of our generation is splitting in two directions. On the one hand, a music is developing with roots in an atmosphere that is in the last analysis social, and which is adapting itself with growing instinctive certainty to the demands and the style of the music festivals. On the other hand, music is remembering its own characteristic aims; it is seeking the lost way to common fellowship, is turning from an artificially exaggerated subjective activity to a new, simple practicality and to the drawing together of a wider circle.

"This last type of music embodies the attitude and aims of the 'Jugendbewegung.' Out of the rebirth of ancient polyphony has grown an increasingly strong connection between this movement and the creative powers of our time. . . . Leading composers are purposely and affirmatively busying themselves with music for youth, since here a rich soil has been prepared by systematic education, an attitude which, nourished on old music, has sought to assimilate the music of the present."

In the nineteenth century, music became a luxury, but the first war created new conditions and a new audience for whom new music had to be supplied. The radio and the sound film were drawn into the circle to popularize music, and the audience became a participant instead of merely a lethargic listener.

So Hindemith wrote pieces to be sung and played by amateurs (op. 43 and 45), and his *Let Us Build a City*, a cantata for schoolchildren, has been sung in Germany, England, and America. The new opera movement was interested in this phase of music, and young Germans and Austrians besides Hindemith turned their attention in this direction, including Kurt Weill (1900), Ernst Krenek (1900), Philipp Jarnach (1892), Heinz Tiessen (1887), and Heinrich Kaminski.

Throughout his composing career Hindemith has been consistent in his style, although he has displayed tremendous versatility and a strong individuality characterized by spirit and vigor. Coincidental with the coming of the Hitler regime, Hindemith seemed to turn his interests to the German Gothic period. He came under the influence of the fifteenth and sixteenth centuries, as may be seen by his use of popular songs from that period in his concerto for viola and small orchestra, *"Der Schwanendreher"* (The Herder of Swans, 1935), which he played during his first American tour, and his opera *Mathis der Maler* (*Matthias the Painter.*) The Middle Ages attracted him also in his ballet *Nobilissima Visione* (1938), based on the life of St. Francis of Assisi, considered one of his most beautiful and sympathetic scores.

Although *Mathis der Maler* (1934) is an opera (page 300), the American public knows it only as a symphony arranged by the composer from material of the opera. The three movements, which form a musical triptych, were inspired by paintings of the Isenheim Altar which are in the museum at Colmar, Alsace. They are the work of Matthias Grünewald, the sixteenth century German painter, and represent the Nativity, called the "Angelic Concert"; the Entombment; and the Temptation of Saint Anthony. Hindemith has used old church melodies, as well as his own, all of which he has treated polyphonically in a masterly style.

Besides *Mathis der Maler* Hindemith has written a number of scores for full orchestra during this period, such as Symphonic Dances (1937); the Symphony in E flat (1941); a concerto for violin (1939); and a "Symphonic Metamorphosis of Themes by Carl Maria von Weber."

In the choral field, Hindemith has done his share also, beginning with an oratorio dating from 1931, *Das Unaufhörliche,* which Aaron Copland translates as "that-indefinable-something-in-life-which-never-ends." It shows, surprisingly, a Brahms and Mahler influence. There are also a revised version of an early score, "In Praise of Music"; more recently a set of six charming *chansons* for four-part chorus of mixed voices, unaccompanied, to French texts by Rainer Maria Rilke; Five Songs on Old Texts for five-part chorus of mixed voices; and "When Lilacs Last in the Dooryard Bloom'd" (Walt Whitman), a requiem "For those we love" (1946), for chorus and orchestra. This last is an exciting score, full of imaginative power in which the Whitman lines are well projected in choral song and skillful use of recitative.

Hindemith has been prolific also in the chamber music field, having composed many sonatas for solo instrument and piano; three sonatas for piano (1936); a sonata for piano, four hands (1938); a sonata for

two pianos (1942); theme and four variations ("The Four Tem-
peraments") for piano and string orchestra (1945); and the *Ludus
Tonalis* (1943).

The *Ludus Tonalis* (a tonal game or a play of tonalities) consists
of twelve fugues connected by means of interludes used as tonal
bridges, with an introductory prelude and a postlude which is a complete inversion and retroversion of the prelude. As Bach's *Well-tempered
Clavier* was a first exposition of all the major and minor scales used
in a composition, so Hindemith has based the *Ludus Tonalis* on the
tonalities developed out of the twelve tones of the chromatic scale as he
explains their use in his theoretical work, *The Craft of Musical Composition.*

This work is in two parts: Book I deals with the theoretical part, and
Book II with exercises in two-part writing. He bases his theory on two
series: tones and intervals. Series 1 contains the twelve tones according
to "tensions" as found in the overtone series:

Series 1

Series 2 contains interval combinations, according to "value-order."
"Series 2," Hindemith states, "tells us that the *skip* of a fifth is stronger
in harmonic effect than the skip of a fourth, which latter, however, is
stronger than the third or the second."

Series 2

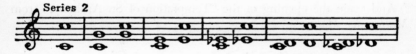

Each of the twelve tones can become a tonal center. He divides
Series 2 into two classes: "those consisting of the first-generation descendants of the progenitor tone (fifths, fourths, thirds, and sixths) and
those formed from the 'grandchildren' (seconds and sevenths)." Hindemith does not treat of chord inversions as other theorists have done. He
states that while three- and four-tone chords may be rearranged so
that their inversions are recognizable, the majority of chords especially
when not built up in thirds are not invertible.

Hindemith states as requirements of a new system of chord analysis:

"1. Construction in thirds must no longer be the basic rule for the erection of chords.

"2. We must substitute a more all embracing principle for that of the invertibility of chords.

"3. We must abandon the thesis that chords are susceptible of a variety of interpretations."

He completes Series 2 with the tritone, "the most distant relative, the eccentric, barred from close association with the interval pairs like Loki among the gods of Valhalla and similarly indispensable." He also says that the tritone has no root and no definite significance, either harmonic or melodic, and its position is determined by a third tone. But tritones take a very important place in his construction of chords. "If we are to be able to make convincing chord-progressions," he states, "we must treat the tritone as their most important constituent."

As an example of Series 1, here is the opening measure of *Ludus Tonalis,* with a melodic passage containing all twelve tones of the chromatic scale:

From Ludus Tonalis   Paul Hindemith

And again the opening of the "Temptation of St. Anthony," from *Mathis der Maler:*

Hindemith's chord and contrapuntal treatment are shown in the arioso of the Prelude in the *Ludus Tonalis,* with the tritone in evidence in the first measure.

The following passage from the second movement of the Piano Sonata No. 2 (1936) shows Hindemith's construction of chords:

In his table of chord-groups, Hindemith has systematized the various classifications which include all the chords of conventional harmony as well as the most extreme tone combinations of ultramodernism. In an article by Bernhard Heiden, "Hindemith's 'System'—A New Approach," in *Modern Music,* Jan.-Feb. 1942, Mr. Heiden states, "The preference of certain periods in music for certain groups of chordal material: Palestrina—Group I; Romantic—Group VI; indicates what is called 'Harmonic Style.' "

Mr. Heiden summarizes a few of the work's most important findings thus: "The conception of 'key' has experienced a radical change. Gone is the idea that there is a definite number of chords in a key or borrowed from another key, with which the composer has to work. Instead, all tone combinations are possible as long as their use is justified by Degree-Progression or other determining factors. Tonality is not a a starting-point but a goal and must be achieved by means of cadences organized according to Series 1. Chords have only one meaning, regardless of the tonal surroundings in which they appear. They stand for themselves, are therefore neither inverted, incomplete, nor in need of relation to some other imaginary sound (Alteration). Melody is restored to its original power after long dependence on harmony, to which the nineteenth century devoted most interest. Finally: Hindemith claims that all his suppositions are only of a physical nature; they are not esthetic nor are they stylistic."

The twentieth century English school is ably represented by William Walton (1902) and Constant Lambert (1905), both of whom have aroused interest at home and abroad. Walton imbibed something of Satie's "music hall spirit" in his setting of "Façade," in which Edith Sitwell's poems were first recited by Osbert Sitwell through a megaphone accompanied by a chamber orchestra behind a curtain. Walton demonstrated his humorous musical talent and clever workmanship. He is the composer of an overture, "Portsmouth Point," which was suggested by Rowlandson's print of a century ago; of a Sinfonia Concertante for orchestra with piano, which is neoclassic but with a warmth which presaged his next work, a truly neoromantic viola concerto; of a violin concerto; and of a choral work, "The Feast of Belshazzar." During the war years he has been writing music for government films, and he also supplied the score for the film *Henry V*. He wrote a successful ballet, *The Quest,* after Edmund Spenser, for Sadler's Wells.

A different type is Constant Lambert. His earliest affinity was with the Russian composers of Borodin's type. He was first brought to public notice through Diaghileff's performance of his ballet *Romeo and Juliet.* The next influence was that of jazz, as evidenced in "The Rio Grande," a tone poem for which Sacheverell Sitwell's poem forms a choral background. He wrote "Elegiac Blues" in memory of Florence Mills, Negro musical comedy singer, and a piano sonata, in which he again shows the jazz influence. As musical director of ballet for the Old Vic–Sadler's Wells enterprise in London, Lambert has had little time for composing. He is the author of a book, *Music Ho! A Study of Music in Decline,* which sounds a pessimistic note. He has commissioned other composers, however, to write ballets, among them Arthur

Bliss, whose *Miracle in the Gorbals,* a story of Glasgow slum life, and *Adam Zero* have been performed.

An older composer who has recently come into prominence is Ernest John Moeran (1894), of Irish descent, who was influenced by Philip Heseltine and the Dutch-English composer Bernard van Dieren. His early works were based on folk material, but after a fallow period he returned to the musical scene with a new style in 1935, with a sonata for two violins unaccompanied, a piano trio (1936), and his First Symphony (1938). More recently he wrote a violin concerto, a sinfonietta, and a cello concerto.

Benjamin Britten (1913), one of the younger English composers, has gained prominence during the war years. He has written chamber music, orchestral and choral works, and songs. Several of his major scores were presented at the festivals of the International Society for Contemporary Music. Britten spent several years in the United States, during which time he wrote a chamber opera on a legendary American figure, *Paul Bunyan.* He has made settings of some Michelangelo poems, which show extreme talent, a fine sense of style, dramatic feeling, and clarity of writing. Britten was commissioned by the Natalie Koussevitzky Music Foundation to write an opera, *Peter Grimes,* which had its première at Sadler's Wells in June 1945, a year before the performance at Tanglewood in the Berkshire Festival series. His latest opera, *The Rape of Lucretia,* opened the Glyndebourne Festival in 1946 (page 307).

Michael Tippett has won acclaim for his Symphony 1945 and his oratorio *A Child of Our Time,* which commemorates the assassination of a German counsellor in Paris by a young Polish Jew.

Edmund Rubbra (1901), who has written much chamber music, is regarded as having an individual style with melodic invention and counterpoint used in a modern and personal way. He has written a double fugue for full orchestra; four symphonies; two piano concertos; Sinfonia Concertante for piano and orchestra; and a setting of Keats' *"La Belle Dame sans Merci"* for chorus and orchestra. He studied with Cyril Scott, Gustav Holst, and R. O. Morris.

Other young Englishmen are Alan Rawsthorne, who served in the army and supplied the music for some army films, and Lennox Berkeley, who studied with Nadia Boulanger in Paris, and Richard A. S. Arnell, who spent the war years in America, where he has had a number of performances of chamber music and orchestral works. Rawsthorne's idiom is compared to the type of composition known as "central European," somewhat favoring Hindemith. W. H. Mellers wrote (*Modern Music,* March-April 1945) that "Rawsthorne and Berkeley represent tendencies in our [English] musical culture which might be intrinsically important, and historically their position is worth studying" because it is both precarious and uncompromising. Development of a cosmopolitan rather than a provincial style "may be a step in the right direction, but it won't produce good music unless it is reborn into the native tradition in such a way that it becomes European without ceasing to be local." Rawsthorne has written an excellent chaconne in his piano concerto, and Symphonic Variations, and more recently a gay overture, "Cortèges."

Alan Bush (1900) was professor of composition at the Royal Academy of Music and served as a soldier in the Medical Corps. He has written many works, including a recent Symphony in C.

Stanley Bate (1912), a pupil of the Royal College of Music and of Nadia Boulanger, lives in the United States. He has written two symphonies, a string quartet, three concertos, sonatas, a ballet, incidental music, and a trio for flute, cello, and piano. His style is neoclassic.

QUARTER TONES is a generic term which has come to mean in particular the division of the half step into two halves, and in general the division of the half step or the whole step into smaller intervals such as the third-tone, the sixth-tone, the three-quarter tone, the eighth-tone, the sixteenth-tone, etc.; that is, into *microtones*. Whether practical or not, the idea is possible. If we concede that musical evolution has traveled along the path of the upper harmonics of a fundamental tone (page 99), then we must admit that with Schoenberg's twelve tone scale we have gone as far as we can without subdividing the half step. The Greeks had a system of quarter tones called the *enharmonic* (page 107), and the Hindus, Arabs, and Orientals use intervals smaller than the half step. For years, those intervals were regarded as resulting from poorly trained ears and badly constructed instruments, but a further study reveals always the same intervals sung and played, which would not be the case if it were just poor intonation.

Today we are more willing to admit the fallibility of man-tempered instruments and music, and we know that change is in the air in this field as in every other.

The Italian pianist and pedagogue Ferruccio Busoni (1866-1924), one of the greatest musicians of his age, was interested in having an instrument manufactured for him that would divide the whole tone into three steps instead of two—a tripartite piano. "No pianist of today is more profoundly of the past. And no pianist today is more truly of the future," said Henry K. Moderwell in the Boston *Evening Transcript* of February 20, 1915. "He is dreaming of harmonies that have never yet been heard, of melodies that notation cannot yet set down."

Busoni felt that the complete revision of harmonics, the extension of the field of dissonance, the search for atmosphere, the liberation of voice-leading—all the things that go to make up "modern" music, have pointed to the further subdivision of the chromatic scale.

In his little book *A New Aesthetic of Music* Busoni made an attempt "to exhaust the possibilities of the arrangement of degrees within the seven-tone scale; and succeeded, by raising and lowering the intervals, in establishing *one hundred and thirteen different scales.*"

He claimed that the tripartite tone has been demanding admittance for some time, and a few who have experimented have discerned that "tripartite tones are wholly independent intervals with a pronounced character, and not to be confounded with ill-tuned semi-tones. They form a refinement in chromatics based, as at present appears, on the whole-tone scale."

Instead of giving up the semitonal system, Busoni recommended its use in a further division of a sixth-tone system.

Since that time Alois Haba (1893), a Czechoslovak, has written string quartets and an opera in quarter tones, and Hans Barth, an American, has a quarter tone piano. He and Charles Ives, the composer, tried playing on two pianos tuned quarter tones apart. As a result Barth induced the Baldwin Piano Company to construct a piano under his supervision, with two keyboards, each tuned in equal temperament; the upper bank is tuned to 440, and the lower to 427.5. Thus the instrument has a tonal range of quarter, three-quarter, half, and whole tones. While at first it sounds distinctly out of tune, the ear becomes adjusted to the finer gradations of tone and the quarter tone establishes its identity rapidly. In 1930 Barth played his Concerto for Quarter-Tone Piano and Strings with the Philadelphia Orchestra under Leopold Stokowski. Mr. Barth invented a notation, as did Haba, to meet the exigencies of writing quarter tone music. Another American, Mildred Couper, of California, wrote compositions in quarter tones played on two pianos tuned quarter tones apart.

In 1926 the League of Composers presented a quarter tone symphony, *"Sonata casi Fantasia"* by the Mexican composer and theorist Julian Carillo. Carillo has spent over thirty-five years in a scientific study of releasing the subdivisions of tone smaller than those included in the chromatic scale. He has invented instruments for his ensemble to include, besides the usual strings, a guitar which produces quarter tones, an *octarina*, playing eighth-tones, an *arpacitera* playing sixteenth-tones which sounds like a fire siren, and a French horn on which may be played sixteenth-tones. Carillo calls his combination *The Thirteenth Tone Ensemble*. I heard a singer with the ensemble who sang quarter tones intentionally and in perfect intonation!

In 1923 a *Manual of Harmony in Quarter-Tones* by Ivan Wyschnegradsky, was published in Paris by *La Sirène musicale*. Wyschnegradsky, a Russian refugee, is one of a group of followers of Scriabin including Nicholas Obouhov, composer of a mystic choral work, *Le Livre de la vie (Book of Life)*, Javorski, and Protopokoff. Obouhov has suggested a very simple solution for the present-day problem of twelve tone notation by indicating the five steps representing the black keys of the piano by means of a symbol on the staff, which remains unchanged whether it indicates a sharp or a flat. Wyschnegradsky has developed a notation for quartertonal music which looks reasonable and logical.

Katherine Ruth Heyman, who with Wyschnegradsky and Obouhov founded the *Groupe Estival* in Paris, gave me the following information: "Quartertonal music is an approach toward the mystical concept of *Pan-tonality*—an ideal perhaps not to be achieved on the plane of material sound, but an idea known to great composers of music as the continuous presence of all music in one place all the time— from which they draw. To Wyschnegradsky it is conceivable on the plane of sound." Quartertonal music has therefore been considered from the standpoint of harmony, of science, and of mysticism, and Wyschnegradsky claims that it is based on a traditional line which relates the music of quarter tones to all the music which preceded it, and that instead of being a *deus ex machina* it has been logically prepared by the evolution of music throughout the centuries.

Wyschnegradsky lives in Paris in poverty and writes symphonies in the conventional system and quartertonal ensemble works for such combinations of instruments as the strings with a quartertonal clarinet, harmonium, and piano. Wyschnegradsky has recently written a symphony *Ainsi parlait Zarathustra* (*Thus Spake Zarathustra*) for four pianos, two tuned a quarter tone higher than the other two. This is the medium he uses for many of his "ultrachromatic" works. His quarter tone piano with three manuals available to the hand is made by Foerster in Saxony. He has had four American students in quartertonal music: Miss Heyman, Margaret Marymount, Cara Verson, and John Appleby, who in 1928 wrote a quartertonal setting of the speech of Socrates in the original Greek.

Leonid Sabaneyeff, writing in *Modern Music* ("To Conquer New Tonal Regions," May-June 1927), believes that "insufficient emphasis has been given to the more natural experiments with ultrachromatic melody. It seems obvious that the introduction of new fractional sounds must be linked to older and related melodic colors—first as timid passing notes, then as neighboring notes, finally as jumps and unprepared sounds. Their very nature demands a gradual reception.... And the beginning should be made with melody, not harmony.... This was the historic development of chromaticism and so it must be for ultrachromaticism."

As interesting as are the electrical experiments in *ether music* such as Leon Theremin and Maurice Martenot have developed, they are extramusical or *instrumentalities* (page 407) and cannot be discussed at length. Henry Cowell working with Theremin has produced an instrument which records various rhythms simultaneously and bears out Cowell's theories of the relationship of rhythm to sound vibration. Joseph Schillinger wrote an "Airphonic Suite for RCA Theremin with Orchestra." There are some new electromagnetic keyboard instruments, such as the Hammond organ and the Novachord, too, which may solve problems, but at the same time create new ones.

Schillinger (1895-1943) collaborated with Theremin in acoustical research and in the construction of electronic instruments. He was a scientist in addition to being a composer, and was a teacher of music, mathematics, and fine arts. He wrote a book, *The Mathematical Basis of the Arts,* a theory and practice of scientific art production underlying all of the arts. He worked out his theories pertaining to music in two volumes which were published posthumously as *The Schillinger System of Musical Composition.* He applied mathematics to music, showing the unifying principles behind its functions. He explained the old, and opened unlimited possibilities for new materials. It represents a lifetime of research and discovery. One goal was the uncovering and classifying of all available resources of our tonal system. But scientific analysis was not enough; he constructed a synthesis in which he applied his mathematical findings to composing. Here is where he may run into conflict with tradition. In his own words, his method implies "the prefabrication and the assembly of components according to a preconceived design of the whole."

Schillinger used the graph system such as one finds in stock reports, in hospital charts, etc., to show the duration of tones and pitch levels. He applied his knowledge of modern physics, modern psychology, and modern mathematics to basic concepts which made possible the working out of his system. The work is a monumental departure in the presentation of the materials and processes of musical composition.

CHAPTER 18

MUSIC, AS AFFECTED BY THE WAR: IN GERMANY, AUSTRIA, CZECHOSLOVAKIA, FRANCE, ENGLAND, POLAND, ITALY, SWITZERLAND, RUSSIA, ETC.

THE effect of the Nazi regime on the future of music in Europe is impossible to estimate at the present. As early as 1933 the cultural life of Germany had been disrupted. Theater directors and conductors were restricted in the performance of their duties, and anyone who had declared sympathy for modern art in any fashion was removed from office. And thousands of "non-Aryan" musicians were uprooted from important posts.

German art became reactionary. The composers were bidden to seek inspiration from Germany's "glorious past," and from Reger, Bruckner, and even Wagner. Dr. Joseph Goebbels regarded modern art as merely fashionable, "the swamp bloom of a democratic sidewalk culture which must be rejected." He is reported to have said that "only a national political art is truly creative and is the only kind of art for which there is justifiable existence."

Before its collapse, artistic life was paralyzed in Germany. All musical activities ceased in September 1944. Many famous opera houses, concert halls, and conservatories were destroyed, among these the Residenztheater in Munich and the Viennese opera house.

Germany had been the center of a musical culture of high level, a culture which embraced Austria, Czechoslovakia, Holland, Hungary, and Switzerland. Mark Brunswick calls attention ("After Munich," *Modern Music,* November-December 1938) to the "individualistic cultivation of chamber music in the home on the one hand, and the communal institution of the opera on the other. In Germany alone there were several hundred opera houses to which the states and municipalities contributed. Recalling the great number of instrumentalists, solo and chorus singers, conductors and coaches that could be educated and absorbed by this system, and further the democracy and liberalism that controlled it, one can form some picture of the intensity of that German musical culture." From this statement one gets a conception of the tragic results the destruction of such a machine involved.

A report from Germany states that after the capitulation hardly any opera groups or complete orchestras were left, and yet artistic life has picked up rapidly, "thanks chiefly to aid from the allied occupation forces." (Arno Huth in "Post-War European Revival," *Modern Music,* Winter 1946.) Symphony and opera have resumed performances in several of the large cities. "The Berlin Philharmonic had a regular concert series this season. In Hamburg, musicians who belonged to the old Bruckner Orchestra of the German Radio have formed a symphony orchestra. Radio Munich has a small instrumental ensemble.... The radio stations of the military governments have become artistic centers, especially in the American zone." Mendelssohn's works have been reinstated, and over Radio Munich, Ernest Bloch's *"Schelomo"* was played.

In Vienna one of the first signs of peace was the revival of the Austrian section of the International Society for Contemporary Music, which had played a most important role in the development of modern music after World War I. Anton Webern was made the president, but he had been killed before news reached him of his election.

The Viennese are hungry for music, as are the Germans. Dr. Karl Krueger on his return from guest performances in Europe related how eager the people were for concerts by the Vienna Philharmonic. To accommodate the crowds the same program had to be given three times. He also told that the men played magnificently and rehearsed for hours although they were weak from hunger. Even for those who could pay for food, there was not enough available to satisfy their needs. Great interest was evinced in new music immediately after the liberation. Alfred Schlee writes (*Modern Music,* Spring 1946, "Vienna Since the Anschluss") : "Enforced abstinence produced a natural reaction. Previously scorned composers were now attractive because they had been forbidden to an audience once alienated by concerts of modern music.... Now seven years of trumpets and concentration camps have, by their terror roused the genius of the thousand-year-old Reich. The next few years will show the extent to which Vienna has grasped the meaning of this history."

Such men as Mahler, Schoenberg, Krenek, Alban Berg, and Webern demonstrated what Austria had contributed creatively to twentieth century music. Hans Erich Apostel, a young representative of the Schoenberg school, is regarded as a worthy successor. He has written a Hölderlin cycle and is at work on a symphony, of which the adagio, written as a memorial to Berg, his teacher, is completed. Other composers are Theodor Berger, who is writing a "Homeric Fantasy" for chorus, orchestra and ballet; Alfred Uhl, who had been badly wounded in the war but has composed actively since the liberation, and has three orchestral works; Alexander Spitzmüller, who has written *"Hymnes à la Paix"* (*Hymns to Peace*) which show strong French stylistic influence; Johann Nepomuk David, who is reconstructing his symphonies which were destroyed. Of the younger generation Schlee says, "New names are bobbing up although the youngest generation has suffered a real setback. It will have a sharper profile when the poison of National Socialism is cast out. Familiarity with contemporary idioms was denied these young men during the Third Reich." He speaks of Anton Heiller, who has written a toccata for two pianos; Gottfried von Einem, who has written a ballet, orchestral pieces, piano works, and songs, and is completing an opera on Buechner's *Dantons Tod* (*Danton's Death*).

New chamber music has been written, although little orchestral music has been listed. A program of the I.S.C.M. premiered two works by Hanns Eisler. These scores, on antifascist texts written just before the Nazi occupation, were hidden in a friend's home behind the flour sacks out of which the underground railroad was fed during the years of occupation.

There is a new Austrian circle which sponsors living composers, and some of the youngest musicians pay tribute to Hindemith with a "Mathis Circle." Great interest is manifested in the music of the outside world, and there seems to be little tendency toward chauvinism.

As the German armies went on their conquering way, in addition to death and destruction they attempted to force their *Kultur* policy on every country. But we learn on all sides of the frantic, and in many cases successful, struggles of the various underground organizations to encourage and keep alive the musical activities of each nation.

Everywhere, too, there were the collaborationists who have since lost caste or in some cases have been reinstated.

Under the head of "Music and Politics," Darius Milhaud wrote for *Modern Music,* Nov.-Dec. 1944, an account of the participation of the French musicians in the resistance. News from Francis Poulenc, who managed to reach him through people who escaped from France, told him that Poulenc, Louis Durey, Georges Auric, and Roger Désormière were active in the resistance. Paul Paray, the conductor of the *Concerts Colonne* refused for four years to conduct any of the performances as long as the name had been changed by the Germans to *Concerts Pierné.* "Claude Delvincourt was offered the post of Director of the Paris Conservatoire by the Vichy government. He accepted because he knew he could help the Resistance. He became one of the important persons of the clandestine movement in which he was known as Monsieur Julien. His office was transformed into a counterfeiting headquarters. None of the Conservatoire students was deported to Germany and during the last weeks they all enlisted in the French Forces of the Interior or in the Maqui for the battle of the liberation of Paris."

New names have arisen among the conductors. Charles Münch, an Alsatian by birth, conductor of the Association des Concerts du Conservatoire, crowded the concert hall from October 1940 on. "Every Sunday for four years he brought escape to an enthusiastic crowd, a few hours of liberation to an oppressed and saddened Paris," Georges Auric wrote in *Modern Music,* March-April 1945, in an informative article, "Paris—The Survival of French Music." Another conductor, Manuel Rosenthal, the head of the Paris National Radio Orchestra, is also a composer. He has written a work called *"Musique de table"* (Dinner Music), which Virgil Thomson describes as program music "pushed to its for the present at least ultimate assertion," and an oratorio, *Saint Francis of Assisi,* on a text by Roland-Manuel. Eugène Bigot was the conductor of the *Concerts Lamoureux.*

Georges Auric also tells of the work of Francis Poulenc, his colleague from the Group of Six days, who, with the singer Pierre Bernac, gave recitals of contemporary song with unqualified success. Poulenc wrote some songs to poems by Louis Aragon in defiance of enemy censorship, and in 1943 he wrote a cantata, *Figure humaine (The Human Face),* including a forceful poem, *"Liberté."*

"The general rebirth in France is especially favorable to contemporary music," Arno Huth writes in *Modern Music,* March-April 1945, "Europe Today: A Report from Switzerland." Compositions by Darius Milhaud, Jacques Ibert, Francis Poulenc, Georges Dandelot, Daniel Lesur, Olivier Messiaen, and Marcel Mihalivici were played. Extracts from the Seven Star Symphony by Charles Koechlin were presented. (The Seven Stars are film stars.) The radio gave an *opéra-bouffe, Isabelle et Pantalon* by Max Jacob and Roland-Manuel. Among new composers Huth mentions Henri Dutilleul, Prix de Rome, 1938. In 1940 Jean Alain, Jean Vuillermoz, and Maurice Jaubert, three young composers, were killed. Their music was presented by Manuel Rosenthal in a memorial concert.

Paris used ballet as a means of escape. In 1942 the Opéra mounted a new work by Poulenc, *Les Animaux modèles (The Model Animals),* based on six fables of La Fontaine. The characters display human qualities, and the stage settings are in the style of Louis XIV.

An International Archives of Contemporary Music has been founded in Paris. The Bibliothèque Nationale will house the collection, which purposes to establish a "complete documentation" for the lives and works of all contemporary composers. Carol-Bérard is the director, and the intention is eventually to have it become a *Musée de la Musique* (a museum of music).

The interest in music showed definite increase in London during and immediately following the war. Many more concerts are taking place than in prewar days. Queen's Hall, a popular center for orchestral concerts and recitals since 1893, was bombed out. Concerts are given in Royal Albert Hall, but as it seats ten thousand, it is too large for satisfactory results, so programs are presented in theaters and any available places.

Foreign artists from Europe and America have appeared, and music is again international in character. Contemporary music was rarely heard during the war, but some works are appearing again on programs. Boosey and Hawkes ran a series of chamber concerts, the B.B.C. (British Broadcasting Company) ran a monthly series called "Music of our Time," and some new works were played at the Promenade Concerts in 1945. A definite increase of interest in new works is apparent.

In the summer of 1946 Erich Leinsdorf, Austrian-American conductor, was invited to act as guest conductor with the London Philharmonic. He appeared in London and on tour with the organization, and reported that concerts everywhere attracted crowds. The orchestras work about thirty hours a week, and with the loss of Queen's Hall it is difficult to find places to rehearse. But he still found much enthusiasm among the musicians.

When Sir Malcolm Sargent, British conductor of the London Philharmonic, visited this country in 1944 as guest conductor of the N.B.C. (National Broadcasting Company) orchestra, he told of the determination of the men to go ahead with their orchestra, and of the difficulties they had to surmount, not the least of which was to find places in which to hold the concerts, as they were bombed out of one hall after the other and had become hardened even to playing to the accompaniment of bursting bombs. On one occasion they borrowed a building much like the old Hippodrome in New York, where a circus was being held. The concert went very well, however, and at the close of one number, while he was bowing, Sir Malcolm heard a great stamping back scenes, and the audience burst into shrieks of laughter. Sir Malcolm turned, to see four elephants ranged across the back of the stage, duly acknowledging the applause.

In 1943 our American composer Marc Blitzstein, whose work with the armed forces took him to London, wrote to *Modern Music* (January-February), "There was evident hereabout a frenzied activity in all fields, and a driving spirit I hadn't remembered in prewar London. They are working, fighting, and playing furiously. Theater-life and concert-life are booming." He wrote of the fine work in ballet at Sadler's Wells; of the radio score, "Christopher Columbus" by MacNeice with William Walton's music; and of other musical activities.

Withal the work of older men like Vaughan Williams and Arnold Bax was handicapped by the war, but gradually conditions are becoming more conducive again to normal existence.

The war work of Myra Hess, internationally known British pianist, won her the title of Dame. She organized noontime concerts at the National Gallery which took place daily, raid or no raid. Once in a while the music was carried on in a shelter. Not only Dame Myra played, but she had the co-operation of many professional colleagues. Concert groups also toured the provinces under her aegis. The courage and solace that that hour of music gave the Londoners during their darkest days cannot be measured.

In Holland a tribunal of Dutch musicians decreed that Willem Mengelberg should never be permitted to conduct in his native land again, because of his collaboration with the Nazis. Also 225 organs in Dutch churches have been destroyed, including several from the eighteenth century.

When Erich Leinsdorf visited London, he was invited also to conduct at the Hague and at Scheveningen. He found the Dutch orchestras in splendid condition and he reported that they are still subsidized. In Holland, too, the people crowded to concerts and were enthusiastic listeners.

German occupation paralyzed Belgian music, but after the first shock a reaction occurred, activities were resumed, and emphasis was laid on Belgian nationalism. The people courageously continued music education with no decline of standards. As was the case in other occupied countries, the Belgians sought respite in music. Popular concerts were organized at the Brussels Conservatory with the assistance of the Department of Public Education. Many of the works presented were by Belgians, old and young, with the twofold purpose of acquainting the youth with native music and of giving opportunity to young talents to have a hearing.

The Belgians' refusal to accept German artists or "collaboration" required courage and stubborn resistance, but it was successful and won praise from a Swiss periodical which said: "In Belgium we find a comforting example of resistance and of dignity which does her honor." The article also stated that the programs of the Philharmonique had "made a heroic appeal to their national musical resources, and drawn for the rest on the best qualified representatives of French art." The famous opera house Théatre de la Monnaie in Brussels was able to carry on. And the orchestra members gave a post-season of concerts under the direction of a talented young conductor René Defossez.

The Belgian radio has again as its head the musicologist Paul Collaer, who put on programs until suppressed by the Germans, including works by Falla, Jean Francaix, Henri Sauguet, and a new work, "Moretus," by the Belgian Marcel Poot. The director of the Philharmonic Society, Marcel Cuvilier, founded *Jeunesses Musicales de Belgique* (Musical Youths of Belgium), and branches of young music lovers were formed in the schools. Symphony concerts were given for their benefit. A group of the same sort was founded also in France. Later these groups united.

The neutrality of Switzerland placed that country in a difficult position. Their music was largely dominated by Germans. But with the close of the war French musicians were heard, and the Swiss conductor Ernest Ansermet did a splendid work through these years with his Orchestre Romand in Geneva. He has presented modern music of the different nations. The exiled Spaniard Pablo Casals, one of the world's great cellists, who is also a conductor, directed his own composition *"Sardana"* in Zurich in 1942. Ansermet played four symphonic pieces by the American octogenarian, Templeton Strong, who has lived in Geneva for fifty years. The Swiss radio presented the work of a young native composer, Pierre Wissmer, whose talent is highly thought of. Another young Swiss is Wilhelm Arbenz, who wrote a school work, *"Jugend im Schnee"* (Youth in the Snow) patterned on Hindemith and Kurt Weill. In Basel, Paul Sacher carries on the work for contemporary music with the Basler Kammer-Orchester (Basel Chamber Orchestra). Many scores by foreign and native composers have been presented, including the Swiss Willy Burkhard and Conrad Beck.

Italy is again released from the kind of propaganda carried on by the Fascist regime. An Italian composer, Luigi Dallapiccola, said he read that a Fascist critic had written that "it was high time to stop writing quartets and chamber music, since these could not be appreciated by audiences of twenty-thousand persons. The 'Theatre for the Twenty-thousand' was part of Mussolinian rhetoric." (*Modern Music,* Summer 1946.)

Dallapiccola speaks of new works by Pizzetti, Casella, Malapiero, and Tommasini. Pizzetti has a new violin concerto; Casella a *Missa Solemnis Pro Pace* (Solemn Mass for Peace); Tommasini a concerto for string orchestra; and Malapiero is completing an extensive oratorio, *Vergilii Aeneis,* based on two episodes from the *Aeneid.*

Of the younger composers, Dallapiccola speaks of Antonio Veretti and his opera *Il Favorito del Re* (*The King's Favorite*); a Passion by Mario Labroca; Virgilio Mortari and Nino Rota; Louis Cortese, a polytonalist who is at work on a "Prometheus Bound"; Gian Luca

Tocchi's Nocturne and Dance for flute, viola, and harp; Frederico Ghedini (1892) and his *"Architectures"* for orchestra; Riccardo Nielsen (1908) and Adone Zecchi, who have turned to twelve tone technic; and Goffredo Petrassi, who has written Four Hymns for baritone and organ, Eight Inventions for piano, and a ballet, *Don Quixote*. Luigi Dallapiccola was the first in Italy to study and apply the principles of the twelve tone system, in "Night Flight" (1940), three cycles of Greek lyrics, and in an opera, *The Prisoner,* on which he is at present working. In it he hopes to express the sufferings of Europe during the last years.

The musicians of Poland were tragically affected by the war. In Warsaw alone the Philharmonic concert hall, opera house, conservatory, musical libraries, and publishing houses were destroyed. Jerzy Fitelberg reported (*Modern Music,* Winter 1946, in "Poland Yesterday and Today") that Polish composers had lost most of their manuscripts and printing plates. "The Nazis burned or robbed collections of Chopin, Moniusko, Paderewski and Szymanowski manuscripts, also the entire music collection of the Warsaw National Library." All musical instruments, old or new, have disappeared. Many of the younger composers have been killed.

Clandestine concerts were held during the occupation in private homes, and an underground musical life flourished. "The Poles are energetically rebuilding their artistic life in spite of staggering handicaps."

Music schools have sprung up by the hundreds, large and small orchestras and opera houses have been functioning, a Central Concert Board sponsors events throughout the country, and the Polish Music Publishing House has been founded in Cracow and has begun activities.

In September 1945 a three-day festival took place in Cracow. "Composers are helping to reorganize the country's musical life; works composed during the occupation are now being performed. Cracow Philharmonic programs have recently included the new *Second Symphony* by Roman Palester, *Grünwald* by Jan Maklakiewicz, *Concerto* for soprano and orchestra by Tadeusz Kassern, *Tragic Overture* by Andrzej Panufnik, besides compositions by Boleslaw Wojtowicz, Tadeusz Szeligowski, Stanislaw Wiechowicz, and of course, Szymanowski."

From a report in *Modern Music,* Summer 1946, we learn that musical life in Czechoslovakia gained in intensity during the war, "and even more," O. F. Korte writes, "became under the occupation, the strongest activating force of the national conscience. . . . For the Czech people music was the only common public medium of resistance, while through it the creative artist found the meaning and substance of his being." He continues that the war "returned honesty and naturalness to the creation of music, gave it a goal, a point for concentration." Works which came out of the war include May Symphony and *"De Profundis"* by Vitezslav Novak (1870), teacher of Jaroslav Kricka, Vaclav Stepan, K. B. Jirak, and Alois Haba; Cantata No. 45 by J. B. Foerster (1859); and from the younger composers, Dobias's "Stalingrad," Kaslik's "Morana," Kabelac's "Don't Retreat" and Stanislav's Red Army Symphony. To Czechoslovakia is credited the first postwar international music festival, "Spring 1946 in Prague," which celebrated also the fiftieth anniversary of the Czech Philharmonic with a series of ninety performances of music from the United States, England, France, and Soviet Russia. Our American conductor Leonard Bernstein was present and introduced his own Jeremiah Symphony and works by his fellow countrymen.

The totalitarianism of Nazi Germany stifled the creative spirit while that of Soviet Russia fostered it. The Russian government dictated terms as to what kind of music it wanted and needed, and from the Western idea of freedom in art, the composers may have been restricted and hampered, but a new type of music was developed. Melodiousness and expressiveness have been stressed, and the result has been *neoromantic*. Personal, subjective mood has been replaced by what might be called collective emotions of joy, sorrow, heroism, optimism—emotions common to men struggling to impress an entire nation with a common cause. This concentration on subject matter and method of treatment, demanded by the Soviet government, has made the composers self-centered and chauvinistic. They have written for their own people, supposedly without having an eye on the outside world.

The aims of the proletariat musician were the re-education and reorganization of the musical masses with the intention of directing their work and creative talents toward the upbuilding of a socialist state, and the complete development and growth of proletarian music through creative production under the necessary conditions.

As part of the policy the working and peasant masses were to be helped in creating their own music through musical education and through work among the masses and the individual circles in workers' clubs, and by organizing choral and orchestral collectives and individual performers.

World War II changed Russia's musical life less, perhaps, than that of any other country because the U.S.S.R. began building its music according to the plans outlined above in its early days following the Revolution. The Soviet state did not try to divert its composers into writing popular war songs, but encouraged the composing of long and serious works which were played before soldiers by members of workers' clubs, groups from the Red Army Ensemble, and amateur art associations.

In an article in *Modern Music,* January-February 1942, "In Time of Bitter War," Henry Cowell describes the development of the clubs growing out of work organizations. "Each farm, each factory, forms its own social circle." He attended some of the stage performances, "partly composed, partly improvised, always subject to informal change, given by factory worker clubs for their own amusement."

"These many activities [music education, production and publication] were steadily increased during the thirties," Cowell continues, "so that when the war broke out there existed an extraordinary number of professional and amateur, centralized urban and far-dispersed local musical organizations." The artists who had been appearing before factory and other mass groups turned to entertaining the soldiers and their families who were left at home.

Musical creative activities were greatly accelerated by the war. Cowell says, "Just imagine anyone in this country suggesting that what our army needs is forty new opera companies! Yet that, among other things, is what has happened there." And the opera companies were supposed to perform newly commissioned operas by native composers.

"As a whole," he says, "the music of Soviet Russia today is much more vivid, more pointed than it was ten years ago. The tendency now is toward simplification—a tendency made inevitable by the necessity of designing music to be played and sung by untrained people."

The gap between the Russian masses and Russian music was never greater than at the end of czardom. The older composers were confused in the presence of the masses. It required a younger generation to solve the problems of reconstruction, and these new men were inexperienced at first.

Soon the older men learned to meet the needs of the new audience and they were called upon to compose songs of revolution for celebrations of the new social order. The Department of Proletarian Culture "ordained the nation's artistic life and promulgated new principles of composition for the mass audience."

A Union of Soviet Composers was formed, and its members were pledged "to support the socialist program of construction with their art." The members included Michael Ippolitoff-Ivanoff (1859-1935), Sergius Vasilenko (1872), Reinhold Glière (1875), Gregor Krein (1880), Alexander Krein (1883), and a group of younger men, Liév Polovinkin (1894), Alexander Veprik (1899), Alexander Mossolov (1900), Vassili Shirinski (1901), Vissarion Shebalin (1902), and Dmitri Shostakovich (1906).

A group organized to spread music for the masses throughout the Soviet Union included Victor Bielyi (1904), Alexander Davidenko (1899), Maryan Koval (1907), and Nikolai Chemberdji. It was disbanded in 1931. There are also Samuel Feinberg, a composer of piano sonatas under Scriabin's influence; Nikolai Roslavetz (1880), Michael Gniessin (1883), and a group of opera writers whose works were compelled to reflect the events of the U.S.S.R. and to build new means of expression in which the emotional standards of the past were to give way to new principles. The ballets were based not on classical lyric themes but on historical events.

The operas from the past include works by Tchaikovsky, Rimski-Korsakov, Borodin, and Moussorgsky. Shostakovich has written two operas, *The Nose* on Gogol's novel, and *Lady Macbeth from Mzensk* on a novel by Leskow. Other opera writers in this pioneer field are Vasilenko, Krein, Paskchecko, Pototsky, Knipper (1898), and Deshevov (1889).

Eugen Braudo finds Soviet music no longer at the crossroad, but has "musical perspectives which are opened up by the new spiritual and social horizon of Soviet Russia."

Nicolai Miaskovsky (1881) is the leading figure in Russian music. He is professor at the Moscow Conservatory and teacher of many of the younger men, including Vissarion Shebalin; Vassili Shirinsky; Vladimir Krinkov; Alexander Mossolov, who is known by the orchestral work "The Foundry," which, in spite of its noisiness, has structure, good orchestration, and climax; Aram Khachatourian, Dmitri Kabalevsky, and Victor Bielyi. He stands as a bridge between the tradition of Tchaikovsky and Glazounov and the development of the young Soviet composers. He may be regarded as the founder of the Soviet symphony, for he has written twenty-four symphonies, besides nine string quartets, piano sonatas, a violin concerto, and many songs.

Shebalin, writing of the "Dean of Soviet Composers" (*Modern Music,* November-December 1943) states: "He dedicated his *Sixth Symphony* to the Russia of after the October Revolution, the theme of the *Twelfth* is life on the collective farm, the *Sixteenth* honors the Soviet 'conquerors of the air,' the *Eighteenth* is based on Russian musical folklore. For the *Twenty-first,* a work of lyric and philosophical content, he was awarded the title, Stalin Prizewinner, in 1941.... The *Twenty-second* depicts the grim events of 1941 ... written in the Caucasus, where the composer spent over a year studying the national music of the Kabardin-Balkar people," which folk themes became the material for his Twenty-third Symphony. Miaskovsky has written songs for the Soviet armies, two-part choruses. One of his war pieces, "Buds are Swelling on the Poplars," has become very popular.

Since 1935 Serge Prokofieff has been aligned with the Soviet composers, of whom he is one of the most important. He returned to his native country in 1934 and had to adjust himself to the new conditions he found there, which differed greatly from what he had had in western Europe. His first work after his return, "Symphonic Song" (1934), called forth unfavorable criticism, in which it was stated that the composer had reflected the declining culture of the urbanized West where art was weary and disillusioned. At the same time he completed the music for the film *Lieutenant Kijé,* from which he made a symphonic suite. It gave him opportunity to write in his own satirical, grotesque style and was successful. The next year he completed his Second Violin Concerto in G minor, and in 1938 he wrote a concerto for violoncello and orchestra. In 1936 Prokofieff wrote the Russian Overture based on national themes; his internationally successful venture in theatrical music, *Peter and the Wolf,* and the ballet music to *Romeo and Juliet,* in which he said he had "taken special pains to achieve a simplicity, which will, I hope, reach the hearts of all listeners."

These last two scores showed the Western world what had happened to his style so far as simplification goes.

Prokofieff gave in his autobiography an illuminating analysis of his composing style as to the lines he followed. First, he was classical because he had heard his mother play Beethoven sonatas. This developed into the neoclassic aspect of his sonatas, concertos, gavottes, the Classical Symphony and the Sinfonietta. After meeting Taneieff, who criticized his rather "elementary harmony," he made a special study of innovation, which consisted first "in a search for an individual harmonic language, but later was transformed into a desire to find a medium for the expression of strong emotions." And he cites "Sarcasms," the Scythian Suite, the opera *Gambler*, "They Are Seven," etc., as examples. The melodic inflection, orchestration, and stage technic were affected as well as the harmonic idiom. The third, Prokofieff calls the "toccata, or motor element," which he claims as having been influenced by Schumann's Toccata. Examples are the Etudes op. 2, Toccata op. 11, Scherzo op. 12, and various movements throughout his works. The fourth is the lyrical element, which Prokofieff states is sometimes "lyric meditation" and "sometimes is found in long melodic phrases." Anyone familiar with his works recognizes the importance of Prokofieff's lyricism as found, for example, in the Third Piano Concerto and the seventh piano sonata. "At later stages I paid more and more attention to lyrical expression"; Nicolas Slonimsky thus quotes the composer in his essay on Prokofieff in *Great Modern Composers*.

Anyone describing Prokofieff's style would naturally speak of his use of the grotesque and of satire, and yet he stated: "I should like to limit myself to these four elements, and to regard the fifth element, that of the grotesque, with which some critics are trying to label me, as merely a variation of the other characteristics. In application to my music, I should like to replace the word grotesque by 'Scherzoness', or by the three words giving its gradations: 'jest', 'laughter', 'mockery'."

In 1938 Sergei Eisenstein produced the film *Alexander Nevsky*, for which Prokofieff wrote the musical score. The film was the outcome of the interest Russians felt in their historical past. The composer developed a cantata for chorus, contralto solo and orchestra, op. 78, out of the film music in 1939, in a series of seven musical pictures from a story of the thirteenth century.

Prokofieff had written five piano sonatas before his Soviet period. In 1940 he finished the sixth, and the seventh and eighth followed in quick succession.

Prokofieff started work on a ballet, *Cinderella,* as a commission, and when Hitler attacked the Soviet Union in 1941, he laid it aside to compose two songs and a march for use at the front. At this time he worked on his opera based on Tolstoy's *War and Peace,* which treated of Napoleon's invasion of Russia in 1812. Prokofieff, using a libretto by Mira Mendelson, retained the lyrical story of the novel. He stated that it was his intention to weave the great range of emotions, the spirit of the Russian people, the beauty of the Russian soul, as Tolstoy portrayed them, into the opera.

Prokofieff's opus 100 is his Fifth Symphony, composed in 1944 and conducted by him in Moscow in 1945. His Fourth, op. 47, had been written in 1929 and was dedicated to the Boston Symphony Orchestra for its fiftieth anniversary. The composer stated that the Fifth has no program, but he said, "It is a symphony about the spirit of man." A mature, beautiful work, it shows the famous Russian at the height of his powers.

Dmitri Shostakovich (1906) rose to fame when his First Symphony, op. 10, reached the public. It was composed when he was eighteen and performed in 1926, before he was twenty. Many feel that he has never surpassed the quality it displays. It has melody, harmony, and rhythm still characteristic of his present style. The second, called the October Symphony, celebrated the tenth anniversary of the Revolution, and the third, called "May First" was dedicated to the international labor holiday. Both symphonies have choral endings. Perhaps he imitated Beethoven's Ninth, because he had said, "Only Beethoven was a forerunner of the revolutionary movement."

In the *New York Times,* December 5, 1931, Shostakovich stated, "I am a Soviet composer, and I see our epoch as something heroic, spirited and joyous.... Music cannot help having a political basis— an idea that the bourgeoisie are slow to comprehend. There can be no music without ideology." Here one sees the manifesto working.

But the manifesto worked both ways, and in 1936 not only did the two symphonies fall into disrepute, but his opera *Lady Macbeth of Mzensk* and his ballet *The Limpid Stream* were both subjected to denunciation from *Pravda,* the official newspaper of the U.S.S.R.

After the opera had had two years of success, the article says that "the listener is shocked by deliberate dissonance, by a confused stream of sounds.... Here we have 'Leftist' confusion instead of natural, human music. The power of good music to infect the masses has been sacrificed to a petty-bourgeois, 'formalist' attempt to create originality through cheap clowning."

The term "formalist" is fraught with special meaning as stated earlier by the Russian Association of Proletarian Musicians. "The decadent subject-matter of bourgeois music determines its form. Under the influence of decadent moods the inner meaning of music becomes diluted; technical elements gain ascendancy and music splits into factions according to its formal elements." The music of the so-called bourgeoisie "makes claim to 'objective', formal, technical 'attainments', rejects the legacy of the classical past, and promotes 'novelty', 'contemporaneity' and 'progress' in a narrow, formal, technical sense." The Soviets objected in the bourgeois music of the West to "the cultivation of sensual and pathologically erotic moods" (this they found in *Lady Macbeth*); mysticism, "a premonition of impending social catastrophe"; a naturalistic streak, "urbanist music that reduces itself to the reproduction of noises"; and "the cultivation of primitive, coarse subjects."

Here is the controversy of the East against the West; a denunciation of the Western *neoclassicism,* which to the Russians is "formalistic," and a setting up of their own standard, which is *neoromantic.* Shostakovich, when he showed leanings toward the methods of western Europe, ran into prejudices which were social rather than cultural. He had a keen satirical streak and a sense of the grotesque as shown in several of his early compositions, and his Second and Third Symphonies showed signs of "formalism" in his use of complex rhythms and complex polyphony. His opera *The Nose* was no doubt influenced by contemporary German opera—Schoenberg, Krenek, Hindemith, and Berg—which was anathema to the ruling powers. So Shostakovich fell into disgrace, and his compositions were taboo—for a while.

He wrote a Fourth Symphony and it was put into rehearsal, but he withdrew it and courageously set to work on his Fifth. He was an ardent believer in Soviet principles and took the criticism sufficiently to heart to be willing to reconstruct his creative work. He said of the Fifth, "The theme of this symphony is the assertion of personality. It was the Man with all his emotions and experiences that I saw as a focus of design in this work, which is lyrical in conception from beginning to end" It was played (1937) twenty years after the October Revolution, and the *New York Times* carried headlines to the effect that the composer had regained his place in the Soviet: "Dmitri Shostakovich, who fell from grace two years ago, on the way to rehabilitation. His new symphony hailed. Audience cheers as Leningrad Philharmonic presents work."

The Russian critics found it a work "based on lofty ideals"; of "a stirring profundity and compelling force"; "of great importance as a milestone in the composer's development"; "the shackles of musical formalism which held the composer captive for so long, and prevented him from writing works profound in concept, have been shaken off."

One cannot resist speculation as to how Shostakovich might have developed had there been no dictating as to how he should write. Be that as it may, the Fifth Symphony opened what is sometimes called his second period, and its success was by no means confined to Russia.

The Sixth Symphony, op. 54, followed the next year and was a success although not such an overwhelming one as the Fifth. A characteristic of the work is the long, slow first movement, distinctly melodic, not in traditional form, followed by a scherzo and finale more according to the customary procedure.

On June 22, 1941, German bombers arrived in Russia, and the Nazis started to march on Moscow. Shostakovich volunteered for the army and was told he would be called when needed. He joined the Leningrad Conservatory fire-fighting brigade. He was asked to become musical director of the people's Voluntary Army Theater. He toured front-line armies with a truck that carried a troupe of entertainers. He composed songs and simple tunes for them.

Early in July he began work on the Seventh Symphony, for which he wrote: "It is to our struggle against fascism, to our future victory, to my native city, Leningrad, that I dedicate my *Seventh Symphony.*" He worked while the city was being bombed from the air and shelled by artillery. He worked intensely and swiftly. "I wanted to create the story of our days, our life, our people, who are becoming heroes and victors for the cause of triumph over the enemy." It was completed in Kuibyshev, where the first performance was given under

the direction of S. A. Samosud, March 5, 1942. The score, photographed
on microfilm, was sent by plane to Teheran, Persia, by automobile to
Cairo, Egypt, and by plane to America, where it was played on the
radio (N.B.C. Symphony Orchestra, conducted by Toscanini) July 19.
This was followed by the first American concert performance at
Tanglewood, Lenox, Mass., under the direction of Dr. Koussevitzky
in a Russian benefit concert, August 14.

A flowing melodic line dominates the first movement in which
Shostakovich has introduced "a requiem in memory of the heroes
who sacrificed their lives so that justice and reason might triumph."
(The words are his own as quoted in the program notes of John N.
Burk in the Boston Symphony Orchestra program of November 21,
1942.) A scherzo recalls "glorious episodes of the recent past. The
thrill of living, the wonder of nature—this is the meaning of the third
part, which is an andante.... The first part is devoted to the struggle
and the fourth is devoted to the victory. A moving and solemn theme
rises to the apotheosis of the whole composition—the presentiment of
victory."

As his works had celebrated the tenth and the twentieth anniver-
saries of the birth of the Soviet Union, so the Eighth was performed
for the first time on the occasion of the twenty-fifth anniversary, in
Moscow in November 1943. Both the Seventh and Eighth are extremely long. They make one think of Mahler in scope and in treatment. The first New York performance was a broadcast on April 2,
1944, played by the Philharmonic-Symphony Society directed by Artur
Rodzinski over the Columbia Broadcasting System. Shostakovich stated
that the symphony is "an attempt to look into the future, into the
post-war epoch," and he expressed his philosophical concept in the
words: "Life is beautiful. All that is evil and ugly will disappear and
beauty will triumph."

Again one feels that melody is uppermost, a melody which is handed
from strings to woodwinds with gradual sonority arising from a full
orchestra still singing but in large harmonic chords. The second
movement is in typical Shostakovich march rhythm. The last three
movements are played without pause, a march with trumpet fanfare,
a passacaglia, and a pastoral, quiet close.

The composer expressed his intention of writing a trilogy of symphonies, to record in music the war consciousness of a nation as ex-

pressed by one of its artists. The Ninth Symphony is shorter, gayer, with a lightheartedness and quiet, reflective sections forming necessary contrasts. Thus Shostakovich celebrates victory and a return to peaceful pursuits. Its American première took place at the opening concert of the Berkshire Festival under the direction of Dr. Serge Koussevitzky on July 25, 1946.

In addition to the symphonies, Shostakovich has written chamber music works, the most important of which are the cello sonata (1934), the string quartet (1938), the piano quintet (1940), and a trio for piano, violin, and cello (1945). For the quintet he was awarded the Stalin prize of one hundred thousand rubles ($20,000), given by the government in recognition of "signal achievements in the arts and sciences."

Aram Khachatourian (1903) is known in America chiefly by his colorful, attractive concerto for piano and orchestra (1935), which reflects something of his Oriental background. He is a native of Tiflis, and brings to his Soviet music an Armenian folk character that adds an individual flavor to present-day music. Khachatourian and Liev Knipper (1898) also from Tiflis have made studies in Asiatic folk music, which they employ in their scores. Khachatourian has written two symphonies and chamber music. The Second Symphony (1943) has as its theme "the wrath of the Soviet people waging a struggle for humanity." He has a violin concerto (1940) and a ballet, *Gayane* (1942), for which he was given the Stalin prize of one hundred thousand rubles. His wife, Nina Makarova (1908), is also a composer, a pupil of Miaskovsky. She has a symphony, a violin sonata, a piano sonatina, and songs to her credit.

Tikhon Khrennikoff (1913) has written two symphonies, one of which was played by Toscanini; two operas on the subject of the Russian civil war; music for films and songs.

Vissarion Shebalin (1902), one of the most representative of the Soviet composers, has written four symphonies which show the growth of an individual modal and contrapuntal style. The Third Symphony (1934) is on the text of Mayakovsky's poem "Lenin," and is regarded as one of the important contemporary Russian symphonies. The work is long and has a choral finale. More recently he has written a musical comedy, *Flight from the Embassy* (period of Catherine II), a fifth string quartet, based on Slav folksongs, and a Russian Overture for orchestra.

Shebalin has been interested in studying the music of Glinka and Moussorgsky, and has completed unfinished scores of both. He has made a version of the latter's *Fair of Sorochintsk*.

Dmitri Kabalevski (1904) has written four symphonies, the first one of which is frequently programmed in this country; also two piano concertos. Of two sonatinas, one has won popularity. He is the composer of an opera on Romain Rolland's story *Colas Breugnon* (1937), the overture to which is frequently played. He has written large works for chorus and orchestra, such as "Poem of Struggle" and "Requiem," which is known as his Third Symphony. He has composed two ballets.

One of the Soviet operas considered to represent a new period in Russia's musical history is *The Quiet Don* by Ivan Dzerzhinsky (1909). The work was first produced in 1935 and was an immediate success. It is dedicated to Shostakovich, and the libretto, written by the composer's brother, is based on Mikhail Sholokhov's novel. The setting is of World War I, closing with a Cossack rebellion led by the hero, Gregor. While the background is war and revolution, the opera is essentially romantic. Cossack folk melodies are used, and the famous marching song "From Border to Border" is sung in the closing scenes.

Dzerzhinsky is the composer of two other operas, and of considerable piano music.

Yury Shaporin (1889) shows the influence of Rimski-Korsakov. He is a conductor and has written much incidental music for plays and for films. He has an opera, *The Decembrists,* which, according to Gerald Abraham in his book *Eight Soviet Composers,* is still unfinished. Shaporin's symphony, "On the Field of Kulikovo," is for chorus, orchestra, and brass band. Abraham says: "It was Borodin inflated to the dimensions of Mahler."

Shostakovich once answered his foreign critics to the extent of telling them that Soviet music—his symphonies—were not written for the ears of sophisticated audiences but for the musically uncultured masses and to inspire them by means of aesthetic ideals. The same may be said of many other Soviet composers who are fulfilling the demands of the government in writing music that shall be an aid to the social development of the people.

Count Leo Tolstoy in his book *What is Art?* seemed many years ago to state the objective of the Soviet Union: "Universal art, by uniting the most different people in one common feeling, by destroying separation, will educate people to union, will show them, not by reason, but by life itself, the joy of universal union reaching beyond the bounds set by life."

While the musical life in the United States was not directly interfered with by the Hitler dictatorship and World War II, their effects were of moment and of importance to our future development. There has been a tremendous cultural movement from the east (Europe) to the Western Hemisphere. Almost all of the composers of note from middle Europe, from France and elsewhere, conductors, musicologists, and artists, migrated to this country, and most of them have become American citizens. They have established new homes all the way from New York to Hollywood. Many famous European musicians are teaching in our music schools and universities. Their new works are performed by our leading orchestras and musical organizations. Many of them have been published in America. Some of the composers are writing for the motion pictures; composers and performers have been employed by the radio; many conductors have found posts or have created new ones; and some of the musical scholars have found positions as music editors, proofreaders, and advisers in our publishing houses. The influence of the migrated Europeans is nation-wide, and in the last decade or so, many have been absorbed into our national life.

While the older composers may be fixed in their own musical ways and idioms, still, unconsciously they reflect in their scores American tendencies and environment. And in turn the teachers are influencing our young composers.

Dr. Paul Nettl in an article, "Alexandrian America," in *Modern Music,* January-February 1941, states his conviction that "musical America is destined to fulfill a tremendous mission of conservation, the conservation of Europe's great cultural values. . . . America today invites comparison with Alexandria of antiquity. After Rome had subdued Greece, Greek culture sought refuge in Egypt." Alexandria became "a brilliant center of Hellenistic culture in which Greek tradition was cultivated and extended. . . . For eight full centuries this Alexandrian culture maintained itself."

"Compared with Europe today America appears to be a second

Alexandria." Dr. Nettl speaks of the growth of musical activity through the radio which carries the works of former centuries "to the most distant parts of the country, to the isolated prairies, to the Arctic. Millions are now acquainted with music." The phonograph preserves works of art, and we have great libraries, "like the great libraries of Alexandria." He also speaks of the extent of music education in our schools.

"This enormous, elaborate cultivation of the music of the past on a scale hitherto unknown in the world, has a significance which, in my opinion," he states, "at present overshadows the cultivation of native music.... It almost seems ... that America has become the land of European music. And that ... is the significance of the present, the latest European migration, which surpasses in importance, all previous musical migrations."

At the present writing (1947), Arnold Schoenberg and Igor Stravinsky, two of the strongest influences in the early twentieth century, live in Southern California. Paul Hindemith teaches composition at Yale University School of Music. Darius Milhaud teaches at Mills College, California. Ernest Krenek teaches at Hamline University, St. Paul, Minn. Before his last illness, Béla Bartók held an honorary professorship in folk music research at Columbia University, New York. Dr. Curt Sachs, one of the great musicologists, is professor in the Graduate School of New York University. Dr. Alfred Einstein, another of the great music scholars, teaches at Smith College. Bohuslav Martinu has written prolifically and has had many performances. He was invited to return to Prague. Herbert Graf is stage director at the Metropolitan Opera House. Ernst Toch has been writing for films in Hollywood and teaching composition at the University of Southern California. Erich Korngold composes for the films in Hollywood. Kurt Weill has written successful light operas, incidental music for the theater, and musical scores for films since his arrival in this country. Richard Arnell and Stanley Bate (British); Gregor and Jerzy Fitelberg, conductor and composer, father and son; Alexandre Tansman, and Karol Rathaus (Polish); Johan Franko (Dutch); Vittorio Rieti (Italian); Karl Weigl (Austrian); Germaine Tailleferre and Yves Tinayre (French); Stefan Wolpe (German); Jaromir Weinberger and H. A. Schimmerling (Czechoslovak); Alexander Gretchaninoff, Arthur Lurié, Nicolai Lopatnikoff (Russian) are a few who have made America their home, and most of them have become citizens of the United States. This list is by no means complete, nor does it include the many musicologists, performers, conductors, etc.

With World War II an epoch of European history closed. We cannot prophesy, but let us pray that the new epoch will produce a constructive social structure that will be conducive to a healthy, wholesome culture and a "golden age" of music and art.

CHAPTER 19

THE NEW OPERA: BERG, HINDEMITH, WEILL, KRENEK, HONEGGER, MILHAUD, GRUENBERG, ETC.

THE twilight of opera has long been prophesied, but as long as there are opera stars who stir the enthusiasm and curiosity of a public which still loves *La Traviata, Madama Butterfly, Rigoletto, Lohengrin, Carmen, Faust,* and *Tannhäuser,* there will be opera. In a few countries, such as Italy, for example, and prewar Germany, the love for opera seems as deeply rooted as the love for folk music.

Of course, there are several opera publics, and some who flock to *Il Trovatore* and *Cavalleria Rusticana* cannot be driven to *Die Goetterdämmerung, Tristan und Isolde, Elektra, Salome, Boris Godounoff,* or *Pelléas et Mélisande.* And there is a third public, a much smaller group, interested in experiment and desirous of seeing the spirit of twentieth century music, dance, and theater inculcated into opera. The feeling has been growing that a new vitality must be brought into the music drama, for it obviously has not kept pace with our changing age.

There are two types who listen to the old Italian operas: those who have heard them all their lives and love the familiar melodies, and those for whom they have a historical value.

Opera reform is not a new story. Since the days of Monteverdi it has raised a hue and cry. So we have had our Glucks, Lullys, Rameaus, Mozarts, and Wagners. (But not many of them!) Wagner, a genius, was able to handle his reforms, but his formulas in the hands of less gifted men proved detrimental rather than constructive. Verdi, strongly entrenched in Italian tradition, was little disturbed by Wagner, and the Verdi of *Falstaff* and *Otello* has been the line of least resistance for the "realism" of Puccini and the later Italians, even for Pizzetti's *Fra Ghirardo* and Respighi's *La Compana Sommersa* (*The Sunken Bell*). Malipiero has had some reforms to offer in Italian opera.

Hans Pfitzner, Franz Schreker, and Erich Korngold (1897) wrote German operas in the Italian *realistic* tradition. Korngold startled the world as a child prodigy by composing a pantomime which was performed at the Court Opera. While living in Vienna he never came under the Schoenberg influence. One of his most successful works was *Die Tote Stadt* (*The Dead City*) in which Maria Jeritza made her debut at the Metropolitan Opera House in New York. Korngold, now an American citizen, has become a well-known composer for Hollywood films.

In America, with the exception of occasional experiments tried outside of the Metropolitan Opera, the current opera has remained practically as it was, with the same repertory, the same demands from both audience and management. The experiments are more necessary to the composers than to the opera-goer or -giver. A small proportion of the public is interested in innovations, but, after all, it is the large public that pays the bills and therefore dictates the policy.

In a day when absolute music reigns, it is understandable that opera should have a difficult time in the hands of young composers. "Of all musical forms dependent on a literary element," says Eric Blom in *The Limitations of Music,* "the opera is answerable for the most radical emancipation from musical conditions. It trespasses most readily on other forms of art and violates its own with the greatest appearance of impunity." He considers that Wagner was a great musician in spite of his reforms and not because of them. "It is significant, also," he continues, "that the one great follower, Strauss, drifts farther and farther away from the Wagnerian system in each successive dramatic work. By the time he reached *Der Rosenkavalier* he had resumed most of the old operatic baggage discarded by Wagner and dropped the *Leitmotiv* as a dramatic agent in favor of musical theme used in a musical way."

The century opened with Debussy's *Pelléas et Mélisande* and Strauss's contributions to opera. Soon the ballet developed in a manner hitherto unknown. As presented by Diaghileff and written by Stravinsky, it was a new movement but it wasn't opera. The opera world went into the archives and brought out old works which were novelties to the twentieth century. Works which a generation ago were discarded as too "melodious" and musically too naïve were held up as models simply because they were at the opposite extreme from Wagnerian theories. *Opera buffa* was a relief after the unsuccessful pursuit of the music drama. In the meantime, the stage became realistic, dealing, as did Gustave Charpentier in *Louise,* with the everyday life of his time. So opera, ready for one of its frequent reforms, has sought to express an artistic truth in which the dramatic and the musical elements could be blended in equitable proportions.

One of the most surprising figures in the account of modern opera is Leos Janacek (1854-1928), who was an old man before his original and dramatic gifts had a chance to be judged by the outside world. With him the modern spirit was introduced into Czechoslovakia, and he has been compared to Moussorgsky for the extraordinary way he united folk music (Bohemian) with characterization. Among his operas are *Jenufa,* which was given at the Metropolitan; *Katja Kubanowa* (*The Cunning Little Fox*), a symbolic fairy tale of animals and humans; *The Makropoulos Affair,* which is one of the first operas to utilize a present-day setting of telephones and hotels, although the prima donna was born in 1576! Without much attempt at making a libretto, he used scenes from Dostoievsky's story of prison life in Siberia, from which he made an opera, *Memoirs from a House of the Dead.* Janacek was an inspiration to the young Czechoslovaks before World War I.

Another Czechoslovak work presented at the Metropolitan was Jaromir Weinberger's comic opera, *Schwanda: Der Dudelsackpfeiffer* (*Schwanda, the Bagpiper*).

Ferruccio Busoni, although a pianist and teacher, had great interest in the problems not only of interpretive music but of original composition. He wrote for orchestra *"Berceuse élégiaque"* and *"Rondo arlecchinesco."* He was interested in a new classicism, in which he attempted to revive the *commedia dell'arte* of the seventeenth century, that flavored his opera *Arlecchino.* Busoni's interest in opera was that of the musician concerned with presenting as "pure" a product as though he did not have the problem of the text. Thus he attempted to carry a new classic spirit into opera. At the time of his death Busoni was completing the score of an opera, *Doktor Faustus,* on which he had worked for many years and for which he had written the libretto.

The finishing touches were added by a pupil, Philipp Jarnach, and it was performed at the fifth festival of the International Society for Contemporary Music at Frankfort in 1927. "A masterpiece of lofty conception," Weissmann called it in an article which appeared in *Modern Music* (November-December 1927), "... it reveals a man completely devoted to his art, bringing to it a mastery both technical and of the spirit...." In the same issue of *Modern Music* Lazare Saminsky expresses surprise at finding no influence of Wagner but rather "the tints of Berlioz and Meyerbeer." Saminsky finds in it "a unity, a style and flexibility of musical action that might serve as a challenge to any creator," and to him "the performance of Busoni's *Faustus* appears a great event in contemporary musical life."

Schoenberg may be held responsible for the introduction of the short, condensed opera such as he wrote in the monodrama *Erwartung,* op. 17, and *Die glückliche Hand,* op. 18, both of which represent experiments in operatic form. *Erwartung* is an attempt to write an opera making one person, a soprano, carry the entire action, and concentrated drama. The text was written at Schoenberg's instigation by Marie Pappenheim. But in the next work, *The Hand of Fate* or *The Lucky Hand,* as the German title is sometimes translated, he wrote his own libretto, and the work is notable for the compactness of its story, action, and music. This time a high baritone carries the burden of the singing and there is a chanting chorus, a *Sprech-chor,* in the orchestra; the woman and another man have no singing but act the roles in pantomime. Here Schoenberg reaches the height of his doctrine of *expressionism* in which all realism is forgotten and, as Paul Stefan says, "one moves in the sphere of poetry, of symbols, of visions."

Whether or not one accepts these early operatic experiments of Schoenberg as symptomatic, there is no doubt that he had both direct and indirect influence on the operas of his pupils and of the younger Germans, and that the history of opera in the last decades reads differently because of his experiments.

During the winter of 1929-30 an opera by Schoenberg was presented at the Frankfort Opera House. It was a happy affair, *Von Heute auf Morgen (From One Day to Another)*, in which the composer, so often accused of morbidity and melancholy, has attempted to prove that his twelve tone system can be applied to the expression of light and cheerful mood. The opera, about fifty minutes long, is on a one-act text in modern setting by Max Blonda. Of the four main characters, each personality calls forth a different type of melodic figure of the twelve tone scale and at the same time a characteristic rhythmic pattern. There are arias and recitatives, and much contrapuntal writing in which a number of experiments are attempted. In the orchestration Schoenberg uses saxophones, mandolins, guitars, piano, a flexaton, besides the usual instruments.

The consensus of critical opinion grants to Alban Berg the achievement of having written in *Wozzeck* the greatest experimental opera since *Pelléas et Mélisande*. Berg spent from 1914 to 1920 on the work which, with its first performance under Erich Kleiber in Berlin in 1925, brought him international fame. Leopold Stokowski presented it in Philadelphia and New York in 1931. Berg used the twelve tone system which he had acquired from his master Schoenberg, but he also infused the work with individuality, passion, and life. It is this warmth combined with the modernity of his technic which is convincing. Berg has added intensity to Schoenberg's expressionism.

Berg chose fifteen scenes from a dramatic fragment by Georg Buechner (1813-1837). He recognized in the century-old work possibilities for new dramatic musical treatment. The phantomlike characters are symbols which Dr. Willi Reich describes in his *Guide to Wozzeck*, a monograph issued by *Modern Music* (taken from an article by R. Schaefke and a lecture by Dr. H. Jalowitz): "The Captain becomes the mask of fear-tormented, moralizing philistinism; the Physician, the demon of cold, materialistic science, hostile to man and his soul; the Drum-Major, the embodiment of the beast in man; and Marie, simply the poor unfortunate." Wozzeck is akin to Wagner's Parsifal, the "pure Fool," "the primitive being, still outside morality; close to the forces of nature, surrounded by their hidden mysteries and forced to surrender to them. . . . Words cannot convey the idea, which, though barely expressed, becomes embodied in this figure as powerfully as any concept ever has been on the stage. Thus Wozzeck has something of the force of a mythological being and for that reason is well cast as the central figure of an opera." He is the incarnation of elemental feelings and passions.

Berg made the fragmentary sketches into a well-proportioned libretto which he divided into three parts: exposition, dénouement, and catastrophe. Dr. Reich says: "Indeed the sociological undercurrent of the

Buechner play is not untimely today. The grotesque element in the delineation of the characters, especially of the Physician, finds its echo in modern art. The interpolated folk-tunes and the opportunities for the use of tone-color in various episodes must have attracted the musician.... The method by which the poetic material is developed contains the germ cell of Berg's music."

Wozzeck was the first work in which the system of atonality was applied to an extended composition. Heretofore there had been no atonal symphonies, oratorios, or grand operas. Berg has utilized old forms in a surprising way in *Wozzeck,* adopting them with amazing fluency and skill to the demands of an atonal technic.

The scheme of musical forms in *Wozzeck* is analyzed by Dr. Reich as follows:

Act I. Five character sketches: Suite, Rhapsody, Military March and Cradle Song, Passacaglia, Andante Affetuoso (quasi Rondo).

Act II. Symphony in five movements: Sonata Form, Fantasie and Fugue, Largo, Scherzo and Rondo Martiale.

Act III. Five Inventions: on a Theme, on a Tone, on a Rhythm, on a Key (D Minor), on a Persistent Rhythm (*Perpetuum Mobile*).

There are certain unforgettable scenes, such as Marie's reading of the Bible; the incessant pounding of the tone b in the scene in which Wozzeck kills Marie; the playful indifference of the child in the face of tragedy. In spite of the early controversies caused by the opera, it always created a profound impression by its desperate sincerity and spontaneity. "Despite the protests of reactionary spirits," Adolf Weissmann wrote in *Modern Music* ("Unexpected Developments in Germany," March-April 1926), "a work which denies the old tradition of bel-canto and relentlessly pursues its own direction in a search for truth, has miraculously achieved not only a first night success, but an enduring place in the opera repertoire ... it is, in the truest meaning of the word, an independent and original work."

Alban Berg wrote in *Modern Music,* November-December 1927, that he never entertained the idea of reforming the artistic structure of opera through *Wozzeck*. "Neither when I started nor when I completed this work did I consider it a model for further operatic efforts, whoever the composer might be. I never assumed or expected that *Wozzeck* should in this sense become the basis of a school.

"I wanted to compose good music; to develop musically the contents of Buechner's immortal drama; to translate his poetic language into music; . . . to give the theater what belongs to the theater."

His answer to the "much discussed utilization of old and new musical forms and their application in an absolute music," is that it was "imperative to use everything warranted to create individualizing characteristics on the one hand, and coherence on the other."

In his own words, he believes his achievement to be that "from the moment the curtain parts until it closes for the last time, there is no one in the audience who pays any attention to the various fugues, inventions, suites, sonata movements, variations and passacaglias . . . no one who heeds anything but the social problems of this opera, which by far transcend the personal destiny of Wozzeck."

At the time of his death, December 24, 1935, Alban Berg left his opera *Lulu* completed except for some of the orchestration. These few measures were worked out by Schoenberg, and the work was presented at Zurich in 1937. The five excerpts which Berg extracted for orchestra met with various reactions, arousing storms of criticism for and against his music.

The libretto of *Lulu* was taken from two plays by Frank Wedekind, *The Earth Spirit* and *Pandora's Box* (1893-1905). These were translated by S. A. Eliot as *Tragedies of Sex,* which title is significant. Lulu not merely represents a beautiful woman with irresistible sex attraction but she is "a completely natural primal spirit,"—"the eternal feminine manifestation of evil." The story is revoltingly disagreeable. It was chosen not for its pornographic character, however, but obviously for the moral it preaches. No doubt the degeneracy of the period impressed Wedekind, who pictures the destructive fascination of this primal type whom he calls "a wild, lovely creature" and represents in the prologue as a snake. Lulu attracts everyone, and like the flame, she unwittingly lures the human moths to their destruction, but in turn she sinks to the deepest degradation and is finally destroyed.

An innovation is the use of a silent film with music which serves as the entr'acte. Berg has constructed the music to the entire opera upon a single twelve-tone row: bb-d-eb-c-f-g-e-f♯-a-g♯-c♯-b. Berg stated that he used vocal forms like arias, duets, trios, ensembles, and also employed sonata form to depict one character, rondo form another, and "an exotic pentatonic scheme" for another.

In the *Musical Quarterly* for October 1936 Willi Reich, a Viennese critic and friend of the composer, wrote an important and detailed account of the plot and an analysis of the twelve tone treatment in an article entitled "Alban Berg's *Lulu*."

Egon Wellesz, the biographer of Schoenberg and a member of the Schoenberg circle, is his own librettist in his opera *Die Bachantinnen* (*The Bacchantes*) after the drama by Euripides. From his studies of Byzantine music, Wellesz has brought an archaic flavor into the melody and rhythm of the work, although the harmony is modern. His interest in Greek classics is shown in his use of the chorus, which is placed in the foreground and carries the burden of telling the story. In fact, it is a choral opera. A ballet by Dr. Wellesz, *Die Nächtlichen* (*The Phantoms*) is written in the form of a dance symphony.

Wellesz's most recent works have been, for orchestra, Piano Concerto, op. 49, and the symphonic suite based on Shakespeare's *Tempest* (1936-1938); two masses op. 51 and 58; choruses; chamber music— suite for violin and piano, and Little Suite for flute solo; and Five Sonnets from Elizabeth Barrett Browning for soprano and string quartet (1936). He wrote a textbook, *Die Neue Instrumentation* (*The New Instrumentation*, 1928-1929). For twenty-five years he carried on in Vienna a successful career as composer and musicologist, which ended in March 1938. Dr. Wellesz was then given a chair in Oxford University, England.

Paul Hindemith, after writing four dramatic works—*Mörder, Hoffnung der Frauen* (*Mörder, the Hope of Women*), a one-act opera on a text by the painter-writer, Oskar Kokoschka, who was one of the instigators of Schoenberg's painting; *Das Nusch-Nuschi,* music for a burlesque puppet show for Franz Blei's Burmese play; a one-act opera on August Stramm's *Sancta Susanna;* and a dance panto-mime, *Der Daemon*—wrote *Cardillac,* an experimental opera.

The libretto for this dramatic opera after a romantic story by E. T. A. Hoffmann, in which Hindemith wished to express his principles of neoclassicism, is by Ferdinand Lion. Adolf Weissmann said in "Germany's Latest Music Dramas" (*Modern Music,* May-June 1927), "In his conviction that the score of an opera should not differ fundamentally from the score of any other composition, he [Hindemith] has literally retraced his steps to the forms of Bach.... The style is that which we associate with the chamber orchestra; it is contrapuntal and linear and therefore as remote as possible from the operatic convention." His uncompromising attitude kept *Cardillac* from winning the public's approval.

More experiments followed. *Hin und Zurück* (*There and Back*) is a comedy of chamber music proportions, a *Sketch mit Musick* from Charlot's Revue, in which the action borrows Schoenberg's *motus cancrizans* and in crab fashion the second part is reversed and the entire action and music are played backwards. *Neues vom Tage* (*News of the Day*) is a tabloid opera on a libretto by Marcellus Schiffer, a writer of revues, who also supplied the text for *Hin und Zurück.*

Why Hindemith, the serious young composer, the shining hope of interwar Germany, should have been attracted to a burlesque of mediocre caliber is interesting psychology. Not so long ago a contemporaneous topic was thought unfit as a subject for opera. With the realist movement in art, however, everyday life, shorn of all vestige of prettiness—vulgar, raw, showing up human weaknesses and foibles with a pitiless spotlight—has replaced Wagner's world of myths and medieval characters teaching and preaching nobility of sentiment and redemption through love. A passing phase perhaps, a result of war brutality? Yes, but obviously a symptom of a world sick in mind and spirit. Hindemith, Kurt Weill, Ernst Krenek, and Heinrich Kaminski: had they sold their birthright for a mess of pottage? *Gebrauchsmusik, Jugendbewegung!* Bach wrote "useful music" too when he supplied his choir with a new cantata every week. But what would the youth of today want with a cantata? Tabloid newspapers, jazz "hot," detective stories, pornographic literature, radio, movies, prize fights, sports, joy rides, bootleggers, racketeers, are these the ideals that are to determine the art of tomorrow?

The political situation in Germany interfered with the première of Hindemith's opera *Mathis der Maler,* written in 1932-1934. It was finally presented in Zurich, and proved to be one of Hindemith's greatest achievements. Arno Huth reported (*Modern Music,* November-December 1938) in "Forbidden Opus—Protestant": "The composition, which is national opera in the very best sense, and gives powerful expression to a part of German history, German art and German mores, was lifted out of the baptismal font in the very hour when Hindemith's scores were being pilloried in the Düsseldorf exhibition of 'Degenerate Music' as un-German."

The libretto is his own, and the story concerns the painter of the Isenheim altar (page 258), Matthias Grünewald, who to Hindemith became the symbol of the German artist. The composer makes the painter of the time of the Reformation and the Peasant Wars the center of a personal conflict between art and the call to arms. But the artist is disillusioned because the peasants fight in revenge, not for a better way of life. In Huth's words, "his belief in himself and the world shattered, he hears the voice of his outraged soul, is tormented by visions of his paintings. The answer to doubt comes at last in a dream." (In the symphony this is "Temptation of Saint Anthony" section.) "The artist must follow his divine mission, neither questioning the goal nor asking for reasons. Obedient to the mandate, he begins to labor as in a trance, and absorbed in a sacred passion, produces work after work until he collapses, the task complete."

Kurt Weill, a disciple of Busoni, went into the Youth Movement and produced several operas which had popular success, one of which, *Dreigroschenoper* (*Three Penny Opera*) is supposed to be a modern German version of Gay's *The Beggar's Opera*. It smacks of the music hall and is clever, commonplace, and artificial. Among his works is *Der Jasager* (*The One Who Says Yes*) based on an ancient Japanese legend and written in a simple idiom for performance by school children. Jazz has played an important role in this popular type of opera, for example in Weill's *Royal Palace* on a libretto by Ivan Goll, in which a ballet of waiters and bellhops appears and a film is projected, and his *Mahagonny*, a chamber opera which the composer calls a *Singspiel* (early German *opera buffa*) with "pseudo-popular songs in the jazz manner."

After Kurt Weill came to America, he continued the ideas he had started in Germany for the "musical theater." He worked with Paul Green and created a successful incidental music score for *Johnny Johnson* which resulted in typically American theater. Weill was the composer of the music in Franz Werfel's *Eternal Road,* Maxwell Anderson's *Knickerbocker Holiday,* Moss Hart's *Lady in the Dark,* and Elmer Rice's *Street Scene.*

Ernest Krenek's *Jonny spielt auf* had its fling at the Metropolitan, but New York felt that the American writers of revues and musical comedy knew their business better than the German pseudo-jazzists. *Jonny* really succeeded, however, in making Europe believe that "The new world had come sailing over the sea in splendor and had conquered old Europe by means of the Dance." *Jonny* also was a financial success.

Under the name of *Orpheus and Euridice* Krenek had previously composed a serious opera on a text by Oskar Kokoschka, in which Euridice is a modern woman and resents Orpheus's domination. Krenek opened up a new lyricism which could eventually lead to a neoromanticism, and showed, as well, a psychoanalytic tendency.

Jonny made it hard for America to understand that Krenek is a serious talent, a radical and uncompromising composer. He understands the demands of opera and has been particularly interested in problems presented to opera writers by the changes which have taken place in the musical idiom of the twentieth century.

In 1930, although only thirty years of age, he wrote his eighth stage work, *Leben des Orest* (*The Life of Orestes*) a grand opera in five acts with eight scenes for which he was his own librettist. He attempts to combine jazz with Greek classicism. "Hellenic Jazz!" His mixture of styles is deliberate, done apparently for theatrical effect only. H. H. Stuckenschmidt writing in *Modern Music,* April-May 1930, finds the composer too uncritical of his work. "The opera has been wonderfully successful. And this, not only because it is so dulcet and tuneful, or has good choruses, or is really so effective theatrically, but because it is a symbol of the stylistic chaos of our times."

Krenek has espoused the cause of twelve tone technic; in fact one of his most important stage works, *Karl V,* is written in twelve-tone. The composer wrote the book, and has used spoken dialogue as well as operatic song. After Krenek had left Europe, the work was performed at Prague (1938) just before experimental opera ceased to be presented there. The story, written between 1931 and 1933, concerns the Austro-Spanish Emperor, and the subject, Karl's attempt in the sixteenth century to hold together his imperial power over Rome, Germany, France, Spain, Turkey, and South America, was timely.

Jürg Jenatch by Heinrich Kaminski is, according to Lazare Saminsky, a spoken drama in a framework of orchestral preludes and finales, interpolated with dialogues and mass scenes. It is based on an event in Swiss history. Kaminski used his well-developed contrapuntal technic and showed strong dramatic gifts. It strikes a different note in the mass of experimental operas so much of which seems to be artificial and artistically barren.

Opera has paid its tribute to the Machine Age in a lyric drama, *Maschinist Hopkins,* by Max Brand. Serious and dramatic, it still flavors of the music hall and pays its respects to jazz.

"His [Brand's] real achievements in this work are the two industrial scenes whose vitality have a machine-like throb, and the creation, in Hopkins, of a character who is himself an avenging machine," writes Oscar Thompson (*Modern Music,* December-January 1929-30). "The great clanking upbuildings of sound at the finale, when the huge industrial plant is in full operation, with Hopkins in control, and a multitude of puny workers going through their machine-like routine, have their power in the theater, and transcend in their weight and clangor the mechanistic music that has its place in ballet and orchestral programs."

What the next step in German opera will be is impossible to foresee. Perhaps the Nazi regime and World War II have led it into a blind alley or at least attempted to turn it back to a "straight and narrow path." But in spite of physical setbacks such as war, political prejudices, world depressions, etc., the spirit of art has in the past had a way of turning catastrophes to its own account. Perhaps the shades of Mozart, Gluck, Weber, Wagner, and even Meyerbeer—all radicals in their day—will lend their aid.

A slogan for German impresarios might be, "A Mozart! A Mozart! My kingdom for a Mozart!" But copying a former style will not do it. The new Mozart will have to have an inner conviction and genius. Digging up the past reeks too much of the mummies that are unearthed—and too much of the earth!

The after effects of World War I were worked off in France through the ballet (page 187), but there, too, experiment in opera has been rife. Stravinsky's contribution to opera has been small when one discounts the ballets, but many of his ideas have been the source of new developments. *L'Histoire du soldat, Renard,* and *Mavra* encouraged the development of chamber music opera which should, from a practical and economic point of view, prove indispensable. It offers tremendous opportunities for originality and satisfactory stage performance. *Le Rossignol* flavored too much of *Le Coq d'or* to be considered a new influence, but *Oedipus Rex* in its attempt to solve the problem of reducing dramatic effect through less action could indicate a direction both for music of the stage and in choral works (oratorios, cantatas).

When Arthur Honegger turned the incidental music of Morax's poem into the opera *Judith* (page 241), he expressed his intentions thus: "From the moment when a number of young musicians returned voluntarily to the old Italian *opera buffa,* I wanted to use again the old Italian background of *opera seria.*" The splendid choral treatment of *Judith* gives special power to the score in which chorus and orchestra are treated independently of each other. "He has no need of an immense orchestra and rare instruments to produce impressions of strength and extraordinary strangeness. His distinction lies in achieving the unusual by the simplest means," said Henry Prunières.

André Coeuroy contended that the only original operas are those which reveal a study of declamation which conforms to language. In this sense opera will be national, not because of its subject but because of its "aesthetic will." Coeuroy quoted as examples of this linguistic nationalism, Moussorgsky's *Boris Godounoff,* Debussy's *Pelléas et Mélisande,* Bartók's *Blue Beard's Castle,* Janacek's Moravian dramas, Szymanowski's *Roi Roger,* and Honegger's *Antigone.*

Honegger said of *Antigone,* "I wanted to give the exact *plastique* of the voice, to find a natural form of vocal expression, and I sought a melodic line created by the word itself, by its own *plastique,* designed to accentuate the contours and to bring the word into relief." To achieve his intentions, Honegger has used a rapid recitative comparable to the old Italian system called *quasi parlando.* Even more than in *Judith* Honegger claims to have kept the song and the orchestra independent of each other. (Freely transcribed by the author from André Coeuroy's *Panorama de la musique contemporaine.*)

Darius Milhaud's setting of Paul Claudel's *Christophe Colomb* had its world première in Berlin (1930) under the direction of Erich Kleiber, who had given many first performances of German and foreign works at the Staatsoper. It was regarded as a significant event. Its first claim to innovation is that it introduces the cinema into grand opera. Raymond Petit in *La Revue musicale* cited as examples of its successful usage the storm at sea and the arrival of the boats in the New World. Another innovation is the introduction of song and the spoken word, performed in rhythm and held together by percussion instruments, accomplished without shock to the artistic sensibilities. Milhaud had already tried the effect of declamation in rhythm with accompaniment of percussion in his choruses to *Choéphores,* one of the triptych of operas which includes *Agamemnon* and the *Euménides.*

"The use of the moving pictures permits the most interesting studies in the domain of time, as Claudel has done in his libretto, when he brings simultaneously before the eye, the parleying of the Mexican gods on the stage, and the departure of the ships from Spain on the screen," Petit writes.

A powerful personality is revealed in the treatment of the music, its unity, depth, and creative strength. Petit finds the first act a great memory in his operatic experience, and in it he sees "a *genre* of theater very new, more epic in nature than tragic." The choruses create a grandeur and dramatic effect comparable in Petit's estimation to those of *Boris Godounoff.*

Milhaud is one of those composers upon whom it is impossible to fasten a characteristic style, as he has the Protean faculty of adapting his music to the demands of the moment. *Le pauvre matelot* (*The Poor Sailor*) is a simple, direct story told with simple, unpretentious music, in which the characters sing songs, some folklike and others romantic in character. It is in the regular repertory of the Opéra Comique.

In addition to *Le pauvre malelot* Milhaud continued his experiments in a condensed type of opera in *Les Malheurs d'Orphée* (*The Misfortunes of Orpheus*); *Esther de Carpentras;* and the three "minute operas," *L'Enlévement d'Europe* (*The Abduction of Europa*), *L'Abandon d'Ariane* (*The Abandonment of Ariadne*) and *La Délivrance de Thésée* (*The Deliverance of Theseus*). Another short opera is *Médée* (*Medea*). Milhaud said that "the shorter works were a natural reaction against Wagnerian music drama and that composers turned instinctively to the earlier operatic forms, such as the *opera di camera,* which fitted in with the neoclassic spirit that had permeated twentieth century forms. Eighteenth century forms also lent themselves more successfully to new harmonic schemes, the 'music hall spirit' (similar to the spirit of the earlier *opera buffa*), and popular rhythms and melodies." (*Musical Quarterly,* April 1942, "Darius Milhaud" by Marion Bauer.)

Milhaud's *Maximilien* had its première in Paris in 1932. The hero is the ill-fated Archduke of Austria who became emperor of Mexico.

In 1934 Milhaud collaborated again with Claudel in incidental music for the drama *L'Annonce faite à Marie* (*Announcement Made to Marie*) presented in Brussels. In all he has written seventeen stage works, the most recent being the opera *Bolivar* based on the life of Simon Bolivar, the South American patriot. The book is by his wife, Madeleine Milhaud.

The opera *Chartreuse de Parme* by Henri Sauguet was presented in Paris in 1939. It is neoromantic in style and stems from early nineteenth century opera. Sauguet also wrote *Le Plumet du Colonel* (*The Colonel's Plume*), which belongs in the group of modern operas and attempted definitely to get away from Wagnerian ideas by reverting to pre-Wagnerian idioms. His opera *La Gageure imprévue* (*The Improvised Wager*) was presented at the Opéra Comique in 1944.

The Soviet contribution to opera has been considerable, and the government has directed its course and dictated its policy. Subjects from Russian history or stories of foreign origin having patriotic import were stressed. The composers were expected to reflect the psychology of the proletariat and to choose subject matter close to revolutionary ideas. Several of the operas were discussed in Chapter 18, especially the controversy over Shostakovich and his *Lady Macbeth of Mzensk*.

To sum up the achievements in Russian opera in the twentieth century we name *The Quiet Don* (or *Quiet Flows the Don*), *Virgin Soil Upturned,* and *Volochaevko Days* by Ivan Dzerzhinsky; *The Master of Clamecy* (after Romain Rolland's *Colas Breugnon*) by Dmitri Kabalevsky; *North Wind, Cities and Years,* and *The Rising Sun* by Liév Knipper; *Simeon Kotko* and *War and Peace* by Serge Prokofieff, who wrote earlier operas such as *The Gambler* and *The Love of Three Oranges*; and *The Nose* and *Lady Macbeth of Mzensk* by Dmitri Shostakovich.

Many of the Soviet composers have written ballets that have been performed in Russia, although few have been seen outside the Soviet Union except those by Prokofieff.

Although a group of nineteenth century Italians proved that they could compose outside of the form fastened to them by tradition, the twentieth century has brought about a rebirth of Italian opera. Pizzetti represents one angle of the new movement, but his work is closely related to that of the nineteenth century. Malipiero, on the other hand,

THE NEW OPERA

307

made a public gesture when he wrote the prologue of the *"Sette canzoni,"* *"La Morte delle maschere"* (*The Death of the Masque,* i.e., of the *commedia dell' arte*). In this he presents Orpheus who locks up, one after the other, the classic figures of the *commedia dell' arte!* Following this, Orpheus, in the role of an impresario, calls forth the characters of the *Sette canzoni* to sing, not music of the stage, but songs sung by real people to old poetic texts. Malipiero has supplied a stage setting, and the opera consists of these disparate scenes connected by means of orchestral intermezzi—"synthetic music drama." The epilogue of the *Orfeide* of which *"La Morte delle maschere"* and *"Sette canzoni"* are two parts, is *"Orfeo"* in a symbolic and original aspect.

From some of the Goldoni comedies Malipiero has made one-act librettos for which he has written music: *La Bottega di caffe, Sor Todero Brontolon, Le Baruffe chiozzotte.* In this last Malipiero has condensed the dialogue to short, rapid, exclamatory sentences for which he has used a *recitativo parlato,* reproducing the inflections of the speaking voice, with orchestral accompaniment creating mood and color.

Malipiero uses the idea of synthetic drama for comedy, tragedy, lyricism, for small pictures or great scenes. *Il Mistero di Venezia,* for example, celebrates the city in a trilogy: *Le Aquile d'Aquilera,* a legend of the founding of Venice; *Il finto Arlecchino* (*The False Harlequin,* from the last days of the *commedia dell'arte*), and *I Corvi di San Marco,* present day Venice in which the spirit of the past stalks through a city controlled by jazz bands, would-be artists, and antique dealers.

Casella (d. 1947) wrote, besides the ballet *La Giara,* an *opera buffa* on a text by Carlo Gozzi, *La Donna serpente,* a style adapted to present day environment by several older and younger Italians. Among these are Alfano, Castelnuovo-Tedesco (*La Mandragola* on Macchiavelli's text), Virgilio Mortari, Antonio Veretti, Nino Rota Rinaldi, etc.

A new figure in the opera-making world is the British composer Benjamin Britten, whose recent work, *Peter Grimes,* was written as a commission from the Koussevitzky Music Foundation granted in 1941 (page 263). Britten was drawn to George Crabbe's poetry about the seacoast of Suffolk, which was his native country as well as the poet's. He found the story of Peter Grimes in the poems *The Borough* (1810), and Montagu Slater used it as the basis of his libretto. Grim and tragic, it deals with types characteristic of the fishing town bordering on the sea. "My life as a child was coloured by the fierce storms that sometimes drove ships on to our coast and ate away whole stretches of the neighboring cliffs," Britten says. In the opera he wanted to express his "awareness of the perpetual struggle of men and women whose livelihood depends on the sea—difficult though it is to treat such a universal subject in theatrical form." Peter Grimes, a harsh and solitary fisherman with a streak of poetic imagination, too, has taken boys from an orphanage to help him at sea. When a second helper is accidentally killed, he is held responsible for the death of the two of them. To avoid his infuriated neighbors who thought he maltreated the boys to the point of murder, he goes out in his boat and never returns. The opera was described after the London première as "a milestone in the history of British music." In the London *Times* of June 1945, Ernest Newman wrote: "Peter Grimes is a work of great originality"; but to him it is outside "the category of standard opera," and the casual listener will be unable to "apply to it his standardised formulae of appreciation." ... "The whole milieu has been strikingly framed in an orchestral sea picture that begins and ends the main action."

As with Milhaud, whose première of *Christophe Colomb* took place in Germany, so George Antheil's first opera, *Transatlantic,* had its initial performance, not in his native country, but in Frankfort. The plot deals with up-to-date characters—an oil magnate, a presidential candidate, a beautiful woman—and the story unfolds with villain, hero, and beautiful woman, just as it would if the setting were a baronial castle with a drawbridge instead of Brooklyn Bridge, night club, an ocean liner, New York skyscrapers and "elevated." The music depends considerably on jazz for local color and rhythmical verve, and from the European standpoint, is not harmonically modern.

Antheil's next opera, *Helen Retires,* on a libretto by John Erskine, was presented in New York by the opera students of the Juilliard Graduate School under the direction of Albert Stoessel.

What German composers were trying to do in the years before World War II, which is also the basic idea of *Transatlantic,* stems evidently from the American revue and musical comedy, only the primary object in Europe was to treat political, social, and economic problems with a satirical flippancy which passes for humor in music.

This same satirical mood won the Pulitzer Prize for Ira Gershwin's libretto to *Of Thee I Sing,* for which his popular brother, George Gershwin, wrote the music. We seem to lead the world in musical comedies. Such works as Gershwin's *Of Thee I Sing,* Irving Berlin's *Face the Music,* Jerome Kern's *The Cat and the Fiddle, The Show Boat, Music in the Air,* Arthur Schwartz's revue numbers in *Band Wagon,* are fresher and less artificial than Krenek's *Jonny spielt auf* and Kurt's Weill's *Three Penny Opera.*

More recently Richard Rodgers, of the Rodgers and Hart combination, working with Oscar Hammerstein, has produced two "best sellers," *Oklahoma!* and *Carousel.* The former is an approach to an American folk opera based on a real folk play, *Green Grow the Lilacs,* by Lynn Riggs. The closest relation to folk material is the ballet as planned by Agnes de Mille, who was the gifted choreographer of Aaron Copland's *Billy the Kid* and *Rodeo. Oklahoma!* is still too much a "Broadway show" to achieve the real folk opera that is on the way. But it is a step in that direction. *Carousel* is a free adaptation of Ferenc Molnar's tragedy *Liliom* transferred from Budapest to Maine. Again, the ballet in *Carousel* is one of the most poignant scenes in the work.

The American writers of musical comedy are not sophisticated composers seeking an escape, but they have their own established conventions and definite aims. We have also had a Victor Herbert whose light operas are classics in their line, second only to the English classics of Gilbert and Sullivan.

Marc Blitzstein (1905) found his medium in two stage works, *The Cradle Will Rock* and *No for an Answer,* which moved in the direction indicated by Weill, Krenek, Hindemith, etc. But Blitzstein knew how to adapt his work to the American scene. It is "musical theater," a cross between opera and musical revue. He writes his own texts, which consist of spoken dialogue, recitative, and solos, concerted numbers, and choruses.

In *Our New Music,* Aaron Copland says that in *No for an Answer* "Blitzstein finally found his own musical style. You can recognize it in the short, clipped musical sentences, the uneven phrase lengths, the nervous energy, the unerring sense of design. There is subtle use of a talky prose rhythm over a musical background that is very personal to the composer. His melodic line, as a rule, is straightforward, but the accompaniments may be exceedingly complex, though almost never obtrusive. ... His style, as musical theater, is always enormously effective, whether the mood is one of heartsick yearning or punch-like sarcasm, social uplift or the dregs of dejection."

Of quite another character, yet original (aboriginal in fact) have been some experiments in the theater in which plays about Negroes performed by Negroes have employed incidental Negro music with thrilling effect. Among these are Marc Connolly's *The Green Pastures* with the Hall Johnson Choir, Dorothy and DuBose Heyward's *Porgy* and *Run, Little Chillun,* by Hall Johnson. Here are spontaneity, local color, and sincerity of expression, and in addition the touch of true primitivism for which modern artists are groping.

That Louis Gruenberg should have chosen Eugene O'Neill's famous play *Emperor Jones* as the basis for his opera is not surprising, for he made use of all these elements. His preparation for the American opera which created a furore at the Metropolitan (1932-33) was long and arduous. He was a pupil of Busoni for both piano and composition, which meant that he was thoroughly grounded in the fundamentals of classicism, romanticism, and modernism. The stage has interested him for years, and he has written several operas which included apprentice works. The problem of jazz as an American gesture has been for him the subject of serious consideration and experimentation. He perfected his technic of composition and of instrumentation through a series of orchestral and chamber music works which will be discussed in Chapter 20.

Gruenberg made a delightfully humorous setting of Anatole France's *The Man Who Married a Dumb Wife,* which has never been performed because he never was able to obtain the English rights. Some years ago he wrote a jazz operetta, *Lady X,* under the pseudonym of George Edwards. Few knew the identity of Edwards, and yet the work had many performances and an English critic in the *Chesterian* called it the first successful jazz opera.

On a book by John Erskine, Gruenberg wrote an opera, *Jack and the Beanstalk,* which was performed many times by the Juilliard Opera School under the baton of Albert Stoessel. It reflects credit on Gruenberg's talent that he had the versatility to turn from this charming, childlike fairy opera bristling with humor, fun, realistic scenes, a modern impressionistic technic, and delicate effective orchestration to the gruesome tragedy and dark hue of *Emperor Jones.*

Gruenberg arranged his own libretto for *Emperor Jones* and has held the dramatic picture which O'Neill created throughout the short two-act opera. The movement of the music timed to the dramatic action was expertly done. The mood of Jones, first in his braggadocio, then in his panic as it increases, is mirrored in the music. Gruenberg has achieved a new and original effect in opera in treating the orchestra as a background to the exciting and moving drama. Although incidental, the music, played apart from the opera, would probably be one of the most extraordinary scores of modern times. The composer has lost all sense of personality in the primitive force of the music. Short-breathed phrases follow each other in rapid succession. The deeper-toned instruments are used to create a somber, sinister web over which the highest registers of the woodwinds and violins flare up shriekingly. Rhythmically, Gruenberg has made some remarkable effects.

It is a one-man opera. Lawrence Tibbett made the most of a character part such as never before has come to a singer to perform. Much of the vocal score is semispeech and shouts with occasional breaking into song. The composer carefully indicated the speech intonation of the vocal line. The choruses are shouted rather than sung, and they enhance the primitivism of the work greatly.

In the *New York Times* (January 8, 1933), Olin Downes said: "For an American opera to appear, which not only stands on its own feet, but represents a treatment of the form that could only come from a new country and a young people, fully alive to the present day, is the thing which makes this success of Mr. Gruenberg so gratifying and important to the future."

Another pioneer work in the modern American theater was George Gershwin's (1898-1937) *Porgy and Bess,* his setting of the Heyward play *Porgy*. It was in direct line with the Negro plays mentioned above, as it also had an entire Negro cast. It was presented by the Theatre Guild in 1935. The score, which has some of the earmarks of opera, also carries the stamp of musical comedy. Through the combination of the two styles Gershwin created a work which has become a milestone in the history of the American stage. Just such music as "I Got Plenty o'Nuttin'," "Bess, You Is Mah Woman Now," "A Woman

Is a Sometime Thing," "Oh, de Lawd Shake de Heaven" has made
Porgy and Bess acquire the right to the title "folk opera."

Virgil Thomson (1896) added a milestone to American opera with
Four Saints in Three Acts on a text by Gertrude Stein. This was
also performed by an all-Negro cast, but two works could hardly be
further apart in treatment, result, aesthetics, and music than *Porgy
and Bess* and Thomson's witty, sophisticated, satirical caricature of
old operatic clichés. His most recent work is a new opera on a libretto
by the late Gertrude Stein (1947), *The Mother of Us All.*

America is slowly but surely evolving her own opera, a type that
differs from the traditional in many respects. American folk operas
or works characteristic of various sections of this country might not
meet the requirements of opera houses devoted to accepted classics.
On the other hand, a number of Americans have been interested in
creating a "lyric theater," and of recent years a number of stage works
on American subjects by Americans have been written and produced.
Most of these would be lost in the vastness of a Metropolitan stage,
are written primarily as chamber opera with small cast and small
orchestra, and are often short. One exception was *Merry Mount* by
Howard Hanson, on a story of Puritan New England by Nathaniel
Hawthorne, made into a libretto by Richard Stokes, which was presented at the Metropolitan Opera House (1933).

Since then the Juilliard Opera School presented Gruenberg's *Jack
and the Beanstalk,* Antheil's *Helen Retires,* Stoessel's *David Garrick,*
Beryl Rubinstein's *The Sleeping Princess,* and Robert Russell Bennett's
Maria Malibran, which had an American setting. It gave a prize to
Joseph Wood for a one-act opera, *The Mother* (1942), and the pro-
gram was shared with Randall Thompson's *Solomon and Balkis.* The
Juilliard School has recently given a commission to Burrill Phillips
for an opera.

Thompson's *Solomon and Balkis,* also a one-act opera, was a joint
commission from The League of Composers and the Columbia Broadcasting System, and was a first step toward the establishment of a
lyric theater that should be modeled on the "little theater" movement
throughout the country. The World War II interfered with a con-
tinuation of plans, and in turn Douglas Moore, one of its prime movers,
developed the lyric theater idea in Columbia University with the
Columbia Theater Associates, after his own opera *The Devil and*

Daniel Webster on a libretto by Stephen Vincent Benét had had unusual success. With the assistance of the Alice M. Ditson Fund, several operas were composed and performed. These included Ernst Bacon's *The Tree on the Plain;* Bernard Wagenaar's *Pieces of Eight;* Normand Lockwood's *The Scarecrow* after Percy Mackaye's play; Benjamin Britten's play *Paul Bunyan;* and Gian-Carlo Menotti's *The Medium.*

Gian-Carlo Menotti (1911) is an Italian whose musical training was American, under Rosario Scalero at the Curtis Institute of Music. His first bid for fame was *Amelia Goes to the Ball,* in the style of the old *opera buffa,* on his own libretto. It started in Philadelphia and reached the Metropolitan in 1938. His next success was *The Old Maid and the Thief,* a radio opera commissioned by the National Broadcasting Company in 1939, for which he again wrote the libretto. Next Menotti wrote a short grand opera, *The Island God,* which was produced at the Metropolitan (1942). His recent operatic venture, *The Medium,* shows again his unusual talent for stage works, and is ideally suited for chamber opera, as is also a later work, *The Telephone* (1947). These were produced on Broadway.

Aaron Copland's one attempt at a stage work was eminently successful. He wrote a "play-opera," *The Second Hurricane,* for the children of the Henry Street Settlement Music School, New York. It is simple, original, and far from conservative, and is in the same category as Hindemith's *Let Us Build a City.*

A discussion of the stage music of the twentieth century would be incomplete without reference to the tremendous development of the ballet, especially as it has touched the American composers. The history of the Russian ballet goes back to the days of Catherine the Great, under whose aegis it developed notably. The Russian ballet under Diaghileff has been discussed elsewhere (Chapter 14). The Russian ballet has been largely responsible for the direction ballet has taken in this country. In 1932 the Ballet Russe de Monte Carlo was founded, with George Balanchine and Leonide Massine as choreographers and de Basil as impresario. The next year Balanchine was invited to visit America to found a school of American ballet, out of which the American Ballet Company arose (1934). "As Russia is a collective expression of Asia and the East," writes Lincoln Kirstein, in *Dance,* "so is America a collective expression of Europe and the West. Their theatrical dance is an inscription of their life that has been, that is and as it might be."

The work of Martha Graham, Charles Weidman, and Doris Humphrey, and many other American dancers, has been responsible for original music scores by American composers.

In 1945 there were the Ballet Russe de Monte Carlo and the Ballet Theatre. In 1946 the cards were reshuffled and redealt, and ballet companies have come and gone. But the roster of American composers who have written music for ballets has grown in length and importance. The Ballet Caravan under Lincoln Kirstein's direction brought into existence scores for *Billy the Kid* (choreography by Eugene Loring) and *Rodeo* (Agnes de Mille) by Aaron Copland, and *The Filling Station* by Virgil Thomson (Lew Christiansen). Other composers who have written for ballet include Marc Blitzstein, Paul Bowles, Elliott Carter, Ray Green, Clair Leonard, Robert McBride, Jerome Moross, Walter Piston, Wallingford Riegger, etc.

The idea of original music scores, created in collaboration with the choreographer, has grown vastly. This seems a more legitimate art than that of arranging masterpieces to fit choreography.

The following list, although incomplete, shows the extent of the recent movement of new ballets from 1938 to April 1947:

BALLET	COMPOSER	CHOREOGRAPHER
Nobilissima Visione	Paul Hindemith	Massine
City Portrait	Henry Brant	Eugene Loring
Great American Goof	Henry Brant	Eugene Loring
Every Soul Is a Circus	Paul Nordoff	Martha Graham
Waltz Academy	Vittorio Rieti	Balanchine
Fancy Free	Leonard Bernstein	Jerome Robbins
Interplay	Morton Gould	Jerome Robbins
Danses Concertantes	Stravinsky	Balanchine
Sailor Bar	Arthur Honegger	Mary Jane Shea
Evocation	Paul Bowles	Sets by Dali
The Last Flower	N. Nabokoff	Wm. Dollar
Sebastian	Gian-Carlo Menotti	Edward Caton
Sea Gull	Virgil Thomson	Schwetzoff
Sentimental Colloquy	Paul Bowles	Eglevsky
Imagined Wing	Darius Milhaud	Martha Graham

BALLET	COMPOSER	CHOREOGRAPHER
Appalachian Spring	Aaron Copland	Martha Graham
Herodiade	Paul Hindemith	Martha Graham
The Man from Midian	Stefan Wolpe	Eugene Loring
Undertow	William Schuman	Antony Tudor
On Stage	Norman Dello Joio	Michael Kidd
Gift of the Magi	Lukas Foss	Simon Semenoff
The Bells	Darius Milhaud	Ruth Page
Facsimile	Leonard Bernstein	Jerome Robbins
Dark Meadow	Carlos Chavez	Martha Graham
Serpent Heart	Samuel Barber	Martha Graham
Mute Wife	Vittorio Rieti	Antonia Cobos
Pocahontas	Elliott Carter	Lew Christiansen
Minotaur	Elliott Carter	John Paras
Night Journey	William Schuman	Martha Graham

CHAPTER 20

JAZZ AND AMERICAN MUSIC:
WHAT IS JAZZ? ITS INFLUENCE ON EUROPEANS
AND AMERICANS.
IVES, RUGGLES, MOORE, PISTON, HANSON,
GERSHWIN, THOMSON, HARRIS, ETC.

JAZZ, for better or for worse, is a twentieth century American product. It has come to be a generic term rather than to specify a type. Everyone knows what it is, but no one will undertake to define it.

Winthrop Sargeant, whose book *Jazz, Hot and Hybrid* is recognized as an authority on the subject, says: "Jazz may include: (1) the sort of spontaneous improvisation known as 'hot' jazz or 'swing music'; (2) the rehearsed music played by a large professional dance orchestra in pseudo-Negroid manner including occasional solos and 'breaks' that are technically 'hot'; (3) rehearsed music by a sophisticated orchestra based on Tin Pan Alley tunes of purely European character which are subjected to the process known as 'jazzing'; (4) the same type of music based on a tune pirated from the work of some classical composer; (5) something written down on paper by a Tin Pan Alley composer in imitation of the Negro method of playing, and so on."

"The least European, hence the most purely Negroid, variety of Afro-American music," Sargeant states, "is to be found in the embryonic spiritual of the shoutin' congregation. It is less standardized in pattern, more varied in style, freer in form than the hottest of hot jazz. A comparison with African tribal music will show it to be related to its jungle prototypes. Hot jazz, on the other hand, exhibits the influence of sophisticated city life, and something of the standardization usually associated with commercial products. The mere fact that hot jazz is played upon complex standardized instruments of European origin ... gives it a sophisticated character totally lacking in the shoutin' spiritual. The human voice, feet, and hands are instru-

316

ments common to both the American and the African Negro; the piano, trumpet, silver-plated banjo, and saxophone are not."

Whether we like it or not, Europe considers jazz the one original contribution that America has made to modern music. And to Europeans, music is not typically American unless it reflects the Negro or the Indian. The composers abroad appreciated, especially after World War I, how rejuvenating it was to introduce a primitive impulse into a tired sophisticated music. Stravinsky had done it by means of going back to pagan Russia; Bartók had uncovered a new melodic impulse through his studies of Hungarian folk song; Debussy listened attentively to the exotic harmonies of a Javanese gamelang. Jazz was another American shot that was heard around the world! And it has beaten its insidious rhythms into every corner of the globe.

Darius Milhaud said that jazz was like a beneficent thunder clap which cleared the art-sky. His tribute to jazz was his ballet *La Création du monde*. In it he realized a project to release jazz from the narrow confines of the dance. He even dreamed of writing a jazz symphony, but wrote the ballet instead.

Stravinsky, in his concerto for piano, has the same curious combination of Bach and jazz influences which Milhaud used (page 239). The vigorous rhythm which characterizes all of Stravinsky's neoclassic works was present in *Le Sacre du printemps,* but later it took on something of the jazz individualities and was widely imitated. The *Piano-rag-music, Ragtime, L'Histoire du soldat,* all reflect jazz.

Debussy, too, was interested in this curious American popular music. Before the day of jazz, it was the ragtime and coon songs which he found intriguing. "Minstrels," "Golliwogg's Cakewalk," and "General Lavine: Eccentric," in which he celebrated an American music-hall comedian, show that his ears were open to the new rhythms.

Jean Wiéner wrote a jazz sonata, and Clicquet-Pleyel has many compositions in jazz idiom.

Ravel succumbed to its fascinations to a small degree in his ballet *L'Enfant et les sortilèges* (*The Child and Its Sorceries*), but he showed in the concerto for piano and orchestra that he had quietly been assimilating its rhythms. The concerto, Ravel claimed, was written in the tradition of Mozart and Saint-Saëns, in other words it is in classic form. The first movement brings to mind Ravel's own delightful early classic style; the second is a long cantilena which sounds as though the composer had had a "back to Bach" aria in mind. But the last is a movement in which deftness and speed supply technical interest for a background of jazz in supple, graceful effect. It is musically more interesting and secure than the disappointing sonata for violin and piano which Ravel wrote for his American tour in 1926-27.

Alexandre Tansman wrote a *Sonatine Transatlantique,* first for piano and then in an orchestral version in which he employs an alto saxophone, the high range of the clarinet, and jazzlike brass. Its three parts are Fox-Trot, Spiritual and Blues, and Charleston. Tansman's *triptyque* for string orchestra borrows, in the first section, its regular pulsation from jazz with its deplaced accents.

Constant Lambert's "The Rio Grande" is jazz, and Eugene Goossens has used the rhythms, as have also Honegger, Casella, and many lesser lights.

Paul Hindemith has jazz rhythms in some of his piano pieces, but chiefly in the operas, as have the other writers of the new opera in Germany (Chapter 19).

When we consider that in the seventeenth and eighteenth centuries the suites were based on popular dance tunes (page 23), and in the nineteenth century the *Ländler* and waltz made their way into the music of the day, is it surprising that the twentieth century drew inspiration from its most popular dance music? Especially in view of the fact that World War I superinduced a state of hysteria which found its satisfaction in jazz. Krenek ended *Jonny spielt auf* with Jonny, the Jazz king, on the top of the world. Either consciously or unconsciously he was symbolizing the fact that jazz had destroyed lyricism and was playing fast and loose with moral codes and venerated customs. European composers have finished with jazz, it seems, but with Americans it is a different matter.

We had never developed our own musical speech. Until the twentieth century we allowed ourselves politely to be guided by Europe. We had not shown the same fearlessness in creating musical modes as we had in our inventions and more practical affairs. We have an American architecture, an American theater, and a wide range of local colloquial literary styles, so why should not our composers consider jazz seriously in modified forms as an original impulse on which to build? It must be recognized as a means to an end, but not as the end. It cannot be dropped by Americans as easily as by Europeans, because it has become an unconscious part of our musical heritage. It is our folk music in so far as it is the popular music we have heard since childhood. "Jazz, ragtime, Negro spirituals and blues, Southern mountain songs, country fiddling, and cowboy songs can all be employed in the creation of American art-music, and are actually used by many composers now," George Gershwin said in Henry Cowell's *Symposium, American Composers on American Music*. "Jazz I regard as an American folk-music; not the only one, but a very powerful one which is probably in the blood and feeling of the American people more than any other style of folk-music. I believe that it can be made the basis of serious symphonic works of lasting value, in the hands of a composer with talent for both jazz and symphonic music."

Aaron Copland wrote in *Modern Music* in 1927, "Possibly the chief influence of jazz will be shown in the development of the polyrhythm. This startling new synthesis has provided the American composer with an instrument he should appreciate and utilize. It should stir his imagination; he should see it freed of its present connotations. It may be the substance not only of his fox-trots and Charlestons, but of his lullabies and nocturnes. He may express through it not always gayety but love, tragedy, remorse."

And in 1924 Louis Gruenberg wrote in the second number of the League of Composers Quarterly, *Modern Music* ("For an American Gesture"): "In an effort to appraise music today in Paris, London, Berlin and Vienna, it becomes my firm conviction that the American composer can only achieve individual expression by developing his own resources, instead either of submitting to the prevailing tendencies of various countries, however vociferous they may be in their appeal and in their success, or of blindly following the traditions of classical form.

"These resources are vital and manifold, for we have at least three rich veins indigenous to America alone,—Jazz, Negro Spirituals and Indian themes. . . . It seems to me that it is the indefinable and at the same time unmistakable atmosphere in America that must be youthfully interpreted in a new idiom, not merely exploited in a characteristic melody.

"A new technic should be invented which will combine a knowledge of tradition and the modern experiment, if for no other reason than to avoid the pitfall of imitation. Music in Europe today is suffering from over-sophistication and perhaps America's trouble is under-sophistication."

At that time, Gruenberg was writing a series of compositions in which he was trying out these theories, including "Daniel Jazz," on a text by Vachel Lindsay; also a group of songs, *Animals and Insects,* to Lindsay's poems; James Weldon Johnson's Negro Sermon, "The Creation"; "Four Indiscretions" for string quartet; *Jazzberries* and *Jazz Epigrams* for piano; some jazz pieces for violin; the Jazz Suite, and "Vagabondia" for orchestra.

The Fox-Trot from *Jazzberries* * is not atonal, in fact it is in the key of C major, but Gruenberg uses chromaticism and sudden polytonal effects whenever his fancy dictates, syncopated rhythms, and bursts of banal melodies, as for example this bit, which is characteristic of his treatment of a bass:

* Quoted with the permission of the original editor, Universal-Edition A.G., Vienna, copyright, 1925.

Or this:

Universal Edition (1925)

Gruenberg was made a member of the National Institute of Arts and Letters in 1947.

The *spiritual,* which is actually of Negro origin, contrary to the "white man's jazz," has made a decided impression on Gruenberg as it has on other composers. Its traces are evident in "The Creation."

John Powell and Harold Morris are Southerners whose works show the unconscious influence of the Negro. With them the Negro spiritual takes on true folk song significance. Powell, who is interested also in the Anglo-Saxon folk songs of the South, wrote a Negro Rhapsody for piano and orchestra before the "Jazz Age," which, as pioneer work, pointed a direction. His most recent work is a symphony on American folk themes, a commission from the National Federation of Music Clubs. Another pioneer was Henry F. Gilbert (1868-1928), who investigated not only the music of the Indian (page 71) but of the Negro, and wrote orchestral works based on Negro themes and a ballet produced at the Metropolitan (1918), *The Dance in Place Congo,* based on Louisiana Creole songs. Rubin Goldmark also wrote a Negro Rhapsody in 1922, and Daniel Gregory Mason has a string quartet based on Negro themes. Morris reveals the environment of his childhood in almost every score he writes: his Piano Concerto; the variations on the Negro spiritual "Dum-a-Lum"; his sonata for piano and violin; trio; quartet, and quintet. This is not a matter of rhythm alone but of the use of a long melodic line which naturally takes on the proportions of a spiritual and is quite different in effect from the works of Gruenberg or Copland.

Whatever jazz is or is not, it has created its own method of instrumentation unlike that of any other school or nationality. Not only is the rhythm syncopated, but the harmony also presents a syncopation by means of anticipating and retarding entire chords. It has also made use of polyrhythms in a thoroughly modern and complicated manner—a counterpoint of rhythms. One tires quickly of the monotonous thump-thump of the drum marking the even beats, but against this in the best jazz are interwoven the fascinating irregularities of the uneven beats. H. O. Osgood, in his *So This Is Jazz*, said, however, that "it is the spirit of the music, not the mechanics of its frame... that determines whether or not it is jazz." And so we include *blues*, the slow melancholy jazz invented by W. C. Handy in this category.

Jazz, which has developed into an art, started as an improvisation, and even though we call it a white man's invention, the Negro has taught him how to play his own concoction. The first Negro jazz players knew the tune, but all the quirks and turns which made it "jazzy" they made up as they went along, each man for himself, blending, syncopating, gliding, harmonizing, throwing in off-beats and rhythmic patterns which somehow or other held together and made jazz. The American learned from his black brother—by listening, imitating, missing it, and trying again until he caught on to the tricks, wrote them down, repeated them, and standardized them. The European never quite caught the secret of playing jazz the way the colored musicians, or for that matter, the best jazz bands do.

Like Caesar's *Gallia* which *est omnis divisa in partes tres,* three types of jazz writers have developed: the Zez Confrey, George Gershwin (when he was a song plugger in Tin Pan Alley), Irving Berlin, Youmans, Jerome Kern type—those who wrote and still write real jazz in and out of musical comedy. Then the kind created by Paul Whiteman, who was both directly and indirectly responsible for Gershwin's "Rhapsody in Blue"; for Ferde Grofé's inimitable instrumentations, which created a real jazz orchestration, or as it is often called, a "modern American" orchestration; for such works as Gershwin's

"An American in Paris," Werner Janssen's "New Year's Eve in New York," Grofé's Grand Canyon Suite, Thomas Griselle's Two American Sketches, Robert Russell Bennett's "Sights and Sounds," etc. And the type developed by John Alden Carpenter in "Krazy Kat" and "Skyscrapers," by Copland, Gruenberg, and many other Americans and the Europeans enumerated earlier in this chapter.

In this last type must be included William Grant Still, a Negro who uses Negro music as the basis of his composition in modern vein, which includes an Afro-American Symphony, "Africa" for orchestra, "From the Black Belt" and "Log Cabin Ballads" for chamber orchestra, and two stage works, *La Guiablesse* and *Sahdji*. "Our [Negro] music possesses exoticism without straining for strangeness," Still writes in Henry Cowell's *Symposium*. "The natural practices in this music open up a new field which can be of value in larger musical works when constructed into organized form by a composer who, having the underlying feeling, develops it through his intellect." More recently Still wrote a moving work, "In Memoriam: The Colored Soldiers Who Died for Democracy," also Poem for Orchestra.

Several colored composers have, by their authentic arrangements of Negro spirituals, preserved their music for the future. Among them are H. T. Burleigh, the famous baritone soloist at St. George's in New York; R. Nathaniel Dett (1882-1943), former conductor of the Hampton Choral Union and of a radio chorus in Rochester, N. Y., whose cantata *The Ordering of Moses* is based on a well-known spiritual; Hall Johnson; J. Rosamond Johnson; Lawrence Brown; Clarence Cameron White, successor to Dett at Hampton Institute, Virginia, etc.

Louis Armstrong wrote a book, *Swing That Music,* that gives the history of jazz and explains the difference between jazz and swing. "Jazz is the grand daddy of today's swing music," he says; "and though they both came from the same soil, along the lower Mississippi, they have come to be very different kinds of music.... Jazz came up slowly and out of the old Negro folk songs and the spirituals, and the regular beat of the jazz syncopation probably came out of the strumming of the banjos which the slaves had learned to play before the Civil War. Some say it went back to the tom-toms of our people in Africa before we were civilized...."

Armstrong talks about Dominick James La Rocca of "The Old Dixieland Jazz Band" of New Orleans which became famous and went down into history. "Nick" La Rocca was "one of the great pioneers of syncopated music." It took a quarter of a century for jazz to make the trip from New Orleans to New York—"and to bring it finally to the music we know today as *swing*."

Swing is improvisation. A swing musician "just plays, feels as he goes, and swings as he feels," says Armstrong. "It is just the liberty that every individual player must have in a real swing orchestra that makes it most worth listening to. Every time they play there is something new swinging into the music to make it hot and interesting." *Hot* "is used when a swing player gets warmed up and 'feels' the music taking hold of him so strong that he can break through the set rhythms and the melody and toss them around as he wants without losing his way. That creates new effects and is done whether the music is loud or soft, or fast or slow.... They all play together, picking up and following each other's 'swinging', all by ear and sheer musical instinct."

Armstrong sums up swing and jazz by saying, "Swing music is America's second big bid to bring forth a worthwhile music of its own. The first big attempt was in the early days of jazz." But jazz "got side-tracked.... Jazz lost its originality and freshness and stopped growing.... As it came to be written down and recorded in all the thousand and one jazz songs of later years, it was not musically rich enough." Hearing it over and over, it gets tiresome, but swing players vary the treatment constantly although it is based on one tune; they break up "the worn-out patterns," and they call their music *swing* because it is different "from the stale brand of jazz they've got so sick of hearing."

We have been long in recognizing that there are American composers of the twentieth century whose work could be the result of no other environment. And perhaps in time through better acquaintance with American music in general, Europe will come to recognize certain subtleties that reflect the unconscious nationalism of music made in America, even though it has no suggestion of the Negro or the Indian.

A most interesting example is Charles Ives (1874), the more interesting because quietly and without wide recognition he has worked out his experiments for years while engaged in business. He is a New

Englander, and it has pleased him to try to catch the idiosyncrasies of the village band, of a fiddler at a dance, the village choir with its wheezy harmonium, or a Fourth of July celebration. "Typically American, they distinguish our folk art from the folk art of the Europeans," says Henry Cowell (*Modern Music,* November-December 1932). "Yet the 'cultivated' musicians who have collected and published these songs of our people unconsciously and without question have weeded out all irregularities, so that not the slightest suspicion of original, indigenous, or truly American feeling remains in the published versions. . . .

"All these elements of back-country New England music were assimilated by Ives and made a deep impression. With sure creative instinct and sensitive ear, he began early to build himself a music in which he could express them."

Ives combined this native sense with a fine musical training and a rhythmic curiosity, which enabled him to get away from European methods. Long before his works reached the public, he was trying ideas which later turned out to be poly- and multirhythmic, polytonal and atonal experiments, but which before the day of Stravinsky and Schoenberg seemed eccentric and contra-musical.

Another side of his New England nature is shown in his sonata, "Concord, Massachusetts, 1840-60," in which the movements are entitled Emerson, Hawthorne, The Alcotts, and Thoreau. He has over one hundred songs, four symphonies, and many other scores.

Carl Ruggles (1883), the "Cape Cod composer," although his output is small, is regarded by many as having elements of genius. He is strongly individual and has developed independently a harmonic and rhythmical scheme of distinction and refinement. Having heard "Portals" for string orchestra, one never forgets the elusive beauty of its last pages. Among his orchestral works are "Men and Angels," "Men and Mountains," and "Sun-Treader." A choral work, *Vox Clamans in Deserto* for voice and chamber orchestra was performed by the International Composers' Guild, as were also "Angels" for six trumpets, "Men and Mountains," and "Portals." He has had more performances abroad than at home. His most recent work is a series of piano pieces called *Evocations.*

Arthur Shepherd (1880) shows his Western patrimony in his compositions. He has a piano sonata in which, without using Indian themes, he has brought the spirit of Indian music into one of the movements in his characteristic rhythmic and melodic line. Particularly interesting from an American point of view, is his orchestral work "Horizons," in which he has used as thematic material several famous cowboy ballads: "The Dogies," "The Dying Cowboy," and "The Old Chisholm Trail."

Wallingford Riegger (1885) is a neoclassicist whose early training along reactionary lines seems to have given him technical freedom for his experiments in "Study in Sonority" for ten violins, "Dichotomy," Suite for flute alone, Canon and Fugue for strings, Three Canons for Woodwinds. Riegger was the first American to win the Elizabeth Sprague Coolidge prize, in 1924, with *"La Belle Dame sans Merci"* for chamber orchestra and four solo voices. He won the Paderewski prize in 1921. He has written scores for modern dancers such as Martha Graham, Doris Humphrey, and Charles Weidman. His craftsmanship is of a high order, and he has worked out an atonal, dissonant style based on twelve tone technic. One of his most recent works was a string quartet (1945) in that medium.

John J. Becker (1886) was a member with Riegger, Adolph Weiss (1891), an American disciple of Schoenberg; Ruth Crawford, Henry Cowell, and others of a pan-American group. The North American section was neoclassic and experimental, interested almost without exception in linear music, absolute in character. Becker has remained in Minneapolis and St. Paul, working out a musical style of his own based on the Palestrina type but using dissonant intervals.

Philip James (1890) is known both as composer and conductor, and is chairman of the music department at New York University. For seven years he was conductor of the Bamberger Little Symphony Orchestra (Station WOR, New York). In 1932 he won a prize in the National Broadcasting Company's competition with a satirical symphonic radio suite, "Station WGZBX." He has written many successful choral works, among them *Missa Imaginum* (*Mass of the Pictures*) and a setting of Vachel Lindsay's "General Booth Enters Heaven." In 1937 he was awarded honorable mention in the Philharmonic-Symphony Society of New York contest for his overture "Bret Harte"; and the same year his suite for string orchestra won the publication prize of the Juilliard School of Music. James is an officer of the American Institute of Art and Letters, and in 1946 he was elected president of the Society for the Publication of American Music, succeeding Oscar Wagner.

Although Edwin John Stringham (1890) has composed a symphony, three symphonic poems, a nocturne for orchestra which was played by the Philharmonic-Symphony Orchestra (1935), a *notturno* for wind instruments and harp, and a string quartet, his chief influence on twentieth century music has been as teacher and music editor. He was dean of the Denver College of Music before coming to New York in 1930; he taught composition at the Union Theological Seminary, and acoustics at the Institute of Musical Art of the Juilliard School; he was a member of the music faculty at Teachers College, Columbia University; chairman of the Music Department at Queens College in Flushing; head of the music section of the University overseas; and on his return to the United States was appointed (1946) as guest professor to teach composition at the University of California in Los Angeles, following Arnold Schoenberg, who was retired.

Stringham was formerly general music editor of the American Book Company, and is the author of a book, *Listening to Music Creatively* (1946).

Frederick Jacobi (1891) has a special gift for poetic expression, as may be seen in his earlier scores: "The Eve of Saint Agnes"; a symphony; "The Poet in the Desert" for mixed voices and baritone solo; Two Assyrian Prayers for voice and orchestra. This same gift for modern romanticism is to be found in his concertos for violoncello, for piano, and for violin. He wrote a first string quartet on Indian themes which he collected in New Mexico. Two other string quartets followed. He also made the Indian material into an orchestral work, Indian Dances. Jacobi's innately religious temperament is shown in his Sabbath Evening Service which was commissioned by the Temple Emanu-El in New York; his *"Hagiographa,* Three Biblical Narratives" for string quartet and piano; "From the Prophet Nehemiah: Three Excerpts for Voice and Two Pianos"; six organ pieces; a Palestinian folk song arrangement, etc. Among more recent compositions are a scherzo for flute, oboe, clarinet, bassoon, and horn; *"Ave Rota:* Three Pieces in Multiple Style" for small orchestra and piano; Rhapsody for harp and string orchestra; "Ode," which was played by the Boston Symphony Orchestra; Ballade for violin and piano; and an opera in three acts, *The Prodigal Son,* based on four early American prints.

Bernard Rogers (1893), a member of the faculty of the Eastman School of Music in Rochester, New York, was an early holder of a Pulitzer traveling scholarship (1918). He handles rhythm in a characteristic fashion that Howard Hanson compares to the complex rhythms of primitive man. His treatment of percussion illustrates this point. He has a special gift for stage works, and a one-act opera of his, *The Warrior,* on a libretto by Norman Corwin, won the Alice M. Ditson Fund Contest, sponsored in collaboration with Columbia University, and was presented in 1947 at the Metropolitan Opera. Rogers has received several commissions from the League of Composers for orchestral and radio performances. Among his orchestral works are "To the Fallen," dedicated to the dead of the last war; "The Faithful"; "Fuji in Sunset Glow"; three symphonies; "The Supper at Emmaus," Five Fairy Tales, and "In Memory of Franklin Delano Roosevelt." He was made a member of the National Institute of Arts and Letters in 1947.

Douglas Moore (1893), who is head of the music department of Columbia University, not only writes American music but encourages others to do so. His constructive spirit has carried his endeavors into the theater (page 312) and in 1945 to the founding of an annual Festival of Contemporary American Music, sponsored by the Alice M. Ditson Fund and Columbia University. He also advances the cause of American music as president of the National Institute of Arts and Letters.

Besides his opera *The Devil and Daniel Webster,* his orchestral works "Pageant of P. T. Barnum," "Moby Dick," "Village Music," "Dirge" (passacaglia), "Symphony of Autumn," "Overture on an American Tune" have established his name. He has written a string quartet, characteristically American; choral works; and the music to two documentary films, *Power and the Land* and *Youth Gets a Break.*

Moore expressed an artistic credo in the *New York Herald Tribune* (May 17, 1931) which may well be taken into serious consideration by many young composers: "I feel very strongly that we are all of us overconscious today of the problems of idiom and esthetics. Most of us compose under the deadly fear of being either not modern enough or too modern. Too many of us worry about whether our music is properly a reflection of America, or suitably international, in order to please whatever faction impresses us most. The particular ideal which I have been striving to attain is to write music which will not be self-conscious with regard to idiom, and will reflect the exciting quality of the life, the traditions, and country which I feel all about me." (Quoted from the program notes of the Philharmonic-Symphony Society of New York, January 11 and 12, 1945.)

It was fortunate for American music that Walter Piston (1894) changed his mind about becoming a painter and turned to music when he entered Harvard, where he has for some time been a professor. In the interim he spent several seasons in Paris studying with Nadia Boulanger. His style is neoclassic and individual. Few composers can boast of having written three symphonies under commissions. His first symphony was commissioned by the League of Composers for a performance by the Boston Symphony Orchestra (1938). He was commissioned by the Alice M. Ditson Fund of Columbia University to write his Symphony No. 2, which won the New York Music Critics' Circle award of 1944-45. Dr. Koussevitzky commissioned a third symphony for performance in 1947.

One of his best-known scores is the music for a ballet, *The Incredible Flautist,* which presents Piston in a light and pleasing mood. He wrote a concerto for violin and orchestra, a concerto for orchestra, and one for piano, and a beautiful sonata for violin and piano. His chamber music includes also three string quartets, a sonata for flute and piano, and a passacaglia for piano. Piston has also written two books on musical theory.

The premature death of Albert Stoessel (1894-1943) robbed this country of one of its most constructive musicians. He showed decided talent in an early violin sonata, his *Suite Antique* for two violins and chamber orchestra, etc. He made a name as choral and orchestral conductor. Through the various organizations of which he was director— the Oratorio Society of New York, the Worcester (Mass.) Festival, the Chautauqua Symphony Orchestra and Opera Association, the Juilliard Orchestra and Opera School—he was of invaluable assistance to American composers by producing their works and being instrumental in commissioning and publishing scores. He produced some of the most important modern choral works, such as Honegger's *Le Roi David* (*King David*), Stravinsky's *Symphonie de Psaumes*

(Symphony of Psalms), Holst's "Hymn to Jesus," Malipiero's "The Princess Ulalia," Kodaly's *Psalmus Hungaricus;* and he conducted many opera premières, such as Gruenberg's *Jack and the Beanstalk,* Antheil's *Helen Retires,* Bennett's *Maria Malibran,* Thompson's *Solomon and Balkis,* Beryl Rubinstein's *The Sleeping Princess,* and his own *Garrick.* He also gave the first performance in America of Richard Strauss's *Ariadne auf Naxos* at the Juilliard Opera School.

Garrick is a charming work which Stoessel wrote (1936) on a libretto by Robert A. Simon, who was also the librettist of *Maria Malibran. Garrick* had performances in New York, Chautauqua, and Worcester under the composer's direction. More recent works included a concerto grosso for string orchestra, "Festival Fanfare" for chorus and orchestra, choral works, and musicianly arrangements of Bach, etc. Albert Stoessel died with his baton in his hand, while conducting Walter Damrosch's "Dunkirk" at a concert of the American Academy of Arts and Letters, of which he was a member.

Robert Russell Bennett (1894) is one of the few men who has achieved fame in the two different musical fields of arranging and orchestrating other men's works and of composing his own. Many Broadway successes in musical comedy bear his imprint, among these are *Oklahoma!* and *Show Boat.* He took up this special work as an economic measure in the early days of his career, in order to enable him to pursue his studies and serious composing. Many of the other American composers are college professors and teachers for the same reason.

Bennett's studies took him to Paris to Nadia Boulanger. While there he wrote a symphony which won honorable mention in the *Musical America* contest (1927-28). He also won two prizes in the Victor contest (1929-30), for "Sights and Sounds" and "Abraham Lincoln, A Likeness in Symphonic Form." In addition he wrote Eight Etudes for Orchestra (1942), dedicated to Walter Damrosch, Aldous Huxley, Noel Coward, "King" Carl Hubbell (baseball pitcher), "to all Dictators," to the Grand Lama, to the painter Ernest Speicher, and "to the Ladies," which shows the wide range of Bennett's interests and culture; a symphony, "The Four Freedoms" (1943) on four paintings by Norman Rockwell; the opera *Maria Malibran* (1935); a concerto for violin and orchestra (1944); and *"Hexapoda,* Five Studies in 'Jitteroptera' " for violin and piano, which are clever and humorous. He composed the music for the fountain displays at the World's Fair (New York, 1939).

Another composer who won fame as an arranger and orchestrator is Ferde Grofé (1892). He is deservedly acclaimed for having developed a special line of instrumentation which was introduced by Paul Whiteman and the early works of George Gershwin. His best known work is the Grand Canyon Suite.

Leo Sowerby (1895), the first composer to hold the fellowship in the American Academy at Rome, has written in many styles from church music to jazz. He has set folk music using the type of harmonization made popular by Percy Grainger, with whom he studied. One of these is the whimsical piano piece "The Irish Washerwoman." He has three symphonies, the third composed for the golden jubilee of the Chicago Symphony Orchestra in 1941 and played under the direction of Frederick Stock. He has also written for orchestra: "From the Northland"; a ballad, "King Estmere," for two pianos and orchestra; Concert Overture; a concerto for piano and orchestra, and one for violin; and Passacaglia, Interlude, and Fugue. In addition, he has written a quantity of organ and chamber music, including a clarinet sonata. Sowerby lives in Chicago, where he is a teacher and organist. He is a member of the American Institute of Arts and Letters.

Howard Hanson (1896) has had an unusual opportunity to further the interests of the young American composers in his position as director of the Eastman School of Music in Rochester, New York, which provides a composer's experimental laboratory. For two decades Hanson has operated on the principle that the crusading spirit is important and that all-American programs are necessary and useful to give young talents an opportunity to hear their orchestral scores in order to promote their development. The changes that have been wrought in these twenty years and the developments that have occurred in American music have been mirrored in the programs of these American Composers' Concerts.

Not only young Americans are heard, but the programs have included works by Horatio Parker, Loeffler, Carpenter, Charles Ives, Bernard Rogers, Roy Harris, Frederick Jacobi, Lazare Saminsky, Mabel Daniels, William Grant Still, Deems Taylor, Daniel Gregory Mason, Douglas Moore, Robert Russell Bennett, Edward Burlingame

Hill, and many others. In the spring of 1933 Hanson presented several concerts of American music abroad.

His own compositions include four symphonies—the Nordic, the Romantic, and two others. Although the Third and Fourth have no titles, he stated that the Third was temperamentally related to the Nordic, and that it pays tribute to the epic qualities of the northern pioneers who founded the first Swedish settlement in this country three centuries ago and helped to conquer the West. Hanson is of Swedish parentage. The Fourth is in memory of his father, and carries Latin subtitles for the four movements of *Kyrie, Requiescat, Dies Irae* and *Lux Aeterna. "Lux Aeterna"* is also the title of one of his earlier works, which, like "Pan and the Priest," is a symphonic poem. He wrote an organ concerto, and made a suite from his opera *Merry Mount.* Among his choral works are "The Lament of Beowulf," "Heroic Elegy," Songs from *Drum Taps* by Walt Whitman, and a transcription for chorus and orchestra of Palestrina's Pope Marcellus Mass. His chamber works include a string quartet, a piano quartet, and a piano quintet. He held a fellowship in the American Academy at Rome during the time that Leo Sowerby was there.

At the time of the première in Boston of his Romantic Symphony, Hanson set forth his artistic creed by stating that the symphony represented for him his "escape from the rather bitter type of modern musical realism which occupies so large a place in contemporary thought. Much contemporary music seems to me," he continued, "to be showing a tendency to become entirely too cerebral. I do not believe that music is primarily a matter of the intellect, but rather of the emotions. I have therefore, aimed in this symphony to create a work that was young in spirit, lyrical and romantic in temperament, and simple and direct in expression."

He said in the program notes of the Philharmonic-Symphony Society of New York of January 17 and 18, 1946 (signed L.B.—Louis Biancolli) that by making this statement he added to his worries the job of explaining a few thousand times what he meant by "romantic." "I believe that there are essentially two types of music, warm-blooded music and cold-blooded music, and every possible admixture of the two. The 'Romantic' is definitely warm-blooded music." (One wonders whether the explanation is as simple as Dr. Hanson states it!)

Again, he said of the Third Symphony that it stands, like the Romantic, as an avowal against "a certain coldly abstract, would-be non-sentimental music professed by certain composers of high gifts." (From the *Concert Bulletin* of the Boston Symphony Orchestra by John N. Burk, March 14 and 17, 1945.)

Virgil Thomson (1896) has long been a "problem child" in music, especially to those who do not know his self-avowed heritage as an American product of Erik Satie, and of Jean Cocteau as well. Thomson, who since 1940 has been the music critic of the *New York Herald Tribune* wrote on January 5, 1941 (quoted from his book *The Musical Scene*), that Satie's firmest conviction was that "the only healthy thing music can do in our century is to stop trying to be impressive" (Chapter 16). He states that Satie is the only influential composer "whose works can be enjoyed without any knowledge of the history of music. These lack the prestige of traditional modernism, as they lack the prestige of the Romantic tradition itself, a tradition of constant Revolution. They are as simple, as straightforward, as devastating as the remarks of a child." And this might be a criticism of Thomson's own works. "To the uninitiated they sound trifling," as true of Thomson as of Satie. French music, says the critic, "has eschewed the impressive, the heroic, the oratorical, everything that is aimed at moving mass audiences. . . . It has directed its communication to the individual.

"It has valued, in consequence, quietude, precision, acuteness of auditory observation, gentleness, sincerity and directness of statement." Thomson admits that because of these qualities, people who admire them in private life are embarrassed by encountering them in public, and therefore this embarrassment "gives to all French music, and to the work of Satie and his neophytes in particular, an air of superficiality, as if it were salon music written for the drawing-rooms of some snobbish set."

Thomson, no doubt, is sincere in this statement, although it may sound to many who are outside of the Satie cult like rationalization. This composer from Kansas came to the conclusion stated above during his years in Paris following his Harvard student days and three years as assistant instructor in his alma mater. His own style is of a simplicity and homeliness that is apt to annoy sophisticated audiences. His melodies are often "corny," one of his own favorite adjectives, and his compositions frequently are "slick." He takes his material from old-fashioned songs, a Methodist hymn tune, Gregorian chant, Handel, Rossini—a veritable musical ragbag.

Thomson has written many works: symphonies, string quartets, masses, chamber music, and "musical portraits." In 1944 his Suite for Orchestra was played by Eugene Ormandy and the Philadelphia Orchestra. In the program notes of November 21, the composer tells that he first started making musical portraits in 1928. "The gallery of them now includes over a hundred." They are scored for all sorts of instruments and combinations. They are drawn from life. "The subject sits for his likeness," says Thomson, "as he would for a painter, and the music is composed in front of him, usually at one sitting.... The musical style of the pieces varies with the personality of the subject. Sometimes it is harmonious, sometimes dissonant, sometimes straightforwardly tuneful, sometimes thematically or contrapuntally developed."

This suite contains portraits of Pablo Picasso; a young painter of Russian birth, Nicolas de Chatelain; Alexander Smallens; and two ladies. Obviously the Mayor La Guardia Waltzes, commissioned for radio performance by Andre Kostelanetz, belong to the portrait type.

Thomson came into fame with his opera *Three Saints in Four Acts* (page 312). Here, as elsewhere, he shows his ability to write for voices. His Stabat Mater for soprano and string quartet is one of his best works. Some of his most spontaneous and successful ventures are the scores he wrote for documentary films, *The River* and *The Plough That Broke the Plains,* and his music for the ballet *Filling Station.* In 1946 a set of piano études was published. In 1947, his opera *The Mother of Us All* was produced (page 312).

Roger Sessions (1896) is regarded as one of the most gifted and serious American composers. He has written two symphonies, and is best known by his piano sonata, a string quartet, and an early score based on incidental music for Andreyev's *Black Maskers.* He has also a violin concerto, which illustrates Aaron Copland's statement that "he writes his music for Titans"; Three Choral Preludes for organ; and a song, "On the Beach at Fontana." Much of his technical development he owes to the teaching of Ernest Bloch, and in turn he is regarded as an important teacher. He has a keen sense of form and a real appreciation for the value of the melodic line. His harmonization is polytonal, and he is a master of counterpoint.

Sessions held scholarships from the Guggenheim and Carnegie

Foundations and from the American Academy in Rome. He was on the music faculty of Princeton University for some years, and in 1945 joined that of the University of California.

Henry Cowell (1897) is first and foremost an experimenter whose keen mind keeps him on the jump from one problem to the next. He took up the study of primitive and folk music which lead to a Guggenheim fellowship in 1931, and he has done valuable research in both lines. He and Charles Seeger, one of America's most erudite musicologists and one of Cowell's first teachers at the University of California, gave courses of study far from the beaten track at the New School for Social Research in New York. Cowell was interested in finding new percussion possibilities in the piano, and acquired fame for his use of "cluster chords" which he played with his forearms. He was the founder of the *New Music* Quarterly which has published scores and records of contemporary North and South American and European composers. He has been an indefatigable worker in the Pan-American Association, the League of Composers, and other of his various interests. With Leon Theremin he developed the *rhythmicon,* an instrument which produces complex rhythmic combinations (page 267). In 1940 he became consultant in music for the Music Division of the Pan-American Union, and during World War II he served as music consultant and senior music editor for the Office of War Information.

Cowell's *American Composers on American Music,* a symposium by the various composers, which he compiled and edited, and to which he contributed many sections, is a valuable addition to information about American music. Another important book is his *New Musical Resources,* in which he discusses modern music from the standpoint of harmonic and rhythmic overtones and combinations. Cowell has written chamber music, piano music which reveals his Celtic ancestry, and many works for chamber and for full orchestra, including a symphony and a piano concerto. He has been greatly interested in writing for school bands and orchestras, for which he simplified his style, as in "Tales of Our Countryside," "Old American Country Set," etc. The Celtic strain is apparent in his Gaelic Symphony and "Schoontree" for band. A new and eloquent style appears in a series of hymns with fuguing tunes, which he developed from his study of William Billings and other eighteenth-century Americans.

Few modern composers are as versed in the music of rural America as is Ernst Bacon (1898). This knowledge shows itself in the mood and style of his songs, many of them settings of folk melodies, in his opera *The Tree on the Plain* (page 313), and his orchestral work "From These States (Gathered along Unpaved Roads)." In the program notes of the Second Annual Festival of Contemporary American Music presented at Columbia University, New York, Bacon writes of the orchestral work: "These songs are in a sense geographical; for do not the vista, the altitude, the humidity, the vegetation, the crops, the desert, the sea-coast, the fertile inland valleys, the characteristic sky and clouds, the temperature, wind and rainfall—all affect the people's song no less than their national, racial and cultural heritage?

"As a painter uses as models men and women, buildings and trees, skies and water, so the composer may use as his models sequestered tunes.... But the composer, no less than the painter, considers such material as something through which to discover and reveal his own personality...."

In both folk song treatment and his settings of Emily Dickinson's poems—songs, and a cantata for women's voices, *From Emily's Diary*—Bacon shows skill in handling prosody and in writing simple accompaniments that are neither harmonically overloaded nor naïve. He is unique in his backward look "toward an ideal and primitive America without snobbery, self-deception or truculence. It is honest and skillful and beautiful," says Virgil Thomson in the *New York Herald Tribune*, March 4, 1946.

Ernst Bacon was supervisor of the San Francisco and Los Angeles Federal Music Projects, was head of the music departments of Converse College, Spartanburg, S. C., and later of Syracuse University, and he held Pulitzer and Guggenheim fellowships.

Chronologically, George Gershwin's work belongs here, but his opera *Porgy and Bess* was discussed in Chapter 19, and mention has been made of his "Rhapsody in Blue" and "An American in Paris" (page 323). He began his career as a "song-plugger" in Tin Pan Alley, reversing the customary process of trained composers who try their hand at the popular game as did Victor Herbert and Rudolph Friml. He made a great popular success in the musical comedy field, won a Pulitzer prize with his brother Ira for *Of Thee I Sing,* and with

"Rhapsody in Blue" became a pioneer in combining the popular field with the art world.

Virgil Thomson finds in the rhapsody "a passionate cry for deliverance from the cement-and-steel canyons of New York City in this deeply emotional, nervously actuated rhapsody. The bells echoed in the Gershwin opus are those of the Elevated and Underground, are workshift bells all of which Gershwin's New Yorkers, for whom this rhapsody is written, beg to forget." (*The Musical Scene*.)

Besides the rhapsody and "An American in Paris," Gershwin wrote a piano Concerto in F as a commission from Walter Damrosch, and a second rhapsody. His untimely death cut off a rapidly evolving talent, which would probably have added many more scores to musical Americana.

Randall Thompson (1899) has a notable place in American music as a composer of distinctive choral music, in which he has been particularly successful in setting the English language. "Americana," a satirical chorus on excerpts from Henry L. Mencken's column in the *American Mercury* quoting selections from newspapers, is written as a burlesque of oratorio in most amusing fashion. On the other hand, *The Peaceable Kingdom* is a serious work based on Biblical text and commissioned by the League of Composers in 1936. More recently *The Testament of Freedom* for men's chorus and orchestra was written (1943) in celebration of the two hundredth anniversary of the birth of Thomas Jefferson. Thompson chose quotations from Jefferson's speeches as his text for one of the most important choral works of its type produced in this country. *Pueri Hebraeorum* to a Latin text and his frequently sung Alleluia have added to his reputation.

In 1942 his opera *Solomon and Balkis,* which had been composed for radio on a commission from the Columbia Broadcasting System, was presented. The little opera received stage performances as well.

Thompson's best-known orchestral work is his Second Symphony, regarded as a representative American composition. He is a meticulous workman with a strong individual touch without having been influenced by radical tendencies. He handles rhythms in an original way and he occasionally writes melodies quite deliberately which just escape being in the class of popular song. Yet his music must be admitted as contemporaneous, and he has won a wide public.

His song "Velvet Shoes" is frequently programmed, and he has written others equally charming, and chamber music also which in 1941 won him the Coolidge Medal for distinguished service to chamber music.

Thompson was a fellow of the American Academy in Rome and held a Guggenheim fellowship. He has taught at Wellesley, Harvard, and the University of California, was director of the Curtis Institute of Music in Philadelphia (1939-1941), head of the music department at the University of Virginia, and is now on the music staff at Princeton University.

Another composer whose individuality and method of working is characteristically American is Roy Harris (1898), of whom his first teacher, Arthur Farwell, says (*Musical Quarterly,* January 1932): "Already a peculiar feeling of vitality attaches to the mention of his name, which in a fugitive way is coming to be regarded as a symbol of the most advanced modern musical thought." Harris has much of the "wild and woolly West" in his independent and pioneering spirit. He has worked out his own technic not by accepting the dictum of teachers, although he studied abroad with Nadia Boulanger, who has been the teacher of many young Americans, but by blazing his own trail, by weighing the worth of every time-honored rule and regulation, and by trial and rejection of innumerable suggestions made to him. Without musical training and background in the accepted sense of the terms, he acquired his own culture, and withal he obeyed "the still small voice" that since childhood has assured him that salvation for him lay in developing this inner urge for self-expression in musical composition.

Farwell suggests that "it may be that he will prove to be the protagonist of the time-spirit, by which I do not mean that passing phase which worships the machine, or machine-made sport, but of the new time-spirit which seeks the truer human values beneath the surface of present phenomena, and which must presently posit the deeper aspirations of the Twentieth Century."

Harris's style is austere, polychordal, and multirhythmic. He has worked things out logically for the outsider, if the listener can approach his compositions from his point of view. And many, who have faith in his talent, do. As to musical form, he tries to develop everything from a germ motive, allowing the composition to unfold naturally from the central idea. In the Piano Sonata this development amounts almost to a form of free variations, and of geometrical design. He frequently harmonizes by means of open fifths and chords used in a modern organum fashion (page 140). He constantly combines unrelated chords bitonally, and seeks unity and balance by means of rhythmic patterns.

The nucleus of the prelude of the Piano Sonata, as stated in the opening measures, is:

a. Piano Sonata, Prelude
Maestoso con bravura

Cos-Cob Press (copyright, 1931)

A second theme, used as counterpoint to the main theme, is:

In the eighteenth measure this develops into a bitonal combination in which the germ motive in the left hand is repeated in inversion in the right:

In the *andante ostinato,* the first measure of irregular groupings shows the theme which forms the basis of the *ostinato,* a modern treatment of the ancient passacaglia idea, and the second measure discloses his harmonic (polychordal) scheme:

Roy Harris, op. 1

Cos-Cob Press (copyright, 1931)

This tonal design is not unlike the Hindu *ragas,* to which I have compared the arbitrary selection of notes from a scale system indulged in by many twentieth century composers (page 108).

The scherzo, interesting rhythmically, is in two-part dissonant counterpoint. The sonata closes with an extended coda which is a return to the material of the prelude.

His reputation rests on his Piano Sonata op. 1; three string quartets; Concerto for piano, clarinet, and string quartet; Sextet for flute, oboe, clarinet, bassoon, horn, and piano; Chorale for string sextet; Prelude and Fugue for string orchestra; six symphonies, including the best-known Third Symphony, the Folksong Symphony for chorus and orchestra, one dedicated to Russia, and a Lincoln Symphony; a quintet for piano and strings; and choruses, including the two *a capella* works on Whitman texts, "Song of Occupations" and the Symphony for Voices.

Harris has worked out his own technic in which a long spun-out melody is an important issue. The spontaneous flow of his melodic line was not hurt by the sophistication of European study. He has remained distinctly an American composer, although his work is more successful when he is unconsciously so, and less satisfactory when he sets out to write American music as in some of his works composed during the war years.

He made an intensive study of plainsong which shows definitely in a work generally considered his best—the Third Symphony (1938-1939), which opens with a sweeping melody in plainsong style:

From Third Symphony
Con moto   Roy Harris

Cello f

(G. Schirmer, Inc., copyright, 1939, 1940)

After twenty-four measures of a free-flowing melody, he injects fourths which give the effect of a modern organum. According to his own analysis of the symphony it is in five sections. Section I, which follows this opening part, is tragic; the second section is lyric; and the third, in which most unusual treatment of the strings appears, is pastoral. The woodwind melody has a polytonal accompaniment of arpeggiated chords which carry on for 166 measures with a most curious and interesting whirring effect. Section IV is a fugue based on a subject in unusual rhythm:

Third Symphony   Roy Harris

(Strings) ff   ffz

ffz   etc.

(G. Schirmer, Inc., copyright, 1939, 1940)

Although in an entirely different rhythm, this reminds one of a theme in Stravinsky's *Petrouchka*. The symphony has an imposing chorale-like close based on the melody of the first section, with a long pedal point on the tympani.

Harris writes both tonally and polytonally. His harmony is based on triads, major and minor. He uses modes as a means of producing tone color, and to him every inversion of the triads has a bright or dark color. The final section (the chorale) is constructed along the lines of "triads as color." He uses as a basis of his work a system of "harmonic polytonality."

An illuminating article, "The Harmonic Idiom of Roy Harris," appeared in the Spring 1946 issue of *Modern Music*. It is by Robert Evett, a pupil of his at the University of Colorado at Colorado Springs, where Harris holds the post of composer-in-residence. Evett analyzes Harris's "evolving concepts of tonal relations," the first of which concerns his use of harmony as "mass resonance"; the second, as a means "for the inflection and modification of melodic line," and the third "for purposes of architectural definition." Harris has applied his observation of Bach's use of "complex and inventive cadences," as well as the methods employed by Gesualdo and other pre-rococo composers, to his own work, resulting "in a merciless intensification of his own expression at the point of conclusion."

Evett gives a clear description of many of the Harris methods which hitherto have been kept secret from the public. Among these are the problems of brightest and darkest simple harmonies, "a very precisely calculated concept of tonality relationships" illustrated by a chart, and their application in polytonal textures, calculated according to over-tones and their "graduated color values," with a chart. The article closes with the statement that Harris will soon publish a book dealing with these problems.

One situation in America which does not exist to the same degree in Europe is the presence of the foreign-born composer who has become a naturalized citizen. Those who came to this country during the Nazi regime have been discussed elsewhere (page 289), but before that time several important men who have become an integral part of the American scene did the major portion of their work in this country.

Edgar Varèse (1883), who spent a short time in his native France after a sojourn in this country, is particularly interested in percussion and rhythmic problems. Pitts Sanborn said, "It is easy to relate the music of Mr. Varèse to that modern movement in the visual arts which is represented by Matisse, Picasso ... and Brancusi. And Mr. Varèse himself has authorized us to believe that his *Hyperprism* aims its facets hopefully toward the elusive desideratum of the Fourth Dimension...." For orchestra he has written *"Ameriques," "Arcana"*; for chamber orchestra, *"Integrales," "Offrandes,"* "Hyperprism," "Ionisation"; and for chamber music, *"Octandre."* Varèse was the founder with Carlos Salzedo of the International Composers' Guild, a pioneer movement in presenting modern music in America. The purpose of the guild was to give living composers—innovators and pathfinders—the opportunity to have their work performed, and to present the public with auditions of the latest music.

Carlos Salzedo (1885), the world famous harpist, has been an indefatigable worker in the cause of modernism. His experiments, of which his compositions are tangible examples, have extended the possibilities of harp technic. He has written a concerto for harp and seven wind instruments; *"Préambule et Jeux"*; "Four Preludes to the Afternoon of a Telephone," in which the themes are worked out from his friends' telephone numbers; Sonata for Harp and Piano; Sonata for Two Harps, etc.

Lazare Saminsky (1882), eminent writer, composer, and authority on Hebrew and liturgical music, was born in Russia and was trained at the conservatories of Moscow and Petrograd. Since 1920 he has been identified with music in this country, as choir director at the Temple Emanu-El in New York, and for many years as one of the directors of the League of Composers, of which he was a founder. He is the head of the annual Three Choirs Festival and has conducted American and Russian works in Europe, South America, and Canada. He is the author of *Music of Our Day* and *Music of the Ghetto and the Bible*.

Saminsky has written five symphonies; symphonic poems; *Gagliarda of the Merry Plague* and *Jephtha's Daughter,* opera ballets; "Litanies of Women" for mezzosoprano and ten instruments, and other chamber music; "By the Rivers of Babylon," Psalm 137, for mixed chorus, soprano, baritone, and four instruments; *"De Profundis,"* for chorus, tenor, and organ.

Werner Josten (1888), of German birth, has been in this country since 1921 and has been professor of music at Smith College since 1923. One of his most serious scores, *Concerto Sacro* I and II, was inspired, like Hindemith's *Mathis der Maler,* by the sixteenth century triptych of the Isenheim altar at Colmar, Alsace, painted by Grünewald. Another fine score is the ballet *Joseph and his Brethren,* produced by Albert Stoessel in 1936 at the Juilliard School of Music. Other ballets include *Batouala* and *Endymion.* He has written two symphonies, symphonic movements, choral works, and chamber music.

Bernard Wagenaar (1894) was a pupil of Johan Wagenaar in his native Holland. He came to this country in 1921 and was a member of the New York Philharmonic, which was then directed by a fellow countryman, Willem Mengelberg. In his Sinfonietta, which was performed at the Liége (Belgium) Festival of the International Society for Contemporary Music in 1930, Wagenaar shows a distinctly neo-classic style. His three symphonies display the same traits, with all the modern polytonal and atonal equipment. Everything he writes, including his Triple Concerto for flute, harp, and cello with orchestra, and his adventure in the operatic field, *Pieces of Eight,* displays a sensitive elegance of style and a cultured personality. He has written three string quartets, a sonata for violin and piano, and a sonatina for cello and piano which show a high degree of musicianship and technical knowledge. Both Wagenaar and Frederick Jacobi are teaching composition in the Juilliard School of Music.

Leo Ornstein (1895), although a child when he came from Russia, has many national characteristics in his music. His first attempts at composition came in a wild burst of dissonance and experimentation which marked him as an *enfant terrible.* "Wild Men's Dance" and "Poems of 1917" are examples of his first style. Later he became interested in classical forms and wrote a concerto for piano, a symphony, sonatas for cello and for violin, a quintet and a quartet, in which he has gone to the extreme of long developments of good thematic material. Among his later works are Six Preludes for Cello and Piano, in which he has successfully combined mastery of technic and a dissonant style.

A score in which he showed a delightful humor was a pantomime, "Lima Beans," on a text by Alfred Kreymborg. The League of Composers commissioned Ornstein to write an orchestral work in 1935.

It was "Nocturne and Dance of the Fates," presented by the St. Louis Orchestra under Vladimir Golschmann.

Other naturalized musicians influential in the present day composing field include Nicolas Slonimsky (1894) of Russian birth, who, in addition to compositions for piano and chamber music, is author of *Music since 1900* and *Music of Latin America;* Dane Rudhyar (1895), a French mystic, writer, and composer, who was searching for an individualistic and spontaneous expression, and worked in the development of rituals manifested in the dance, music, and other arts; Alois Reiser (Czechoslovak, 1884), winner of several prizes; Rudolph Ganz (Swiss, 1877), an important pianist, conductor, and pedagogue; Carl Engel (French, 1883-1944), editor and musicologist in addition to composer; Joseph Achron (Russian, 1886-1943), whose last years were spent in California; Arthur Lourié (1892), a Russian who made his home in Paris until World War II drove him to America, where a serious, mystical work was presented by Koussevitzky; Eugene Goossens (British, 1893), a member of the early twentieth century group of gifted English composers, who became an American citizen and was for some years conductor of the Cincinnati Orchestra until 1946 when he resigned his post to go to Australia to conduct and head a university music department; Stefan Wolpe (1902), a gifted composer from Berlin, who studied with Herman Scherchen and Anton von Webern, was head of the composition department of the Palestine Conservatory of Music from 1934 to 1938, and has written much choral, orchestral, and chamber music which was heard in important European centers before he arrived in America; Joseph Yasser (Russian, 1893), musicologist; and Aurelio Giorni (Italian, 1895-1938), pianist and composer of much piano and chamber music.

In 1921-22 a group of American composers formed the American Music Guild with the object of encouraging any serious efforts in musical composition that might be or had recently been made by American composers. Its primary reason was for the members to become acquainted with each other's works through informal hearings, helpful criticism, and frank opinion. As one of the original members of the guild, I can attest to the stimulating effect of the short-lived organization in fulfilling its mission. It gave the members a definite opportunity to measure their talents and to seek the right channels for further development. The founders included, besides myself, Louis

Gruenberg; Sandor Harmati, who made his career as a conductor as well as composer before his untimely death (1936); Charles Haubiel, winner of the Schubert Centennial Prize with his symphonic variations "Karma," and a well-trained polyphonist; Frederick Jacobi, whose recent works are neoromantic; A. Walter Kramer, eminent song writer, whose orchestral works include a symphonic rhapsody for violin and an orchestration of Bach's Chaconne, and a famous critic and writer on musical subjects; Harold Morris, who has won many awards, from the Juilliard Publication Award in 1933 to that of the Fellowship of American Composers in 1946; Deems Taylor, opera composer, two of whose works were commissioned by the Metropolitan Opera Company; and Albert Stoessel.

A number of composers have done serious work and have added materially to the catalogue of American compositions. Among these, to mention a few, are: Richard Donovan, Mabel Daniels, Mary Howe, Rosalie Housman, John Beach, Avery Claflin, Wesley La Violette, Eric Delamarter, Ethel Glenn Hier, Richard Hammond, Edward Ballantine, Edward Royce, John Duke, Frederic P. Hart, David Stanley Smith, Eugene Bonner, Fanny Charles Dillon, Antonio Lora, George McKay, Donald Tweedy, Celius Dougherty, Frances McCollin, Lee Pattison, Wintter Watts, Carl Deis, Herbert Elwell, Elliot Griffis, Harrison Kerr, Adolph Weiss, Walter Howe, Samuel L. M. Barlow, Seth Bingham, Gena Branscombe, Albert Elkus, David Guion, Harl McDonald, Timothy Spelman, Lamar Stringfield, Burnet Tuthill, Paul White.

CHAPTER 21

AMERICAN COMPOSERS OF THE 1900's:
COPLAND, BLITZSTEIN, SCHUMAN, BARBER, GOULD, DELLO JOIO, CAGE, DIAMOND, BERNSTEIN, FOSS, ETC.

THE division of composers born in the 1900's may seem an arbitrary one, and yet these younger men have an aesthetic aim and have achieved a goal differing definitely from the accomplishments of the older composers. Naturally there is no clear-cut division between those born in the last decade of the nineteenth century and those of the early part of the twentieth. There is, however, a growing nationalism, belated but evidenced in the work of many. There is also a technical dexterity that was formerly missing when the criticism used to be that the Americans had talent but no technical equipment. They also vary greatly in style, and are quick to seize composing opportunities that did not exist in an earlier generation, and are utilitarian rather than merely following "art for art's sake."

Aaron Copland (1900), one of the most gifted of the twentieth century Americans, in many ways is a product of his period. He has a facile technic, an architectural sense, a complete understanding of dissonance in the Stravinsky and Milhaud manner, has absorbed the Jazz Age, turning what he wished to his own ends, and has gone his own way to an expression in which jazz is merely a memory of past glories, a part of his unconscious cerebration. The Concerto for Piano and Orchestra (1926) represents the jazz period in its most dazzling aspect—dissonant unleashed primitivism—but handled with an unexpected mastery of material for a young composer of twenty-six. His "Music for the Theater" (1925), one of the first works to bring him before the public, remains a significant score. The Symphonic Ode (1929), written for the fiftieth anniversary of the Boston Symphony

Orchestra, is in the later idiom *sans* jazz, and the Piano Variations (1930) show the experimental spirit in his attempts to use the instrument in its percussive propensities.

Aside from his own compositions, Copland has a splendid musical intellect and a fearless attitude that has made him a leader among the younger musicians. He has done much to encourage the writing of individual music in this country, first by means of the Copland-Sessions concerts and the early Yaddo Festivals of Contemporary American Music, and then as a member of the executive board of the League of Composers and as founder and first president of the American Composers Alliance.

Copland is definitely a child of his environment and his works reflect the present day trends. He has a technical security and musical foundation that result from the thoroughness and conservativeness of his early training with Victor Wittgenstein, Clarence Adler, and Rubin Goldmark. The impact of Parisian musical life, study with Nadia Boulanger, hearing the music of Stravinsky and the French composers of the early twenties, helped to mold his style. It was formerly claimed that his Russian-Jewish heritage shows in the quality of his melodic line, but he seldom consciously sought out Jewish folk melodies. An exception is his piano trio "Vitebsk" (1934).

A definite and original musical personality emerged from his early period. In the *Book of Modern Composers* edited by David Ewen, I wrote of him as "a clear, logical thinker; a richly endowed musicality; a brilliant craftsman; a non-sentimentalist; a man of high-strung, nervous vitality, one who works with directness, fearlessness, honesty, supreme concentration, and with little superfluous detail, development, or decoration." In fact, this statement concerning Copland describes characteristics that have become those of American music.

Today Copland is working along two seemingly opposing lines. The one is the outcome of the sophisticated style developed in his twenties; the other is a conscious simplification resulting in works definitely American in character. In this latter are his ballets *Billy the Kid* (1938), *Rodeo* (1943), and more recently the lovely *Appalachian Spring* (1944), composed on a commission from Mrs. Elizabeth Sprague Coolidge for Martha Graham. Here he has achieved supreme simplicity and the American folk expression that indicates the belated nationalism cultivated by many Americans. In this same group may be included *The Second Hurricane* (1937), a play-opera for high schools probably suggested by Hindemith's *Let Us Build a City;* An Outdoor Overture (1938), composed for and played by the High School of Music and Art in New York; the music for the documentary film *The City* and the more important film for Thornton Wilder's play *Our Town;* and the "Portrait of Abraham Lincoln" (1942), a commission from Andre Kostelanetz. In *El Salón México* (1936) Copland has used Mexican popular airs in a brilliantly orchestrated composition that is a blend of his earlier and later styles.

In the earlier works one finds orgiastic moods side by side with the nostalgic. The gentler Copland may be sought in some of the short works, such as the song with flute and clarinet accompaniment "As It Fell upon a Day" (1929), and the *a cappella* setting for women's voices of Edward Arlington Robinson's "The House on the Hill" (1925), and the first of the Two Pieces for string quartet (1939). The "Quiet City" is distinctly of nostalgic mood. The wild boisterous mood, held in check through his intellectual and technical mastery, is the result of his extraordinary rhythmical sense, the brilliancy of his orchestration (with his characteristic use of the trumpet), and the pungent effect of his polytonality. His harmonic scheme is more polytonal than atonal.

Practically every composition comes to life by reason of the vitality of his rhythmic patterns, a completely American characteristic. Swift changes of meter, a contrapuntal web of rhythms, "a fearless bravado, an ironic wit, all are offshoots of his inherent response to a fundamental rhythmic urge" ("Copland" from the *Book of Modern Composers,* edited by David Ewen).

In Copland we find angles, lines, and planes, but no soft contours, pastel harmonies, or long developments. Sharply defined motifs, reiteration of short figures and of bits of thematic material are employed in a style of development sometimes described as *cumulative.*

This style is clearly seen in his Piano Sonata (1942) and the Violin Sonata, which followed rapidly. These two compositions form one of those sharp contrasts in Copland's work. They represent the carefully planned, austere, serious style in which one finds an uncompromising harmonic starkness, and frequently planes of juxtapositions of melodic and harmonic resources that create the Copland individuality.

The following quotation from the second movement of the Piano Sonata shows the cumulative treatment of a melodic line:

(with permission of Boosey & Hawkes, Inc., N.Y. 1942)

In September 1946 Copland completed his Symphony No. 3. Commissioned by the Koussevitzky Music Foundation, it is dedicated to Natalie Koussevitzky. His first symphony, for orchestra with organ, dates from 1924–25. Nadia Boulanger played the organ part on her first visit to America. His second, entitled "Short Symphony," is rhythmically complex and was first performed in Mexico by Carlos Chávez in 1934. It had a radio performance under Stokowski's direction over NBC in 1944.

The Third Symphony in four movements is an epitome of Copland's work of the last years, a combination of the simplicity and national idiom achieved in *Appalachian Spring,* without any folk quotation, and the highly skilled workmanship of the Piano Sonata and Violin Sonata. He uses dissonance, polytonality, sophisticated rhythms, but no jazz effects, and yet it is not as complicated in sound, form, rhythm, harmony, or melody as his earlier scores. There is a smoothing out of line and idiom, and the achievement should prove of signal importance in Aaron Copland's further development.

In the Boston Symphony program notes of November 16, 1946, Copland is quoted as having stated: "Harold Clurman put my meaning well when he wrote recently that music is a 'reflection of and response to specific worlds of men: it is play, it is speech, it is unconscious result and conscious statement all at the same time.'"

Copland is the author of two books, *What to Listen For in Music* and *Our New Music.*

The first reward for merit of the Boston Symphony Orchestra (1947) was given to Aaron Copland for his Third Symphony; it won the 1947 award of the New York Music Critic's Circle also.

Four other composers born in 1900 are Otto Luening, George Antheil, Nicolai Berezowsky, and Anis Fuleihan. Otto Luening, composer and conductor, is associate professor of music at Barnard College, Columbia University, and conducts the opera performances of the workshop of Columbia. He was for some years head of the Music Department at Bennington (Vt.) College, and succeeded Aaron Copland as president of the American Composers Alliance. He has written for full and chamber orchestras; also chamber music works, a four-act opera, *Evangeline,* and with Ernst Bacon a two-piano piece, "Coal Scuttle Blues." He also has songs on texts by Whitman, choral works, and piano pieces. Among recent publications are "Prelude to a Hymn Tune by William Billings" and a "Fuguing Tune" for five wind instruments. He has experimented with a wide variety of styles and forms and written in many mediums.

George Antheil came back into the musical picture in 1944, when Leopold Stokowski presented his Fourth Symphony over the NBC network. He has been writing for films in Hollywood. After his sensational *Ballet Méchanique* in 1927, he returned to Europe, where he had previously spent a number of years (page 308).

Nicolai Berezowsky made a romantic escape from his native Russia at the time of the Revolution. His studies in composition were completed at the Juilliard Graduate School and his career has been developed in America. In an interesting violin concerto (1930) he crystallized his neoclassic tendencies. He has written four symphonies; chamber music including string quartets and woodwind ensembles;

a harp concerto; "Concerto Lirico" for the cello; a string quartet with orchestra, etc. His wife, Alice Berezowsky, has told the building of his career as violinist, composer, and conductor in an entertaining book, *Duet with Nicky*. He has been the recipient of a prize from the NBC, and a grant from the American Academy of Arts and Letters.

Anis Fuleihan was fifteen when he came to this country from the island of Cyprus, and his training was acquired here. He is largely self-taught in composition and has a long catalogue of works, including many piano compositions and orchestral scores.

Like Hugo Wolf or Gabriel Fauré, Theodore Chanler (1902) is best known for his contribution to song literature. Eight Epitaphs, and a second series of Epitaphs; Four Rhymes, a commission from the League of Composers sung by Dorothy Maynor; "The Children," "These, My Ophelia," a number of choral works including a mass for women's voices, and "Seven Recreations" for women's voices, oboe, viola, cello, and piano, and other songs, mark him a scrupulous workman, a gifted composer with an aristocratic sense of style.

Chanler has written chamber music and piano compositions, among which is one of his most sensitive creations, "The Second Joyful Mystery," a fugue for two pianos. He has worked in music criticism, and was a pupil of Arthur Shepherd, Percy Goetschius, Ernest Bloch, and Nadia Boulanger.

Ruth Crawford (1901) was the first woman composer to hold the Guggenheim fellowship (1930). She has written a violin sonata; a suite for piano, "The Adventures of Tom Thumb"; preludes for piano; a string quartet; a suite for small orchestra and one for five wind instruments and piano; and five songs to poems by Carl Sandburg. In 1933 her Three Songs for contralto, oboe, piano, and percussion with orchestral ostinato was presented in Amsterdam at the Festival of the International Society for Contemporary Music.

Ruth Crawford is the wife of Charles Seeger, whom she assisted in the Resettlement Administration, which work brought her in touch with American traditional music. She has collaborated with John and Alan Lomax in their books on American folk songs and ballads, for which she transcribed from phonograph discs several hundred songs recorded in the field. She has used some of these traditional melodies for children's pieces for piano.

Louise Talma, a fellow of the American Guild of Organists, and a 1946 holder of the Guggenheim fellowship, is assistant professor of music at Hunter College. Her advanced studies were made with Isidore Philipp and Nadia Boulanger at the Fontainebleau School of Music in France, where she also taught. She has frequently worked at the MacDowell Colony, Peterborough, N.H., as have many other of the twentieth century American composers. Among her compositions are choral works, a serious piano sonata, a group of French songs of lovely mood and excellent workmanship, and a Toccata for Orchestra.

A number of gifted American women belong to this younger group, including Miriam Gideon; Vivian Fine; Evelyn Berckman; Dorothy James; Radie Britain; Ulric Cole, who has had two works published by the Society for the Publication of American Music; Margaret Starr McLain; Jeanne Behrend; Florence Galajikian; Beatrice Laufer, whose first symphony was played at the Festival of American Music in Rochester (1945); Ursula Lewis and Virginia Seay, both of whom won prizes with orchestral scores in the Young Composers Contests of the National Federation of Music Clubs, Dika Newlin, and others.

Among the composers who studied the possibilities of jazz must be mentioned Marc Blitzstein (1905), whose early work "Triple-Sec" (1928) is an example of its clever employment. At the time he did "Triple-Sec" he had written other works in other styles, principally neoclassic, but the humor and entertaining rhythms of the little "opera-farce" stand out in one's memory. His penchant for writing for the stage found a successful outlet in *The Cradle Will Rock* (1936), *No for an Answer* (1937–40), and the short radio opera *I've Got the Tune*. These are not properly opera; Aaron Copland calls them "musical theater," but in them Blitzstein found his real medium for musical and social expression. They are truly American, although his models may have been works by Kurt Weill and Hanns Eisler.

He has written his own texts for all his stage works and for the Airborne Symphony. Blitzstein, almost more than any other composer, has made the twentieth century amalgamation of popular idiom and so-called "serious" music seem feasible.

During World War II he was a sergeant in the Eighth Army Air Force, stationed in London, where he worked in radio and films. His symphonic piece "Freedom Morning" was composed for concerts that he arranged, featuring a chorus of two hundred Negro soldiers. He used melodic and rhythmic material that the soldiers improvised or suggested, giving the work an American folk character.

Blitzstein was commissioned by the Eighth Army Air Force to compose a work, and his efforts resulted in the Airborne Symphony (1943–44). He calls it a symphony, but it is not one in the usual meaning of that term. It deals with the history of human flight and is in twelve sections, on his own text in everyday, homely, sometimes commonplace language. It is scored for a speaker, called "Monitor," male chorus, solo tenor (for a Negro voice), baritone, and full orchestra. Its original treatment, the effective combination of speech, choral declamation, and singing, the dramatic music for the soloists, the expert handling of the orchestral sections, all make it a significant experiment in a new type of musical composition.

Paul Creston (1906), an American of Italian parentage, a holder of a Guggenheim fellowship, and the recipient of an award from the American Academy of Arts and Letters, is unique in that he is practically self-taught in composition. His most recent works include a suite for saxophone and piano; a sonata and a concerto for saxophone; a partita for flute, violin, and string orchestra; two Choric Dances; Pastorale and Tarantella for orchestra; a concertino for marimba and orchestra; many songs and piano pieces, a string quartet, and two symphonies, the second of which received the New York Music Critics' Award in 1943.

In 1906, several composers important in the American scene were born. Among these are David van Vactor, first flutist of the Chicago Symphony Orchestra; Normand Lockwood, composer of choral works, whose chamber opera *The Scarecrow* brought him before the New York public in performances by the Columbia Theater Associates of Columbia University in 1944; Arthur Kreutz, a Guggenheim fellow and winner of the *Prix de Rome* in 1940, whose "Music for Symphony Orchestra" was played by Dr. Rodzinski following a "reading rehearsal" of the Philharmonic-Symphony Orchestra in 1944; Ross Lee Finney of the faculty of Smith College, composer of string quartets and piano sonatas; and Robert L. Sanders, a fellow of the American Academy in Rome (1920), who won an award in the New York Philharmonic-Symphony contest in 1938.

Burrill Phillips (1907) of the Eastman School of Music faculty has struck an American note with two orchestral works, *Selections from*

McGuffey's Readers based on: "The One-Hoss Shay," "The Courtship of Miles Standish," and "The Midnight Ride of Paul Revere"; and "Courthouse Square," which depicts in music life in an American town. He has written chamber music; a concerto for piano and orchestra; "Three Informalities; Blues, Scherzo, and Sonatina" and Five Divertimenti for piano; Concert Piece for Bassoon and Strings; and other compositions showing an individuality. He won the American Academy of Arts and Letters and the National Institute of Arts and Letters award (1944), and the same year the Koussevitzky Music Foundation gave him a commission for an overture, premiered at the Third Annual Festival of Contemporary American Music (Columbia University, 1947).

Elie Siegmeister (1909) is well known for his research in musical Americana and his use of folk music in his compositions. *A Treasury of American Song,* edited with Olin Downes, several collections of early ballads and songs, and his training and conducting of the American Ballad Singers are indicative of his interests and achievements.

Also born in 1909 are Paul Nordoff, writer of many songs and chamber music; and Israel Citkowitz, a pupil of Copland, Sessions, and Nadia Boulanger, who has made a choral setting of Blake's poem "The Lamb" and has written song cycles to poems by Blake, Frost, and Joyce.

Two of our composers have been attracted by the lure of exotic music, and have built their careers along highly specialized lines. Colin McPhee (1901), of Canadian birth, studied at the Peabody Institute in Baltimore, also in Paris, and in New York with Edgar Varèse. His early works were along traditional lines, but in 1931 he went to Bali, where he remained for six years. Since that time, his chief interest has been a book on Balinese music, *A House in Bali,* for the preparation of which he had a Guggenheim fellowship.

Paul Bowles (1910), a pupil of Copland and of Virgil Thomson, traveled in Spain, Northern Africa, the Sahara, the Antilles, and South and Central America, to study the folk music in these various countries. His music has been strongly influenced by these exotic strains. The Ballet Caravan performed his *Yankee Clipper* in 1936, and he has written incidental music for plays directed by Orson Welles, and others written by Saroyan, Philip Barry, and Lillian Hellman, scores for films, and other ballets. He has written chamber music and piano pieces, and was a critic on the *New York Herald Tribune* for a few years.

William Schuman (1910) has developed a style of his own, an individuality, however rooted it may have been in the teachings of Roy Harris. There is a deeply serious, learned side to Schuman's work, especially in his skilled use of counterpoint, which is the basis of his technic. But there is a youthful energy, a buoyant exuberance also that is equally characteristic. He has written five symphonies, the third (1941) having received the first award in 1942 of the New York Music Critics' Circle. The fifth is for strings alone.

The Third Symphony is an excellent example of the "neobaroque," as its movements are a passacaglia, a fugue, a chorale, and a toccata. The technical framework may be baroque, but the treatment is contemporary.

One finds the energetic drive in his American Festival Overture (1939), which was commissioned by the League of Composers and was one of the first works to bring Schuman into the public eye. A score in serious vein is "Prayer in Time of War" (1943). He has been unusually successful in his choral settings of "This Is Our Time" and "Holiday Song" (Genevieve Taggard); "A Free Song," Secular Cantata No. 2, and "Pioneers" on texts by Walt Whitman; Prelude for Voices, text by Thomas Wolfe; *"Requiescat"*; Four Canonic Choruses, text by Edna St. Vincent Millay; "The Orchestra Song" (Marion Farquhar), and many others composed for his chorus when he was teaching at Sarah Lawrence College in Bronxville, N.Y.

Schuman has written three string quartets, one of which received a Town Hall award for representative chamber music by an American composer. His Concerto for Piano and Small Orchestra is in the chamber music category, but since its appearance in 1943 Schuman has reorchestrated it for large orchestra. "Newsreel in Five Shots" and "Side Shows" are scores demonstrating his humor and ability to handle light material.

One of his successes is *Undertow* (1945), a forty-minute ballet presented by the Ballet Theatre, which was given in concert form by the New York Philharmonic-Symphony under Artur Rodzinski in 1946 as "Choreographic Episodes for Orchestra." The program annotator called it "a bold excursion into the Freudian jungle." It showed Schuman's gift for composing for the stage and for dramatic expression in music. The composer stated that the ballet "concerns itself with the emotional development of a transgressor. The choreographic action depicts a series of related happenings, the psychological implications of which result in inevitable murder." As a result of his crime "his soul is purged" as he realizes that "he will no longer be called upon to endure the anguish of being a misfit and an outcast among his fellow men."

In addition to two Guggenheim fellowships, he received the grant in music from the American Academy of Arts and Letters and the National Institute of Arts and Letters (1943). He left Sarah Lawrence College to be manager of publications at G. Schirmer, Inc., in 1945, from which position he resigned to become, at the age of thirty-five, the president of the Juilliard School of Music.

Samuel Barber (1910) presents a curious anomaly in an age when all the young composers, and the older ones too, for that matter, write works that are in some way or other problematical—atonal, polytonal, folkish, jazzish, simplified, or going back to medieval methods. But Barber has gone his own independent way, a romantic way in his earlier scores such as the Adagio for Strings (1936) and the two Essays for Orchestra (1937 and 1942). He has gained international recognition, and his works are frequently programmed. For one reason, they are easy to listen to, again they can be understood, they are extremely well written, and have a decided aristocracy of style.

His music has been accused of being conservative; nevertheless he has used his materials with beauty of design and knowledge of the architectural and tonal structure he was building, and it is never commonplace.

Barber's name is high on the list of American song writers. His first published work is "The Daisies" on a text by James Stephens. The same poet's "Bessie Bobtail," A. E. Housman's "With rue my heart is laden," and three songs from James Joyce's *Chamber Music* followed in the next years. Barber knows how to write for the voice because he himself sings. He is a nephew of the late American opera contralto Louise Homer, and was surrounded by music from babyhood. In fact, he had piano lessons at six and tried to compose at seven. He attended the Curtis Institute of Music in Philadelphia at thirteen, where he had piano, singing, and composition lessons. He studied composition with Rosario Scalero, from whom he received a thorough and conservative education. In 1935 he was awarded the *Prix de Rome* and later received the Pulitzer Prize.

Barber's choral works show the same understanding of the treatment of voices and setting of texts as the songs. His choice of poets, Emily Dickinson, James Stephens, and Stephen Spender, displays his cultural taste. In 1940 he made a setting of Spender's "A Stop-watch and an Ordnance Map" for unaccompanied men's chorus and kettledrums. In this work and other compositions written while he was in the Army, one sees a sterner mood, a rapidly developing individuality, and increasing fearlessness in handling harmonic materials.

Of his symphonies, the first, dating from 1936, was revised and played by Dr. Rodzinski and the Philharmonic-Symphony in 1944. The same week Dr. Serge Koussevitzky performed the Second Symphony, op. 19, with the Boston Symphony Orchestra in New York. The latter was commissioned by the Army Air Forces, to which it is dedicated. Although the composer claims it is not program music, in the second movement Barber uses a specially constructed electrical "tone generator" that simulates the sound of a radio beam, "a code signal used in night or blind flying, or over unknown territory, in order to keep the pilot to his course." In 1945 Barber wrote his Capricorn Concerto for flute, oboe, trumpet, and strings, which had a citation from the Critics' Circle (1947). He received a commission from the Alice M. Ditson Fund to write a ballet, *Serpent Heart,* in collaboration with Martha Graham for performance at the Second Annual Festival of Contemporary American Music at Columbia University, in May 1946.

A month earlier Koussevitzky conducted the first New York performance at a Boston Symphony concert with Raya Garbousova of Barber's Concerto for Violoncello and Orchestra. It received the New York Music Critics' Award. It was called a work of "quality and distinction" by Irving Kolodin in the *Sun.* "Its effect was immediate, unmistakable."

Earl Robinson, A. Lehman Engel, and Richard Franko Goldman have little more in common than a birth year, 1910. Robinson jumped into fame with his "Ballad for Americans" on a text by John La Touche, originally a WPA production (1939). This he followed with a setting of Carl Sandburg's "The People, Yes," to write which he received a Guggenheim fellowship; "The Lonesome Train," a cantata describing the funeral train of Lincoln; "Battle Hymn" on a text by John La Touche and Robinson, based on President Roosevelt's "State of the Union" speech; "The House I Live In," on which a radio play was based; and other works with a social message.

A. Lehman Engel, who conducted in the Great Lakes Naval Training School during World War II, conducted and trained the Madrigal Singers under the WPA Music Project in New York, and has directed the music of a number of modern stage works in addition to writing incidental music to plays such as Eliot's *Murder in the Cathedral,* Aristophanes' *Birds,* Shakespeare's *Macbeth,* and O'Casey's *Within the Gates.*

Richard Franko Goldman is an authority on band music, the assistant conductor of the Goldman Band, of which his father, Edwin Franko Goldman, was founder and its first conductor. During World War II, Richard Goldman was in the Office of Strategic Services of the United States Army. He is the author of two books on band music, and with Roger Smith he compiled, edited, and arranged *Landmarks of Early American Music.* He studied in Paris with Nadia Boulanger and has written a sonatina for piano, a divertimento for flute and piano, two "Monochromes" for flute alone, scores for concert band and orchestra, etc.

Bernard Herrmann (1911), a staff conductor of the Columbia Broadcasting System, has become well known through his music for several successful motion pictures, radio scores, and for his dramatic cantata *Moby Dick.* He has composed a symphony, a violin concerto, a string quartet, orchestral suites, and ballets. He was a student under Albert Stoessel and Philip James at New York University and later at the Juilliard Graduate School under Stoessel and Bernard Wagenaar.

One of his classmates, Jerome Moross (1913), has also written for the motion pictures and for radio, and has several ballets, one on the "Frankie and Johnny" theme.

Robert McBride (1911) got his early training in Arizona, playing the saxophone or the clarinet in school bands, theater orchestras, and jazz bands. Although he teaches at Bennington (Vt.) College, the influence of those early years shows in his titles and musical style, "Strawberry Jam," "Jam Session," "Wise-Apple Five," "Workout and Swing Stuff," "Rumba." He had a Guggenheim fellowship and was granted an award by the American Academy of Arts and Letters.

The year 1913 brought to earth a group who developed varying styles: Morton Gould, Norman Dello Joio, Henry Brant, John Cage, Gardner Read, and Kent Kennan.

Morton Gould never loses an opportunity to state that he has tried "to fuse the elements of our popular American idioms with the classical form and structure." This was the basic idea in his four *Symphonettes,* the second of which is called the American Symphonette, and contains one of his most frequently performed compositions, Pavane. This has been danced and played by concert groups and school orchestras. Other works with the same combination of American popular music and classical forms are an orchestral Chorale and Fugue in Jazz; a piano concerto; "Foster Gallery," based on Stephen Foster melodies; a symphony; an American Suite, "Lincoln Legend," and three piano sonatas and a sonatina.

In 1941 Gould completed his Spirituals for String Choir and Orchestra, which has had frequent performances by major orchestras. The composer said that here he "sought to convey the mood and idiom of White and Negro Spirituals, without resorting to literal exposition of specific tunes." As a rule his aim was to use the idiomatic elements of the spiritual in conjunction with much original material. To the annotators of the Philharmonic-Symphony programs, Gould said, "I have tried to write music the way one speaks. I tried to make it as direct and simple as possible." The movements are called "Proclamation," "Sermon," "A Little Bit of Sin," "Protest," and "Jubilee." In the last the composer utilized a boogie-woogie pattern. And he finds that "many contemporary jazz effects coincide with certain rhythmic patterns in our Spirituals." The two groups, white and Negro spirituals, "make a tremendous body of folk material.... Our White songs are influenced by our Negro songs, and the other way around." He used the strings as he would have used voices. The wood winds, brass, and percussion provide the background.

Norman Dello Joio started his musical career as an organist, following in the footsteps of his father, but when he went to the Juilliard School of Music his interests turned to composition and he studied with Bernard Wagenaar. He also was a pupil of Paul Hindemith. Dello Joio won the Town Hall Composition Award for his orchestral work "Magnificat," two Guggenheim fellowships, and a grant from the American Academy of Arts and Letters.

His work is neoclassic and of serious character. He has written Concert Music for orchestra; Concerto for Two Pianos and Orchestra; Concerto for Harp and Orchestra; two concertinos, one for flute and strings, the other for piano and orchestra. He writes well for voices, and among his works for chorus are "The Mystic Trumpeteer" and "Jubilant Song" on texts by Whitman; "Madrigals"; and a Symphony for Voices and Orchestra with narrator on Stephen Vincent Benét's "Western Star." Dello Joio composed the music for a widely performed ballet, *On Stage*.

His most recent work was the *Ricercari* for piano and orchestra, three pieces that have the character of a concerto although they bear the name of a fugal form of the sixteenth and seventeenth centuries. Dello Joio states that they preserve the trait of the *ricercare* in the development of a germinal idea in fantasia form. The first movement exploits a harmonic feature, the second a melodic idea, and the third a rhythmic pattern. He had in mind a sort of twentieth century Scarlatti style, "one not overly complex in its contrapuntal texture." Dello Joio was invited to play the *Ricercari* in Poland (1947).

Henry Brant, of Canadian birth, was a student at the Juilliard School, and he also studied with George Antheil. He has been an experimenter and his work usually is called "clever" rather than profound or subtle. When Brant was eighteen, Henry Cowell wrote, "Of all very young composers in America Henry Brant...has the most original things to say and the most perfect technic for saying them." Cowell finds also that he has courage as well as original ideas and knowledge. He has had much experience as orchestrator for the American ballet and Paramount Pictures, and was formerly secretary of the Pan-American Association, which was founded in 1928 by Edgar Varèse.

Brant's titles show something of the humor his music displays: "Galloping Colloquy," a scherzo ballad; "Five-and-Ten-Cent Stores Music"; "Hand Organ Music"; *Miss O'Grady,* theater-opera; *"Entente-Cordiale,"* satire; and *Alisaunde,* platform opera, earth-rite satire. But he also has written two symphonies, a concerto for flute and ten instruments, variations for orchestra, Lyric Cycle for soprano, three violas, and piano, and a sonata for two pianos. In 1946 Henry Brant was granted a Guggenheim fellowship.

One of the most daring and original talents seems to be that of

John Cage from California, who is a pioneer if not a folklorist. A pupil of Schoenberg, he has attempted to express himself through rhythm without melody and harmony in their accepted meanings. His is the melody and harmony of percussion instruments, sound machines, and of "prepared" pianos, of "sensuous sound and independent rhythm," with a complete breaking away from tonal customs and conventions of the past.

The piano is prepared by applying all sorts of gadgets to the strings, such as weather stripping, bolts, screws, pennies, slats of bamboo, etc. He has written a *Book of Music for Two Pianos,* which calls for two such instruments.

The effect of the prepared piano is thus described by Kurt List in the *New Republic* of December 24, 1945: "...the compositions for what some facetious listeners have called the well-tampered clavichord sound more like a movie-mogul's dream of a Balinese orchestra [Paging Colin McPhee!] than a mechanical rumpus. This impression is strengthened," Mr. List continues, "by Cage's sensitive and free-flowing imagination, which... impresses one as spontaneous and intuitive experimentation in sound and rhythm."

Gardner Read has been awarded several coveted prizes. His First Symphony, written at the MacDowell Colony in New Hampshire, was given the first prize by the Philharmonic-Symphony in 1937, and with the Second Symphony he won the Paderewski Prize, 1943. The Boston Symphony played his Suite for String Orchestra in 1938, and he conducted the Second Symphony with that orchestra in 1943. Read is from Illinois and was trained at the Eastman School of Music.

Kent Kennan, who won the *Prix de Rome* in 1936, has shown a sensitive talent in some short works for piano, and "Night Soliloquy" for flute and strings, and his compositions have frequently been played at the American Composers' Concerts of the Eastman School, where he was a student.

Gail Kubik (1914), a student of the American Conservatory in Chicago and of the Eastman School in Rochester, was occupied during World War II as music consultant for the Motion Pictures Bureau of the Office of War Information, and as composer of documentary films for the United States Maritime Commission and for the Army Air Force. He has held a postwar Guggenheim fellowship.

One of the most arresting talents of the younger generation is David Diamond (1915), who has held two Guggenheim fellowships; the American Academy in Rome fellowship; a prize for chamber music given by the Paderewski Fund for the Encouragement of American Composers; and the award of the American Academy of Arts and Letters and the National Institute of Arts and Letters.

His teachers, among others, include Roger Sessions, Bernard Rogers, and Nadia Boulanger. Many of his scores have been played at the Festivals of American Music, at the Eastman School, at which he was a student, and by the principal orchestras all the way from Boston to San Francisco.

Diamond has written three symphonies, which show seriousness of purpose, creative ability, a well-equipped technic, and promise for the future. He has also written other orchestral scores, including Rounds for String Orchestra, which was commissioned by Dimitri Mitropolous for the Minneapolis Symphony Orchestra. In this he used canonic construction and fugal imitation.

He has written much chamber music, a Concerto for Two Solo Pianos, and many songs of serious character. He wrote a documentary film, *A Place to Live,* and the musical score for Glenway Wescott's ballet *The Dream of Audubon,* which was awarded first prize by the Ballet Guild. His third string quartet, commissioned by the Koussevitzky Foundation, received honorable mention from the Critics' Circle (1947), which gave Ernest Bloch the chamber music award.

Other composers of 1915 include Norman Cazden; Homer Keller; Joseph Wood, whose opera *The Mother* won the Juilliard Opera Competition in 1942; and Robert Palmer, one of our most serious composers of chamber music, who has written also a "Poem" for violin and orchestra and a piano sonata.

Joseph Wood's name appears in a list of Post Service Fellowship Awards 1945–46 of the Alice M. Ditson Fund. Other composers on the list include Jacob Avshalomoff; John Barnett; Jack Goodwin; Andrew Imbrie, a pupil of Sessions, who won the New York Music Critics' Award (1945) with a string quartet; Ulysses Kay; Ellis Kohs, who has written a concerto for piano and orchestra, and chamber music of unusual promise; John Lessard; Milton Rosenstock; Frank G. Stewart; Robert Ward, whose Symphony No. 1 shows exceptional talent; Hugo Weisgall; and Frank Wigglesworth.

A group of young composers from California includes several experimentalists such as John Cage; Ray Green, who is head of the composition department of the San Francisco Conservatory, a pupil of Ernest Bloch and Albert Elkus; Gerald Strang, who has been an assistant to Arnold Schoenberg since 1935 and is managing editor of the New Music Publications; Ingolf Dahl, a member of the faculty of the University of Southern California and a follower of Stravinsky; George Tremblay; and Lou Harrison, who lives in New York and is a music critic of the *Herald Tribune,* also a pupil of Schoenberg and a disciple of the twelve tone technic.

One of the first times that I came within range of Leonard Bernstein's talent was in 1943 at a concert of the League of Composers at the New York Public Library, a program of first performances by young American composers. Young Bernstein's Sonata for Clarinet and Piano was played, and so was a Duo for Cello and Piano by Lukas Foss, a twenty-one-year-old composer. Leonard Bernstein (1918) was just beginning to make his way as a composer. He was a Bostonian, a graduate of Harvard and of the Curtis Institute, and had attended Dr. Koussevitzky's conducting classes at Tanglewood, the Berkshire Music Center. He has made a meteoric success in three fields, that of pianist, composer, and conductor. He was assistant conductor to Artur Rodzinski of the Philharmonic-Symphony Orchestra (1944–45), and in 1945 he succeeded Leopold Stokowski as conductor of the City Symphony of the New York City Center.

As a composer he has exhibited a many-sided facility; his works include the Jeremiah Symphony, the ballet *Fancy Free* from which was derived the musical comedy *On the Town,* and another ballet *Facsimile.* In 1944 Dr. Koussevitzky invited Bernstein to conduct Jeremiah at a concert of the Boston Symphony Orchestra. It is Judaic in subject and character. In the last movement, "Lamentation," the composer employs the Hebrew language to represent the voice of the prophet, which is sung by a contralto. The other two movements are "Prophecy" and "Profanation." This second movement is a savage scherzo in which he makes use of a traditional Hebrew chant. The New York Music Critics' Circle gave the symphony an award in 1944.

The first ballet and *On the Town* show the use of rhythmic devices that stem from jazz and Latin-American dance. Bernstein handles the lighter music facilely and with a naïveté that gives way easily to sophistication. His critics feel that he is especially gifted for the theater.

A fellow student of Bernstein at the Curtis Institute was Lukas Foss (1922). Also a protégé of Koussevitzky, he is the youngest composer to be performed by the Boston Symphony. In 1943 an orchestral piece, "The Prairie," based on themes from his cantata, was conducted by Dr. Koussevitzky. In 1944 he became official pianist of the Boston Symphony Orchestra.

The sixteen-year-old boy was introduced, on January 17, 1939, in the boardroom of G. Schirmer's in a recital of his own works including a Set of Three Pieces for Two Pianos, a Sonata for Violin and Piano, and solo numbers for piano. Those who heard him on that occasion, including the writer, were impressed by the spontaneity and contemporaneity of his gift and prophesied a brilliant career, which prophecy he has fulfilled.

At that time he was studying composition (Scalero), conducting (Reiner), and piano (Isabelle Vengerova) at the Curtis Institute in Philadelphia. He had for four years been a student at the Paris Conservatoire, continuing the work he had begun with Julius (Goldstein) Herford in Berlin. By citizenship and predilection he is an American composer, although of foreign birth. While a member of Dr. Koussevitzky's conducting classes, he also followed Paul Hindemith's course in composition, and he continued to work with Hindemith at Yale University.

The Hindemith influence is a strong one in Foss's technical approach, although Aaron Copland has also been intriguing to him, as representing a phase of Americanism, which is close to his heart and a never ending source of inspiration. His first large work to reach the public, *The Prairie,* is proof of this deeply felt interest. *The Prairie,* a cantata for mixed chorus, four solo voices, and orchestra, is a setting of Carl Sandburg's poem "Prairie" adapted by Lukas Foss. He recognized in Sandburg's epic "new possibilities in its earthy and almost religious approach...a new expression of an old faith drawn from the native soil." (Quoted from the printed program when the work was first performed by the Collegiate Chorale under Robert Shaw's direction in 1944.) And thus he developed a work in oratorio style based on the American soil and spirit.

The incident is told that Dr. Rodzinski, formerly conductor of the Philharmonic-Symphony, tuned in late one night on the broadcast of a work that interested and excited him to the extent that he decided he must present it himself. At the end of the broadcast the announcer gave him the information he was seeking. It was *The Prairie* by Lukas Foss, and the conductor produced it in January 1945.

Two months later George Szell, as a guest conductor of the Philharmonic-Symphony, gave the first performance of Foss's Ode for Orchestra—"Ode to those who will not return." While the composer attaches no program, he states that the general idea conveyed in the Ode is "crisis, war and ultimately faith."

Foss's First Symphony in G was given its première in Pittsburgh under the direction of Fritz Reiner, and later he conducted it with the orchestra of the New York City Center. He conducted and played his piano concerto at a CBS broadcast in 1944. He wrote incidental music for a Theatre Guild production of Shakespeare's *The Tempest,* which won him a Pulitzer scholarship in 1942. *The Prairie* two years later was cited for its musical distinction by the New York Music Critics' Circle, as the best new dramatic composition of the season 1943–44. Foss has also written three ballet scores: *The Heart Remembers* for the Humphrey-Weidman company, *Woman of the Hour* (*Within These Walls*), and *The Gift of the Magi,* produced by the Ballet Theatre. The League of Composers commissioned him to write compositions at different times, the most recent having been a setting from The Song of Songs for soprano and orchestra, scheduled for performance in 1947 by Dr. Koussevitzky and the Boston Symphony Orchestra, with Ellabelle Davis as soloist. He has also written a work on a Biblical text for baritone solo and orchestra. The Koussevitzky Foundation commissioned Foss to write a capriccio for cello and piano.

As an example of his individual and striking style, here are the opening measures of a recent piano piece, "Fantasy Rondo":

Fantasy Rondo

Lukas Foss

Later he treats eighth-note groups in fascinating rhythmic variety, one motif of which follows; although this does not represent Foss of the important orchestral scores, it still has a characteristic freshness and a recognizable profile.

Harold Shapero (1920), like Bernstein, is from Massachusetts and studied at Harvard. Among his teachers were Nicolas Slonimsky, Ernst Krenek, Piston, Hindemith, and Copland. Shapero has won many awards, among them the Prix de Rome (1941), the Guggenheim fellowship, and the B'nai B'rith prize.

William Bergsma (1921), a Californian who attended Stanford University and was trained at the Eastman School, became a teacher of composition at the Juilliard School in 1946. He has written two string quartets, other chamber music works, two ballets, and choral works. He won the Town Hall 1942 Commission, for which he wrote a symphony for chamber orchestra. His first string quartet won him the Bearns Prize, Columbia University, and the Society for the Publication of American Music award. The second quartet was written on a commission from the Koussevitzky Foundation, and in 1945 he received a grant from the National Institute of Arts and Letters. He is a Guggenheim fellow for 1947. He has written several orchestral scores, among them "Music on a Quiet Theme," a "nonprogrammatic piece . . . not always quiet," he says, in free variation form. The score won a publication award in 1946 in a competition sponsored by the Arrow Press and the Independent Music Publishers.

Among the composers born in the early 1900's are several of Russian birth who came to America after the Russian Revolution. One of these, Nicolai Berezowsky, was discussed above. Vladimir Dukelsky (1903) fled from Russia in 1920 after having studied in Moscow with Glière and in Kiev. After some time spent in Constantinople and in this country, he went to Paris, where he was commissioned by Diaghileff to write music for a ballet. On his return to America, he made a career in the commercial field under the name of Vernon Duke. Dukelsky continued as a serious writer, however, numbering among his scores two symphonies; "Epitaph" for soprano solo, chorus, and orchestra; "On the Death of Diaghilev"; *Dedicaces* for piano, orchestra, and women's voice obbligato; a piano concerto with a prologue and epilogue with a soprano voice, singing or reciting some French poems by the Parisian Guillaume Apollinaire. He has written more recently a violin concerto (1943) and a violoncello concerto (1946).

Boris Koutzen (1901), a violinist and composer, had his early training at the Moscow Conservatory. His is a serious, well-balanced talent, and he has written chamber music and orchestral scores including a concerto for five solo instruments and orchestra in a contemporary concerto grosso style. His string quartet won the award of the Society for the Publication of American Music.

Nicolai Lopatnikoff (1903) was a pupil at the St. Petersburg Conservatory, and spent some years after the Revolution in Finland and in Germany, where he was a pupil of Ernst Toch. He became a member of the new, advanced school in Berlin, and his works were heard at festivals of modern music. His Second Symphony was performed by Serge Koussevitzky in 1939, shortly after his arrival in New York. A violin concerto in contrapuntal, linear style, showing clever thematic invention and constructive skill, had several performances. He has a sinfonietta, op. 28, in neoclassic style, a concertino for orchestra, op. 30, commissioned by the Koussevitzky Foundation, and a piano sonata in contrapuntal style, with canonic imitation and shifts of interesting rhythmic patterns.

Another young composer who has made a definite place in our American music is Alexei Haieff (1914) of Siberian birth. He came to this country in 1932 and was educated at the Juilliard School, where he studied with Rubin Goldmark and Frederick Jacobi. He was a pupil of Nadia Boulanger at Cambridge, Mass., and in Paris in 1939-1940. In addition to a Guggenheim fellowship, he had one from the American Academy in Rome, and commissions from the Koussevitzky Foundation and from the Juilliard Foundation for piano pieces. His compositions, which are notable for their vitality and refinement of style, include a symphony; two piano sonatas; an orchestral divertimento which was turned into a ballet by Balanchine and was presented by the Ballet Society (1947).

Jacques de Menasce (1905), a recent addition to American composers, is of Austrian birth and was educated in Vienna. He came to this country in 1941 and has become a constructive member of our musical circles. His style is neoclassic and he writes with a well-schooled technic. Among his compositions are two concertos for piano and orchestra, a divertimento for piano and strings, a violin sonata, sonatinas, and works for piano and for voice.

Johan Franko (1908) was born in Holland where he studied with Willem Pijper. He is one of the many American composers who served in the armed forces. He has written much chamber music and orchestral scores in dissonant, atonal style and some excellent songs of mystic character.

A young foreign-born composer of unusual promise was Charles Naginski (1909–40), whose career was cut off by his early death. He was born in Cairo, Egypt, and was trained in New York at the Juilliard Graduate School under Rubin Goldmark. He received a commission from the League of Composers in 1937 for a chamber music work to be broadcast over WOR. He completed two symphonies, two string quartets, and a sonatina. He is well remembered for a group of charming songs.

Before Roger Sessions left Princeton for a post at the University of California, he had trained several young composers who have shown special talents: Edward T. Cone, Carter Harman, and Andrew Imbrie, all of whom were in the armed forces.

The American composer has been given tremendous encouragement for the development of his talents through the awards of fellowships and prizes of publication made by the American Academy in Rome, the John Simon Guggenheim Memorial Foundation, the Eastman School of Music, the Juilliard Foundation, the Curtis Institute of Music, the Naumburg Foundation, the National Federation of Music Clubs, the Pulitzer Traveling Scholarship and Prize Awards in Music, the National Broadcasting Company, the Columbia Broadcasting System commissions, the Paderewski Prize, the Society for the Publication of American Music, the New Music Publications, the Arrow Press with which was inaugurated the Cos Cob Press sponsored by Alma M. Wiener, the Victor Talking Machine Company, the Alice M. Ditson Fund commissions, the Bearns awards at Columbia University, the League of Composers, the Elizabeth Coolidge prizes and commissions for chamber music, the Koussevitzky Foundation commissions, the A.C.A.–B.M.I. prizes, and others.

Fellowship holders of the American Academy in Rome include: Samuel Barber, William Denny, Herbert Elwell, Vittorio Giannini, Howard Hanson, Walter Helfer, Herbert Inch, Werner Janssen, Hunter Johnson, Kent Kennan, Arthur Kreutz, Normand Lockwood, Charles Naginski, Robert L. Sanders, Roger Sessions, Leo Sowerby, Alexander L. Steinert, Randall Thompson, Frederick Woltmann.

The following composers have held Guggenheim fellowships: George Antheil, Ernst Bacon, Stanley Bate, Robert Russell Bennett,

William Bergsma, Marc Blitzstein, Paul Bowles, Henry Brant, Carl Bricken, Juan José Castro (Argentina), Theodore Chanler, Carlos Chávez (Mexico), Aaron Copland, Henry Cowell, Ruth Crawford (Seeger), Paul Creston, Robert Delaney, Norman Dello Joio, David Diamond, Alvin Etler, Ross Lee Finney, Dante Fiorillo, Lukas Foss, Anis Fuleihan, Alberto Ginastera (Argentina), Alexei Haieff, Roy Harris, Hunter Johnson, Arthur Kreutz, Gail Kubik, John Lessard, Normand Lockwood, Alan Lomax (American folklore), Otto Luening, Robert McBride, Carl McKinley, Colin McPhee, Quinto Maganini, Leopold Damrosch Mannes, Gian-Carlo Menotti, Douglas Moore, Paul Nordoff, Harry Partch, Burrill Phillips, Walter Piston, Quincy Porter, Earl Robinson, Bernard Rogers, William Schuman, Roger Sessions, Harold Shapero, Robert Shaw (choral director), Theodore Stearns, William Grant Still, Louise Talma, Randall Thompson, John Verrall, Adolph Weiss, and Mark Wessel.

Some of the winners of the Pulitzer prize have been: Ernst Bacon, Carl Bricken, Samuel Gardner, Sandor Harmati, Quinto Maganini, Leopold Damrosch Mannes, Douglas Moore, and Lamar Stringfield. Since 1942, there have been Pulitzer prize awards for special compositions. Winners included William Schuman for "A Free Song"; Howard Hanson for Symphony No. 4; Aaron Copland for *Appalachian Spring,* ballet; Leo Sowerby for "Canticle of the Sun" for chorus and orchestra.

The Alice M. Ditson Fund, left by the will of Mrs. Charles H. Ditson to be administered by Columbia University, since 1942 has brought out some valuable additions to musical Americana through commissions: Walter Piston's Symphony No. 2, which won the New York Music Critics' Circle award; Leo Sowerby's "Canticle of the Sun"; Bernard Wagenaar's "Pieces of Eight"; a symphony by Randall Thompson; Roger Sessions' Symphony No. 2; Normand Lockwood's chamber opera *The Scarecrow;* Paul Creston's Poem for Harp and Orchestra; Gian-Carlo Menotti's chamber opera *The Medium;* Lazare Saminsky's Requiem for Chorus and Orchestra; a chamber opera by Virgil Thomson and the late Gertrude Stein; and a ballet, *Serpent Heart,* by Samuel Barber and Martha Graham.

The League of Composers, organized in 1923 to promote contemporary compositions, has acted as a national and international clearinghouse for presenting contemporary music, and has been a source of stimulation and assistance to the last generation of composers in

Europe, America, and Latin America. Over one thousand works have been presented, one half of which were by American composers. Of valuable benefit to creative workers has been the league's commissions, which number over seventy. In addition to commissioning a work, the league arranges its first performance. *Modern Music,* the official organ of the League of Composers, has, in the twenty-three years of its existence as a magazine, been an invaluable record of contemporary composers, works, and trends. Minna Lederman has been its editor. Claire R. Reis has been executive chairman of the League of Composers since its foundation.

Another organization that has been of benefit to the composer, particularly in Europe, is the International Society for Contemporary Music (I.S.C.M.), which from 1922 to World War II was of great importance in the production and performance of contemporary works. The annual festivals in different countries of compositions chosen by an international jury drew interest from both sides of the Atlantic. The U.S. Section worked valiantly during the war to carry on the organization, and the first American festival took place in 1940 in New York. The U.S. Section has been a haven for expatriated European musicians. Edward J. Dent, professor of music at Cambridge, England, was the first president of the I.S.C.M. Among the presidents of the U.S. Section have been Oscar Sonneck, Alfred Human, Louis Gruenberg, Roger Sessions, and Mark Brunswick.

The National Association of American Composers and Conductors (N.A.A.C.C.), founded by Henry Hadley, with Leon Barzin as its present president, encourages native composers by performance and by giving awards for compositions.

The Society for the Publication of American Music was founded in 1919 by Burnet Corwin Tuthill. It is supported by subscription and publishes two chamber music works annually. Since 1932, S.P.A.M. has published scores by Vittorio Giannini, Quincy Porter, Wallingford Riegger, Daniel Gregory Mason, Frederick Preston Search, Frederick Jacobi, Arthur Shepherd, Leroy J. Robertson, David Stanley Smith, Douglas Moore, Edward Burlingame Hill, David Holden, Bernard Wagenaar, Ulric Cole, David van Vactor, David Diamond, Gail Kubik, Leo Sowerby, Isadore Freed, Boris Koutzen, William Bergsma, Charles Jones, Normand Lockwood, and Lehman Engel. The last three presidents have been A. Walter Kramer, Oscar Wagner, and Philip James.

The New York Music Critics' Circle was formed by a group of critics in 1942, to encourage American composition through awards made to composers for works in different categories—orchestra, chamber music, choral or stage works—judged best during each current year. The awards are an annual index to the quality of work done and serve to draw attention to gifted Americans. In 1947 a special citation was made to Virgil Thomson for *The Mother of Us All,* as being a member of the Circle precluded his winning an award.

Another source of encouragement to American composers was the founding of the American Music Center for the purpose of disseminating American works, and as a central depot for unpublished and published scores. The board of directors includes Otto Luening, chairman, Marion Bauer, Aaron Copland, Howard Hanson, Philip James, Harrison Kerr, Douglas Moore, Quincy Porter, and Oscar Wagner.

In *Modern Music,* January–February 1943, Aaron Copland wrote on the young composers "From the '20s to the '40s and Beyond" saying, "If in no other way, the experience of the past two decades has been different from earlier periods of our native music in the number and quality of our young men. Whitman's prophecy is coming true ("I hear America singing")—there are scads of them about. It is significant that in technical dexterity they rival their elders. ... It is further significant that they no longer exclusively look abroad for their influences. ... They come now in all types and sizes: the transcendental Robert Palmer, the elegant Paul Bowles, the noise-inspired John Cage, the rapturous David Diamond, the swing fan, Robert McBride; we have also the simple purity of John Lessard, the lyricism of Norman Dello Joio, the neo-classicism of Edward Cone, the physical violence of Jerome Moross, the folksong of Earl Robinson, the sensitivity of Alexei Haieff, the smooth wit of David van Vactor, the ordered intensity of Harold Shapero."

Among the younger Americans who have gone their own way without assistance from the various organizations are: Arthur Berger, Dai-Keong Lee (Hawaiian-born), Donald Fuller, Charles Mills, Harold Cone, Harry Hewitt, Vincent Persichetti; Harrison Kerr, who was recently appointed chief of the Music Division, Reorientation Branch, of the United States Army; Thomas Scott, Irving Fine, Kurt List (naturalized), Norman Cazden, Mark Brunswick, Arthur Cohn, Edwin Gerschefski, Herbert Haufrecht, George Kleinsinger, H. Merrills Lewis, Goddard Lieberson, Alexander Lipsky, Conlon Nancarrow, Joseph Wagner, Allan Willman, Roger Groeb, etc.

Under the cloak of experimentation, composers have occasionally tried to palm off glitter for gold, and many crimes have been perpetrated against the listening public in the name of "modernism." We do not need to worry about the effect of these experiments on the future of music because posterity will retain what it needs and desires, and the rest will be lost through "innocuous desuetude."

This book was intended primarily as a study of tendencies and schools rather than a chronicle of individuals, and these chapters dealing with "home brew" have overflowed their confines. Even at the risk of having neglected many whose achievements justify inclusion, this American section must be brought to a close.

CHAPTER 22

LATIN AMERICANS: SOURCES, NATIONALISM, VILLA-LOBOS, CHAVEZ, REVUELTAS, ETC.

THE various influences and backgrounds of Hispano-America, or Latin America, have created a music which differs fundamentally from that of North America. True, we have had the Negro and the Indian, both of whom have left their stamp in varying degrees upon our music, with the Negro far in the lead. In Latin America, the Indian has been a greater force than in the North, and the music of the Negro has developed in an entirely different way. In the United States the music of the Indian has been regarded, not as folk expression, but as primitive. South of us, however, Indian music has been amalgamated and treated as folk music. The Negro of North America reflects the surroundings of a different type of civilization from the Negro of Latin America.

This difference is reflected in the two civilizations. North Americans have been more closely connected with England, Germany, Scandinavia, France, and Italy, while South Americans' connections have been with Spain, Portugal, and in a lesser degree, with Italy. The separation is carried out in race, religion, language, discovery, and exploration.

The Indian, Negro, and Spanish ingredients appear in varying proportions in different parts of Latin America. The east coast line, Cuba, the West Indies, Haiti, Santo Domingo, and Puerto Rico show a strong Negro influence. The Indian is strong in Mexico, Peru, Ecuador, and Bolivia. The Spanish predominates in Argentina, Chile, Uruguay, Paraguay, Colombia, and Costa Rica. In several countries the effect of mixed backgrounds is in evidence: Portuguese, Negro, and Indian in Brazil; Negro and Indian in Venezuela; Portuguese,

375

Spanish, Indian, Negro, and North American in Panama. Argentina dominates Uruguay, and European influences are strong in Guatemala and Paraguay. A pronounced native music is not found in Nicaragua, Salvador, Honduras, or Costa Rica.

The language in Brazil, which covers a larger area than the United States, is Portuguese. Haiti has a French-speaking population, and English, Dutch, and French are spoken in different outposts.

When the Spanish explored and conquered South America, they found a rich native music which was used for religious and secular celebrations. Although the religious teachers tried to supplant the heathenish cult music with their own, the vitality of the aboriginal art was great enough to survive and to combine with that of the conquerors and missionaries. Thus Inca and Gregorian chants may still be traced occasionally in the same composition.

"When the African Negroes were imported, they brought a new element which was fused with Indian and Christian lore. The *Voodoo* ritual of Haiti is a mixture of African and Indian elements, and during festivals singing, dancing, and beating of drums continue for days." (*Music through the Ages.*)

The antiquity of some of the music may be realized when we recall that Mexico City was the center of the Aztec confederacy for at least two centuries before Cortés conquered the country (1521), and the ancient cities of Cuzco and Quito had a history that reached into a mythical past. The Peruvian musical system was the most advanced on the early American continent. Quito in Ecuador remained Indian.

The dance was an important part of the folk music in all parts of Latin America, and many of our popular dances, such as the tango, rumba, and conga, originated "below the Equator."

Heitor Villa-Lobos (1888), the foremost composer of Brazil, is an example of the power these various elements have had in the forming of a typical Latin-American style. He is an interesting combination of European sophistication in technical means, in his use of dissonance, of harmony, and tonality, with a barbaric richness of color, rhythm, native atmosphere, and folk characteristics.

Villa-Lobos has given much study to the problem of using Brazilian primitive and folk music as a basis of his art. Through frequent trips into the interior, he collected material from the Indians and absorbed the character of the music of Brazil from the coast cities to the jungle.

He has written over a thousand works, original compositions, transcriptions, arrangements, in which he displays a gigantic technic of composition, based on his own harmonic methods and the use of individual timbre.

A new influence appeared in his music when he visited France in 1923 and came in touch with impressionism, neoclassicism, and Stravinsky's music, which he drank in as avidly as he had his own native idiom. At this time he wrote much chamber music, and also became one of the idols of Paris, which is always susceptible to the strange and the exotic.

The influence of the neoclassic movement he encountered in Paris was manifested in his *Bachianas Brasileiras,* a group of seven suites in which Villa-Lobos combined Bach's technic with Brazilian folklore, giving to each movement a traditional and a Brazilian title. In the first suite, an unusual but fascinating ensemble of eight cellos, he marks the movements Introduction (*Embolada*), Prelude (*Modinha*), Fugue (*Conversación*). To Villa-Lobos Bach's universality seems to flow directly from the folk, and he becomes "an intermediary between all peoples."

Villa-Lobos wrote twelve *Chôros,* a title which he uses for compositions "in which the various aspects of Brazilian music, Indian and popular, achieve their synthesis." *Chôros* means a street band of players of popular songs. Villa-Lobos's pieces range from a guitar solo, a duet for flute and clarinet, a quartet for brass, a piano solo, to works for full orchestra and native percussion instruments, a mixed chorus depicting the primitive, and a work for piano and orchestra.

Villa-Lobos became supervisor and director of music education in 1932. He has made many experiments in educational problems and has written hundreds of choruses for children.

This prolific writer has a list of oratorios, orchestral suites, symphonic poems, concertos, operas, symphonies, many piano pieces and songs. Much of his piano music was inspired by Artur Rubinstein, for whom he wrote the *"Prole do Bébé"* (Baby's Dolls) and the *"Rudepoema,"* a powerful and primitive work which the composer orchestrated later. Darius Milhaud, who was in the consular service in Brazil, introduced Villa-Lobos to Debussy's music before he went to France. In 1945 he first visited North America, and many of his works were played.

São Paulo is the home of two famous Brazilians, Francisco Mignone

(1897) and Camargo Guarnieri (1907). Mignone's first opera on an Italian libretto was written while he was a student in Milan, where he went in 1920. *"Congada,"* a popular orchestral piece, is from the opera. Brazilian folklore inspired him from early childhood, when he first began to compose. Under the pseudonym of Chico-Bororó, he has written popular dances and songs. Bororó is the name of an Indian tribe. His music reflects the Negro dance of Brazil.

L'Innocente, his second opera, also on an Italian text, was performed in Rio de Janeiro, as was his first, *Contractador dos Diamantes* (*The Diamond Merchant*).

Among Mignone's many compositions are *Fantasia Brasileira* for piano and orchestra; *Suite Brasileira Batucajé,* dance for modern orchestra and native instruments; several ballets; chamber music, the most important of which is a sextet for piano, flute, oboe, clarinet, bassoon, and horn; and piano works, including a sonata, preludes, "Transcendental Etudes"; piano versions of orchestral works; and many songs. Mignone has written a *Sinfonia de Trabalho* (Symphony of Labor), music of a social character, in which the movements are Song of the Machine, Song of the Family, Song of the Strong Man, and Song of the Fruitful Work. He visited North America in 1942, when he conducted the NBC Orchestra in a performance of his *"Festa das Igrejas,"* representing in music four cathedrals of Brazil.

In 1942, the United States was host to Camargo Guarnieri, one of the most modern of Brazilian composers. He conducted his works in concerts of the Boston Symphony Orchestra and other organizations. He was sent abroad on a government fellowship (1938), and he studied in Paris with Charles Koechlin. Although he does not use folk music, his music is characteristically Brazilian, which spirit he combines with contemporary polyphony.

Among his many compositions are a Tragic Cantata, *"A Mortedo Aviador"* (The Death of an Aviator) for orchestra, chorus, and soprano solo; orchestral scores; concertos for piano, for violin, and violoncello; chamber music; many songs and choral works, some in Portuguese and some in Afro-Brazilian dialects; Three Brazilian Dances; a comic opera, *Pedro Malazarte;* three piano sonatas, five children's pieces, and a *Toada Triste,* based on a Brazilian folk form, the *toada.*

Other composers who have added materially to the development of contemporary music in Brazil and have given it an outstanding position among South American countries are: Alberto Nepomuceno (1864-1920), Francisco Braga (1868), Luciano Gallet (1893-1931), Oscar Lorenzo Fernândez (1897), W. Burle Marx (1902), Fructuoso Vianna (1898), Barrozo Netto (1881-1941), and Claudio Santoro (1919), who writes in the twelve tone technic. Several of these including Carlos Gomes (1839-1896), composer of the opera *Guarani,* and Alexander Levy (1864-1892) were pioneers in the use of the native elements of Brazilian music.

Mario de Andrade and Renato Almeida have written authoritatively on native Brazilian music. In a contribution, "Brazil Mirrors its own Nature," in *Modern Music,* March-April, 1939, Ceiçao de Barros-Barreto wrote: "Today a widespread, earnest seeking for a more genuine accent marks the work of our Brazilian composers. Deliberately relegating the European concepts of their education to the past, they have set their goal toward a music which is to be national according to our necessities and interest. Therefore material is now gathered from all indigenous sources, Indian, Negro and half-caste. Out of such elements they strive to create a music which shall truly express this American nation, blended of so many different peoples, living together in a setting of prodigal nature, of blazing light and heat, amid forests and rich valleys, mountains, seas and impetuous rivers, a sun-drenched land that has molded a Brazilian personality, proud, intelligent and generous."

In Mexico Carlos Chávez (1899) not only is the most important composer, but he has been a leading factor in its musical life. He founded (1928) and directed the Orquesta Sinfónica de México, and he has worked to make Mexico City a music center. He has composed music contemporary in spirit, and by teaching and performing he has encouraged the modern spirit in the younger composers such as Luis Sandi (1905), choral conductor; Daniel Ayala (1908), an Indian who uses the ancient Mayan folklore as the basis of his compositions and his work in Yucatan; Salvador Contreras (1912); and Blas Galindo (1911), who studied with Aaron Copland at the Berkshire Summer Academy. The last three with Moncayo formed a group of four, *Grupo de los Cuatro.*

The Mexican revolution of 1910, which resulted in a cultural awakening in the arts, provided Chávez, the eleven-year-old son of an

Indian mother, with the impulse to become the mouthpiece of the new nationalism. With the *Canciones Mexicanas* of Manuel M. Ponce (1886) national melodies were brought to the attention of the Mexican people. The folk material in the hands of Carlos Chávez became a modern vocabulary in which the native spirit and the technical sophistication of European innovations were blended. Chávez studied classical forms in addition to the primitive scales and instruments which accompanied native ancient rites. These he absorbed in his annual visits to the Indian villages. He wrote his first symphony before he went to Europe to continue his studies, and then he passed several years in New York. During this time he became expert in handling the European idioms of our own age. Aaron Copland, in his book *Our New Music,* sees in Chávez's music that he had to face the problems of modern music: "the overthrow of Germanic ideals, the objectification of sentiment, the use of the folk material in its relation to nationalism, the intricate rhythms, the linear as opposed to vertical writing, the specifically 'modern' sound images."

The first work in which Chávez tried experiments with native material and percussion instruments was the ballet *El Fuego Nuevo* (*The New Fire*). After that he wrote the Sonatinas for violin and piano, cello and piano, and piano solo, in which the amalgamation of national characteristics and modern methods is complete. This blending of musical elements dominates the later works, by means of which he has helped to create a Mexican tradition. Two more ballets followed, *Los Cuatro Soles* (*The Four Suns*) and "H.P." (Horsepower), a symphony from the ballet material which is symbolic of the "machine age." Two symphonies, *Sinfonía de Antígona* and *Sinfonía India* are distinct types of Chávez's writing. The first, originally incidental music for Sophocles' *Antigone,* contains no native Mexican material although it is characteristic of its composer's style. The second is made up of native tunes, and in it Chávez has sought to express the Mexican soul.

In concerto form are the Concerto for Four Horns and the Concerto for Piano and Orchestra performed in New York in 1942. Adolfo Salazar in *Music in Our Time* considers that "this work, so concise, well knit and finely balanced, reaches a culminating point in Chávez's music and perhaps in the music of Latin America today."

While Chávez desired to incorporate into the music of today the culture of the aborigines, another gifted composer, Silvestre Revueltas (1899-1940), sought to give in music a picture of Mexico, "with the festivities of its market places, the comical, sad atmosphere of the *carpas*—the crude little playhouses of the capital—, the tumult of the crowd in the street, the shrill colors of the people and the land-scapes, the songs and music of the country as it exists today," writes Otto Mayer-Sera in the *Musical Quarterly* of April 1942, "Silvestre Revueltas and Musical Nationalism in Mexico."

Chávez and Revueltas were friends and, early in their careers, col-leagues. Chávez gave encouragement and performances to Revueltas, and made him assistant conductor of his orchestra from 1929 to 1936, when Revueltas became conductor of a new group, Orquesta Sinfónica Nacional. He did not remain in this post long, as he went to Spain during the Civil War to take part in the cultural activities of the music section of the Loyalist government. His untimely death occurred shortly after his return to Mexico City.

Revueltas was a violinist, and at seventeen went to Austin, Texas, and to Chicago to study. He conducted theater orchestras in Texas and Alabama, and toured Mexico. At the moment of his death his ballet *El Renaucuajo Paseador* (*Polliwog Takes a Stroll*) was being produced in Mexico City. Another ballet, *La Coronela* (*The Girl Colonel*) was produced posthumously after it was finished by Blas Galindo and Candolario Huizar, a composer of Indian origin.

Revueltas was interested in the people, "the types, the gestures, the way women speak and walk, children with their games and shouting," says Mayer-Serra. He was deeply moved also by the sorrows of man-kind, the sufferings of the oppressed; and yet in his last period he expressed an "optimism for a rebirth of humanity," as Mayer-Serra points out, in the predominant note of two works suggested by the tragedy of Spain, an incomplete score *"Itinerario"* and *"Homenaje a García Lorca"* (Homage to Garcia Lorca).

Revueltas gave titles to his symphonic works, but the music was not descriptive. He never used authentic folk melodies, Mayer-Serra stated. "If . . . his themes always bear the unmistakable mark of being Mexican, it is because they are fashioned on the melodic-rhythmic and harmonic patterns of folk melody. The endless number of melo-dies heard in the streets and on the highways, at the traditional *fiestas* and native dances, have left their impress upon the constantly alert sensitiveness of the composer." But the melodies were always transformed and stylized.

Revueltas, like other Mexican composers, was a rich colorist in orchestration. Color was the keynote, not only of his orchestration, but of his harmony and melody also. One of his compositions, *"Colorines,"* was named for the beads worn by Indian women made from the fruit of a tree of the same name. It was one of the few Revueltas works to reach this country, as it was conducted by Nicolas Slonimsky with the Pan-American Orchestra in 1933 in New York. *"Sensemayá,"* a symphonic poem inspired by the Afro-Cuban poet Nicolas Guillén, was performed by Leopold Stokowski in New York in 1945.

Rodolfo Halffter (1900), a Spaniard and brother of the composer Ernesto Halffter, was actively associated with the musical life of Spain, and when the Republic fell, he found a refuge and citizenship in Mexico (1939). He wrote a ballet and a violin concerto in Mexico. Although well grounded in Spanish folklore, he shows neoclassic influences of both Schoenberg and Stravinsky.

A group of composers and musicologists, including Adolfo Salazar, Carlos Chávez, Luis Sandi, Blas Galindo, Rodolfo Halffter, Pablo Moncayo, and Jesus Bel y Gay, organized a series of concerts in 1946 to present their works and those of other modernists.

Salazar, a Spanish musicologist, has been in Mexico several years, where he lectures, composes, teaches, and recently has completed a book, *Music in Our Time.*

Local orchestras have been formed in various parts of Mexico, due to Chávez's example and encouragement.

Buenos Aires, Argentina, is the home of one of the most important opera houses in the Western hemisphere. The Teatro Colón has been the center of a strong Italian following in opera and ballet. The younger generation has been interested in folk research, but the nationalistic tendency has had opposition in the *Grupo Renovación* which has encouraged the writing of absolute music and is considered the "left wing" in music. The *grupo* was founded in 1929 to encourage contemporary music, and to contribute to the progress of musical culture. Its first members included José Maria Castro (1892) and his brother Juan José, (1895), Juan Carlo Paz (1897), and Jacobo Ficher (1896). Honorio Siccardi (1897) became a member in 1932, and Juan José

Castro withdrew. Paz left the group in 1936 to form a "New Music" society. The *Grupo Renovación* has given no concerts since 1944. A new Argentine Youth Orchestra came into existence under the direction of Luis Gianneo (1897) primarily to give performances for the "World Radio" broadcasts, but it has also been playing publicly and has been successful. Juan José Castro is the conductor of the Buenos Aires Philharmonic and has presented many contemporary works.

Of importance to the encouragement of contemporary composers was the founding of the Argentine Music Publishers; under the direction of José Maria Castro, Jacobo Ficher, and Luis Gianneo, works by local composers have been published and performed. The first concert programmed quartets by the directors, by Washington Castro (1909), the youngest brother of the family, also by Juan José Castro and Gilardo Gilardi (1889).

The French composer and conductor Alfred Wolff is in Argentina conducting concerts and operas at the Colón. Among recent works presented were Psalm CL for chorus and orchestra by Alberto Ginastera (1916), and "Three Paintings of Paul Klee" by Roberto García Morillo (1911), whose ballet *Harrild* proved to be a successful novelty, revealing personality and mastery.

José Maria Castro has helped to develop chamber music, is a cellist and conductor of a chamber orchestra Profesorado Orquestal. He won the post of director of the Buenos Aires Municipal Band through competition. In his compositions he uses bitonality and polytonality, and does not lean on folk material.

Juan José Castro's interest in chamber music led him to play violin in a quintet with his brother. He has written in all forms except opera. He wrote a symphony in which his use of chromaticism approaches atonality. Two later symphonies, *Sinfonía Argentina* and *Sinfonía de los Campos,* show his turning to native themes. He spent five years in Paris as a student of Vincent d'Indy. He has conducted throughout Latin America and since 1930 has occupied the post of conductor at the Teatro Colón.

Juan Carlos Paz is regarded by some as the most advanced contemporary composer of South America. His style has undergone changes from neoclassicism (1920-1927) to the use of atonal melody and polytonal harmony (1927-1934) to the twelve tone technic. In his Concerts of New Music, Paz has been responsible for the hearing of much chamber music of Europe and the Americas. His criticism of his own works and those of others is severe but constructive. Francisco Curt Lange has stated in the preface to *Latin American Art Music for the Piano* (G. Schirmer, Inc.) that Paz has arrived "at freedom from any stumbling" through an aesthetic development resembling "that of the great European musicians with its significant return to Bach *via* Hindemith and Stravinsky," and has undertaken "the arduous road of anti-sentimentality, through Schoenberg, towards a music bare, absolute, athematic, without repetition, without padding, without melodic sequence."

Paz's music includes nine ballads, two piano sonatas, orchestral works, incidental music to an Ibsen play, Three Jazz Movements, Polytonal Variations, sonatinas for various instruments, and chamber music.

Honorio Siccardi (1897) an Italian-trained Argentinian, studied with Malipiero. He writes in a contrapuntal, dissonant style, not national in character.

Alberto Ginastera, as the recipient of a Guggenheim fellowship, spent some time in New York, during which period his works were frequently programmed and published. He is considered one of the most gifted of the younger Argentinians. He reconciles national characteristics of rhythm and melody to international traits of harmony, method, and technic. Among his works are *Sinfonía Porteña* (Buenos Aires Symphony); two ballets; a *Concierto Argentino* for piano and orchestra; *Cantos del Tucumán* (Tucumanian Songs) for soprano, flute, violin, harp, and two drums; and piano pieces.

Jacobo Ficher, whose name appears frequently in accounts of Argentine music, was born in Russia and made his studies with Glazounov at the Leningrad Conservatory. He arrived at Buenos Aires in 1923 and became the head of the conservatory there. In 1937 he was the recipient of a Coolidge prize for his Second String Quartet, op. 55, and in 1941 his Third Symphony, showing a Mahler influence, was given a prize by the National Culture Committee in Buenos Aires. Nicolas Slonimsky in *Music of Latin America* says that "his early music is inspired by Hebrew melos, while his later compositions reflect a Russian influence." Only in three Argentine dances (1943) has Ficher displayed any predisposition to use the native idiom of his adopted country. The Second Symphony (1933) shows Hebraic character, as it was written under the emotional stress of the Nazi persecution of the Jews. He has written much orchestral and chamber music, and some of his piano compositions have been published in North America.

Among the younger men, Carlos Suffern (1905) has written much piano and chamber music which Lange finds in an idiom which "derives from his poetical temperament, and often manifests itself in a literary and plastic symbolism of delicate texture, especially in its harmonic aspects."

Washington Castro, like his brother José Maria, is a cellist; Siccardi was his teacher in composition, and he continued his studies in Paris. He is regarded as a valuable acquisition to the *Grupo Renovación*. Among his works are four pieces for piano, *"Homenaje";* variations for piano; a cello sonata, a piano sonata, and Festive Overture for chamber orchestra.

Roberto García Morillo (1911) is a composer and music critic. His compositions were influenced by Scriabin, Stravinsky, and Falla, of whose works he has made extensive analyses. He has written a piano concerto; a Poem for symphony orchestra; a suite inspired by the paintings of Goya; "The Fall of the House of Usher" after Poe, for guitar and small orchestra; and a cantata, *Saul*.

Even as brief an account as this would be incomplete without mention of the dean of Argentine music, Alberto Williams (1862), whose grandfather on his father's side was English. His mother's father was Amancio Alcorta, a musical pioneer among Latin Americans. Alberto Williams has the distinction of being one of the few remaining pupils of César Franck, an advantage he has used in establishing several conservatories since 1893. He also founded a publishing house, La Quena, which issued over a hundred of his own compositions besides many other works. He has composed nine symphonies, much piano music, chamber music, etc., in a style which combines Franck and the French impressionists, but he has also used native forms.

The great Spanish composer, Manuel de Falla, spent the last years of his life in Argentina, where he worked on his oratorio *Atlántida*. He died in December 1946 (page 248).

Another Spanish composer, Julian Bautista (1901) reached Buenos Aires in 1940, having left his native country after the fall of the republic. He had previously won recognition as one of the most talented of the younger group. Slonimsky says: "His style of writing is terse and compact, with diatonic harmonies enhanced by added tones. His instrumentation stresses colorism in a neoimpressionist manner." Bautista has recently finished Four Galician Poems to texts by Lorenzo Varela and is writing a cantata with the poet Rafael Alberti.

Chile has an important place in the history of Latin American music of the twentieth century both in composition and in education. A representative school of composition has been developed in which modern European technics have been blended with the national-folklore tendencies into what Carleton Sprague Smith calls "a curiously homogeneous quality" with "a style which one comes to recognize." ("The Composers of Chile," *Modern Music,* November-December 1941.)

The aborigines of Chile were the Araucanians, whose songs, dances and instruments have been studied by the musical historians, including Eugene Pereira Salas, whose important work on the origins of Chilean music was published in 1941. He writes at length about the folk and popular music of the country.

In Chile, as in other Latin American countries, its independence (1818) marks the beginning of a real development in music. The first orchestral society was founded in 1827. Gradually a school of native composers reached an important point in the 1880's, which saw the births of Humberto Allende (1885), Prospero Bisquertt (1881), Carlos Isamitt (1885), Carlos Lavin (1883, folklorist), Alfonso Leng (1884), Enrique Soro (1884).

Dr. Smith divides the Chilean school into three groups. The first, under Italian influence, is headed by Enrique Soro. Its followers are known as the Sociedad de Compositores Chilenos (Society of Chilean Composers).

Humberto Allende heads the second group. He studied at the National Conservatory of Music in Santiago and has championed the cause of modern music. He has taught a number of the younger men, among whom are René Amengual Astaburuaga (1911), Alfonso Letelier Llona (1912), Nuñez Navarrete (1906), and Jorge Urrutia Blondel (1905). Twelve piano pieces by Allende, *Tonadas de Carácter Popular Chileno* have had success on two continents. The *tonada* comes from a popular Spanish song (in Brazil it is called *toada*) and is in two contrasting moods, a slow section in three-four and a lively section in six-eight. Allende won a competition with a Symphony in B flat offered in 1910, for the centennial of Chile's independence, and with the prize money he traveled in Europe. In 1911 he became a member of the Society of Folklore of Chile. Two symphonic suites reflect Chilean musical characteristics. One of these, *"La Voz de las Calles"* (The Voice of the Streets) is described by Slonimsky as "based on the tunes of the street cries of Santiago vendors of eggs, lemons, or bottles." Allende has written a concerto for cello and one for violin. In 1921 he wrote *Cantos Infantiles,* in which polytonal influences are apparent. While his String Quartet (1926) is abstract in style, his chief contribution has been in the colorful national characteristics of his work. He has spent much time in studying educational problems and has devoted himself to school music and the education of the young.

The third group has as its head Domingo Santa Cruz, one of the foremost educators and most constructive spirits in South American music. In 1918 he founded the Bach Society. From being professor of music history at the National Conservatory in Santiago (1928), he became dean of the Faculty of Fine Arts of the University of Chile (1933). For a few years Santa Cruz was in the diplomatic service and spent some time in Madrid. He has founded several musical magazines and in 1940 was appointed president of the council of the Instituto de Extención Musical, which organized the musical activities in Chile. He has furthered interest in national music, arranged publication and supervised recordings of native works.

Santa Cruz's early works were impressionistic, but he turned to an abstract style influenced by polytonality, which earned him comparison with Hindemith. He has written *Viñetas* for piano in the form of a classical suite; two *Canciones* for four voices, which Slonimsky calls "modern counterparts of Bach's chorales"; five *Poemas Tragicos* for piano, which reflect the sadness characteristic of many Chilean works. Dr. Smith says that "he possesses more depth than most of his contemporaries.... He has distinction and skill and his work is always personal."

Carlo Isamitt, both painter and composer, has studied the music of the Araucanian Indians and is famed as a folklorist. Bisquertt and Urrutia are members of the third group, as is also Alfonso Leng, of whom Dr. Smith speaks as "a sensitive poet whose intuitive qualities have made him an outstanding scientist and physician as well as a composer."

One of the most gifted of the young Chileans is Juan Orrego-Salas (1919), who held a Rockefeller fellowship in musicological research and a Guggenheim fellowship in composition. He has written a sonata for violin and piano, and choral works, including a Christmas cantata in four parts for soprano and orchestra which was performed in Rochester, N. Y., at an American Composers Festival. While here Orrego wrote a score *Escenas* (Scenes), to be used as a ballet in Chile. He studied with Randall Thompson at Princeton University and wrote a piano sonata and variations for piano. He teaches in a Chilean conservatory.

Another Guggenheim fellow is Hector Tosar-Errecart (1923) of Uruguay, who has been in New York studying and working in musicology. His teachers in South America were W. Kolischer in piano and Lamberto Baldi in composition. He is regarded as a very gifted composer and has written a concertino for piano and orchestra which had its première in Montevideo under the direction of Erich Kleiber (1944); Sinfonia No. 1; *Salmo* (Psalm) for soprano, chorus, and orchestra; a string quartet; piano pieces; and songs published by the Instituto Interamericana.

Uruguay has a high place among South American countries for the quality of its art music. Its leading composer is Eduardo Fabini (1883). A list of native-born composers includes Vicente Ascone (1897), Alfonso Broqua (1876), Benone Calvavecchial (1886), Cesar Cortinas (1893-1918), Luis Cluzean Mortet (1893); Carlos Pedrell (1878-1941), who migrated to the neighboring Argentina; Ramon Rodriguez Socas (1890); and among the younger men Luis Pedro Mondino (1903), Guido Santórsola (1904), Carlos Estrada (1909), etc.

One of the most important figures in the inter-American musical field is the musicologist Francisco Curt Lange (1903), who emigrated to Uruguay from Germany in 1923. He is founder and director of the Instituto Interamericano de Musicologia at Montevideo. In 1935 he issued the first volume of the *Boletín latino-americano de música,* planned to promote a campaign for releasing music in Latin America from European roots, and for cultivating an interdependence among the various countries of the Western hemisphere. Five volumes have been published, the first in Montevideo with a musical supplement of works by Juan José Castro, Gianneo, Isamitt, Paz, Allende, Villa-Lobos, J. T. Wilkes, Fabini, Guarnieri, Fernandez, Mignone, and Enrique Casella. Volume II was published in Lima, Peru, in 1936; Volume III in Montevideo in 1937, the musical supplement of which contains works by Guattali, Mortet, Valdés, Ascone, Frederico Gerdes, and eight Colonial Songs of the XVII Century, transcribed and harmonized by Josué T. Wilkes. Volume IV, published in Bogotá, Colombia, in 1938, also has a musical supplement with compositions by Siccardi, Julio Perceval, Suffern, Morillo, José Maria Castro, Ficher, Isabel Aretz-Thiele, Paz, Eduardo Caba, Vianna, Villa-Lobos, Santa Cruz, Bisquertt, Amengual, Negrete, Isamitt, Leng, Allende, Málaga, Abraham Jurofsky, Inzaurraga, Carlos Posada Amador, Guillermo Uribe Holguin, Andrés Sas, Estanislao Mejia. A veritable Latin-American musical Who's Who!

Volume V, which was published in 1941, was edited by Lange with the assistance of Charles Seeger, the North American musicologist, and the musical supplement is devoted to the works of thirty-four United States composers.

According to his plans, Dr. Lange is working on the sixth volume of the *Boletín* which is to be published in Brazil and will be devoted to Brazilian music and musicians.

Another of Francisco Curt Lange's important posts is that of music librarian of the OSSODRE, the Orquesta Sinfónica del Servicio Oficial de Difusión Radio Eléctrica, for which Montevideo won the reputation in 1931 of having produced one of the finest orchestras in Latin America. This radio service has enhanced the musical culture of the city, and in addition to the orchestra it sponsors a chorus, chamber music groups, and schools of music and ballet. Dr. Lange is responsible for the movement known as *Americanismo Musical*.

Volume IV of the *Boletín* includes a detailed account of the music of Colombia written by José Ignacio Perdomo Escoba, musicologist of Bogotá. He traces its history from the period of the Indians before that of the missionaries in the seventeenth century to the musicians of the twentieth, the most important of whom is Guillermo Uribe Holguin (1880). Gilbert Chase in *A Guide to Latin-American Music* states that in the autobiography of this leading composer, music educator, and conductor he "gives an interesting picture of musical and social life in Bogotá around the turn of the century and of the development due in large part to the efforts of Uribe Holguin himself."

He began as a violinist, studied composition with Vincent d'Indy at the Schola Cantorum in Paris, and in 1910 became director of the Conservatorio Nacional de Música in Bogotá, an outgrowth of the Academia Nacional de Música which had been founded in 1881 by Jorge W. Price. He was also founder, and until 1035 conductor, of the Sociedad de Conciertos Sinfónicos del Conservatorio.

Uribe Holguin has written orchestral works, concertos for piano and for violin, much chamber music and about three hundred piano pieces, most of which are still in manuscript. Nicolas Slonimsky says of him in *Music of Latin America* that the style and technic of his music "are impressionist, in the French manner, and his harmonic texture often approaches polytonality, while the basic rhythms and melodic inflections are native in inflection."

Outstanding in an account of Colombia's music is Guillermo Espinosa (1905), who studied in Milan and Berlin, and was made conductor of the Orquesta Sinfónica Nacional of Bogotá in 1936. This organization developed from the Sociedad de Conciertos Sinfónicos del Conservatorio, which in 1938 presented a festival of Ibero-American music for the celebration by the Colombian government of the four hundredth anniversary of Bogotá's founding.

In Cuba contemporary music is represented by the work of two men who died before they were forty: Amadeo Roldán (1900-1939) and Alejandro García Caturla (1906-1940). Henry Cowell called them "two of the most colorful and exciting composers of the Western Hemisphere" ("Roldan and Caturla of Cuba," *Modern Music,* January-February 1941). "Their general outlook was similar, they were above all interested in developing the extraordinarily vivid native musical resources of their native country," Cowell stated, "although both composers wrote chiefly for symphony orchestra and smaller chamber combinations, and both had a sound European training, their work produced quite different results."

A mulatto, born in Paris, Roldán studied violin in Madrid and composition in Havana with Pedro Sanjuán, a Spanish composer who migrated to Cuba. He used Afro-Cuban rhythms and introduced native percussion instruments. "Nowhere else in America has the native African rhythm been so well preserved as in Cuba," says Cowell, "and no other composer has made so significant a develop-

ment of these ritualistic and secular rhythmic modes." Roldán's ballet
La Rebambaramba is a reflection of the spirit of Negro ritual music.

Alejandro García Caturla was in Paris for a while, during which
time he studied with Nadia Boulanger. He was also a pupil of Sanjuán
in Havana. He combined Afro-Cuban folk melodies with modern
harmonic means. Cowell compares the two composers thus: "Although
less close to genuine native music, Caturla's orchestral works are more
telling and effective as show pieces than those of Roldán.... At times
he has used native themes, adding discordant notes not to be found
in native scales. Roldán, on the other hand, often used actual native
melodies, preserved as accurately as possible, and composed original
melodies in native style which are almost impossible to tell from the
really indigenous ones."

Caturla was born in Remedios, where he was a judge, and where
he was assassinated. His orchestral works include three Cuban Dances;
"Bembé," an Afro-Cuban suite for fourteen instruments written in
an ultramodern harmonic style; *"Yamba-O,"* a ritualistic symphonic
poem, based on a Negro liturgy; and a rumba which is regarded as
one of his best works.

Cuba's popular music has had a strong influence on our own, as
may be seen in the rumbas and congas. The name of Ernesto Lecuona
(1896) is the most famous in the popular field, and his piano pieces
have a vogue. The popular music, like the art music, is a combination
of the rhythm of the Negro and the melody of the Spaniard.

A modern music society, Grupo de Renovación Musical, more interested in neoclassicism than in the national folklore tendency, was
founded in 1943. A Spaniard, José Ardévol (1911), settled in Havana
in 1930 and founded a Society of Chamber Music Concerts. Many of
his pupils and of Roldán were members of the *grupo,* among whom
are Juan Antonio Cámara (1917), Virginia Fleites (1916), Hilario
Gonzalez Iñiguez (1920); Harold Gramatges (1918), who studied at
the Berkshire School with Aaron Copland; Gisela Hernandez (1910),
Edgardo Martin (1915), Julian Orbón (Spain, 1925), Esther Rodriguez
(1920).

Peru has always aroused interest and stirred the imagination because of the music of the fabulous Inca empire of the pre-Columbian
period. Raoul and Marguerite d'Harcourt of France made extensive
research in Peru of Incan instruments and music, and published books

based on their findings. José Castro discovered the pentatonic basis of the Inca musical system in 1897, and many Peruvian musicians have made further investigations of the fascinating subject. Daniel Alomía Robles (1871-1942), of Indian blood, dedicated years to collecting Peruvian and Bolivian folk material. He wrote an opera, *Illa-Cori;* symphonic poems, songs, and piano pieces. Like Robles, Teodora Valcárcel (1900-1942), an Indian, wrote a ballet-opera, *Suray-Surita;* symphonic music, songs, and piano pieces based on Indian themes.

Andrés or André Sas (1900), although born in Paris of Belgian and French parentage, has worked indefatigably for the cause of Peruvian indigenous music. Since he went to Peru in 1924, he has taught in the conservatories, with his wife has given concerts of contemporary music, and has written for musical journals. His compositions for violin and for piano are based on Peruvian melodies and rhythms fused with modern French harmony.

Contemporary music in Venezuela has tried to develop a national idiom based on indigenous melodies and rhythms. Some native composers have been seeking to free themselves from the imitation of European methods and idioms. The choral group Orféon Lamas, with Vicenté Emilio Sojo (1887) as conductor, has been a stimulating influence.

Juan Bautista Plaza (1898) is called by Lange "a towering figure in the Venezuelan musical scene because of the many-sidedness of his genuinely musical personality and the vigor with which he has carried out his projects and expounded his ideas in newspapers and magazines" (preface to *Latin-American Art Music for the Piano*). Plaza was educated in France and in Rome. He became organist and choir master of the cathedral in his native Caracas. He transcribed the archives of Venezuelan colonial music into modern notation. He read a paper on "Music in Caracas during the Colonial Period (1770-1811)" before the Greater New York Chapter of the American Musicological Society in 1942. He has composed choral music, religious works, three symphonic poems, Seven Venezuelan Songs, and piano works.

In other countries of Latin America the same tendencies of *"americanismo musical"* as have been traced in this chapter are to be found. Gilbert Chase points out in *A Guide to Latin American Music* (Introduction) that "since the turn of the century the majority of 'art music' compositions written in Latin American countries have made use, more or less freely, of traditional tunes and rhythms." This "primitive or indigenous element" plays an important part in the nationalist movement that has been consciously cultivated in the Latin American countries as well as in the United States. "In its broadest interpretation," Dr. Chase wisely states, "musical nationalism means simply the definite awareness of the full musical potentialities of a given country, and a deliberate effort to realize those potentialities in every sphere of musical activity."

CHAPTER 23

THE NEW AESTHETIC:
EFFECT OF WAR, THE MACHINE, PHONOGRAPH, RADIO, TELEVISION, MOTION PICTURES, ETC. THE NEW "AMERICANISM"

EVERY artist, as a creator, has something in him which calls for expression (this is the element of personality).

"Every artist, as child of his age, is impelled to express the spirit of his age (this is the element of style)—dictated by the period and particular country to which the artist belongs (it is doubtful how long the latter distinction will continue to exist).

"Every artist, as a servant of art, has to help the cause of art (this is the element of pure artistry, which is constant in all ages and among all nationalities)." (*The Art of Spiritual Harmony* by Wassily Kandinsky; translated with an introduction by M. T. H. Sadler.)

A clearer statement of aesthetics would be difficult to find. The "element of pure artistry" has made us recognize the value of Palestrina, Monteverdi, Bach, Mozart, Beethoven, Brahms, Wagner, and Debussy. It is that which in common parlance stands the test of time, or, as Clive Bell states it, makes some movements become part of the great tradition.

And yet in a discussion of contemporary problems, the elements of personality and style mark the period. They are the hands of the clock that mark the hour, while pure artistry marks eternity (page 190).

As we look back over the past, the personalities and the styles of the different ages are recognizable. We know what the composers of various epochs were aiming to do; we have seen how their problems were solved; we have traced the changes that gradually came over the most deeply rooted conventions. In other words, we know the aesthetics of the past. But our interest now is to solve the riddle the Sphinx propounds today. Every artist, the child of our own day, impelled to express the spirit of his age, expresses what? What is the spirit of our age? What is it that this period dictates? And in what do the dictates of one country differ from those of another? What are our musicians aiming to do? How are they solving their problems? And what are the problems? What is the aesthetic of the present generation of composers?

In the first place, the artist of the twentieth century has had a phobia against any display of feeling. In the fear of being sentimental he has sacrificed sentiment. He rationalizes to the point of revolting against the nineteenth century, the epoch of romantic thinking and belief in a soul, and of establishing an affinity with the eighteenth century, when art and thought were intellectual, classic, and "pure." Our artist, however, has been building a false foundation for his declaration of faith, if he has thought that Bach, Mozart, or Haydn was coldly classical and chastely intellectual! They were expressing their emotions in the means at their command, but the eighteenth century musician had not yet learned the trick of calling on the other arts for heightened dramatic, literary, or pictorial effect. The dawn of personal expression had not yet appeared. Having gone through the experience of a close correlation of the arts, the world in the twentieth century has emerged with one very definite decision—poetry must not be used merely to tell a story; a picture must not tell a story, nor must music.

"Sound for sound's sake," Stravinsky decrees; "sound for sound's sake," echo answers. "Our young musicians—I mean those who have something to say—our young musicians, immured in their laboratories, are trying to discover a music wholly free from extra-musical appeal," André Coeuroy wrote ("The Esthetics of Contemporary Music," *Musical Quarterly,* April 1929), "just as our painters envisage a painting that shall obey the laws of line and color only. This is the real objective of their experiments, and, even when they fail, they never weary of beginning over again."

"Back to Bach" has been the slogan of the musicians since World War I, but Bach would turn in his grave could he hear some of the compositions committed in his name. The truth is that the young musicians have not really gone back to Bach, they could not even though they would. They have not been concerned with the "inner spirit" that is the "element of pure artistry," the eternal quality of Bach, but they have taken a few technical means and twisted them to fit their ideas of a revolt against the romantic spirit. *Neoclassicism* is the result. Out of the experiments of the few a style has arisen that must stand or fall by its own might.

Out of the experiment, if it contains the proper ingredients, must come *the* art for *the* age. We see it today, the type of art that expresses our age. Deplore the art expression if you will, but do not search Art for the cause of something you do not approve of, and with which you cannot become attuned. It goes deeper. We must blame the turbulence and maladjustments of social conditions and economic pressure; the instability of the ground under our feet and the roof over our heads. After 1914, the world lived in the crater of an active volcano that broke forth with even greater vehemence in 1939. Time-honored customs, shaken to the very foundations, have fallen about our heads, creating havoc in the art world as well as in every other phase of human activity. The old forms fail to satisfy the newly aroused sensibilities. Contemporary experiences demand contemporary expression, and the old machinery is inadequate.

There will always be those who try to hold on to the last shreds of a past gentility, and the artists of that type walk into the future with their faces turned to the past. There are just as many who go into the future burning their bridges before they have fairly cleared them.

Interpreters play safe and pin their faith to experiments of a past age that have proved their right to "a place in the sun," and leave the performance of most contemporary music to societies organized for that purpose. And individuals choose concert programs as they do motor cars and sewing machines, unwilling to take chances on an unstandardized label. The composers—that is, the experimenters—are usually about a generation ahead, so the works of Strauss and Debussy, the earlier scores of Stravinsky and Schoenberg are now off the black list.

The new classicism has reached the audience and the performer and the *need* for Bach has induced a *love* for Bach beyond the dreams of Mendelssohn, who worked more than a century ago to create the very kind of appreciation for this neglected eighteenth century composer that he is receiving at the present time. For the same reason the last works of Beethoven and the symphonies and chamber music of Brahms have been more frequently heard than formerly. Haydn and Mozart, too, have experienced something of a renaissance.

We speak of this as the Mechanical Age and sometimes as the Jazz Age. Both terms give a clue to our aesthetics. Matthew Arnold pointed out the important function of culture in his *Culture and Anarchy,* and of its especial importance in our modern world, "of which the whole civilization is, to a much greater degree than the civilization of Greece and Rome, mechanical and external, and tends constantly to become more so.... The idea of perfection as an *inward* condition of the mind and spirit is at variance with the mechanical and material civilization in esteem with us...."

If this statement was true in his day, how much more so is it now? Not only the power of the machine grows, but man's worship of its power and his respect for the mechanical principle increase. He finds beauty in the perfection of its mechanism, and in the rhythm of its movement. He personifies the Machine in literature, painting, drama, dance, and music. It has changed the face of the physical world and has created "a new mental attitude toward the world of the spirit," Thomas Craven says in *Men of Art.* "America is the land of machines, and our new attitude toward the world—our indifference to cultural precedences and observances—is both the cause and the effect of our mechanized civilization. Our psychology is profoundly conditioned by our changing instruments and our control over them."

The recognition of the era of the machine shows a direct effect in the neoclassic aspect of music. The tendency is to break with the expression of personal emotion and supersensibility, to replace it with a speculative intellectualism, to tear away extraneous material, to modify dynamics not inherent in the musical line, to perfect the form and technic of composition. To be more interested in the *how* and the *why* than in the *what* aligns the artists more closely with the classic spirit than the romantic. The classic spirit shows itself in the formal structure, in the linear, contrapuntal character of melodies, in the harmonic textures, in clever musical compositions rather than inspired, and in the interest in instrumentation not as a means of calling out emotion but for creating characteristic timbres and nonartificial effects. Texture, line, architecture, and tonality are the problems, not an imperative need for expressing profundities of feeling and heights of ennobling emotion. The science of composition seems of greater import than the art of composing.

The English critic Edwin Evans ("Stocktaking 1930," *Music and*

Letters, January 1931) regarded the first thirty years of the twentieth century as an age of experiment that "set in because it was needed and the time was ripe for it. It has come to an end because it has performed its function of providing a sufficiency of new expressive resources. It has yielded a profusion of new material none of which has been fully exploited, and much of which has scarcely been developed." He felt that "a time of experiment is not likely to be fertile in master-pieces," but those years "created the material in which the artist of the next phase is to work."

Taking it for granted that Evans is correct in regarding Debussy's first impressionistic work as inaugurating a period of experiment and "the contemporary works of Strauss as the last great manifestation of the era that was passing," we may hope for more tangible results in the near future. With the crystallization of Schoenberg's teachings, Stravinsky's experiments, Hindemith's attempts at simplification, Russia's propaganda music, and America's rhythmic contributions, the next decade may succeed in bringing composer, interpreter, and audience into closer relationship by the creation of more masterpieces.

We must work toward a combination of what John Burroughs (*Whitman: A Study*) calls the two phases of art: formal art, "which makes a direct appeal to our sense of form,—our sense of the finely carved, the highly wrought, the deftly planned," which has been the aim of the last decades; and creative art, "that quickening, fructify-ing power of the masters, that heat and passion that makes the world plastic and submissive to their hands, teeming with new meanings and thrilling with new life." And this seems to be in the air.

That a new aesthetic sensibility exists in both the art creator and the public is heartening. In 1930 José Ortega y Gasset ("The Dehumaniza-tion of Art," *The Symposium,* April 1930, translated by Pedro V. Fernandez) stated: "On looking for the most generic and charac-teristic feature of the new work, I find it in the tendency to dehumanize art."

Ortega speaks of the painter who "has proposed boldly to deform reality, to break its human aspect, to dehumanize it." He finds the need to create and invent new ways of dealing with these unaccus-tomed forms. He finds the new life, in which spontaneous life is annulled, not lacking in sentiments and passions, but they "belong to a psychic flora very different from that which covers the landscape of our primary and human life.... They are specifically *esthetic* sentiments."

The "ordinary reality that becomes the substance of the aesthetic whole" was formerly the nucleus of works of art. But the young artists question, "Why should the old always be in the right against the young when the future always agrees with the young against the old?"

In Ortega's answer is the basis of contemporary aesthetics: "Our most rooted, our most indubitable convictions are the ones most to be distrusted: they are our limitations, our confines, our prison. Life is indeed unimportant if there does not stir in it a great eagerness to expand its frontiers. We live only so far as we are eager to live more, and all obstinacy in remaining limited by our habitual horizon means weakness, a decadence of vital energies. The horizon is a biological line, a living organ of our being; and while we enjoy plenitude the horizon flees, swelling and undulating with an elasticity almost in the rhythm of our breath. But when the limits of the horizon are fixed, it is because they have become rigid, and we have entered old age."

Ortega here answers an often asked question: Why does the musician of today deny the nineteenth century so vigorously? "It was necessary to root out private feelings from music, to purify it by an exemplary objectification. This was the achievement of Debussy.... This conversion from the subjective to the objective is of such importance that all exterior differences disappear for it. Debussy dehumanized music and for that reason it is from him that we date the new musical era."

Roger Sessions, one of the most gifted of American composers, states this credo thus: "Younger men are dreaming of an entirely different type of music—a music which derives its power from forms beautiful and significant by virtue of inherent musical weight rather than intensity of utterance; a music whose impersonality and self-sufficiency preclude the exotic, which takes its impulse from the realities of a passionate logic; which, in the authentic freshness and simplicity of its moods, is the reverse of ironic and in its very aloofness from the concrete preoccupations of life, strives rather to contribute form, design, a vision of order and harmony. Such a music, like all that is vital in art, seeks affinities in the past. Bloch, in his splendid enthusiasm for the masters of the sixteenth century, for Bach, for Haydn, has helped more than one of his pupils to comprehend the true nature of such an art, and to appreciate the forces in the culture of today which make our impulse toward it inevitable." ("Ernest Bloch," *Modern Music*, November–December 1927.)

One phase of the mechanical age, which has had direct bearing on the history of music, is the invention of mechanical instruments—radio, gramophone, player piano, reproducing piano, and the sound film.

The phonograph, after a number of years of experimentation during which it was regarded as a nuisance and was called "canned" music by musicians, who fought it because they claimed it would kill the art, has found its place as an invaluable aid to education in schools and in homes. An extraordinary library of records is extant. These include the music of primitive peoples and savage tribes recorded in Africa, Australia, Asia, North and South America; folk music of many nations, such as the collections made by Percy Grainger of Danish, English, and Australian songs; records of Gregorian plainsong and of the religious music of the golden age of polyphony; of all the great classics, from Bach, Haydn, and Mozart to Beethoven, Brahms, Wagner, and the nineteenth century romanticists; and music of the twentieth century.

Of particular significance is the rapidly growing catalogue of contemporary compositions, which is of incalculable value to those interested in the question of how to become familiar with modern music. The only way to know whether or not you like modern music is to hear it repeatedly. This being virtually impossible even to those within reach of the great orchestras, as their repertory of new works must of necessity be limited, it is obvious that owning records of accredited modern compositions, or being within reach of libraries where soundproof rooms and a collection of records are available, is a practical way of solving the problem. And one should read the orchestral score while listening to the records. Listen to the recordings of Debussy's *"La Mer"*; Stravinsky's *Petrouchka, Le Sacre du printemps,* Symphony of Psalms, or *Scenes de ballet;* Strauss's *Der Rosenkavalier,* "Don Quixote," and "Till Eulenspiegel's Merry Pranks"; Schoenberg's *"Verklärte Nacht"* or *Pierrot Lunaire;* Sibelius' symphonies; Scriabin's "Poem of Ecstasy" or "Prometheus: The Poem of Fire"; Hindemith's String Quartet, op. 22, and *Mathis der Maler;* Berg's Violin Concerto and Lyric Suite; Ravel's *Daphnis et Chloë* or the Piano Concerto; Copland's *Appalachian Spring* and *El Salón México;*

Harris's Third Symphony; Shostakovich's First and Fifth Symphonies; Prokofieff's Third Piano Concerto, and many other twentieth century compositions. You will then be more ready to appreciate concerts directed by Koussevitzky, Stokowski, Rodzinski, Ormandy, Mitropoulos, Reiner, Leonard Bernstein, Golschmann, or any other conductor addicted to modernism, also to the concerts in New York City of the League of Composers, the National Association of American Composers and Conductors, the U.S. Section of the International Society for Contemporary Music, the series at the Juilliard School, and the festivals of American music at the Eastman School of Music in Rochester, N.Y., at Columbia University, and at Yaddo in Saratoga Springs, N.Y.

The fact that you can put on any record you please with frequent and necessary repetitions makes the phonograph a more valuable ally in fostering an appreciation for twentieth century music than the radio.

The recording piano was valuable, too, but it had a more limited library of modern records and is no longer found in many places.

Gradually some of the works by American contemporaries have reached the discs, in addition to jazz classics such as those by George Gershwin, Ferde Grofé, Jerome Kern, Vincent Youmans, the popular literature by Rudolf Friml, Sigmund Romberg, Cole Porter, Richard Rodgers, etc., and the vast collections of dance records and modern jazz. Among scores that have been recorded are Charles Griffes' "The Pleasure Dome of Kubla Khan"; Loeffler's "Pagan Poem" and Music for Stringed Instruments; Copland's *El Salón México* and the suite from *Appalachian Spring;* Ernest Bloch's *Schelomo,* Concerto Grosso, Concerto for Violin and Orchestra; Blitzstein's *The Cradle Will Rock* and *No for an Answer;* Carpenter's "Adventures in a Perambulator" and *Skyscrapers;* the Mexican Carlos Chávez's *Sinfonía de Antigona* and *Sinfonía India;* Paul Creston's Suite for Saxophone and Piano; Hanson's Romantic Symphony, No. 2; Harris's Third Symphony, Quintet for Piano and Strings, and Symphony for Voices; Ives's "New England Holidays" and Violin Sonata; Jacobi's *"Hagiographa";* George Kleinsinger's "I Hear America Singing"; Harl McDonald's symphony "The Santa Fé Trail"; Piston's "The Incredible Flutist" and String Quartet No. 1; William Schuman's American Festival Overture and Choral Etude; Sowerby's "The Irish Washwoman" and Symphony in G major for Organ; Still's Afro-American Symphony (Scherzo); and Deems Taylor's "Through the Looking Glass."

Some important titles have been allowed to go out of stock, perhaps temporarily, and there are still many fine unrecorded American scores, among which might be mentioned Louis Gruenberg's "Daniel Jazz," Arthur Shepherd's "Horizons," Carl Ruggles' "Portals," Edward Burlingame Hill's "Lilacs," Roger Sessions' Piano Sonata, William Schuman's Third Symphony (or his Fourth), Harold Morris's Piano Concerto, Walter Piston's Second Symphony, and Griffes' Piano Sonata, as the recording made by Harrison Potter for Friends of Recorded Music can no longer be obtained. The New Music Recordings have brought the works of a number of younger composers into circulation, and Jeanne Behrend, pianist and composer, made a volume of recordings of American piano music. Every year adds to the growing list of new American works that are performed by major orchestras and are worthy of being recorded.

In 1929 the RCA-Victor Company announced a $25,000 prize for an orchestral work by an American. The sum was divided between four composers: Ernest Bloch, Louis Gruenberg, Aaron Copland, and Robert Russell Bennett, who won two awards. But at that time, the works were not recorded.

Radio, one of the greatest inventions of the age, has made gratifying progress, and like the phonograph in its early history, has passed out of the stage of being regarded largely as a toy. Its function, besides being a medium for the dissemination of news, has come to include an educational program, with a portion devoted to music. A few such programs in music have been experimented with by the Columbia Broadcasting System (American School of the Air) and the National Broadcasting Company (University of the Air, inaugurated in 1942). The development of music in the Americas has been traced in a three-year cycle, "Music of the New World," worked out by Gilbert Chase, Ernest La Prade, and John Tasker Howard, three authorities in the field of South and North American musicology. In 1946–47, the subject is the story of opera, ballet, and music meant for dramatic performance. In addition to the broadcasts, Gilbert Chase is the author of handbooks distributed by NBC that form a notable addition to musical bibliography.

In a little volume, *Music in Radio Broadcasting,* edited by Gilbert Chase, Samuel Chotzinoff says a word of aesthetic import: "... The

possibility of someday achieving absolute fidelity to the living model
is precisely what justifies our calling radio an art and not merely a
gadget. For no matter how much radio may progress as a science, its
artistic result will depend in a great measure on the imagination, the
ingenuity, and the integrity of those who have the responsibility for
supervising the transmission of music over the air waves." *

Ethel Peyser claims that radio "is without doubt the greatest of all
inventions since printing and the gasoline engine." In defense of those
who still claim that "radio programs are so bad," we cite those of the
New York Philharmonic-Symphony, the Boston, Philadelphia, Chicago, Detroit, NBC, and other orchestras, National Orchestral Association concerts, the concerts of the New Friends of Music, Saturday
matinees of the Metropolitan Opera Association, as well as many special radio hours, and the annual Festivals of American Music presented
by the New York City station WNYC between the birthdays of Washington and Lincoln. Think what it must mean to thousands who never
had the chance to listen to cosmopolitan music to be educated and
entertained by such broadcasts.

Naturally its artistic results have been handicapped by the fact that
the radio has been used by "commercial hours" as an advertising medium, and that its programs are subject to what the sponsors think
the radio listeners want. Because of the "fan" mail, the sponsors may
have been misled as to what the air audience likes, because serious listeners may not take time to write in to the stations.

The claim that through radio America is becoming musical is not
exaggerated. If the radio must cater to what it thinks the public wants,
then we must understand that the standard will be mediocre until
public taste is improved and listeners become familiar, through frequent repetitions, not only with the finest in the accepted repertories,
but with the newest music as well. This is one of the most important
means that radio has in educating the masses. Even though these programs do not carry the label "educational hours," which would
frighten many away, they are truly educational and cultural.

In New York both stations WQXR and WNYC have programs of
the best recorded music in addition to programs of "live" talent, that
is, by the artists in person. The others, nation-wide networks, NBC,
CBS, ABC (American Broadcasting Company), and WOR (the Mu-

* By permission, from *Music in Radio Broadcasting,* by Gilbert Chase, editor. Copyright, 1946, by McGraw-Hill Book Co., Inc.

tual Broadcasting Company), have programs of wide range including high-class music, excellent dance music, "jam sessions" of swing, "slapstick" comedy, the most famous "torch" singers, "blues" singers, crooners, or the singing of a famous musical comedy star or prima donna, the debut of a foreign conductor, or the playing of a pianist, violinist, or other instrumentalist of international reputation who appears on one of the many radio "hours."

Ernest La Prade states the purposes of program scheduling as follows: to provide a desired type of entertainment, instruction, or information; to appeal to the presumed mood of the audience at a given hour of the day; to exploit featured talent; to preserve a balanced schedule; and to meet competition. (*Music in Radio Broadcasting*.)

A radio triumph was the formation in 1936 of the NBC orchestra with the great Italian maestro Arturo Toscanini as conductor. It has been maintained both as a sustaining and as a commercially sponsored (General Motors Corporation) hour. Samuel Chotzinoff wrote that its creation was not "the indulgence on the part of the NBC of a desire to own its own symphony orchestra. On the contrary, it came indirectly as a response to our government's mandate to operate radio for the public interest, convenience, and necessity." This necessity was to supply the public "which demands and expects to get the finest interpretations of the finest music over the radio." These demands and expectations have been supplied by Toscanini and other famous men of the baton engaged as guest conductors.

The first major orchestral broadcast was that of the Boston Symphony Orchestra under Serge Koussevitzky in November 1926, under the auspices of the NBC. The same year the first grand opera broadcast, a performance of *Faust* in Chicago, took place. Dr. Koussevitzky has been responsible for many broadcasts and concert performances of new works by both American and European composers.

Radio audiences have also had the opportunity of learning that we have an American folk music that is rapidly being absorbed into our art music.

We can learn a few lessons from Europe, just as Europe can get ideas from us in broadcasting. Abroad, even before the war, the radio was supported by means of a tax on every receiving set, and, in most countries, was subsidized by the government. The British Broadcasting Company has made a special feature of presenting contemporary works of English and Continental composers. Recently it inaugurated its Third Program, which may be had by all owners of sets for an additional tax of eleven shillings a year. It operates daily from six P.M. until midnight. The director general of the BBC, Sir William Haley, described it as "intended for the attentive and not as a background to work, to reading or to washing up." The prospectus (as told in the *New York Times* by Morris C. Hastings, December 22, 1946) states that the plan is "to give the finest available performances of music of every style and epoch, with special emphasis on works of interest and beauty which are rarely heard in the concert hall or, hitherto, on the radio." The program has already included a performance of Benjamin Britten's new opera, *The Rape of Lucretia,* of William Walton's First Symphony conducted by the composer, in addition to music by Monteverdi and Purcell. The Third Program hopes to encourage composers to do original works for it without limitations of time, subject, or form. "In short," Mr. Hastings concludes, "the Third Program reaches for a level never before attained by radio, certainly never by commercial radio. If it is successful, it will prove, to quote Sir William Haley once more, 'the greatest value both to the individual and to the community as a whole' of all post-war developments in radio."

In pre-Nazi Germany some of the prominent composers were in control of the stations, while others, such as Hindemith, Kurt Weill, Ernst Toch, and Fitelberg, before they migrated to America, and Graener and Butting wrote special compositions for the radio, and the stations fought for "first performances" of new works.

After having been forbidden modern music during the German occupation, Belgium used its radio to present modern concerts, and through the instance of the National Broadcasting Institute, contemporary music has been reinstated. The institute levies obligatory taxes by means of which it can be a cultural force with no commercial obligations. Belgium has heard many of the important works, most of which were written in America, during the war years. The composers listed include Bartók, Hindemith, Martinu, Milhaud, Schoenberg, Stravinsky, also the Americans Barber, Blitzstein, Copland, Creston, Harris, and Schuman, and the Mexican Chávez, the Russians Prokofieff and Shostakovich, and the English Britten and Michael Tippett. Of their own composers, many of whom are connected with the radio, Paul Collaer, musical director of the Belgian Radio, mentions in *Mod-*

ern Music (Fall 1946) Jean Absil, Raymond Chevreuille, Victor Lengley, and David van de Woestyne as four of the most gifted.

In this country radio opera is a field still not overcultivated. The late Charles Wakefield Cadman's *The Willow Tree,* an opera based on an Indian subject, Louis Gruenberg's *Green Mansions,* Gian-Carlo Menotti's *Old Maid and the Thief,* and Vittorio Giannini's *Beauty and the Beast* were written specially for radio production, and were commissioned by the broadcasting companies.

The CBS commissioned compositions for radio performance in 1936 and 1937. And in 1932, Philip James won first prize in a competition of the NBC for works by American composers. Another distinctly American phase of musical encouragement was the now extinct nationwide singing contests of the Atwater Kent Radio Auditions, which lent aid to many young artists. Walter Damrosch spent several years in bringing music to the school children of America in the NBC Music Appreciation Courses and Dorothy Gordon acquainted them with the folk music of many countries. These were followed by the broadcasts mentioned above.

Ethel Peyser, my collaborator in *Music through the Ages,* wrote on recent radio developments as follows: "The youth of radio is apparent in its yet unsolved problems on which engineers, composers, orchestra leaders, and radio-set manufacturers are working. Much has been accomplished by inventors, technicians, and musicians. Much must be done by the listener to understand and appreciate the problems and advantages, and the glory which can be and often is ... Radio."

Ethel Peyser recommends that more composers write for the radio and study its demands. "The composer of radio music has to know frequency ranges, dynamic ranges; timbres of sound as effected by transmission and reception; the effects of 'lonesomeness' on the listener and his resultant psychological reactions; and many another vagary of loud-speaker and audience."

No doubt in the near future the radio itself will undergo great changes. The possibilities opened up by "Frequency Modulation" (the F.M. circuit) alone have already made new kinds of receivers and transmitters necessary. (For more detailed information see Chapter 45, "Electricity's Influence on Instruments and Music," in *Music through the Ages.*)

Leopold Stokowski, the famous conductor, was instrumental in many acoustical experiments on the radio. While he was still at the head of the Philadelphia Orchestra, the Bell Telephone Laboratories conducted some interesting experiments in wiring halls and constructing systems by which to carry the radio waves over wires.

These experiments, which are going on constantly, will no doubt revolutionize the existing conditions, and the radio of the future will probably influence and improve musical development greatly. Perhaps the use of mechanical instruments, or "instrumentalities," as Ethel Peyser prefers to call them, is a part of the dehumanizing, or depersonalizing, process in art.

While television is an accomplished fact, it has not yet found its way generally into the homes, nor has music found its rightful place in television. How it is to be used successfully for musical programs is still in a highly experimental stage. The dramatization of music in concert might be worked out satisfactorily. Perhaps the type of program used by the film *Fantasia* in the Stokowski-Disney production might be transferred to television with real people acting, singing, or playing instruments, in a visual interpretation of music. One difficulty would be in trying to interpret music that has no programmatic intention. For this reason *Fantasia* was offensive to many musicians who wish to listen to music as music, and do not care to have their Bach and Beethoven "interpreted" by extramusical means.

In an essay on "Opera in Television" in *Music in Radio Broadcasting,* Dr. Herbert Graf points out three possibilities for televising music: by "concert photography—as if we were attending the concert with a camera in the concert hall"; by "producing suitable optical background for music"; and by "visual illustration of the contents of music" by realistic or surrealistic treatment, or by kaleidoscope. (He speaks of *Fantasia* as surrealistic treatment.) Dr. Graf sees television as "a really legitimate medium" to present "those forms of music which are meant to be visual: musical comedies, operettas, ballets, and opera." Through the radio broadcasts of the Metropolitan, opera has developed a vast new audience, and this interest, so necessary to the life of opera, can "be greatly expanded by television, which, by bringing sight to sound, makes the picture of an opera performance complete." Several experiments have been tried successfully, but the most satisfactory way to produce television opera will be to write scores especially for the purpose. Dr. Graf sees television as "the democratic medium that will make opera take off its top hat and speak in every way the language of the people," thus contributing "decisively to the opening of a new chapter in the history of opera in this country. . . ." *

In motion pictures we have had many experiments that show the possibilities of the sound film as a revolutionizing medium for music. The ephemeral life of the film is an argument against its being of cultural import to the serious musician, as is also the fact that the average film audience seeks entertainment of a popular rather than a high-class order. On the other hand, before World War II, some Russian films, Hindemith's Film-Music Studio in Berlin, and a few highly specialized pictures in France and America opened new vistas in the art world.

In 1931 a picture was shown at a Copland-Sessions concert in which a film by Ralph Steiner, *Mechanical Principles,* was accompanied by an orchestral score composed for it by Colin McPhee. Despite the fact that the screen movement and the music were not perfectly synchronized, it was an extraordinary realization of the spirit of the mechanical age imprisoned in an art expression. "Dancers, stage directors, painters, and musicians all attended the occasion to seek novelty of form, motion and design in this imaginative regrouping of the arts," said Richard Hammond in *Modern Music* ("Pioneers of Movie Music," March-April 1931). *Mechanical Principles* presented "a ballet of the screen, with pistons for dancers, the *battements* of levers, the *pirouettes* of fly-wheels, *glissades* of worm-gears, *fouettés* of pendula and *jetés, cabrioles* and *entrechats* of spring valves. . . . For almost every art there was supplied a healthy opportunity to take fresh stock of its component elements. . . . To the film creator especially, new vistas were opened. The slave of realism, the purveyor of every day, he finds stretching before him vast fields of the imagination. . . . It is entirely conceivable that the future may beget emotion from motion, aphrodisiac reaction from hypno-mechanical movement and spiritual elevation from abstract forms of beauty."

Hollywood has made a place for an army of musicians, composers, arrangers, copyists, orchestral players, singers, pianists, coaches, conductors, etc. Regardless of the fact that successful music for a picture must be of secondary importance, many well-known composers, both European and American, have been employed to write for the screen.

* By permission, from *Music in Radio Broadcasting,* by Gilbert Chase, editor. Copyright, 1946, by McGraw-Hill Book Co., Inc.

Among the men who, coming to this country to escape the persecutions of the Nazis, found a haven and profitable reward in Hollywood are Erich Korngold, a Viennese writer of operas, Ernst Toch, Hanns Eisler, Kurt Weill, Miklos Rozsa, and others. Korngold supplied music for, among many other films, *Midsummer Night's Dream, Juarez, The Constant Nymph,* and *King's Row.* In 1946 he returned to Europe perhaps only for a visit, as he, no doubt, was "fed up" with writing to order for the films. Among Ernest Toch's scores were *The Outcast, Ladies in Retirement,* and *First Comes Courage.* He is teaching music in the University of Southern California and is an American citizen, as is also Korngold. Hanns Eisler, a pupil of Schoenberg in Vienna, attempted some film music in twelve-tone technic for *White Floats;* he also wrote the music for *Spanish Main, 4,000,000* on the situation in China, *None but the Lonely Heart,* and *Forgotten Village.* Miklos Rozsa wrote the scores to *Spellbound, Jungle Book,* and *The Lost Weekend.*

Hollywood has made famous a number of composers who have turned out expert scores. Among these are Alfred Newman (*The Song of Bernadette*), Max Steiner (*Mission to Moscow*), Roy Webb (*The Human Comedy*), David Raksin (*Smoky*), Franz Waxman (*Objective Burma*), Herbert Stothart (*Mrs. Minniver* and *Mme. Curie*), Victor Young (*For Whom the Bell Tolls*), Hugo Friedhofer (*The Lodger, Marco Polo*), etc.

Many composers well known in the symphonic field have supplied scores to famous pictures. Aaron Copland wrote music for Thornton Wilder's *Our Town,* also *North Star* and *Of Mice and Men;* Bernard Herrmann, a radio conductor, wrote music for *Jane Eyre, Hangover Square,* in which a specially composed piano concerto appears, *Citizen Kane,* and *All That Money Can Buy;* George Antheil wrote *Once in a Blue Moon;* Dimitri Tiomkin wrote *San Pietro;* Werner Janssen wrote *The General Died at Dawn, Peter Ibbetson,* and *Captain Kidd;* Earl Robinson brought American folk music into the movies in *Old California* and *The Romance of Rosy Ridge;* Louis Gruenberg wrote *Thus Ends Our Night* and *Commandos Strike at Dawn,* and he was chosen to participate in the production of *Arch of Triumph.*

Gruenberg contends that he has spent ten years in Hollywood, watching, writing, and waiting for a real chance to prove that film music can be an art form worthy of the best that is in a composer, and he believes there is a real film-opera technic.

Documentary films have reaped a rich harvest among American composers. One of the finest was Gruenberg's *A Fight for Life;* and other important ones were Copland's *The City;* Virgil Thomson's *The River* and *The Plow That Broke the Plains;* Thomson and Blitzstein's *Spanish Earth;* Blitzstein's *Native Land;* Douglas Moore's *Power and the Land* and *Youth Gets a Break;* the English composer Richard Arnell's *The Land,* etc.

During World War II, the Office of Emergency Management Film Unit produced "factual shorts" with music by Gail Kubik (*Men and Ships, Memphis Belle, The World at War*) and Morton Gould (*Ring of Steel*); and the Office of War Information distributed "shorts" by Norman Lloyd (*Valley of the Tennessee*), Kurt Weill (*Salute to France*), William Schuman (*Steeltown*), and Kubik (*Paratroops*), besides others.

Some of the foreign composers have written important films, such as *Pygmalion* by Arthur Honegger, *Henry V* by William Walton, *Alexender Nevsky* by Prokofieff, *The Love of Paris, Blood of the Poet,* and *Caesar and Cleopatra* by Georges Auric, and scores by Alexandre Tansman, Darius Milhaud, Shostakovich, Kabalevsky, etc.

Motion pictures are bringing music to a very wide public, second only in size to the radio listeners and larger than the phonograph "fans." The *art* of film music is in its infancy, but it has tremendous possibilities for further development, and as Virgil Thomson said in *The Musical Scene,* "The gramophone, the cinema, and the radio are what make the difference between today's music and that of preceding centuries."

The term Jazz Age does not designate a period dominated by jazz. Jazz is merely a symptom. The restlessness, the search for diversion, the avoidance of facing facts, the fear of being fearful, and, above all, the ruthless materialism of the day, are taking toll of our art. The reaction from World War I assumed a humorous twist. Life had been too serious. Humor in itself is not an unworthy adjunct of art, but when it is abused, when it supplants dignity, and is treated by inexperienced hands, it becomes frivolous and commonplace. Democracy in art is the vogue, but democracy is in danger of becoming a synonym of vulgarity. As Charles Koechlin says: "The tendency towards familiar art easily drifts into vulgar art: the spirit of simplification, if it brings us 'light tones' (not without charm sometimes...) on the other hand may end in anemia, with commonplace ideas; the fear of sadness that impels one to flee from all depths will engender none but rather childish things. Serenity will no longer even be understood...." ("Sensibility in Contemporary Music," *Pro Musica Quarterly,* December 1927.)

Psychologists tell us that the strong hold exciting rhythms had exerted during the 1920's was an aftermath of the war and that dancing has always been a diversion in times of war, panic, and epidemic. So Europe's discovery of jazz was timely and its influence on serious music inevitable. It revitalized a tired art. It put energy in place of lyricism, and brutality in place of power. But these are inevitable reflections of an overtaxed world in which many find it none too pleasant to live.

World War I was responsible for breaking up the "corner" Germany had on music. It was a monopoly that had served its purpose, and not without fruitful results, from 1685 to 1914. With the prejudice that arose at that time against German composers, the musical world was forced to close time-honored portals and to open other doors. In America, particularly, this fanaticism led to a ban on German works and, consequently, to cultivating music the existence of which previously had hardly received recognition. The Russian nationalists, French Impressionists, and English, Spanish, and Italian contemporaries, as well as the Russian modernists such as Stravinsky, Scriabin, and Prokofieff, were received with more consideration than they had heretofore been given. And even the American composer was admitted by the front door instead of having to steal through a window.

As interesting as this awakening to an existence of many tongues was, it also hastened the erection of a Tower of Babel the foundations of which had been laid in the nineteenth century, and which has led to a confusion of purposes in the twentieth.

As we look back we see how music was dominated by definite trends, even though other tendencies existed, and in time overrode the established direction. When Bach wrote suites and fugues, every one else wrote suites and fugues; when Beethoven wrote in sonata form, every other composer was doing the same; and this is true of program music and of impressionism. What characteristics of the interwar period will go down in history as permanent? Will the cloak of neo-classicism cover it? Atonality, polytonality, linear counterpoint, new chord formations, new rhythmic formulas, a new idea of melody, short phrases, short compositions, condensed music dramas, chamber music works, small instrumental groups, new choral works, music in which the untrained musician can participate, music especially written for the films or the radio, perhaps for a super-radio in which television will re-establish the contact between performer and audience—will this be the foundation for the music of the future?

In the last generation, the world has been going through a crisis that must leave its effect on art. How will this crisis be met in music? Many of us have spent the greater part of our lives creating cultural standards for ourselves and for others, working to realize a goal that would build constructively for the future. Are past efforts to be brushed aside by the oncoming hordes of youths with other aims, other ideals? Will they know how to turn to account these unprecedented conditions, in carrying on the great musical tradition?

Is the apparent breaking up of traditions in art, in politics, in social conditions, in religion, symptomatic of the death struggles of an old civilization, or are they the birth pangs of a new era?

As an aftermath of World War II a new nationalism seems to have sprung up in music, following in the wake of political, social, and cultural oppression. Nationalism as developed in nineteenth century Europe did not reach the United States. But among several recent tendencies in this country the pursuit of an American idiom is being stressed through accent on our folk music, which lay dormant for so long, through employment of jazz rhythms and popular tunes in art music, through the exhuming of works by such composers as William Billings, and through belated recognition of the "Americanism" and genius of Charles Ives. In other words, at long last our national consciousness has been aroused.

In 1926 Henry F. Gilbert was quoted by Philip Hale in the program book of the Boston Symphony Orchestra as stating his creed: "My constant aim has been to write some American music—i.e., some music which would not naturally have been written in any other country, and which should reflect, or express, certain aspects of the American character, or spirit, as felt by myself. That spirit, as I see it, is energetic, optimistic—nervous—impatient of restraint and in its highest aspect, a mighty protest against the benumbing traditions of the past. This new birth—renaissance—of the human spirit, which is America, is a joyous, wildly shouting demonstration. . . ."

This is a clear statement of American aesthetics of the 1920's. This recently awakened nationalism is still somewhat self-conscious, but is rapidly becoming part of the inheritance of the younger men. The public acceptance of this Americanism is in the hands of the conductors and performers. The concert goers still "know what they like," and they like principally what appeared on the programs listened to by their parents and grandparents. But as Eugene Goossens wrote in *Modern Music,* January-February 1943, "... conductors and composers alike can, and must, combine to win over, intrigue, educate, and entertain the public... ; not by offering it syrupy concoctions in the manner of a weak compromise, but by strong, vigorous doses of first-rate, important music, as American as the painting of Grant Wood and Thomas Hart Benton, and the writings of Steinbeck and Hemingway."

A new audience is developing, such an audience, young, enthusiastic, intelligent, and full of curiosity, as has been created since 1945 by Leonard Bernstein for the orchestral concerts at the New York City Center. A number of other conductors, in proportion to their own interest in contemporary music, have introduced new works to their subscribers. Often boards of directors stand in the way of too many experiments, and the box office directs the policies of program building. Leopold Stokowski has been an intrepid soul when it came to experiments with new scores. Serge Koussevitzky, throughout his leadership of the Boston Symphony Orchestra, has fed the public accepted masterpieces, well larded with contemporary European and American scores.

Dr. Koussevitzky laid the cornerstone of a great monument in 1942, when he established the Koussevitzky Music Foundation, in memory of his wife, Mme. Natalie Koussevitzky. Through the Foundation the veteran conductor has commissioned many important works, mostly by Americans and Europeans in America. A list of the commissions speaks for itself: Nicolai Berezowsky's Symphony No. 4; Bohuslav Martinu's Symphony No. 3; Béla Bartók's Concerto for Orchestra; Igor Stravinsky's Ode for Orchestra; William Schuman's Symphony for Strings; William Bergsma's Second String Quartet; Robert Palmer's String Quartet; Darius Milhaud's Second Symphony; Aaron Copland's Third Symphony; Nikolai Lopatnikoff's Concertino for Orchestra; Lukas Foss's Capriccio for Cello and Piano; Burrill Phillips' Overture for Orchestra, "Tom Paine"; Villa-Lobos' *Madona Poema Sinfónica;* Alexei Haieff's "Eclogue" for cello and piano; *Peter Grimes,* an opera by Benjamin Britten; operas by Samuel Barber and Marc Blitzstein; and works by Olivier Messiaen, Howard Hanson, David Diamond, Harold Shapero, Walter Piston, and Paul Hindemith.

There is a tendency today to look down on the accomplishments of the twenties and thirties, just as the twenties and thirties turned away from the impressionism of the first decade of the century. The present is always suspect of the immediate past, regardless of whether the time be 1947, 1847, or 1747. All of our composers have not turned to "Americanism." Many of them are nourished by the works of these earlier decades whether or not the indebtedness is acknowledged. The technics of today have grown out of the experiments of yesterday, only the experiments have come to be accepted as a matter of course and exist as part of the unconscious memory of the present generation of composers. Atonality, polytonality, modal harmony, dissonant counterpoint, all are used in greater or lesser degree, just as the nineteenth century composers enlarged on the harmonic material of the eighteenth century. The difference lies in the fact that the present generation has simplified much that it helped itself to. In fact, much of the new Americanism is part of the simplifying process. Also, there is a definite swing away from dissonance used in exaggeration as it was by many in the previous generation. The pendulum leads back to diatonicism and neoromanticism; back to homely sentiment; but it eschews the sentimentality that seemed to have weakened the postromantic movement; both the public and the young composer have in many ways become reactionary.

The reactionary attitude of the public and of the young composer, however, seems to have turned the tide. The young are desperately in earnest and are determined to tear down the unnecessary scaffolding. They take what they need from the past and build their share of the musical edifice with tools that they teach themselves to use. They learn, as has every generation before them, by experimentation, failure, and reconstruction.

But the writing on the wall points to a new romanticism, a renaissance of beauty and of simplicity—but a romanticism composed of the new materials. The spirit of beauty must be born again. It must be released from the fetters that have held it earthbound. It will be a new beauty to fit a new epoch that is gradually rising from the ashes of the old, for "the former things are passed away."

EXPLANATION OF MUSICAL TERMS

THE readers of *Twentieth Century Music,* especially in applying "How to Listen to It" practically, may find it useful to understand something of the theoretical terms employed in its pages. For the musician this explanation of musical terms will be superfluous; to the untrained music lover or the student it may be helpful.

An INTERVAL is the distance from one tone to another. The smallest interval on the keyboard is the half step. Half steps are *diatonic* (c to d♭) and *chromatic* (c to c♯). Diatonic half steps appear between the 3rd and 4th, and 7th and 8th degrees of the major scale. All the rest are whole steps or *whole tones.* From the 1st degree of the scale to the 2nd is a *second;* from 1 to 3, a *third;* from 1 to 4, a *fourth,* etc.

All intervals are measured according to the major scale. In the major scale, therefore, primes, fourths, fifths, and octaves are perfect intervals; seconds, thirds, sixths, and sevenths are major. In the minor scale, thirds and sixths become minor.

Fourths, fifths, primes, and octaves are perfect consonances; seconds, thirds, sixths, and sevenths are imperfect consonances.

Intervals are major, minor, perfect, augmented, diminished. By raising or lowering either tone of an interval by means of a sharp, flat, or natural (called *chromatics*), an interval is altered. A minor interval is a chromatic half step smaller than a major interval; a diminished interval is a chromatic half step smaller than minor, an augmented interval is a chromatic half step larger than major. Perfect intervals become diminished or augmented by reducing or increasing them a chromatic half step. For example:

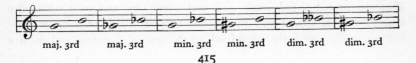

maj. 3rd   maj. 3rd   min. 3rd   min. 3rd   dim. 3rd   dim. 3rd

An interval may be inverted, that is, the position of the two tones forming the interval may be turned upside down: A prime inverts to the octave; a 2nd inverts to the 7th; a third, to the 6th; a 4th, to the 5th; a 5th, to the 4th; a 6th, to the 3rd; a 7th, to the 2nd; an octave, to the prime.

Major intervals invert to minor; minor to major; perfect to perfect; augmented to diminished; and diminished to augmented. For example: a major 3rd inverts to a minor 6th, a perfect 4th to a perfect 5th; a diminished 5th to an augmented 4th, etc.

DIATONIC refers to the consecutive tone degrees of a scale, or to tones within a given key. A diatonic melody is one in which no tones foreign to the key are used.

CHROMATIC means literally color (*chroma*)—a different color of the same tone, altered by means of sharp, flat, or natural. It means also intervals proceeding by half steps: the *chromatic scale* of twelve half steps, the new twelve tone system of Schoenberg.

A SCALE is a succession of tones within an octave. The DIATONIC SCALE is a definite succession of tones within an octave written on adjacent staff degrees. The diatonic scales in common usage are *major* and *minor*. They are based on the Greek tetrachord or half scales. A *tetrachord* is the name of the Greek instrument of four strings tuned thus: ef g a (natural tetrachord); e f♯g a (minor tetrachord); e f♯ g♯a (major tetrachord); ef g♯a ("chromatic oriental" tetrachord).

Our major scale is a combination of two major tetrachords: c d ef g a bc. They are formed of two whole steps and a half step, and are a whole step apart. Every tetrachord may be the first or second half of a major scale. For example g a bc is the second half of the scale of C major, and the first half of the scale of G major. This gives rise to the *circle of fifths* (page 110). Although there are actually twelve different sounding major and twelve minor scales, including the enharmonic scales, there are fifteen different notations of each. *Enharmonic* means different notations for the same pitch (f♯, g♭). The enharmonic scales are B major–C♭ major, F♯ major–G♭ major, C♯ major–D♭ major, and their relative minors.

There are three forms of the minor scale: natural, harmonic, and melodic. All three forms have a minor tetrachord as the first half of the scale. The form of the scale depends on the second half:

a b͡c d (minor tetrachord)
e͡f g a (natural) Natural Minor
e͡f g͡♯a (chromatic-oriental) Harmonic Minor
e f♯ g♯a (major) ascending Melodic Minor

The descending melodic minor is the natural minor scale.

If you play from the 6th degree of the major scale to its octave you will find the *natural minor scale*. The minor system is regarded as a part of the major system, so that every major scale has its relative minor (based on the 6th degree of the scale) and both are indicated by the same key signature, that is, one sharp indicates either the key of G major or of E minor.

The *harmonic minor* developed, not by consciously making use of the Greek chromatic-oriental tetrachord, but by borrowing the seventh degree from the major scale as leading tone. The *melodic minor* arose because theorists claimed that the augmented step between 6 and 7 (f-g♯) was not logical scale movement, so the sixth degree was raised to avoid the unvocal step (f-g♯). Then a compromise was made so that the second tetrachord of the melodic minor read: e f♯ g♯ a g♮ f♮ e.

For convenience I call the first tetrachord the Tonic Tetrachord (starting on the first degree of the scale) and the second tetrachord, the Dominant Tetrachord (starting on the fifth degree of the scale).

Chapter 9 will have shown the reader that scales are man-made conventions and that there are many varieties: the pentatonic or five tone scale in which the half steps are missing, used by Chinese, Scotch, and primitive races; the modal scales of the Greeks passed on to the early Christian Fathers and becoming the Ecclesiastical Modes (page 109); the diatonic major and minor scales; the whole tone scale of Debussy, and the twelve tone system of Schoenberg.

With the breaking down of the modal system and the adoption of the diatonic scale system came the use of *key* or *tonality* and key signatures, symbols to indicate the key or tonality.

KEY is any particular scale of tone series forming a unity through relation to a tonal center which gives the key its name (key of F major, or key of A minor). TONALITY, like a key or mode, relates all the degrees of a scale to a tonal center.

HARMONY is the science which treats of chords—their construction, interrelation, and logical progression. It is vertical music in contradistinction to Counterpoint which is horizontal or linear music.

COUNTERPOINT means literally note against note. Notes were formerly called *points*. Counterpoint is the science of sounding two or more melodies simultaneously. It is *polyphonic* or many-voiced. It is written according to rules governing the permissible combinations of intervals. The theme of a contrapuntal composition is called the *cantus firmus* (fixed song), and the counter melody (or melodies) is the counterpoint. Following the age of *Organum,* came the *Polyphonic Era* in which vocal counterpoint prevailed. The first music for instruments was contrapuntal. (See FORMS.) Today composers are writing *dissonant counterpoint* (page 253).

The basis of Harmony is the three-voiced chord or TRIAD, consisting of a root, third, and fifth (c-e-g). On each degree of the diatonic scale, major or minor, a triad may be constructed:

MAJOR MODE   HARMONIC MINOR SCALE

I II III IV V VI VII   I II° III+ IV V VI VII°

Triads are major, minor, augmented and diminished.
A major triad has a major 3rd and perfect 5th.
A minor triad has a minor 3rd and perfect 5th.
An augmented triad has a major 3rd and augmented 5th.
A diminished triad has a minor 3rd and diminished 5th.

The triads are distinguished by Roman numerals and names, as follows: I, tonic; II, supertonic; III, mediant; IV, subdominant; V, dominant; VI, submediant; VII, leading tone.

In the *major mode,* the *primary triads* (I, IV, V) are major triads;

the *secondary triads* (II, III, VI) are minor; and the triad on the leading tone (VII°), also a secondary triad, is diminished (page 114).

In the (harmonic) *minor mode,* I and IV are minor triads; V and VI are major, II° and VII° are diminished, and III+ is augmented.

In the diatonic system all chords are built in thirds: triads, chords of the 7th (g-b-d-f), chords of the 9th (g-b-d-f-a), chords of the 11th and 13th (page 114). And every chord is subject to inversion, that is, to re-arrangement of parts so that some other than its root serves as the bass. Today other systems of chord building are used arbitrarily, such as Schoenberg's chords in fourths (page 217).

Up to the twentieth century, practically all music since the introduction of the diatonic major and minor modes can be analyzed by means of these chord combinations plus modulations and alterations. It can be reduced to a few harmonic formulas and cadences. A system of indicating chord combinations by means of figures over the bass was invented to accompany recitatives and to facilitate the reading of scores. It was known as *thorough bass* or *figured bass.*

CADENCE is derived from the Latin *cadere,* to fall, and means the close or ending of a phrase, period, part, movement, or work. It is a harmonic formula which gives a sense of temporary or complete finality.

MODULATION is a change of tonality. Modulations may be transient, or auxiliary, or they may indicate a permanent change of key in a composition. Greater freedom in the use of modulation has been one of the most noticeable changes in music. A comparison of a Haydn and a Wagner score will prove this statement.

ALTERED CHORDS have become an important factor in modern music and are accomplished by means of raising or lowering chromatically one or more voices of a chord. The object of chord alteration is usually to bring a tone closer to its note of resolution. For example:

Dominant 7th with 5th lowered   (1) Supertonic with 3rd raised
                                 (2) Dominant with 5th lowered

RHYTHM is defined as "measured movement in time." The term is often erroneously employed instead of meter. Meter is the pulsation, the reiterated beats in which a composition is written: $^6\!/\!_8$, $^3\!/\!_4$, $^{12}\!/\!_8$, $^9\!/\!_{16}$, etc., which means that there are six eighth notes, three quarter notes, etc., to the measure. Rhythm is the movement within the meter, the design or pattern in time woven around the reiterated beat. The modern methods of shifting meter (multirhythms) and of combining rhythmic patterns (polyrhythms) have been discussed in the text. The boundaries of a metrical measure are determined by accents.

FORM is the plan or design of a piece of music. Rhythm, melody, harmony, and structure are the ingredients of musical composition, combined according to the canons of art in unity, balance, and contrast. The materials out of which a composition is constructed include musical figures or patterns; phrases, periods, or sentences; larger sections or movements. Themes, one, two, three, or more, are announced, developed, interwoven, repeated, manipulated in symmetrical order to produce definite effect.

Forms throughout the ages have changed as the character of music has changed. The principal music forms chronologically listed, include:

MOTET: a vocal polyphonic work to sacred text.

MADRIGAL: a vocal polyphonic work to secular text.

CANON: a form in which a melody or subject is imitated by one or more parts, note for note at a given distance, either at the same or at a different pitch.

FUGUE (From Latin: *fuga,* flight): a polyphonic work for voices or instruments; the highest form of contrapuntal art. It is the apotheosis of canon. The design of the fugue calls for the exposition in which are set forth a *subject,* a short phrase announced as a single melody, the *answer* corresponding to the subject but usually a fifth above it, the *counter subject,* contrapuntally fitted to the answer; the episodes which are developed from the material of the exposition; and the final section, in which frequently the exposition is recapitulated, with *stretti, organ point,* and closing cadence. Stretto is a passage in which the subject (and sometimes the answer) is treated canonically so that the voices overlap and crowd upon one another to produce an effect of climax. Organ point is a stationary tone or tones usually in the bass, over which the other voices move freely and dissonantly.

SUITE: the first important instrumental form to be developed (seventeenth and eighteenth centuries). A series of compositions of folk dance origin from the different countries; the principal dances are:

Allemande, in moderate movement, in common time, of German origin.

Courante or *Corrente,* fast, in duple or triple measure, of Italian or French origin.

Sarabande, a slow stately dance in triple measure of Spanish origin.

Gigue, very fast dance in duple or triple measure, of Italian or English origin.

The other dance forms include *gavotte, minuet, chaconne, passacaglia, bourrée, rigaudon, tambourin,* etc. Suites are also called *partitas, exercises, lessons, ordres, sonate da camera, partien.* (See *Music through the Ages,* Bauer and Peyser, pages 126-128.)

SONATA: a composition of three or four contrasting movements. The early sonata was derived from the Italian *sonata da chiesa* (church sonata), one of the first instrumental forms. The *classical sonata* as developed by Karl Philipp Emanuel Bach, Haydn, Mozart, and Beethoven is the form in which *concertos, symphonies, string quartets,* and chamber music of the eighteenth and nineteenth centuries were written. The first movement of these compositions is usually in *sonata form* often called *sonata allegro.*

Sonata form consists of:

Exposition: *Principal subject,* modulating to *second subject,* and *codetta* or *closing subject;*

Development or free fantasia in which the exposition is handled freely according to the imaginative fertility and technical skill of the composer;

Recapitulation: a repetition of the exposition with prescribed changes of key, and frequently the addition of a coda.

The second movement of a sonata is usually in slow tempo. It is in two-part song form (A-B) or, more frequently, three-part song form (A-B-A) so named because it was derived from the early vocal aria.

The SCHERZO (literally, a *joke*); a development of the *minuet.* In large three-part form: Scherzo-Trio-Scherzo repeated.

The sonata finale is often a RONDO, derived from the old French round dance, or *rondeau.* It is based on the principle of a frequent return to a primary subject interspersed with secondary subjects. The first rondo form has two themes: A-B-A; the second rondo form has three themes: A-B-A-C-A; and the third has four themes, A-B-A-C-A-D-A, or three themes distributed thus: A-B-A-C-A-B-A.

VARIATION form, that is, *theme and variations:* an old type which has been developed by the various composers through the centuries. It can replace any movement in the sonata.

Many sonatas begin with a slow, impressive *introduction* and end with an additional section called a *coda.*

CONCERTO GROSSO: the precursor of the modern concerto for solo instrument and orchestral accompaniment, a form in common usage in Bach's and Handel's time. It was a composition for a group of solo instruments called *concertante* and the accompanying instruments called *ripieno*.

SYMPHONY: developed from the *sinfonia,* which was the instrumental passages in operas, cantatas, and masses, and was sometimes called *ritornella* and *overture*. Later, it became a sonata for orchestra.

With the coming of romanticism, the long sonata was broken into short forms such as the *étude* which was the first type of music written for the perfected pianoforte; *ballade, rhapsody, impromptu, nocturne,* etc. The short piano piece with programmatic names, the *symphonic tone poem* (also program music), and the art song were products of the nineteenth century. Many of these are based on three-part form with a wide range of modifications.

The tendency today is to cut out all superfluous developments and to return to modified classic forms, the suite and the early sonata.

OPERA, ORATORIO, and CANTATA have come down through the centuries with various metamorphoses. The *aria, candenza,* and *recitative* belong distinctly to these vocal forms.

Since twentieth century terms, such as impressionism, polytonality, atonality, neoclassicism, etc., have been fully discussed in the text, they are not included in this section.

BIBLIOGRAPHY

Music through the Ages. Marion Bauer and Ethel Peyser. G. P. Putnam's Sons, New York, 1932, 1946.

How Music Grew. Marion Bauer and Ethel Peyser. G. P. Putnam's Sons, New York, 1925, 1939.

Carlo Gesualdo, Prince of Venosa, Musician and Murderer. Cecil Gray and Philip Heseltine. Lincoln MacVeagh. The Dial Press, New York, 1926.

Monteverdi. Henry Prunières. Librairie Felix Alcan, Paris, 1924.

The Progress of Music. George Dyson. Oxford University Press, London, 1932.

Johann Sebastian Bach. C. Hubert H. Parry. G. P. Putnam's Sons, 1909.

Bach: The Historical Approach. Charles Sanford Terry. Oxford University Press, London, 1930.

Musical Taste and How to Form It. M. D. Calvocoressi. Oxford University Press, London, 1925.

A History of Music. Paul Landormy (trans. by Frederick H. Martens). Chas. Scribner's Sons, New York, 1923.

Beethoven: His Spiritual Development. J. W. N. Sullivan. Alfred Knopf, New York, 1927.

The Limitations of Music, A Study in Æsthetics. Eric Blom. The Macmillan Company, New York, 1928.

Beethoven: The Man Who Freed Music. Robert Haven Schauffler. Doubleday, Doran & Co., Inc., New York, 1929.

A History of Music. John Frederick Rowbotham. Richard Bentley & Son, London, 1893.

Musical Acoustics. John Broadhouse. William Reeves, London, 1892.

New Musical Resources. Henry Cowell. A. A. Knopf, New York, 1930.

Music: A Science and an Art. John Redfield. A. A. Knopf, New York, 1927.

A Theory of Evolving Tonality. Joseph Yasser. American Library of Musicology, W. W. Norton & Co., New York, 1932.

New Harmonic Devices. Horace Alden Miller. Oliver Ditson Co., New York, 1930.

How to Enjoy Music, First Aid to Music Listeners. Ethel Peyser. G. P. Putnam's Sons, New York, 1933.

A Study of Modern Harmony. René Lenormand. The Boston Music Co., Boston, 1913, English trans., 1915.

Modern Harmony: Its Explanation and Application. A. Eaglefield Hull. The Boston Music Co., Boston, 1914.

The Relation of Ultramodern to Archaic Music. Katherine Ruth Heyman. Small, Maynard & Co., Boston, 1921.

A New Esthetic of Music. Ferruccio Busoni. G. Schirmer, New York, 1911.

Acoustics for Musicians. Percy C. Buck. Oxford University Press, London, 1918.

The Musician's Arithmetic. Max F. Meyer (Ed. University of Missouri). Oliver Ditson Co., New York, 1929.

The Evolution of Harmony. C. H. Kitson. Oxford University Press, London, 1924.

Jewish Music in Its Historical Development. A. Z. Idelsohn. Henry Holt & Co., New York, 1929.

"The Elastic Language" from *A Musical Motley.* Ernest Newman. A. A. Knopf, New York, 1925.

The History of Music. Cecil Gray. A. A. Knopf, New York, 1928.

Music and the Romantic Movement in France. Arthur Ware Locke. E. P. Dutton & Co., New York, 1920.

The Book of American Negro Spirituals. Introduction by James Weldon Johnson. The Viking Press, New York, 1925.

The Romantic Composers. Daniel Gregory Mason. The Macmillan Company, New York, 1906.

The Unknown Brahms: His Life, Character and Works, Based on New Material. Robert Haven Schauffler. Dodd, Mead & Co., New York, 1933.

Music: An Art and a Language. Walter R. Spalding. Arthur P. Schmidt & Co., Boston, 1920.

Afro-American Folksongs, A Study in Racial National Music. H. E. Krehbiel. G. Schirmer, New York, 1914.

Musicians of Today. Romain Rolland, trans. by Mary Blaiklock. Henry Holt & Co., New York, 1917.

Modern French Music. Edward Burlingame Hill. Houghton Mifflin Co., Boston, 1924.

The Problems of Modern Music. Adolf Weissmann, trans. by M. M. Bozman. E. P. Dutton & Co., New York, 1925.

Contemporary Russian Composers. M. Montagu-Nathan. Frederick A. Stokes Co., New York, 1917.

Modern Russian Composers. Leonid Sabaneyeff. International Publishers, New York, 1927.

Arnold Schoenberg. Egon Wellesz, trans. by W. H. Kerridge. E. P. Dutton & Co., New York, 1925.

Sibelius. Cecil Gray. Oxford University Press, London, 1931.

The New Music. George Dyson. Oxford University Press, London, 1924.

A Survey of Contemporary Music. Cecil Gray. Oxford University Press, London, 1924.

Claude Debussy: His Life and Works. Leon Vallas, trans. by Maire and Grace O'Brien. Oxford University Press, London, 1933.

French Piano Music. Alfred Cortot, trans. by Hilda Andrews. Oxford University Press, London, 1932.

La Musique française d'aujourd'hui. G. Jean-Aubry. Perrin et Cie., Paris, 1916.

Panorama de la musique contemporaine. André Coeuroy, "Les Documentaires." Simon Kra, Paris, 1928.

La Musique française moderne. André Coeuroy. Delagrace, Paris, 1922.

Panorama de la radio. André Coeuroy, "Les Documentaires." Simon Kra, Paris, 1929.

Music of Our Day. Lazare Saminsky. Thomas Y. Crowell Co., New York, 1932.

Modern Composers. Guido Pannain, trans. by Michael R. Bonavia. E. P. Dutton & Co., New York, 1933.

Our American Music. John Tasker Howard. Thomas Y. Crowell Co., New York, 1930-31, 1946.

American Composers on American Music. A Symposium edited by Henry Cowell. Stanford University Press, Palo Alto, Cal., 1933.

American Composers. A Catalogue compiled by Claire Reis, U. S. Section of the International Society for Contemporary Music. New York, second edition, 1932.

An Hour with American Music. Paul Rosenfeld. J. B. Lippincott, Philadelphia, 1929.

Dictionary of Music and Musicians: Sir George Grove. The Macmillan Company, New York, 1927.

Manuel de Falla and Spanish Music J. B. Trend. A. A. Knopf, New York, 1929.

A Russian Tone Poet: Alexander Scriabin. Eaglefield Hull. Kegan Paul, Trench, Trübner Co., 1916.

Music: Classical, Romantic and Modern. Eaglefield Hull. E. P. Dutton & Co., New York, 1927.

The Art of Spiritual Harmony. Wassily Kandinsky, trans. with an Introduction by M. T. H. Sadler. Houghton Mifflin Co., Boston, 1914.

Strauss's Tone-Poems. Thomas Armstrong, from "The Musical Pilgrim" edited by Sir Arthur Somervell. Oxford University Press, London, 1931.

"The Lyceum of Schoenberg." Adolph Weiss. *Modern Music,* New York, March-April, 1932.

"Wozzeck: A Guide to the Words and Music of the Opera by Alban Berg." Willi Reich, trans. by Adolph Weiss. *Modern Music,* New York, 1931.

"The Esthetics of Contemporary Music." André Coeuroy. *The Musical Quarterly,* New York, April, 1929.

L'Ecran des musiciens. José Bruyr. Les Cahiers de France, Paris, 1930.

Gustav Mahler: Song-Symphonist. Gabriel Engel. The Bruckner Society of America, New York, 1932.

L'Essor de la musique espagnole. Henri Collet. Max Eschig, Paris, 1929.

Stocktaking, 1930. Edwin Evans. Music and Letters, London, 1931.

The Dehumanization of Art. José Artega y Gasset. The Symposium, New York, April, 1930.

"Sensibility in Contemporary Art." Charles Koechlin. *Pro Musica* Quarterly, New York, Dec., 1927.

Modern Music. Ed., Minna Lederman. A Quarterly Review, pub. League of Composers, New York, 1924-1933.

The Rise of Music in the Ancient World East and West. Curt Sachs. W. W. Norton & Co., New York, 1943.

Music in the Middle Ages. Gustave Reese. W. W. Norton & Co., New York, 1940.

Music in Western Civilization. Paul Henry Lang. W. W. Norton & Co., New York, 1941.

A Short History of Music. Alfred Einstein. A. A. Knopf, New York, 1938.

Grove's *Dictionary of Music and Musicians.* The Macmillan Company, New York, 1940.

The International Cyclopedia of Music and Musicians. (Ed. Oscar Thompson) Dodd, Mead & Co., New York, 1944.

The Oxford Companion to Music. Percy A. Scholes. Oxford University Press, New York, 1938.

The Style of Palestrina and the Dissonance. Knud Jeppeson. Carl Fischer, New York, 1927.

The History of Music in Performance. Frederick Dorian. W. W. Norton & Co., New York, 1947.

Music in History. McKinney and Anderson. American Book Co., New York, 1940.

Opera. Edward J. Dent. Penguin Book, Ltd., London, 1940.

The Bach Reader. Hans David and Arthur Mendel, eds. W. W. Norton, New York, 1945.

Handel. Herbert Weinstock. A. A. Knopf, New York, 1946.

Gluck. Alfred Einstein (trans. Eric Blom). E. P. Dutton & Co., New York, 1936.

Haydn: A Creative Life in Music. Karl Geiringer. W. W. Norton & Co., New York, 1946.

Mozart: His Character, His Work. Alfred Einstein. Oxford University Press, New York, 1945.

Florestan: The Life and Work of Robert Schumann. Robert Haven Schauffler. Henry Holt & Co., New York, 1945.

Clara Schumann: A Romantic Biography. John N. Burk. Random House, New York, 1940.

The Musical Quarterly. Issue devoted to Liszt. G. Schirmer. New York, July, 1936.

The Changing Opera. Paul Bekker. Trans. Arthur Mendel. W. W. Norton & Co., New York, 1935.

The Opera: A History of its Creation and Performance: 1600-1941. Wallace Brockway and Herbert Weinstock. Simon and Schuster, New York, 1941.

The Life of Richard Wagner (3 vols.). Ernest Newman. A. A. Knopf, New York, 1933, 1937, 1940.

Brahms: His Life and Works. Karl Geiringer. Houghton Mifflin Company, Boston, 1936.

Tchaikovsky. Herbert Weinstock. A. A. Knopf, New York, 1943.

Beloved Friend. Catherine Drinker Bowen and Barbara von Meck. Random House, New York, 1937.

Free Artist: The Story of Anton Rubinstein and His Brother. C. D. Bowen. Random House, New York, 1939.

Our New Music. Aaron Copland. Whittlesey House, New York, 1941.

The Music Lover's Handbook. Ed., Elie Siegmeister. William Morrow & Co., New York, 1943.

Debussy: Man and Artist. Oscar Thompson. Dodd, Mead & Co., New York, 1937.

Bolero. The Life of Maurice Ravel. Madeleine B. Goss. Henry Holt & Co., New York, 1940.

Great Modern Composers. Ed., Oscar Thompson. Dodd, Mead & Co., New York, 1941.

The Book of Modern Composers. Ed., David Ewen. A. A. Knopf, New York, 1942.

The Musical Scene. Virgil Thomson. A. A. Knopf, New York, 1945.

About My Life. Igor Stravinsky. Simon & Schuster, New York, 1936.

Music, Here and Now. Ernest Krenek. W. W. Norton & Co., New York, 1939.

Schoenberg. Ed., Merle Armitage. G. Schirmer, New York, 1937.

"To Arnold Schoenberg on His Seventieth Birthday: Personal Recollections." Darius Milhaud. *The Musical Quarterly*. G. Schirmer, New York, October, 1944.

"Darius Milhaud." Marion Bauer. *The Musical Quarterly*. G. Schirmer, New York, April, 1942.

"The War Years." S. Prokofieff. *The Musical Quarterly*. G. Schirmer, New York, October, 1944.

Bohuslav Martinu: The Man and his Music. Milos Safranek. A. A. Knopf, New York, 1944.

Eight Soviet Composers. Gerald Abraham. Oxford University Press, London, 1943.

Music of Latin America. Nicolas Slonimsky. Thomas Y. Crowell Co., New York, 1945.

Music of the New World. Handbooks Vol. IV and Vol. V. Gilbert Chase N. B. C., University of the Air. 1944.

Studies in Counterpoint. Ernst Krenek. G. Schirmer, New York, 1940.

Challenge to Musical Tradition. Adele T. Katz. A. A. Knopf, New York, 1945.

Music in Our Time. Adolfo Salazar. Trans. from the Spanish by Isabel Pope. W. W. Norton & Co., New York, 1946.

A Guide to Latin American Music. Gilbert Chase. Library of Congress. Music Division, Washington, D. C., 1943.

Modern Music. Composers and Music of Our Time. Max Graf. Philosophical Library, New York, 1946.

Serge Koussevitzky. The Boston Symphony Orchestra and the New American Music. Hugo Leichtentritt. Harvard University Press, Cambridge, 1946.

Dmitri Shostakovich. The Life and Background of a Soviet Composer. Victor I. Seroff. A. A. Knopf, New York, 1943.

What to Listen for in Music. Aaron Copland. McGraw-Hill Co., New York, 1939.

The Catholic Choirmaster. Articles by Cyr de Brant and J. Vincent Higginson.

The Music of Spain. Gilbert Chase. W. W. Norton & Co., New York, 1941.

Latin-American Art Music for the Piano. Preface: Francisco Curt Lange. G. Schirmer, New York, 1942.

Boletino latino-americano de música. 5 Vols. Francisco Curt Lange, ed. Montevideo.

"Silvestre Revueltas and Musical Nationalism in Mexico." Otto Mayer-Serra. *The Musical Quarterly.* G. Schirmer, New York, April, 1941.

Toward a New Music. Carlos Chavez. W. W. Norton & Co., New York, 1937.

Science and Music. Sir James Jeans. The Macmillan Company, New York, 1937.

Music for All of Us. Leopold Stokowski. Simon & Schuster, New York, 1943.

Files of *Modern Music.* Minna Lederman, ed. League of Composers Quarterly, 1933-1946.

Files of *The Musical Quarterly.* G. Schirmer, New York, 1933-1947.

Program notes of New York Philharmonic-Symphony Society of New York. Robert Bagar and Louis Biancolli.

Program notes of the Boston Symphony Orchestra. John N. Burk.

Changing Forms in Modern Music. Karl Eschman. E. C. Schirmer, Boston, 1945.

Music in Radio Broadcasting. Gilbert Chase, ed. NBC-Columbia University Broadcasting Series. McGraw-Hill Co., New York, 1946.

The Craft of Musical Composition. 2 vols. Rev. Ed. Paul Hindemith. Associated Music Publishers, New York, 1941 and 1945.

Bruckner, Mahler and Schoenberg. Dika Newlin.

PRONOUNCING GLOSSARY OF FOREIGN NAMES

THE symbols in this Glossary are those used in Webster's New International Dictionary.

āle, câre, ăm, ärt, ȧsk, all
ēve, dê-pend', ĕnd, evĕr, thère
īce, ĭll
ōld, ô-bey', ôrder, ŏdd, sȯn, oil, fōōd, fŏŏt, out=owl
ūse, ûrn, ŭp, the French u *
y=used as in yet or yard
c=k as in cake, or s as in cite
g=ġ as in go, or j as in gem, or zh (French) as in azure †

A

Albeniz, Isaak	äl'bā-nēth, ē-zäk'
Alfano	äl-fä'nô
Also sprach Zarathustra	äl'zō shpräк(ch) zä-rä-tōō' strä
Amati	ä-mä'tē
Apollon Musagetes	à-pŏl-lôn' mü-zà-jĕt' (Fr.) or
	à-pŏl'ō mū-sä'gē-tēs (E.)
Ariadne auf Naxos	ä-rē-äd'nĕ ouf näk'sōs
Artusi	är-tōō'zē
Aubert, Louis	ō-bêr'
Auric, Georges	ō-rēk', zhôrzh
Aus Italien	ous ê-täl'yĕn

B

Bacchantinnen	bäk-kän'tēn-ĕn
Baïf, Jean Antoine	bà-ēf', zhôn ôn-twán'
Balakireff, Mily	bä-lä-kē'rĕf, mē'lē

* The French u and the German ü have no equivalent in the English language. It is obtained by pursing the lips and trying to say e=ü.

The French nasals, *in, an, on, un,* have no equivalents in English: *in* (indicated by àɴ) *im, ain, aim, ein, eim,* are pronounced somewhat like *an* in anxious if divided thus: *an-kshŭs.*

an, am, en, em, are indicated by äɴ, and pronounced approximately like the English word *on.*

on is indicated by ôɴ and is pronounced like the *on* in the English word *long.*

un is somewhat like *un* in the English word *under* (ŭɴ = u-nder).

The German *ch* is impossible to indicate exactly. Webster uses к but that does not give the guttural sound as though clearing the throat.

The French *e* is a cross between the English ā and ĕ. The ā would be close enough if we did not give a compound sound (ā-ē) to our long *a,* therefore, I have generally used ĕ to indicate the French unaccented *e.* While we have no exact equivalents for the French *é* and *è, é* is close to ā, and *è* to ĕ. The symbol ē indicates the French mute *e* like the *e* in the English word *her*—thus: lē, dē, etc.

Another problem is the accentuation in French of strong syllables as the primary accent invariably falls on the last syllable, though they are almost of even value.

† The French *g* is indicated by *zh.*

Barbieri, Francisco	bär-byâ′rē, frän-chēs′kō
Bardi	bär′dē
Bartók, Béla	bär′tŏk, bā′lä
Baudelaire	bō-d′-lâr′
Beethoven, van	vän bā′tō-věn
Bellini, Vincenzo	běl-lē′nē, vĭn-chěn′zō
Berezowsky, Nicolai	bě-rě-zǔf′skē, nē-kō-lī′
Berg, Alban	bârg, äl′bän
Berlioz	bēr-lē-ōz′
Bielyi	by-ě′lē
Bizet, Georges	bē-zě′, zhôrzh
Boccherini	bôk-kē-rē′nē
Boieldieu	bwäl-dyů′
Bordes, Charles	bôrd, shârl
Boris Godounoff	bō-rēs′ gō-dōō-nôf′
Borodin	bŏ-rŏ-dĭn′
Borowski	bŏ-rǔf′skē
Boulanger	bōō-laɴ-zhä′
Brahms, Johannes	bräms, yō-hän′něs
Bréville, Pierre de	brä-vēl′, pyâr dē
Brouillards	brōō-yàr′
Bruckner, Anton	brŏŏk′nēr, än-tōn′
Buechner, Georg	büκ′nēr, ḡä-ôrḡ′
Busoni, Ferruccio	bōō-sō′ni, fēr-rōōch′yō
Bussine, Romain	büs-sēn′, rō-màɴ′
Butting	bōōt′tĭng
Buxtehude	bōōks-tē-hōō′dě

C

Caccini, Giulio	kä-chē′nē, jōōl′yō
Calsabigi	käl-sä-bē′jē
Calvocoressi	käl-vō-cō-rěs′sē
Camerato	kä-mē-rä′tō
Canteloube	käɴ-tē-lōōb′
Caplet, André	kàp-lě′, äɴ-drä′
Carillo	kä-rēl′yō
Casella, Alfredo	kä-sěl′lä, äl-frä′dô
Castelnuova-Tedesco	käs-těl-nwô′vä-tě-děs′kō
Castillon, Alexis de	kàs-tē-yòɴ′, à-lěk-se′ dē
Cathédrale engloutie, La	kä-tä-drál′ äɴ-glōō-tē′, là
Caturla, Alejandro	kä-tōōr′lä, ä-lē-hän′drō
Cavalieri	kä-vä-lyä′rē
Cavalli	kä-väl′lē
Cavos, Catterino	kä′vōs, kät-tě-rē′nō
Chabrier	shà-brē-yä′
Chambonnières	shäɴ-bòn-yêr′
Charpentier	shàr-päɴ-tyä′
Chausson	shō-sòɴ′
Chavez	shä′věz
Chemberdji	shěm-běr-djē′
Chevillard	shē-vē-yàr′
Chopin	shò-pàɴ′
Christophe Colomb	krēs-tôf′ kô-lōmb′
Clavecin	klàv-sàɴ′

Clicquet-Pleyel	klē-kä-plä-yĕl'
Cocteau	kôk-tō'
Coeuroy, André	kûr-rwä, äN-drä'
Corelli	kô-rĕl'lē
Corsi, Jacopo	kôr'sē, ja'kô-pō
Cortot, Alfred	kôr-tō'
Cotapus, Acario	kô-tä'pōōs, ä-kä'rē-ō
Couperin, François	kōō-pē-ràN', frän-swä
Cristofori, Bartolommeo	krēs-tō-fō'rē, bär-tō-lōm-mä'ō
Cui, César	kwē, sä-zàr'
Czerny, Carl	chĕr'nē, kärl

D

Daquin	dà-kàN'
D'Aranyi	dà-rän'yē
D'Archambeau, Iwan	där-shäN-bō', ē-vän'
D'Arezzo, Guido	dä-rĕt'zō, gwē'dō
Dargomijsky	där-gō-mĭsh'skē
Davidenko	dä-vē-dĕn'kō
De Vitry, Phillippe	dē-vē'trē, fē-lēp'
Debussy, Claude	dē-bü-sē', klōd
Delamarter, Eric	dē-là-mär'tēr, ĕr'ĭk
Delius	dē'ly-ŭs
Dello Joio	del'-lo jo'-yō
Delvincourt	dēl-vàN-kōōr
Derain	dē-ràN'
Deshevov	dĕsh'ē-vŭv
Diaghileff, Sergei	dē-ä'gē-lĕf, sâr-ġä'
D'Indy, Vincent	dàN'dē, vàN-säN'
Dohnanyi	dō-nän'yē
Doktor Faustus	dôk'tôr fou'stōōs
Don Juan	dôn hwän
Donna Serpente, La	dôn'à (or dôn'nä) sêr-pĕn'tē
Don Quixote	dôn kĭ-hō'tē
Dostoievsky	dôs-tō-yĕf'skē
Drei Klavierstücke	drī klä-vēr'shtü-kĕ
Dreyschock	drī'shòk
Dubois, Theodore	dü-bwä', tā-ō-dôr'
Ducasse, Roger	dü-käs', rò-zhä'
Dufranne	dü-fràn'
Dukas	dü-kàs'
Dukelsky	dōō-kel'skē
Duparc	dü-pàrk'
Durey	dü-rā'
Dussek	dōō'chĕk or dōō'sĕk
Dvorák, Antonin	dvôr'zhäk, än'tō-nĭn

E

Eichheim	īк(ch)'hīm
Ein Heldenleben	īn hĕl'dĕn-lā"-bĕn
Enesco	ĕn-ĕs'kō
Enfant Prodigue, L'	läN-fäN' prô-dēġ'
Epitaphe	ä-pē-tàf'

Erwartung	êr-vär′tŏŏng
España	ĕs-pän′yä
Etude	ā-tüd′
Eugen Oniegin	oi-g̣ĕn′, ŏn-yĕ′g̣ĭn
Expert, Henri	ĕx-pêr′, äɴ-rē′

F

Falla, Manuel de	fäl′yä, mä′nōō-el dē
Fauré, Gabriel	fō-rā′, g̣à-brē-ĕl′
Fernandez, Pedro	fêr-nän′deth, pä′drō
Fétis	fā-tēs′
Feuersnot	foi′ērs-nōt
Feuilles mortes	fēy′ môrt
Fils des Étoiles, Le	fēs dê zä-twàl′, lē
Flonzaley	flôn-zä′lä
Franck, César	fräɴk, sä-sàr′
Freischütz	frī′shütz
Frescobaldi, Girolamo	frĕs-kō-bäl′dē, zhĭ-rō-lä′mō

G

Gabrieli, Giovanni	g̣ä-brē-êl′ē, jô-vän′nĭ
Galilei, Vincenzo	g̣ä-lē-lā′ē, vĭn-chĕn′zō
Galluppi	g̣äl-lōō′pē
Gamelang	g̣äm′ē-läng
Garcia	g̣är′thē-ä
Garcin, Jules	g̣àr-sàɴ′, zhül
Gatti, Guido	g̣ät′tē, gwē′dō
Gaubert	g̣ō-bêr′
Gauguin	g̣ō-g̣àɴ′
Gautier, Theophile	g̣ō-tyā′, tä-ō-fēl′
Gebrauchsmusik	g̣ä-browĸs′mōō-sēk″
Général Lavine—eccentric	zhä-nä-rál′ là-vēn′—ĕx-äɴ-trēk′
Georg, Stefan	g̣ä-ôrg′, stä-fän′
Gerville-Réache	zhêr-vēl′-rä-àch′
Gesualdo, Don Carlo	zhä-sōō-äl′dō, dôn kär′lō
Gewandhaus	g̣ĕ-vänt′hous
Giannini, Vittorio	jän-nē′nē, vĭt-tō′rĭ-ō
Gigout	zhē-g̣ōō′
Ginastera	hē-nä-stä′-rä
Giorni, Aurelio	jôr′nē, aw-rä′lē-ō
Giraud, Albert	zhē-rō′, àl-bêr′
Glazounoff	g̣lä-zōō-nŭf′
Glière	g̣lē-yêr′
Gniessen	gnyĕ′sĕn
Goyescas	g̣ō-yĕs′cäs
Granados, Enrique	grä-nä′dōs, ĕn-rē′kä
Gretchaninoff	grĕ-chä-nē′nŭf
Grétry	g̣rä′trē
Grovlez, Gabriel	g̣rôv′lĕz, g̣à-brē-ĕl′
Guarneri	g̣wär-nä′rē
Guidiccioni, Laura	g̣wē-dē-chē-ō′nê, lä′ōō-rä
Guilmant	g̣ēl-mäɴ′
Guiraud, Ernest	g̣ērō′ êr-nĕst′
Gurre-Lieder	g̣ōōr′rĕ-lē″dēr

H

Haba, Alois	hä'bä, ä'lō-ĭs
Handel or Händel	hăn'dĕl (E.) or hĕn'dĕl (Gr.)
Harmonielehre	här-mō-nē'lä"rē
Harsanyi, Tibor	här-sän'yĭ, tē'bôr
Haydn	hī'dn
Histoire du soldat, L'	lēs-twâr' dü sŏl-dà'
Holmès, Augusta	hôl'mĕz, ō-güs-tä'
Honegger	ō-nĕ-ġêr'

I

Iberia	ē-bä'ryà
Idée fixe	ē-dā' fēks
Ippolitoff-Ivanoff	ē-pô-lē'tŭf-ē-vä'nŭf
Islamey	ēs-lä-mä'

J

Jachimecki, Zdislas	yà-chē-mĕtz'kē, zdēs'läs
Jalowitz	yä'lō-wĭts
Janacek, Leos	yä'nä-shĕk, lā'ôs
Jardins sous la pluie	zhàr-dàn' sōō là plwē'
Jarecki, Tadeusz	yä-rĕtz'kē, tä-dĕ'ōōsh
Jarnach	yär'näκ(ch)
Javorski	yä-vôr'skē
Jean-Aubry	zhäN-nō'brē'
Jemnitz	yĕm'nĭtz
Jeritza	yĕ-rĭt'zä
Jeux d'eau	zhû' dō
Jonny spielt auf	jŏn'nē shpēlt ouf
Juilliard	jōōl'yärd
Juon	hwŏn, or hōō-ŏn'
Jurg Jenatch	yōōrġ yä'natsh

K

Kabalevsky	kä-bä-lĕv'-skē
Kalevala	kä-lē-vä'là
Kaminsky, Heinrich	kä-mĭn'skē, hīn-rĭκ(ch)
Kandinsky, Wassily	kän-dēn'skē, väs-sē'lē
Katchaturian	kä-tchä-tōō'-ri-an
Kleiber, Erich	klī'bêr, ê'rĭκ
Knipper	knēp'pĕr
Kodaly, Zoltan	kō-däl'yē, zȯl'tän
Koechlin, Charles	kûκ(ch)'làn, shàrl
Kokoschka	kô-kōsh'kä
Koussevitzky	kōōs-sĕ-vĭt'skē
Koutzen	kŏŏt'zĕn
Koval, Maryan	kō-väl', mä-rĭ-än'
Krein	krīn
Krenek	krĕ' nĕk
Kullervo	kŭl-lêr'vō
Kunnecke	kōōn'nĕ-kê

L

Ladmirault	làd-mē-rō'
Laforgue	là-fôrg'
Lahor	là-ōr'
Lajtha, Ladislaw	läzh'tà, lä-dēs-lä'
Lalo	là-lō'
Laloy	là-lwà'
Lamoureux	là-moō-rû'
Landormy	län-dör-mē'
Laparra, Raoul	là-pär'rà, rà-ōōl'
Laranjeiras	lä-rän-yä'räs
Le Jeune, Claude	lē zhûn, klōd
Lekeu, Guillaume	lē-kē', ġē-ōm'
Lenormand, René	lē-nôr-män', rē-nä'
Lesueur	lē-swûr'
Lobaczewska, Stephanie	lô-bä-chĕv'skä, stĕ-fà-nē'
Lourié	loōry-ä'
Lully, Jean Baptiste	lül'lē, zhän bàp-tēst'
Lyre d'Apollon, La	lēēr dàp-pol-lôn', là

M

Machaut, Guillaume de	mà-shō' ġē-yōm' dē
Magnard, Albéric	màn-yàr' al-bä-rēk'
Mahler, Gustav	mä'-lēr, goōs'täv
Mallarmé	mà-làr-mä'
Ma Mère l'Oye	mà mâr l-wà
Manet, Edouard	mà-nē', ĕd-wär'
Markiewitch, Igor	mär-kyĕ'-vĭch, ē'gôr
Marot, Clément	mà-rō', clä-män'
Martinu, Bohuslav	mär-tē'noō, bō'hoō-släv
Martyre de Saint Sebastien, Le	mär-tēr' dē sàn sē-bàs-tyàn', lē
Matisse	mà-tēs'
Mauduit, Jacques	mō-dwē', zhàk
Mazurka	mà-zoōr'kà
Mein Vaterland	mīn fä'tēr-länt
Meistersinger von Nurnberg, Die	mī'stēr-zĭng-ēr fōn nürn'bêrg, dē
Messager	mĕs-à-zhä'
Messiaien	mĕss-ī-yàn'
Methode: L'Art de toucher le Clavecin	mä-tôd' : l'àr dē toō-shä' lē clàv-sàn'
Meyerbeer, Giacomo	mī'ēr-bâr, jà'kō-mō
Miascowsky	mìà-skŭv' skē
Mickiewicz	mētz-kyĕ'vēch
Mignone	mēēn-yō'-nä
Mihailovsky	mē-hī-lŭv'skē
Milhaud, Darius	mē-yō' or mē lō' dä-rē-üs'
Mompou	môm-poō'
Monet, Claude	mô-nē', klōd
Monteux, Pierre	môn-tû', pyâr
Monteverdi, Claudio	môn-tĕ-vâr'dē, klow'dĭ-ō
Moscheles	mōsh'ĕ-lēz
Mossolov	mô'sô-lôf
Moussorgsky	moō-sôrg'skē
Mozart, Wolfgang Amadeus	mō'tsärt, vōlf'gäng, ä-mä-dä'oōs

Muris, Jean de   mü-rēs', zhäɴ dē
Musique Mesurée à l'Antique   mü-zēk' mē-sü-rā' à läɴ-tēk'

N

Nabokoff   nä'bô-kôf
Neue Zeitschrift für Musik   noi-ĕ zīt'shrïft für mōō-zēk'
Noces, Les   nŏs, lä
Nordraak, Rikard   nŏr'dràk, rïk'àrd

O

Obouhov   ô-bŏŏ'khôf
Oedipus-Rex   ĕd'ï-pŭs rĕx
Oiseau de Feu, L'   lwà-zō' dē fû
Opera buffa   ô-pā-rà' bŏōf'fà
Opéra comique   ô-pā-rà' kò-mēk'
Ortega y Gasset, José   ōr-tā'gà y gäs'sĕt, hō-zā'
Ostinato   ôs-tē-nä'tō

P

Pachelbel, Johann   päk(ch)'ĕl-bĕl, yō-hän'
Paderewski   pä-dĕ-rĕv'skē
Pagodes   pà-gòd'
Paladan, Sâr   pà-là-däɴ' sär
Palestrina, Giovanni Pierluigi   pä-lē-strē'nä, jō-vän'nē pyär'lwē-jē
Paniagua, Raul   pä-nē-ä'gwä, rä'ōōl
Paskchenko   pàsh'chĕn-kô
Pauvre Matelot, Le   pō'vr mà-tē-lō', lē
Pavane pour une Infante défunte   pà-vàn' pŏōr ü-nàn-fänt' dā-fûnt'
Pelléas et Mélisande   pĕl-lā-às' ĕ mä-lē-sänd'
Périer, Jean   pä-rē-yĕ', zhäɴ
Petrouchka   pĕt-rōōsh'kà
Petyrek   pä'tē-rĕk
Pfitzner   pfïtz'nēr
Picasso   pē-cäs'sŏ
Pierné, Gabriel   pē-yâr-nā', gà-brē-ĕl'
Pierrot Lunaire   pyĕ-rō' lü-nàr'
Pillois   pē-lwà'
Pique Dame   pēk dàm'
Pizzetti, Ildebrando   pït-tsĕt'tē, ēl-dà-brän'dō
Plaza, Juan Bautista   plä'-thä, hŏŏ-an bow-tēēs'-tä
Plein-air   plä-nâr'
Poème de l'Extase   pō-ĕm'dē lĕks-stàz'
Poldowski   pŏl-dŭv'skē
Polignac, Princesse Edmond de   pŏlēn-yàc', pràn-sĕs' ĕd-môɴ' dē
Polovinkin   pô-lô-vēn'kĕn
Poulenc   pŏŏ-lànk'
Printemps   pràn-täɴ'
Prokofieff, Serge   prō-kó'fyĕf, sēr-ġā'
Protopokoff   prô-tô-pó'kôf
Prunières   prü-nyâr'
Pulcinella   pŏōl-chē-nĕl'lä

R

Rachmaninoff, Serge	rä-κhmä′nē-nôf, sēr-g̣ä′
Rameau, Jean Philippe	rȧ-mō′, zhäɴ fē-lēp′
Rathaus, Karol	rät′hows, kä′rŏl
Ravel, Maurice	rȧ-vĕl′, mạ-rēs′
Rebikoff, Vladimir	rĕ′bē-kôf, vlä-dē′mēr
Reflets dans l'eau	rē-flä′däɴ lō
Reger, Max	rä′g̣ēr, mäks
Respighi, Ottorino	rĕs-pē′g̣ē, ȯt-tō-rē′nō
Revueltas	rĕ-vōō-äl′täs
Rieti	rē-ĕ′tē
Rimski-Korsakov	rĭm′skē-kôr′-sä-kŭf
Rinaldi	rē-näl′dē
Rinuccini, Ottavio	rē-nōō-chē′nē, ot-tä′vē-ō
Roi David, Le	rwȧ dȧ-vēd′, lē
Roldan	rôl-dän′
Rolland, Romain	rôl-läɴ′, ro-mȧɴ′
Rose-Croix	rôz-crwȧ′
Rosenkavalier	rō′zĕn-kä-vä-lēr″
Roslavetz	rŏs-lä′vĕtz
Rossignol	rŏs-sēn-yòl′
Rossini, Gioachino	rŏs-sē′nē, jwä-kē′nō
Rousseau, Jean Jacques	rōōs-sō′, zhäɴ zhȧk
Roussel, Albert	rōōs-sĕl′, ȧl-bêr′
Rudhyar	rōōd-yȧr′

S

Sabaneyev	sä-bä-nyä′ĕf
Sacre du Printemps, Le	sȧkr′dü prȧɴ-täɴ′
Salome	sä′lō-mä
Salut au Monde	sȧ-lü′tō mônd
Sanjuan, Pedro	sän-hwän′, pä′drō
Satie	sȧ-tē′
Saudades do Brazil	sō-dä′däz dō brä-zēl′
Sauguet, Henri	sō-g̣ĕ′, äɴ-rē′
Schéhérazade	shä-hĕ-rä-zäd′
Schloezer	shlü′zēr
Schlagobers	shläg′ō-bērs
Schoenberg	shûn′bêrg
Schola Cantorum	skō′lȧ cȧn-tō′rŭm
Scriabin	skrē-ä′bĭn
Séverac, Déodat de	sä-vē-rȧk′, dä-ō-dȧ′ dē
Shebalin	shĕ-bä′lēn
Shostakovich	shŏ-stä-kó′vĭtch
Sibelius, Jan	sĭ-bāl′yōōs, yän
Smetana, Bedrich	smĕt′ä-nä, bä′drĭκ
Société Nationale de Musique	sȯ-sē-ä-tä′ nä-syô-nȧl′ dē mü-zēk′
Société Musicale Indépendante	sȯ-sē-ä-tä′ mü-zē-kȧl′ äɴ-dä-päɴ-däɴt′
Sonnambula	sŏn-näm′bōō-lä
Sons et les parfums tournent dans l'air du soir, Les	lä sôɴ ĕ lä pȧr-fŭɴ′ tō̆orn däɴ lȧr dü swȧr
Stradivari	strä-dĕ-vä′rē

Sumare	sōō-mä'rĕ
Symphonie de Psaumes, La	sȧɴ-fô-nē' dĕ psōm, lȧ
Symphonie Fantastique	sȧɴ-fô-nē' fäɴ-tȧs-tēk'
Szymanowski	zhĭ-mä-nŭf'skē

T

Tailleferre, Germaine	tī-fêr', zhêr-mĕn'
Tanieff, Sergei	tä-nē'yĕf, sēr-ġä'
Tchaikovsky or Tschaikovsky	chī-kŏĭ'skē
Tcherepnin	chĕ-rĕp-nēn'
Tamara	tä-mä'-rä
Theremin	thê'rĕ-mēn
Tiersot, Julien	tyêr-sō', zhül-yȧɴ'
Tiessen, Heinz	tē'zĕn, hīnz or tēs-sēn
Till Eulenspiegels lustige Streiche	tĭl oi'lĕn-shpē-gĕls lōōs'tĭ-ġĕ shtrī'ᴋ(ch)ĕ
Tijuca	tĭ-hōō'ka
Toch, Ernst	tŏᴋ êrnst
Tod und Verklärung	tōt ŏŏnt fêr-klâ'rŏŏng
Tombeau de Couperin, Le	tôn-bō' dĕ kōō-pē-rȧɴ', lē
Tonadillas	tō-nä-dēl'yäs
Todte Stadt, Die	tō'tĕ shtăt, dē
Turgenieff	tŏŏr-ġĕ'nyĕf
Turina, Joaquin	tōō-rē'nä, hwä'kēn

V

Vallas, Leon	vȧ-lȧs', lä-ôɴ'
Valse, Le Poème chorégraphique	vȧls, lē pō-ĕm' kō-rā-grȧ-fēk'
Valses nobles et sentimentales	vȧls nŏbl ĕ säɴ-tē-mäɴ-tȧl'
Varèse	vȧ-rĕz'
Variations Symphoniques	vȧ-rē-ä-syäɴ' sȧɴ-fo-nēk'
Vasilenko, Sergei	vä-sĭ-lyĕn'kô, sêr-ġä'
Verklaerte Nacht	fêr-klâr'tĕ näᴋ(ch)t
Verlaine	vêr-lĕn'
Vestale, La	vĕs-tä'lȧ, lä
Villa-Lobos	vē-lä lō'-bōs
Voiles	vwȧl

W

Wagenaar	vä'gē-när
Weill, Kurt	vīl, kŏŏrt
Wellesz, Egon	vĕl'lĕts, ĕ-ġŏn' or vĕl'lĕsh
Werkmeister, Andreas	vêrk'mīs-tēr, än'drä-äs
Wieck	vēk
Wiéner	vyä'nêr
Wyschnegradsky, Ivan	vĭsh-nĕ-gräd'skē, ē-vän'

Y

Ysaye	ē-zä'yĕ

INDEX

441

"Composers of Chile, The" (Smith), quoted, 386
Concertino (Carpenter), 160, 161
Concertino (Stravinsky), 189
Concerto da Camera (Martinu), 252
Concerto for piano and orchestra (Copland), 347
Concerto for Quarter-Tone Piano (Barth), 265
Concerto Grosso (Bloch), 167
Concerts Lamoureux, 272
Concerts, a novelty in the 18th century, 28; first public, 29
Concerts Colonne, 272
Concerts Pierné, 272
Concerts spirituels, 29, 77
Conductus, 15
Cone, Edward T., 370, 373
Cone, Harold, 373
Confrey, Zez, 322
Congressional Library, concert hall opened, 201-02
Consonance, 102-05, 216-17
Contreras, Salvador, 379
"Conversations" (Bliss), 155
Converse, Frederick, 72
Coolidge, Mrs. Elizabeth Sprague, 148, 157, 201, 252, 256, 326
Copland, Aaron, 70, 73, 181-82, 258, 313, 314, 315, 347-51, 371, 373; quoted on jazz, 319; wins prize, 402; writes for films, 409, 410, 413
Copland-Sessions Concerts, 348, 408
Coq d'or (Rimski-Korsakov), 60
Coq et l'Arlequin, Le, 241
Coriolanus overture (Beethoven), 34
Cornemuse, La (Loeffler), 159
Corsi, Jacopo, 16, 17
Cortese, Louis, 276
Cortinas, Cesar, 388
Cortot, Alfred, 141
Corwin, Norman, 328
Counterpoint, its development in the 14th century, 14, 15; replaced by harmony, 24; dissonant counterpoint, 113, 216, 254-55; see also chapter on "Explanation of Musical Terms," 415
Couper, Mildred, 266
Couperin, François, 22; his theories of playing the clavecin, 26
Courante, 23
Cours de Composition (d'Indy), quoted, 78
Cowell, Henry, 73, 99, 231, 267, 279, 319, 326, 371; his experiments and some of his works, 335
Crabbe, George, 307
Crab-canon (*motus cancrizans*), 220-21, 300
Cracow Philharmonic, 277
Cradle Will Rock, The (Blitzstein), 309, 353
Craft of Musical Composers, The (Hindemith), quoted, 259-60
Cramer, John B., 27, 36
Craven, Thomas, 397

Crawford, Ruth, 326, 352, 371
"Creation" (Gruenberg), 161
Création du monde (Milhaud), 187, 239
Cremona, Italy, 21
Creston, Paul, 73, 354, 371
Cristofori, Bartolommeo, 36
"Cuckoo" (Daquin), 47
Cui, César, 59, 60
Cullen, Countee, 166
Culture and Anarchy (Arnold), quoted, 397
Curtis Institute of Music, 357
Cuvillier, Marcel, 275-76
Czech Philharmonic, 252, 278
Czerny, Carl, 27, 36

D'Agoult, Countess, 46
Dahl, Ingolf, quoted on Stravinsky, 206
Dallapiccola, Luigi, 276, 277
Damrosch, Walter, 182, 330, 337
Dance music, 318; in Latin America, 376; see also Ballet, Jazz
Dandelot, Georges, 273
"Daniel Jazz" (Gruenberg), 161
Danielou, J., 200
Daniels, Mabel, 331, 346
D'Annunzio, Gabriele, 130
Danses concertantes (Stravinsky), 205
Dante Symphony (Liszt), 47
Danza (Carpenter), 161
Daphne (Strauss), 93
Daphnis et Chloë (Ravel), 147, 187
D'Aranyi, Yelly, 148
D'Archambeau, Iwan, quoted, 8
D'Arezzo, Guido, 14, 107
Dargomijsky, Alexander Sergeivich, 59, 62
"Darius Milhaud" (Bauer), quoted, 305
David, Johann Nepomuk, 271
Davidenko, Alexander, 280
Davis, Ellabelle, 366
"Dean of Soviet Composers" (Shebalin), quoted, 281
Debussy, Claude Achille, 8, 62, 63, 101; prelude cited, 111-12; impressionism as developed by him, 125; some of his works, 129; his innovations in opera, 130; fourth prelude cited, 131; analysis of his methods in *"Feuilles mortes,"* 134, 135; "Jimbo's Lullaby" cited, 135; "Minstrels" cited, 137; *"Jardins sous la pluie"* cited, 138; *"La Cathédrale engloutie"* example of 20th-century organum, 140; *"Voiles"* written in whole-tone scale, 141-42; *"Pagodes"* analyzed, 143-44; *"Reflets dans l'eau"* cited, 144; *"La Puerta del Vino"* analyzed, 145-46; *"Hommage à Rameau"* example of 20th-century plainsong, 149-50; the jazz influence, 317
Defossez, René, 275
Degas, Edgar, 126
Deis, Carl, 346
Delamarter, Eric, 346
Delaney, Robert, 371
Delannoy, Marcel, 243